Non-State Actors
in the Human Rights Universe

Non-State Actors
in the Human Rights Universe

George Andreopoulos, Zehra F. Kabasakal Arat,
and Peter Juviler
editors

Kumarian
Press, Inc.

Non-State Actors in the Human Rights Universe
Published in 2006 in the United States of America by Kumarian Press, Inc.,
1294 Blue Hills Avenue, Bloomfield, CT 06002 USA

The text of this book is set in 10.5/13 Esprit Book.

Production and design by Joan Weber Laflamme, jml ediset
Proofread by Beth Richards
Index by Robert Swanson

Printed in the United States by McNaughton & Gunn, Inc. Text printed with
vegetable oil-based ink.

∞ The paper used in this publication meets the minimum requirements of
the American National Standard for Information Sciences—Permanence
of Paper for printed Library Materials, ANSI Z39.48–1984

Library of Congress Cataloging-in-Publication Data

Non-state actors in the human rights universe / edited by George
Andreopoulos, Zehra Arat, and Peter Juviler.
   p. cm.
   Summary: "This book provides a new approach to the study of human
rights and the issues of globalization and state sovereignty"—Provided by
publisher.
   Includes bibliographical references and index.
   ISBN 1-56549-213-7 (pbk. : alk. paper) — ISBN 1-56549-214-5 (alk. paper)
   1. Human rights. 2. Globalization. I. Andreopoulos, George J. II. Arat,
Zehra F. III. Juviler, Peter H. IV. Title.
JC571.N645 2006
323—dc22
                                                              2005030654

15 14 13 12 11 10 09 08 07 06   10 9 8 7 6 5 4 3 2 1   First Printing 2006

Contents

Part I:
Theoretical Questions and Approaches

Part II:
The Role of Corporate Actors

List of Figures and Tables

Abbreviations and Acronyms

AFDC	Aid to Families with Dependent Children
CAG	cult-awareness group
CCG	counter-cult group
CEDAW	Convention on the Elimination of All Forms of Discrimination against Women
CERD	Convention on the Elimination of Racial Discrimination
CIOMS	Council for International Organizations of Medical Sciences
CoC	codes of conduct
CSCE	Conference on Security and Cooperation in Europe (after January 1995 the OSCE)
CISS	Comparative Interdisiplinary Studies Section (of the ISA)
CTC	Counter-Terrorism Committee (UN)
ECHR	European Convention of Human Rights
ECOSOC	Economic and Social Council (UN)
EU	European Union
FLA	Fair Labor Association
FWF	Fair Wear Foundation
GAVI	Global Alliance for Vaccines and Immunization
GDP	gross domestic product
HRNGO	human rights nongovernmental organization
HRW	Human Rights Watch
IAVI	International AIDS Vaccine Initiative
ICC	International Criminal Court

ICCPR	International Covenant on Civil and Political Rights
ICESCR	International Covenant on Economic, Social and Cultural Rights
ICRC	International Committee of the Red Cross
ICTR	International Criminal Tribunal for Rwanda (UN)
ICTs	information and communications technologies
ICTY	International Criminal Tribunal for the former Yugoslavia
IGO	intergovernmental organization
IHL	international humanitarian law
IHRL	international human rights law
ILO	International Labour Organization
IMF	International Monetary Fund
INGO	international nongovernmental organization
ISA	International Studies Association
ISAC	Inter-Agency Standing Committee (UN)
LRA	Lord's Resistance Army (Uganda)
MNC	multinational corporation
NBAC	National Bioethics Advisory Commission
NGO	nongovernmental organization
NIH	National Institutes of Health
NILE	norms, institutions, legal frameworks, and enabling economic environments
NSA	non-state actor
NSP	non-state perpetrator
OCHA	Office for the Coordination of Humanitarian Affairs (UN)
OECD	Organization for Economic Co-operation and Development
OHCHR	Office of the United Nations High Commissioner for Human Rights

OMCT	Organización Mudial Contra la Tortura (World Organization against Torture)
OSCE	Organization for Security and Co-operation in Europe (before 1995 the CSCE)
PRWORA	Personal Responsibility and Work Opportunity Reconciliation Act of 1996
ROG	research-oriented group
RTLM	Radio Télévision Libre des Mille Collines
SAI	Social Accountability International
TANF	Temporary Assistance to Needy Families
TNC	transnational corporation
TRC	Truth and Reconciliation Commission (South Africa)
TRIPS	Trade-Related Aspects of Intellectual Property Rights
UN	United Nations
UDHR	Universal Declaration of Human Rights (UN)
UNAIDS	Joint United Nations Programme on HIV/AIDS
UNDP	United Nations Development Programme
UNESCO	United Nations Economic, Social and Cultural Organization
UNHCR	United Nations High Commissioner for Refugees
UNICEF	United Nations Children's Fund
WFP	World Food Programme (UN)
WHO	World Health Organization
WMA	World Medical Association
WTO	World Trade Organization

Introduction

George J. Andreopoulos, Zehra F. Kabasakal Arat, and Peter Juviler

PURPOSE AND APPROACH

This volume is concerned with the analysis and assessment of the role of non-state actors as promoters/protectors as well as violators of human rights. Why is the study of non-state actors identified as critical at this juncture?

According to a global estimation provided by the International Labour Organization, there are 250 million child laborers; denied access to education and several other rights, many of them work for extremely long hours in harsh and dangerous conditions, including acting as soldiers in real war zones.[1] In the last decade or so trafficking in human beings has emerged as a major public order issue. Although there are no reliable data on trafficking, "it is believed to be growing fastest in Central and Eastern Europe and the former Soviet Union."[2] According to a CIA report, "an estimated 45,000 to 50,000 women and children are trafficked annually to the United States, primarily by small crime rings and loosely connected criminal networks."[3] Women all around the world suffer from domestic violence, sexual harassment, rape, and other forms of assault, which cumulatively leave them living in a perpetual state of terror.[4] Violations of rights in these examples are usually not inflicted by the state but by private citizens or organizations, although the state can play crucial and alternative roles as the protector of the victims, provider of relief agencies, assistant or

The research assistance of Antigona Kukaj and Mohammad Faridi in preparing this chapter is gratefully acknowledged.

collaborator of the perpetrators, instigator, or an indifferent actor that permits violations. Private individuals, groups, and corporate entities, referred to here as non-state actors, can also function as an advocate through direct action of human rights activism or by respecting and upholding human rights norms.

The purpose of this volume is to identify the complex network of non-state actors that affect human rights positively or negatively, their relationship with the state, and the mechanisms that would help hold them accountable or even turn them from being violators to being promoters of human rights. To fulfill this goal, it employs an interdisciplinary approach and brings together the research and analyses of international scholars who address some critical issue areas and the involvement of non-state actors in them.

PROGRESS AND OBSTACLES IN PROMOTING HUMAN RIGHTS

Recent developments associated with globalization, the proliferation of intrastate conflicts, the increasing power of international financial institutions, and the diffusion of human rights norms have led many commentators to speak of the decreasing relevance of the sovereign state in international relations.[5] Others have questioned the argument that sovereignty is eroding by pointing out that sovereignty has never been absolute; according to this view, the best guide to state behavior is differentials in national power and interests rather than adherence to international norms.[6] The merits of the debate on the absolute nature of sovereignty notwithstanding, few would question that human rights has influenced modern developments in ways unforeseen at the time of the adoption of two key postwar documents: the charters of the United Nations and of the International Military Tribunal (also known as the Nuremberg Charter).

Responding to the horrors of the Second World War, these documents have sought to maintain a delicate balance between the incorporation of aspirational provisions and the grounding of the said provisions by the exigencies of the sovereign prerogatives of key member states. In the Nuremberg Charter, the most forward-looking provision on crimes against humanity was subsumed under the crimes against the peace and war crimes provisions of the charter.[7] In the Charter of the United Nations, although the promotion and encouragement of respect for human rights was listed as one of the main purposes of the organization, in practice that was treated as inferior to the maintenance of international peace and security. The message was clear: leaders could be punished only for those human rights violations that resulted from the commission of interstate aggressive acts. Any advocacy on behalf of human rights had to be conducted on a consensual basis, primarily in collaboration with the states concerned. Thus, the Charter of the United Nations employed the unthreatening language of promotion, as opposed to protection, of human rights and posited a human rights strategy based on a partnership between the UN and member states.

Even the greatest optimists, however, would not have predicted that what began in 1945 would slowly but steadily gather momentum and change the conduct of international politics in a decisive manner. Under the UN auspices, "an impressive normative architecture" pertaining to human rights has gained wide acceptance in the international community, though its implementation still leaves a lot to be desired.[8] This goes beyond the still growing corpus of international human rights law, and encompasses—among other things—the catalytic role of nongovernmental organizations (NGOs). NGOs played a key role in the incorporation of human rights provisions in the Charter of the United Nations, and the Economic and Social Council (ECOSOC) authorized their consultative status as early as 1946, even before the adoption of the Universal Declaration of Human Rights (UDHR).[9] In just a few decades NGOs have transformed themselves from marginal entities into important actors capable of mobilizing support for increasing scrutiny and pressure against governments,[10] as evidenced in the anti-apartheid campaign. The anti-apartheid struggle, coupled with similar broadly based coalition examples at the international and regional levels (like the Conference on Security and Cooperation in Europe [CSCE] Process),[11] clearly demonstrated the potential for transformative politics counterposed to those that rest on violence and armed struggle.[12]

These relative successes exemplified both the strengths and the weaknesses of the legal paradigm, the dominant paradigm in human rights research and advocacy. The legal paradigm is premised on an antagonistic relationship between the individual/group and the state. The focus of human rights work centers on standard setting, and the role of advocacy work is the articulation of credible legal strategies to hold states accountable to the standards already adhered to. The discrepancy between formal adherence to these standards and the actual practice of states provides the opening for public exposure and eventual compliance (the strategy of shaming).[13]

While the successes of this paradigm have been rightly celebrated, its shortcomings are becoming increasingly apparent. Two are of particular relevance here. First, the targeting of the state has failed to capture the existential variety of non-state actors capable of gross and systematic human rights violations. The inadequacy of this approach is reflected in the gap between states' increasing adherence to international human rights standards (via ratification of the relevant legal instruments) and the continuing violation of these standards in practice. Usual explanations relating to the ritualistic rather than substantive nature of this process provide only a partial answer to this problem.[14] The second is related to the first. By promoting the idea of the "rogue state," human rights discourse has often failed to capture adequately the dual nature of the state as both promoter and abuser of rights. In certain instances the shift from a perception of subversion to one of protection is an indispensable precondition for effective human rights advocacy.

While the state's dual role is undermined, the responsibilities of non-state actors are frequently ignored. Yet an acknowledgment of the dual potential (promoter/abuser) of non-state actors can be found in a variety of human rights instruments. The preamble of the UDHR provides that "every individual . . . keeping this Declaration constantly in mind, shall strive by teaching and education to promote respect for these rights and freedoms and by progressive measures, national and international, to secure their universal and effective recognition and observance." Likewise, both the International Covenant on Civil and Political Rights (ICCPR) and the International Covenant on Economic, Social and Cultural Rights (ICESCR) clearly state in their preambles that "the individual having duties to other individuals and to the community to which he belongs, is under a responsibility to strive for the promotion and observance of the rights recognized in the present Covenant." The language used in the subsequent instruments also points to increasing expectations; the consensual tone of the UDHR is replaced with an obligatory one associated with duties in the covenants. More recently, in 1999, the UN General Assembly adopted Resolution 53/144, which stipulates that "individuals, groups, institutions and non-governmental organizations have an important role to play and a responsibility in . . . promoting human rights and fundamental freedoms."[15]

This convergence between the rising profile of non-state actors and the changing notions about state sovereignty[16] poses critical conceptual and analytical problems for the promotion and protection of human rights norms. While the state is clearly relevant, the evolving coordinates of social, economic, and political life add new sources of power to the traditional cartography of authority and accountability.[17]

ISSUES AND QUESTIONS

The study of non-state actors should not be viewed simply as a much-needed corrective to the state-centered nature of the prevailing human rights paradigm. Instead, an analytical focus on non-state actors is a response to noticeable shifts in the boundaries of decision-making contexts and to the reallocation of capabilities within them. As a result of the multiple and often overlapping nature of cross-border networks operating in open-ended/flexible spaces, the frame of reference for the solution of many of the world's problems, including human rights abuses, is clearly evolving. In the process the constant fluidity of inner boundaries is sensitizing us to the fixity of outer (global) boundaries. As Peter Singer aptly notes, "how well we come through the era of globalization . . . will depend on how we respond ethically to the idea that we live in one world."[18]

This realization raises a set of critical issues. Bringing non-state actors into the picture aims at a better understanding of the constitutive elements of the human rights universe in order to minimize sources/pathways to abuse and maximize sources/pathways to promotion and protection. The authors in this volume have sought, through a variety of conceptual and methodological lenses, and with a focus on key questions raised in a range of critical issue areas, to dissect the non-state actor experience and assess its relevance in understanding the challenges confronting the prevailing human rights paradigm.

The first three chapters in this volume attempt to identify non-state actors and define their role in the human rights universe. Zehra F. Kabasakal Arat and Michael Goodhart offer a critique of the current state-centered structure. Arat points out that while the language of international human rights treaties recognizes the role and responsibilities of non-state actors, the narrow legalist approach, which allows only states to be parties to the conventions and lacks proper enforcement mechanisms, has culminated in an ineffective state-centered human rights regime. Nevertheless, she argues that giving proper attention to the role of non-state actors is likely to improve our understanding of the complex network of actors that violate or promote human rights. She urges analysts to consider not only the direct actions and impact of non-state actors on human rights, but also the relationship between non-state actors and the state, as well as the interaction among non-state actors; each actor, whether state or non-state, may instigate and support violations or promote human rights through its work and influence on other actors.

Michael Goodhart locates the prominence of the classical liberal theory of human rights at the heart of the problem. He notes that the artificial separation of the "public" and "private" realms has led to the exclusion of non-state actors and left some people, especially women, particularly vulnerable and subject to violations by private actors who dominate not only the public but also the private domain, including the family. Highlighting certain points, which he calls "puzzles," as challenges to the development of a new approach, he illustrates the inconsistencies and self-contradictions of liberal theory. For example, while the theory claims to leave the private domain out of reach of the state (and thus could justify the indifference of the state toward issues like domestic violence), liberal states actually seek to regulate the private domain through various mechanisms (for example, licensing marriages, birth registrations, regulations of divorce). As an alternative, he proposes a "functional approach" that would locate and focus on violations, no matter who the perpetrator is, especially in places where we see power relations and governance. These involve not only states but also corporations and institutions such as families.

Focusing on violations of human rights, Herbert Spirer and Louise Spirer propose a procedure that would contribute to the assessment of violations perpetrated by non-state actors. They claim that the accounting process for different types of rights and by different kinds of actors would not need to be substantially different. Once we identify the non-state actors, then we can appraise the extent to which those actors respect the provisions of human rights treaties. Just as a state's treatment of people in custody is assessed vis-à-vis several Articles of the ICCPR, a corporation's violation of economic and social rights (such as unhealthy work conditions) can be assessed through the clear definition of the provisions of the ICESCR. Nevertheless, the authors acknowledge that the monitoring of non-state actors would be challenging, and the technical knowledge and other means necessary tend to be beyond the reach of most human rights NGOs (and perhaps that of poor states as well).

If external monitoring is difficult, and better equipped and resourceful actors such as corporations can escape accountability, would there be some other mechanism that would prevent violations and turn violators into protectors? The next three chapters address this question for transnational corporations. Rainer Braun and Judy Gearhart discuss the circumstances under which the corporate codes of conduct would be effective in protecting human rights. Underscoring the political character of human rights, that is, the call for change in power structures, the authors argue that the corporate code of conduct should be designed to empower the workers in order to protect their human rights. They note that human rights can be viewed *narrowly*, by placing the main protective obligation on the state and relying upon its monitoring and regulation of other actors, or *broadly*, by giving voice and choice to the powerless within the power structures. While the former "regulatory approach" typically deals with human rights violations after the fact by seeking remedies for the victims and penalizing the perpetrators to create a deterrent for the future, the broader "participatory approach" is more likely to be preventive, since it would involve the participation of the population that is supposed to be the beneficiary of protective mechanisms, both in defining the norms and monitoring their implementation. However, the participatory approach does not need to replace the regulatory one. The authors insist that they should complement each other, and third-party regulations are necessary to maintain the progress and ensure that the protection of labor rights is not achieved at the expense of other human rights.

James L. Gunderson points out that transnational corporations (TNCs), employing approximately 54 million people around the world and accounting for nearly one-tenth of the world gross domestic product (GDP), are indeed powerful actors that affect the lives of many. He notes that the human rights responsibilities of TNCs are not limited to their employees and that they have to respect the rights of the communities in which they operate, as well as to the consumers of their products, especially in regard to the rights that involve health and safety. Sought in developing countries for creating employment opportunities and introducing new technology, TNCs can use their power to influence state policies (though that influence has often been exercised to repress labor rights and support abusive regimes). Moreover, some companies, due to their place in the value chain, can influence the conduct of other companies; they can use their position and bargaining power to improve respect for human rights by companies that supply raw materials or distribute and advertise their products. Declarations and resolutions of the International Labour Organization (ILO), the 1976 UN Code of Conduct for Transnational Corporations and its 1992 replacement, the Business Council for Sustainable Development, and various instruments of the Organization for Economic Co-operation and Development (OECD), such as the OECD Guidelines for Multinational Enterprises, set the human rights standards for TNCs. However, monitoring corporate conduct and holding corporations accountable is another matter. Gunderson finds poor states in the developing world ill-equipped for this task. He argues that courts in the industrialized countries, consumer boycotts and media coverage, international human rights NGOs, and shareholders are better suited for the task of shaming companies and pressing them for change. With a brief reference to Schlumberger, a technology TNC, he concludes that a better understanding by business of the importance of adhering to human rights standards may lead companies to the adoption of policies more consistent with these standards, even without external pressures.

While external pressures, such as shaming and consumer boycotts, have contributed to some positive changes in the labor practices of TNCs active in the apparel and shoe industries, TNCs in the oil industry continue to face criticism for their blatant disregard of environmental protection standards. Royal Dutch Shell's activities have been targeted not only for environmental but also for social consequences. Paul Martin's chapter examines the human rights conflicts surrounding the Shell Group and the company's response to various criticisms. He notes that while the company has been rather successful in improving its record on environmental rights by adopting more advanced and sound technologies, addressing the violation of social and economic rights has been more complex. Although executives in headquarters have understood the need to "do business differently" and have begun implementing a human rights approach, their promotion of the goal of "sustainable development" does not often generate the type of strategies necessary to achieve the desired effect; moreover, local executives are far from displaying the same level of commitment to such an approach. Thus, while Martin praises the voluntary changes, he finds international human rights law to be more explicit and comprehensive than any codes of conduct and views third parties (states and

NGOs) as essential for enforcement purposes. This case study of the Shell Group, which stayed in South Africa throughout the apartheid period and increased its investments in Nigeria immediately after the execution of the author and environmental activist Ken Saro-Wiwa, also poses critical questions about TNC responsibility when dealing with a repressive regime. Although it is clear that aiding and abetting the rulers in the commission of abusive conduct is inexcusable, the human rights implications of doing business in a state of repression are not as clear: Would it legitimize and enhance the power of the regime, or would it facilitate "constructive engagement" in favor of human rights?

No issue areas have highlighted the abusive potential of non-state actors as powerfully as those involving conflict situations. Richard Falk and George J. Andreopoulos address critical aspects of this issue. Focusing on the impact of the September 11 attacks, Richard Falk observes that the attacks, by unleashing a war of global scope, "disclosed the potency of non-state, non-territorial 'uncivil society actors,' especially when linked by way of transnational networks." According to Falk, both principal antagonists in this global confrontation are post-Westphalian actors: al Qaeda is a "concealed" transnational network, while the United States operates as a global state exerting, in the name of anti-terrorism, geo-political pressures subversive of territoriality considerations. This new configuration in the global landscape, counterposing the threat of the uncontested hegemony of the United States to the threat of mega-terrorism, has had an adverse impact on world order. Among the most prominent manifestations of this impact is the missed opportunity for promoting the "potential utility of a law enforcement approach to global security" and the restrictions imposed on the operating space of progressive civil society actors who, during the previous decade, actively engaged in global reform initiatives. While the challenges that lie ahead are indeed formidable, Falk outlines four key areas in which creative global society actors can and must contribute to transcend the dilemma posed by mega-terrorism and global imperialism, with a note on the critical role of states that share the concern about this dilemma.

In many modern-day conflicts the rise of non-state violence and, in particular, the deliberate targeting of civilians have rendered the task of ensuring the accountability of the perpetrators of such violence imperative. George Andreopoulos examines the prospects for engagement practices with armed groups, so as to ensure conduct consistent with international human rights law (IHRL) and international humanitarian law (IHL) standards. He analyzes key provisions of the relevant bodies of law (IHRL and IHL) and assesses the importance of their growing convergence. While certain gaps in the protective regime remain, he argues that the emphasis should be placed on strategies for more precise identification of already existing standards and promotion of compliance rather than on additional standard setting. This emphasis is reflected in a series of recent initiatives that include the drafting of a document on fundamental standards of humanity, the recently published International Committee of the Red Cross (ICRC) study on customary international humanitarian law, and NGO innovative mechanisms like the one developed by Geneva Call, which seeks to commit armed groups to a total ban on anti-personnel mines. According to Andreopoulos, non-legally-binding documents would appear to constitute the best vehicle for enhancing accountability among armed groups.

In recent years the biomedical field has been engulfed in a series of controversies ranging from ethical questions concerning certain types of research to the responsibilities incurred by all key actors involved in the production and distribution of the benefits of that research. The next three essays by Peter Juviler, Ruth Macklin, and Alice Page address critical aspects of these debates.

Noting that human genetic research carries both promises and threats for human rights, Peter Juviler points out that it also raises complex ethical issues for public policy. Including several actors such as scientists, bioethicists, human rights scholars, corporations, and parents and children, with different levels of power, access, and ability to make choices, the advancements in gene technology and the genetic revolution in human therapy can invoke nightmares from Aldous Huxley's totalitarian, state-centered dystopia of his much-cited *Brave New World*. Along with a growing number of therapeutic benefits, gene testing and therapy raise issues of privacy and access. Prospects of gene enhancement and human cloning raise issues of eugenic consumerism and concerns for secular and religious values regarding human identity. Contradictions of commerce mean that the marketing and patenting of scientific research and its applications, however beneficial they may be, seem to promise also an intensified "biocapitalism," "consumer eugenics," and deepening social stratification.

The issue of access and, more specifically, of making drugs more affordable to the global South, figures prominently in debates about the meaning of the right to health care, "as well as the more difficult to attain 'right to health.'" Ruth Macklin's contribution addresses vital questions concerning the realization of these fundamental human rights claims in the developing world, the identities of the key actors involved, and the nature and extent of the responsibilities incurred by these actors. In examining these issues Macklin surveys basic facts about biomedical research and its implications, and she identifies six models that characterize the relationship between industrialized country sponsors and developing countries. Macklin argues that only a "full partnership" model between North and South can satisfactorily address the pressing international health needs, and do so in the most ethically sound manner. In this context Macklin discusses three recent developments that involve both state and non-state entities: (1) the decision by some large pharmaceutical companies to reduce the price of anti-AIDS drugs or to donate drugs free of cost; (2) public-private partnerships like the Global Health Fund; and (3) the relative "softening" of the pharmaceutical industry on patent protection. What emerges from an analysis and assessment of these developments, in light of the human rights claims that bear on this issue, is the achievement of modest progress at best, with many conceptual, ethical, and policy questions yet to be resolved. Making drugs affordable is only the first step in the direction of realizing these fundamental rights.

The use of "prior agreements" in international clinical trials addresses another critical aspect of the role of non-state actors (the pharmaceutical companies in this instance) and the promotion/protection of human rights in developing countries—the usual site of clinical research for vaccines and cures for global and local pandemics. Alice Page argues that the two ethical assumptions of international research—that research should respond to the needs of the developing host country and that the population of those countries should benefit from such research—are closely related to the human right to health and the right of all people to share in the benefits of scientific advancements. She proposes negotiating prior agreements with pharmaceutical companies as a way of assuring benefits to the developing host country, which may include technology transfers, capacity building, discounted drugs, and post-trial maintenance of primary care clinics. She also addresses the points made by critics of prior agreements as a prerequisite for research in developing countries (for example, these agreements will delay or prevent research), by providing examples of different types of such agreements.

The complex and varied mosaic of sociocultural forces and practices and the challenges that they have posed to the fashioning of credible institutional responses have generated one of the earliest debates on the impact of non-state actors. After all, it was the acknowledged inability of the prevailing human rights paradigm to seriously address culturally and socially sanctioned forms of abusive conduct, whether in the form of "crimes of commission" or "crimes of omission," that triggered a reconsideration of its fundamental premises. The remaining chapters address varying aspects of this issue.

Anne Nelson and Thomas R. Lansner draw on their experience as both reporters and professors to bring home the importance of media for democracy and human rights. Both put the evolution of media in historical perspective, Nelson mainly in the United States, Lansner internationally. Fighting wars and the motives of profit both put pressures on the right to freedom of opinion, expression, and freedom of information through objective reporting in war and peace. That, Lansner points out, is a relatively new historical development. Nelson divides media into commercialized, mainstream reporters of the news, and media associated with advocacy and analysis of issues underlying the news. Lansner devotes attention to the spread of the Internet, its reach to hitherto isolated groups constrained by a still persistent "digital divide." Human rights and humanitarian NGOs find in media important means of disseminating their findings. Clearly, it is not enough to focus only on the "commercialization" of media, or, on the other hand, only on their importance as reporters in war and peace. The balance struck by these two chapters makes for an important contribution to our "looking beyond the state."

The importance of media in human rights struggles is also addressed by Kevin Bales, albeit in a different era. In his chapter, which focuses on the anti-slavery movements, Bales reports how the public relations team of King Leopold II of Belgium, which used journalists and editors to justify his running of Congo as private enterprise based on slave labor in the 1880s, was countered by the anti-slavery groups that used a new tool, photography, to show the evil character of the ongoing exploitation.

In the history of the human rights movement, no human rights campaign has been more durable and wide-reaching than the one associated with the anti-slavery cause. Arguably, it has been the forerunner of others. Kevin Bales argues that the anti-slavery movement featured the energizing and organizing core of a structured NGO, and its durability, reach, and success were possible because it involved a stabilizing bureaucracy, dedicated leadership, and outreach to existing media. Pointing to the TNCs and transnational criminal organizations as best organized and perhaps the most effective beneficiaries of the new phase of globalization, Bales finds the solution to human trafficking (the contemporary version of the slave trade) in equally well-organized bureaucratic NGOs. These counter-forces, however, should be organized not only internationally, but also in a way that could enhance the capacity of NGOs and states in developing and poor countries that serve as the source of labor.

Non-state actors often take advantage of institutional negligence to exploit the very people whose rights the state deems to be too heavy of a burden to protect/promote. The will of the state to interfere on behalf of the disadvantaged or to provide services that would ensure at least a minimum level of social economic rights has been eroding with the rising popularity of neo-liberalism in shaping economic and social policies. The welfare state, which became the epitome of the Western European countries in the post–World War II era, is rapidly becoming an endangered species. In other societies in which the welfare policies have been more limited, the reductions or rolling back of welfare policies are likely to have a more devastating impact on the most vulnerable segments of the population.

In her chapter Dana-Ain Davis analyzes the welfare reform under the Clinton administration and its causal relationship to the violation of human rights in the everyday experiences of the battered black women in the United States. Even though international human rights norms and standards provide for the protection/promotion of human rights for all women and all peoples, Davis argues that the rights of black women and poor peoples in the United States are often violated by "parastatal" and non-state actors when the state refuses to provide basic needs to its citizens. Arguing that the Clinton administration's welfare reform violates several provisions of the UDHR and many human rights treaties, Davis examines the impact of the welfare policies on individual cases. The stories of three women, documented in her larger field research, illustrate the difficulties of documenting the commission of human rights violations by non-state actors, which include retailers and employers, as well as how violations are enabled by policies, case workers, and the media depiction of welfare recipients.

An institution that exerts great influence on the norms and practice of human rights in all societies has been religion. Although the behavioral impact of religious beliefs and teachings varies not only over time and space but also from person to person, for some people and in some societies the authority of religious doctrines can override the rules and policies of the state. In the current discourse of human rights the role of religion is problematized mainly in relation to the treatment of women in certain belief systems[19] or in cases of religious intolerance.

The last chapter, by Willy Fautre, addresses the latter issue by focusing on some recent developments in Europe. With the passing of dictatorships and communism, Europe, East and West, has become an area of relative religious freedom. However, inroads persist on everyone's right to "freedom of thought, conscience and religion" stipulated in the European Convention for the Protection of Human Rights and Fundamental Freedoms and the International Bill of Rights. Discrimination against some minority rights or "new religions" crop up across Europe. Fautre also provides evidence of the part played by organized religion as victim, opponent, and accomplice when it comes to the violations of religious rights. While some groups sue in defense of such rights, some older and larger groups may acquiesce to or even act as accomplices in the violations committed by governments. The ambivalence of organized religion points to the ambiguities of the divine when absorbed into the agendas of religious associations.[20]

As the contributions to this volume make clear, a proper understanding of the human rights universe, let alone the realization of its transformative potential, is becoming increasingly problematic if divorced from the non-state actor experience. To be sure, bringing non-state actors in does not constitute a panacea for the shortcomings of the traditional paradigm. What it does, or better, what we hope to achieve by such a focus, is a clearer and more comprehensive optic for the examination of the increasingly complex web of interactions between state and non-state entities and of the potential pathways toward effective promotion and protection. After all, if the main task of the human rights project is to ensure human well-being, a better understanding of those entities that can sustain, as well as undermine, this task is long overdue.

NOTES

[1] Zehra F. Arat, "Analyzing Child Labor as a Human Rights Issue: Its Causes, Aggravating Policies, and Alternative Proposals," *Human Rights Quarterly* 24, no. 1 (February 2002): 177–204.

[2] United Nations Office on Drugs and Crime, *Fact Sheet on Human Trafficking,* available online. http://www.unodc/en/trafficking_victim_consents.html

[3] Amy O'Neill Richard, "International Trafficking in Women to the United States: A Contemporary Manifestation of Slavery and Organized Crime," Center for the Study of Intelligence (April 2000), iii.

[4] See the special edition on violence against women, Carnegie Council on Ethics and International Affairs, *Human Rights Dialogue,* series 2, no. 10 (Fall 2003).

[5] A typical example of this perspective is Gideon Gottlieb, *Nation against State: A New Approach to Ethnic Conflicts and the Decline of Sovereignty* (New York: Council on Foreign Relations Press, 1993).

[6] Stephen D. Krasner, *Sovereignty. Organized Hypocrisy* (Princeton, NJ: Princeton Univ. Press, 1999), 3–42. In his *Agenda for Peace* document, Boutros Boutros-Ghali observed that "the time of absolute and exclusive sovereignty . . . has passed; *its theory was never matched by reality*" (emphasis added). United Nations General Assembly, Report of the Secretary-General on the Work of the Organization, *An Agenda for Peace: Preventive Diplomacy, Peacemaking and Peace-keeping,* UN Doc A/47/277/S/24111, 17 June 1992, 5.

[7] For this and what follows in this paragraph, see George J. Andreopoulos, "Introduction: A Half Century after the Universal Declaration," in *Concepts and Strategies in International Human Rights* (New York: Peter Lang Publishing, 2002), 2–3.

[8] Richard Falk, "The Challenges of Humane Governance," in Andreopoulos, *Concepts and Strategies in International Human Rights,* 23.

[9] William Korey, *NGOs and the Universal Declaration of Human Rights: "A Curious Grapevine"* (New York: St. Martin's Press, 1998); and Paul Gordon Lauren, *The Evolution of International Human Rights: Visions Seen* (Philadelphia: Univ. of Pennsylvania Press, 1998), 188–90.

[10] See, among others, Margaret E. Keck and Kathryn Sikkink, *Activists beyond Borders: Advocacy Networks in International Politics* (Ithaca, NY: Cornell Univ. Press, 1998); and Claude E. Welch, Jr., *Protecting Human Rights in Africa: Roles and Strategies of Non-Governmental Organizations* (Philadelphia: Univ. of Pennsylvania Press, 1995).

[11] In January 1995, the CSCE was renamed the Organization for Security and Co-operation in Europe (OSCE).

[12] Falk, "The Challenges of Human Governance," 31.

[13] Robert F. Drinan, SJ, *The Mobilization of Shame: A World View of Human Rights* (New Haven, CT: Yale Univ. Press, 2001).

[14] The extent to which the process of adherence to certain rules and standards is devoid of any meaningful impact, except when it suits the interests of the state(s) concerned, is a matter of debate among different schools of thought, in particular between the realists, on the one hand, and the international legal process and constructivist scholars, on the other hand. See John Mearsheimer, "The False Promise of International Institutions," *International Security* 19, no. 3 (Winter 1994–95): 5–49; Abram Chayes and Antonia Chayes, "On Compliance," *International Organization* 47, no. 2 (1993): 175–205; and Martti Koskenniemi, "The Place of Law in Collective Security," *Michigan Journal of International Law* 17 (Winter 1996): 455–90.

[15] United Nations General Assembly, *Declaration on the Right and Responsibility of Individuals, Groups and Organs of Society to Promote and Protect Universally Recognized Human Rights and Fundamental Freedoms*, A/RES/53/144, 8 March 1999.

[16] Richard Higgott, *Coming to Terms with Globalization: Non-State Actors and Agenda for Justice and Governance in the Next Century*, Institute for Globalization and the Human Condition, McMaster Univ., March 1999.

[17] Ibid.

[18] Peter Singer, *One World: The Ethics of Globalization* (New Haven, CT: Yale Univ. Press, 2002), 13.

[19] Zehra F. Arat, "Women's Rights in Islam: Revisiting Qur'anic Rights," in *Human Rights: New Perspectives, New Realities*, ed. Peter Schwab and Adamanta Pollis, 69–93 (Boulder, CO: Lynne Rienner Publishers, 2000): 69–93; and Susan M. Okin, *Is Multiculturalism Bad for Women?* (Princeton, NJ: Princeton Univ. Press, 1999).

[20] Carrie Gustafson and Peter Juviler, eds., *Religion and Human Rights: Competing Claims?* (London: ME Sharpe, 1999).

Part I

Theoretical Questions and Approaches

Looking beyond the State But Not Ignoring It

A Framework of Analysis for Non-State Actors and Human Rights

Zehra F. Kabasakal Arat

INTRODUCTION

The current global human rights regime was initiated as a response to the atrocities of the Second World War and premised on a state-centered paradigm that was negotiated by the members of the United Nations after the war. Although successful in setting a normative framework, the regime has failed to create a political environment or protective mechanisms that would ensure the enjoyment of human rights. Pointing to the state-centered nature of the regime as a partial explanation of its ineffectiveness in protecting human rights, this chapter attempts to present a framework of analysis that incorporates non-state actors as promoters and violators of human rights.

The Origin of the International Human Rights Regime and the Operating Model

With its Charter, the UN started to lead the world toward a political system that redefined not only the interstate relationship, but also the relationship between states and individuals. The Charter placed the promotion and encouragement of human rights among the purposes of the UN, along with the maintenance of international peace and security (Article 1), assigned the task of promoting "universal respect for, and observance of human rights and fundamental freedoms for all without distinction as to race, sex, language or religion" (Article 55), and explicated that "all members pledge themselves to take joint and separate action in cooperation with the Organization for the achievement of the purposes set forth in Article 55" (Article 56). What was initiated with the Charter was later reinforced by the Universal Declaration of Human Rights (UDHR) and the two international covenants, one on economic, social, and cultural rights and the other on civil and political rights.

However, while limiting state sovereignty, the UN Charter, the International Bill of Rights, and other human rights treaties created a human rights regime that is statist. First, parties to the treaties have been states. Second, the language of the documents assigns the primary responsibility for promoting and protecting human rights to the state parties.[1] States are called to refrain from violating the rights of individuals and peoples and charged with taking steps and all appropriate measures to "ensure" or even "guarantee" that the rights are respected and enjoyed equally by all without discrimination. While the emphasis is on states, private individuals' obligation to respect human rights is mentioned in Article 29 of the UDHR: "Everyone has duties to the community in which alone the free and full development of his personality is possible." Moreover, the preambles of both covenants note that "the State Parties to the present Covenant, . . . realizing that *the individual, having duties to other individuals and to the community to which he belongs*, is under a responsibility to strive for the promotion and observance of the rights recognized in the present Covenant, . . . *Agree* upon the following articles" (emphasis added). Nevertheless, the tasks of monitoring the behavior of private individuals and groups, preventing violations by them, and holding them accountable are assigned to the state. In this system the responsibility of monitoring each state stays with the other member states and the agencies of the UN. Consequently, this model focuses on human rights within each state and mainly recognizes (a) *private individuals and groups* only as actual or potential *victims*, (b) *each state* as the violator and protector of the rights of its population, and (c) *each state* and *the UN* as the promoter of human rights that would monitor all states' behavior. Figure 1–1 illustrates this state-centered global human rights regime, which divides the human rights plane into two separate spheres,

Fig. 1–1. Parties held responsible for violating or promoting human rights

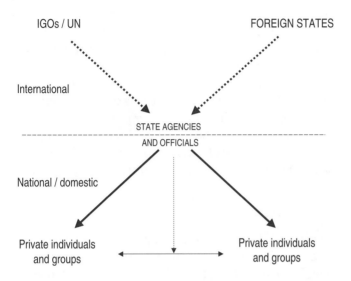

Note: Arrows indicate the direction of action; solid lines stand for responsibility for direct action for protection or violation; dashed lines stand for indirect responsibility (through monitoring, regulation, defining rules, etc.). Tick lines mark the responsibilities emphasized in the current global human rights regime.

domestic and international, and recognizes the states as *active* actors (that violate or protect human rights) and private individuals only as victims.[2]

This statist structure not only has been ineffective in protecting human rights, but when combined with some other factors (that reinforced the state-centered approach as well), it has also led to the selective treatment of human rights. It puts more emphasis on *some* civil and political rights, such as rights claimed by individuals against the state, and almost completely ignores the violations of economic, social, and cultural rights. This has been the case largely because the post–World War II interest in human rights was a response to the Holocaust, which was perceived as a violation of civil and political rights by the officials of Nazi Germany.[3] Moreover, the approach of the several influential states has been shaped by a liberal philosophy that separates the private and public domains of human life, assigns a priority to the protection of the civil and political rights against the state, and focuses on the violations that take place within the "public domain."[4] Finally, even though documentation has proven difficult, connecting a violation to a direct action by state actors tends to be easier in cases of some civil and political rights. The cumulative effect of these assumptions, approaches, and practices has been the violation of the principle of *the indivisibility and interdependence of human rights* and the creation of a *legalistic paradigm* that is premised on an antagonistic relationship between the state and its citizens and relies upon litigation or condemnation. In this context the emphasis is on retrospective rather than anticipatory measures. The ultimate impact has been the lack of enjoyment of human rights by the majority of the world population—despite the proliferation of rights, the treaties that reinforce them, and the countries that sign and ratify these treaties.

An Alternative Framework

The shortcomings of the state-centered approach suggest that the effective protection of human rights requires us to look beyond the state. Monitoring and analyses of human rights violations as well as the development of protective mechanisms have to be extended beyond the conduct of states within their own territories, and the role of non-state actors in violating and protecting human rights has to be examined, with a consideration of the interactions among all actors. Figure 1–2 presents a summary illustration of categories of global actors that are actual or potential violators and promoters of human rights.

By expanding the two-plane analytical model illustrated in Figure 1–1 into a four-plane model, we can acknowledge various forms of *direct* violations/promotions of human rights. Placing individuals at the center, the model acknowledges that any given individual or group is surrounded by a wide variety of national and international actors that can violate his/her/its rights or promote human rights. The *first quarter* highlights the national domain, where both the state and domestic civil actors—private individuals, groups, profit and nonprofit corporations—can be direct violators and protectors (straight arrows) of human rights. They also influence the human rights conditions indirectly by monitoring one another's actions (and imposing sanctions, in the case of the state) to protect human rights, or fail to do so due to ineffective monitoring (circular arrow A). The interaction between the state and non-state actors may also involve collaborative action toward violation or protection of rights.

Fig. 1–2. Global actors as violators and protectors and their interactions

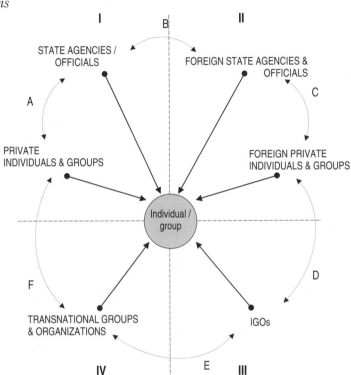

The three quarters that cover the international level include different types of "foreign" actors. The *second quarter* includes the other states and their citizens as the main actors. It denotes that each state not only promotes human rights by monitoring the behavior of other states (circular arrow B), but it can also violate/protect the rights of people who live outside its own territory, the population of other states. Similarly, the residents of each state can affect the human rights of other states' population directly or by exerting influence on other actors.

The *third quarter* embodies intergovernmental organizations (IGOs). Although these organizations are established and guided by state policies, as global actors they are distinct and different from their member states in terms of their goals, power, and procedures. An important distinction for our purposes is the fact that IGOs are not parties to international human rights treaties and consequently are not subject to any formal monitoring mechanisms and sanctions that apply to the states. Here again the straight and circular arrows show that IGOs can affect human rights conditions directly or through their influence on other actors.

The *fourth quarter* includes private transnational actors that have been gaining prominence in global economics, politics and diplomacy. Here we can group them according to their goals as transnational corporations (TNCs) that are guided by profit-making motive and nongovernmental corporate entities, groups, and organizations (NGOs) that are established to achieve different goals that may involve financial or political gains, as well as altruistic missions.

While the post-Westphalian system limits state sovereignty, the current mechanisms of monitoring and maintaining accountability within the human rights regime still operate on the assumption that states are independent entities and free in deciding their internal affairs, formulating policies, and addressing the needs and problems of their residents. Global actors in each of the above-defined categories, however, in addition to their direct role as perpetrators or protectors, can also take actions that may influence other actors and force them to take actions that can affect human rights. Not much different from foreign states and international organizations, which may put pressure on states to promote (and sometimes violate) human rights, civil actors and transnational organizations also exercise pressure on states, as well as on international and other private organizations. Similarly, state agencies can force private groups into violating the rights of others or endorse non-state actors' violations through indifference or even collaboration. Table 1–1 presents an interactive matrix of global actors that can encourage or pressure other actors to pursue activities that can be favorable or unfavorable to the advancement of human rights.

The relationships among the state agencies and non-state actors constitute a matrix because they are multidirectional and dynamic; each actor can be the source and target of pressure at the same time, and such pressure can support *(pro)* or breach *(con)* human rights. In addition to looking beyond the state, we need to look within the state organization as well. An important point about the state, which is often overlooked, is the complexity of its apparatus. With different agencies, which are frequently in conflict or competition with each other, the state is far from being a monolithic entity. Thus, the presented matrix of interaction among global actors acknowledges the pressure that can be exercised by one state agency on another state agency, official, or institution.

There is a host of domestic and international actors that not only violate/protect human rights but also influence the relationship between the state and its population. Among them, some IGOs and transnational organizations have received the attention of human rights scholars and activists.[5] The limelight has been on the human rights NGOs (HRNGOs),[6] which are typically recognized as positive factors in promoting human rights, and TNCs, which attract attention mainly for violating labor and environmental rights.

HRNGOs have been a part of the system from the very beginning. NGOs have been integrated into the international human rights regime, even though their formal position within the system and their relationship with the UN and its agencies have gone through various ups and downs and uncertainties.[7] Expanding their actions beyond monitoring and protests and gaining diplomatic prominence, they have been particularly effective in reframing many issues as human rights issues, as in the case of the campaign to ban land mines (Ottawa Convention), and strengthening the mechanisms of international accountability, as in the case of the creation of the International Criminal Court (Rome Statute).[8]

Although their actions have always had significant implications for human rights, corporations and their conduct have remained a less salient issue in international human rights until recently and have been addressed only in some specific instances. In addition to the Nuremberg Charter, which held corporate managers accountable for war crimes such as pillage, plunder, and spoliation of occupied territories, the Convention against Apartheid stated that corporate involvement in apartheid constituted a crime.[9] More recently, the increasing concern about the impact of environmental deterioration on human rights, as well as awareness of the mobility of capital[10] and its ability to undermine state power, have led some activists and scholars to scrutinize the activities of TNCs.[11]

Missing in the literature is documentation of the *pattern of activities* by the HRNGOs or TNCs that lead to the development of protective measures or systematic violations of human rights. How do these transnational organizations interact with states and other global actors? Which strategies, alliances, and compromises are likely to prevent human rights violations? How can they be held accountable? When does an HRNGO's cooperation with the state allow it to influence the

Table 1–1. A matrix of interactions among global actors: Pressuring/encouraging others to promote or violate human rights

Source \ Target	STATE	DOMESTIC CIVIL ACTORS	FOREIGN STATES	FOREIGN CIVIL ACTORS	IGOs	TRANSNATIONALS
STATE	1.1 **pro.** a state agency regulates state actors to implement human rights norms **con.** the executive restricts courts' autonomy	1.2 **pro.** press publishes information on state violations **con.** corporate executives lobby and pressure the state to ban or restrict unionization	1.3 **pro.** offering aid to monitor elections **con.** providing assistance/guidance in repressive measures	1.4 **pro.** protesting against the state for its violations **con.** selling arms and torture equipment to a repressive state	1.5 **pro.** ILO monitors the implementation of its conventions **con.** IMF forces the recipient state to cut government spending on services/subsidies	1.6 **pro.** international HRNGOs monitor state activities and pressures for improvements **con.** a TNC pressures the state to restrict labor rights
DOMESTIC CIVIL ACTORS	2.1 **pro.** criminalizes human rights violations by law **con.** state actors encourage ethnic hostilities	2.2 **pro.** media produce educational programs on human rights **con.** anti–human rights groups attack human rights activists	2.3 **pro.** supports domestic HRNGOs through political and economic aid **con.** arms a violent militia group	2.4 **pro.** HRNGOs in different countries collaborate **con.** individuals/ groups provide financial support to terrorist groups	2.5 **pro.** UN provides forum for local HRNGOs **con.** forcing the country to sign a treaty deemed unjust by the public and feeding chauvinist sentiments and acts	2.6 **pro.** international HRNGOs assist local HRNGOs **con.** anti-union activity by a TNC
FOREIGN STATES	3.1 same as cell 1.3	3.2 same as cell 1.4	3.3 **pro.** two or more states protest human rights violations in a third state **con.** two or more states conduct an unjust war	3.4 same as cell 1.2	3.5 same as cell 1.5	3.6 same as cell 1.6

Source \ Target	STATE	DOMESTIC CIVIL ACTORS	FOREIGN STATES	FOREIGN CIVIL ACTORS	IGO	TRANSNATIONALS
FOREIGN CIVIL ACTORS	4.1 same as cell 2.3	4.2 same as cell 2.4	4.3 same as cell 2.1	4.4 same as cell 2.2	4.5 same as cell 2.5	4.6 **pro.** international HRNGO informs foreign citizens about violations in a country **con.** a violator TNC misinforms public about its conduct
IGOs	5.1 **pro.** member state proposes human rights resolutions and programs **con.** blocks creation and implementation of human rights instruments	5.2 **pro.** human rights activists monitor the implementation of UN conventions and provide data and reports **con.** a militia group attacks UN aid workers	5.3 same as cell 5.1	5.4 same as cell 5.2	5.5 **pro.** regional and global INGOs collaborate to promote human rights **con.** INGOs support each other in pursuing policies that undermine human rights (e.g., structural adjustment policies)	5.6 **pro.** international HRNGOs monitor and publicize violations by INGOs (for example, the World Bank) **con.** a TNC pressures the IMF to deny funding to a country
TRANSNATIONAL ORGANIZATIONS	6.1 **pro.** regulates TNCs to protect labor rights and environments **con.** bans the activities of international HRNGOs in its territory	6.2 **pro.** local HRNGOs provide information to international HRNGO **con.** religious leaders discredit international HRNGOs working on women's rights	6.3 **pro.** litigation of TNCs for violating human rights **con.** US denying aid to health organizations that work on reproductive health	6.4 **pro.** consumers boycott TNCs for violating human rights **con.** Private groups initiate a discrediting campaign against HRNGOs	6.5 **pro.** UN works with TNCs to develop codes of conduct **con.** An INGO prevents an international humanitarian organization from entering a conflict zone under its control	6.6 **pro.** TNCs adopt codes of conduct **con.** a TNC forces another TNC to undermine environmental or labor rights through fierce competition

state in favor of human rights? When would the HRNGO risk being coopted by the state?

The accountability of some IGOs (better yet, the lack of accountability) has also received some attention. The most overt expression of this has been the chain of protests that started in the late 1990s against the World Trade Organization (WTO), International Monetary Fund (IMF), and the World Bank, in Seattle, Washington, DC, and Prague, respectively. Although these organizations are formed by states, their modus operandi and legal positions are markedly different. Since they are not parties to international human rights treaties, they escape international legal scrutiny to which states are subject. Yet, their decisions have profound direct and indirect impacts on human rights conditions all around the world. Their relationships with the member states are also complex. While they can be used by powerful states as foreign policy tools that serve their national interest and goals, they often restrict the policy options and formulations of the smaller, poorer, and less powerful member states. Especially since the 1970s, the international financial agencies have started to exercise tremendous power over the economic and social policies of debtor states.

The negative impact of the structural adjustment policies (for example, freezing wages, reducing government spending on services and subsidies, and privatization) imposed by the IMF and World Bank on the borrowing states as conditions of lending has been addressed by various advocates of the poor and, more recently, as violations of social and economic rights of the people.[12] The chair of the UN Committee for Economic, Social and Cultural Rights, Philip Alston points out that while demanding "complete transparency" from the borrowing states, the IMF prepares "its structural adjustment policies in utmost secrecy" and "decides on the economic future of entire populations without being accountable to them in any way."[13] The structural adjustment policies have been ineffective in stabilizing or improving economies, except for fighting inflation, and that has been mainly achieved by reducing the purchasing power of the poor and reducing the social services provided by the state. Pierre de Senarclens notes that the IMF and the World Bank "often contributed in the past to the social crisis of developing countries by supporting policies that condemned millions of human beings to a life of misery and grave violations of human rights. . . . As a rule their policy triggered high level of unemployment and increased inequality."[14]

The international economic and political discrepancies, the rapid integration and expansion of international markets, the increasing power of financial agencies, and neo-liberal policies point to the urgency of the political economy of human rights, which has been most neglected yet is essential to the analysis of the violation and realization of social and economic rights.[15]

The largest need, however, exists in addressing the conduct of other non-state actors, both national and transnational, which have been responsible for routine violations of human rights. Among these civil actors we can include the following:

- Organized opposition to the government (for example, political parties, civil associations), some of which may be engaged in armed struggles (for example, guerrilla groups).
- Private enterprises and conglomerates that are engaged in trade, finance, manufacturing, or providing services (for example, hospitals). In addition to the TNCs, the conduct of national and local businesses and corporate entities should be examined in regard to their respect for the rights of their employees, clientele, and the community members at large (see Dana-Ain Davis, Chapter 15 in this volume). They often violate labor and environmental rights. Moreover, they can contribute to the violation of civil and political rights by endorsing repressive regimes.
- Professional organizations, business associations, and labor unions. These are both potential violators and protectors. Their members, staff, and the surrounding community can be subject to discrimination (for example, racism and sexism) and other violations.
- National aid and development organizations, issue-oriented interest groups, including human rights advocacy groups and organizations. Due to their altruistic missions or concerns over public interests, these non-state actors are assumed to be benign or pro–human rights. Nevertheless, due to competition, conflicts of interest, prioritization, or ignorance and miscalculations, their actions may result in human rights violations.
- The media. The state monopoly and control of press and broadcasting has always been addressed as a human rights issue. However, private media, in the form of press, radio, television, Internet, and films, have become increasingly important in promoting human

rights or instigating actions that violate them.[16] Media can play a
crucial role by documenting and reporting violations, increasing
people's awareness and understanding of human rights, and promoting human rights norms. On the other hand, the media can
reinforce stereotypes and discrimination, suppress news about
human rights violations and activists' work, or even serve as a
tool of instigation and mobilization for perpetration, as in the
case of the Rwandan genocide.

- Religious institutions and organizations. By providing spiritual
  and ideological guidance (and in some instances an opportunity
  for organization), they can affect people's approach toward human rights. This may depend on their interest in promoting tolerance or hostility toward other religions, justice or discrimination,
  and equality or hierarchy. Religion and religious organizations and
  groups play a particularly important role in regard to women's
  rights. Their subscription to and promotion of some patriarchal
  norms and values make many religions a source of justification
  for gender discrimination and subordination of women.

- People's tribunals, both local and international. People's tribunals can help hold both states and non-state actors accountable,
  when the powerful states resist accountability (for example, the
  Russell Tribunal on War in Vietnam) or when the state lacks the
  will or power to hold local actors accountable (for example, peas-
  ants' associations in Latin America). However, even though they
  are expected to play a protective role, if they themselves are not
  held accountable, tribunals may be engaged in human rights violations, as well.[17]

- Also important among non-state actors are those groups and organizations that are less formal, and for the same reason, are more
  difficult to define, study, and monitor. They include a wide variety of actors: families; ad hoc and spontaneous groups; religious,
  ethnic, and neighborhood communities; street gangs; and secret
  and underground organizations such as the mafia, mercenaries,
  and militia groups. Yet the scope, severity, and impact of the violations inflicted by these informal groups and organizations may
  be worse than the violations caused by states and other actors.[18]

Women's rights, in particular, are likely to be infringed upon by
private individuals and loosely organized non-state actors in various

forms, including domestic violence; honor killings; dowry burnings; restrictions on freedom of movement; forced marriages, prostitution and labor; trafficking; and female genital mutilation. According to the World Organisation against Torture (OMCT), women are not only subject to torture by the state, but the vast majority of violence against women is committed by private individuals and groups, usually family and community members. For example,

- 14,000 women a year are killed by their husbands in Russia . . .
- In Turkey, at least 200 women and girls are killed every year by their families because they have allegedly violated family "honour" . . .
- In France, in 1999 there were between 50,000 and 90,000 rapes committed . . .
- In Costa Rica, about 3 women die per month at the hands of their husband or partner
- In Eritrea, 89% of women have undergone female genital mutilation . . .
- In Estonia, at least 500 women a year are trafficked abroad and forced into prostitution
- In Mali, 22% of girls are married by the time they are 15, increasing their vulnerability to violence in the family environment
- In the United Kingdom, young Asian women commit suicide at higher rates than the general population because of sexual and physical abuse, domestic violence, immigration issues, forced marriages, and racism.[19]

In the United States, as in many countries, the most dangerous place for women is their home. Of attacks experienced by women, in every category of violent crimes, 50 to 60 percent take place in their homes, according to US Department of Justice statistics.[20]

Non-state actors—individuals or groups, informal or organized, ad hoc or continuous—participate in the violation of human rights not only as the perpetrators but also by permitting and endorsing the violations by others (see Table 1–1) A significant challenge is the transformation of these violators into actors that respect, promote, and protect human rights.

Initiatives by the United Nations

Some recent initiatives by the UN Secretariat and General Assembly imply that the UN has been moving toward appreciating the crucial role played by non-state actors and their potential contribution to the promotion of human rights. In March 1999 the UN General Assembly adopted Resolution 53/144, which stipulates that "individuals, groups, institutions and non-governmental organizations have an important role to play and a responsibility in safeguarding democracy, promoting human rights and fundamental freedoms" (Article 18). The increasing role of NGOs at the UN world conferences and treaty negotiations, as well as the "global compact" initiative of the Secretary General Kofi Annan, are indicative of the UN's interest in revising the state-centered character of the human rights regime.[21] In fact, an annual publication of the UN criticizes the state-centered approach for being anachronistic:

> Developed in a state-centered world, the international system of human rights protection is suited to the post-war era, not the era of globalization. New Actors—global corporations, multilateral organizations, global NGOs—wield great influence in social, economic, even political outcomes.[22]

The report continues with a proposal to build a network for norms, institutions, legal frameworks, and enabling economic environment (NILE) for global actors, and assigns leadership and supportive roles to different government branches (legislative, judiciary, and executive) and non-state actors (NGOs, media, academia, business, and international agencies) in working on ten specific areas of action:

1. Launch independent national human rights assessments
2. Remove discriminatory laws that violate rights
3. Integrate human rights into economic policy and development cooperation
4. Accelerate adoption of codes of conduct, including private sector advocacy for human rights
5. Support debt-for-human development swaps, global compacts and 20:20 initiative
6. Develop more effective early warning systems for conflict prevention

7. Support index for international human rights accountability, and ratification campaigns for human rights treaties and institutions
8. Protect the independence of the judicial system and other
   institutions of accountability
9. Promote human rights norms through the education system
10. Strengthen regional human rights institutions.[23]

The report also presents a chart that identifies in what area each of the above-mentioned actors would play a primary or supportive role. Although this approach constitutes an important step, the actors named and the distribution of the responsibilities among them show that the UN still largely relies on states as the primary actors. Nevertheless, the shift in the UN approach and the emphasis placed on corporations, NGOs, and the media among the non-state actors underscore the power sources that dominate the current phase of globalization. The increasingly common trend toward privatization of state economic enterprises and public services transforms the role of both the state and non-state actors.

Crucial to the analysis is the identification of the will and power of each actor. In addition to the actors' commitment to human rights, their ability to play the role of promoter and protector of human rights would also vary. Domestic civil actors that attempt to promote and protect human rights, for example, are likely to be most effective because of their closeness to the issues and to the actual and potential victims. Yet, they would also be the most vulnerable; the hostile environment created by the state or other non-state actors increases the personal risk and cost of activism. How can women's rights activists be protected? Who will support union activists in their struggle against corporate greed? Can the state create a protective environment for them? Who will protect the activists who are critics of the state or who find themselves at odds with the state about human rights?

CONCLUSION

While the current international human rights regime is state-centered in essence, non-state actors play crucial roles as violators, protectors, and intermediaries. The statist approach, which recognizes states as the only duty-bearers, can be (and in some instances has been) successful in holding states accountable, but it has been ineffective, and doomed to be ineffective, in enforcing respect for human rights. Both lack of will and capacity prevent states from fulfilling their responsibilities. Under the changing human rights regime, the states, which lack the will, would continue to

- treat human rights selectively and define the content and standard for the rights they choose to recognize to suit their other goals and objectives
- assign priority to their "national interests" over the interests of individuals and humanity at large
- invoke the principles of sovereignty and nonintervention

By the same token, despite their will some states fail to prevent human rights violations because they lack the capacity to protect the rights of their own population or of people living elsewhere. While the global human rights regime recognizes states as equals, the international system is inherently unequal. The states that have lesser economic and political power are less likely to monitor or affect the behavior of stronger states.[24] It should be noted that

- states are not completely autonomous and free in choosing among policy alternatives; their actions are restricted by powerful internal and external actors (particularly noteworthy is the United States, whose hegemonic power and commitment to neo-liberalism often result in conditions counterproductive to human rights)
- states are not monolithic institutions; their components that subscribe to different norms can subvert pro-rights provisions of other agencies and make them ineffective
- even those states with limited economic and political power continue to enjoy coercive power within their own territory and can use it to repress the dissident voices and oppress the weak

Thus, while non-state actors enter the center stage, their relationship with the state should not be ignored. Non-state actors have to be scrutinized not only to hold them accountable for the violations that may be direct or indirect results of their actions, but also to be able to identify the causes of state failure and the conditions for state liability. Broadening the scope of analysis would be a step toward the development of monitoring and enforcement mechanisms that can transform the human rights regime into a more inclusive and effective one. In fact, such a transformation may be the only way of counterbalancing the negative and disabling impact of the current form of globalization.

NOTES

[1] While the UN Charter and the UDHR refrained from using "protection" of human rights and limited the state obligations to "promotion," the subsequent documents have employed more forceful language.

[2] Regional human rights systems, such as the European Union, the Organization of American States, and so on, are based on similar assumptions and procedures. Academics, too, tend to employ the same approach and rely upon the state as the main protective agency; for example, see Henry Shue, *Basic Rights: Subsistence, Affluence, and U.S. Foreign Policy* (Princeton, NJ: Princeton Univ. Press, 1980).

[3] It should be noted that the Nuremberg Charter included a provision that authorized the Nuremberg Tribunal to declare private organizations to be criminal enterprises but did not provide for criminal prosecution of those organizations. See Beth Stephens, "The Human Rights Obligations of Multinational Corporations under International Law," paper presented at the Columbia University Seminar on Human Rights, New York, 14 November 2000.

[4] Zehra F. Arat, "Human Rights and Democracy: Expanding or Contracting," *Polity* 32, no. 1 (Fall 1999): 119–44. On the false assumptions of the liberal approach, see also Michael Goodhart, Chapter 2 in this volume.

[5] The categories of non-state actors that have received more attention and their areas of influence are shaded in Table 1–1.

[6] I present HRNGOs as a subcategory of NGOs because not all NGOs have the mission of promoting this or that right, and many serve only their own members' interests (for example, business and professional organizations) and may even undermine the rights of others in the process.

[7] Mary Kaldor, "Transnational Civil Society," in *Human Rights in Global Politics,* ed. Tim Dunne and Nicholas J. Wheeler, 195–213 (New York: Cambridge Univ. Press, 1999); Margaret E. Keck and Kathryn Sikkink, *Activists beyond Borders: Advocacy Networks in International Politics* (Ithaca, NY: Cornell Univ. Press, 1998); Claude E. Welch, Jr., *Protecting Human Rights in Africa: Roles and Strategies of Non-Governmental Organizations* (Philadelphia: Univ. of Pennsylvania Press, 1995); Felix Ermacora, "Non-Governmental Organizations as Promoters of Human Rights," in *Protecting Human Rights: The European Dimension,* ed. Franz Matscher and Herbert Petzold (Cologne: Carl Heymanns Verlag KG, 1988); and David Weissbrodt, "The Contribution of International Nongovernmental Organizations to the Protection of Human Rights," in *Human Rights in International Law: Legal and Policy Issues,* ed. Theodor Meron (New York: Oxford Univ. Press, 1984).

[8] David Davenport, "The New Diplomacy," *Policy Review* 116 (December 2002–January 2003). According to Davenport, HRNGOs have been so influential in the drafting process of these two conventions that they have been changing the diplomatic procedures toward creating a "new diplomacy."

[9] Stephens, "The Human Rights Obligations of Multinational Corporations under International Law."

[10] TNCs and their foreign affiliates produced 25 percent of global output in 1998. See United Nations Development Programme, *Human Development Report 2000* (New York: Oxford Univ. Press, 2000), 79.

[11] For example, see J. G. Frynas, "Human Rights and the Transnational Garment Industry in South and South-East Asia: A Focus on Labour Rights," paper presented at the International Conference of the CISS (Comparative Interdisciplinary Studies Section) of the International Studies Association (ISA), Washington, DC, 29–30 August 2000; and Virginia A. Leary, "Globalization and Human Rights," in *Human Rights: New Dimensions and Challenges,* ed. Janus Symonides, 265-79 (Aldershot, England: Ashgate Publishing, 1998).

[12] The critics of the negative impact of some larger development projects of the World Bank, such as dams that flooded agricultural land and residential areas, tend to employ a human rights language more frequently (for example, violating people's right to shelter, to earn a living, and so on). For a brief discussion of the impact of the IMF and the World Bank decisions on child labor and other human rights violations, see Zehra Arat, "Analyzing Child Labor as a Human Rights Issue: Its Causes, Aggravating Policies, and Alternative Proposals," *Human Rights Quarterly* 24, no. 1 (February 2002): 177–204.

[13] UN Committee for Economic, Social and Cultural Rights, 30 June 1998, E/C12/1998/SR20.

[14] Pierre de Senarclens, "The Politics of Human Rights," in *The Globalization and Human Rights,* ed. Jean-Marc Coicaud, Michael Doyle, and Ann-Marie Gardner, 137–59 (Tokyo: United Nations Univ. Press, 2003), 153.

[15] Zehra F. Kabasakal Arat, "Forging a Global Culture of Human Rights: Origins and Prospects of the International Bill of Rights," *Human Rights Quarterly* (May 2006); and Michael Freeman, *Human Rights: An Interdisciplinary Approach* (Cambridge, UK: Polity Press, 2002), 173.

[16] The role of the private media has been increasing due to the recent trend of liberalization. The state has a monopoly in only 5 percent of the countries (see United Nations Development Programme, *Human Development Report 2000,* 39).

[17] On peasant tribunals in Peru, for example, see John Gitlitz, "Peasant Justice and Respect for Human Rights: Peru," in *Human Rights: New Perspectives, New Realities,* ed. Peter Schwab and Adamanta Pollis, 53–68 (Boulder, CO: Lynne Rienner Publishers, 2000).

[18] For an analysis of the communal invoking of the concepts of honor and shame as a way of violating the rights of women and racial minorities in North America, see Rhoda E. Howard, *Human Rights and the Search for Community* (Boulder, CO: Westview Press, 1995).

[19] OMCT, "Press Release: OMCT Observes the International Day for the Elimination of Violence Against Women," 25 November 2003, Available online.

[20] Bureau of Justice Statistics, Office of Justice Program, the US Department of Justice, http://www.ojp.usdoj.gov/bjs/

[21] The viability of the proposed global compact or other codes of conduct as a protective mechanism of human rights is questionable. In order to be effective, the codes of conduct should be comprehensive and include clearly set standards, auditing systems that are established and run by agencies independent of corporations, and penalties for noncompliance. See Roger Norman, "Privatizing Human Rights: The End of the Rights Regime?" paper presented at the Columbia University Seminar on Human Rights, New York, 8 May 2000.

[22] United Nations Development Programme, *Human Development Report 2000*, 43.

[23] Ibid., 126.

[24] See Richard A. Falk, *Human Rights Horizons: The Pursuit of Justice in a Globalizing World* (New York: Routledge, 2000).

2

Human Rights
and Non-State Actors

Theoretical Puzzles

Michael Goodhart

INTRODUCTION

I argue in this chapter that making sense of the roles played by non-state actors (NSAs) in the real world of human rights practice requires a thorough revision of the conceptual framework of human rights. The editors' introduction makes clear why we must be concerned with NSAs in the first place; my aim is to translate this concern into critique and to suggest what lines a critical reconstruction of the human rights framework might follow.

The argument proceeds in four steps. First, I provide a brief overview of the traditional liberal rights framework that informs contemporary human rights theory, emphasizing three of its most salient features: the ideas that human rights are natural, that governments are created through a social contract to see to their protection, and that this device anchors them practically and conceptually in the public realm. Next, I show how growing awareness of NSAs' role in both the violation and the protection and promotion of human rights raises significant empirical questions about the liberal paradigm adequacy in explaining the real world of human rights practice. The third section draws on these observations in formulating six theoretical puzzles regarding the incorporation of NSAs into our thinking about human rights. These puzzles, in turn, indicate that taking account of NSAs requires a thorough reconceptualization of human rights, a careful, critical reconstruction of the theoretical framework. I cannot develop such an alternative framework here, but in the fourth section I offer some conjectures regarding its construction.

THE LIBERAL HUMAN RIGHTS PARADIGM

No definitive account of the traditional or liberal human rights paradigm exists or could exist. I shall focus here on the most salient common features of various liberal accounts (for example, Locke, Pufendorf, Kant, and Rawls): an emphasis on rights as natural, rational, and universal; a contractual justification for political institutions that protect rights; and a clear distinction between public and private spheres generated by the contract, spheres in which the meaning and realization of rights differ considerably. Let me be clear that my analysis concerns this composite, not any specific theorists, and necessarily sacrifices detail to facilitate useful generalizations of the type indispensable for my purposes here.

In the liberal tradition rights are *natural.* Just what this means is contested, but three ideas stand out.[1] First, natural rights are universal; everyone possesses them merely by virtue of being human. This universality, coupled with the equality always associated with it, entails that everyone has the same rights. Second, natural rights are rational; all rational human beings can know or discern them. Finally, natural rights create a presumption of noninterference that grounds government on consent. Because rights are natural, legitimate government must be consensual. In liberalism these features of rights sometimes have justified denying human rights to certain individuals, those—like women or laborers—whose rationality was deemed inferior or deficient. Even this exclusion frequently assumed the guise of consent, through contracts that were involuntary or to which the excluded individuals were not parties.[2]

Nonetheless, the abstract notion that rights are natural was crucially important to the political projects that the liberal theorists hoped to advance. Ascribing natural rights to individuals has the effect of leveling social and political hierarchies and transforming the justifications for rule.[3] Rule based on birth, rank, or special status (for example, divine right) becomes invalid and illegitimate if one accepts that all people possess rights simply as humans. This latter assertion is devilishly hard to demonstrate, but its radical political appeal ensured its widespread and enduring popularity. Moreover, the logic of natural rights, once introduced, is irrepressible, since their universality provides the theoretical and normative resources to challenge practical exclusions.[4]

The social contract was the mechanism devised by liberal theorists for representing consent to government. Whether treated as a quasi-historical event or a purely hypothetical device, the contract explained how naturally free and equal individuals came to be legitimately ruled. Rational individuals recognize that by transferring their right and power of enforcement to a government established for that explicit purpose, they can avoid certain inconveniences and achieve certain efficiencies. Consent legitimizes rule by making submission to it voluntary and thus consistent with the natural freedom and equality of individuals.[5]

The social contract establishes public and private realms; the public, the realm of civil society and government, is created explicitly by the contract and establishes the legitimate power of the state, at least for so long as the state fulfills its obligation to protect the rights of citizens. The social contract also structures the private realm, both in the immediate sense that what is private is determined by those "reserved" or "retained" rights held by citizens qua natural individuals, and in the mediate sense that public authority regulates and maintains the private sphere through various laws and institutions. The two realms are mutually constitutive. Because rights are natural (and thus pre-political), a presumption of noninterference governs the relations between the two spheres; only those rights and powers explicitly transferred to the state through the social contract can override this presumption.

The liberal paradigm, then, explicitly charges states with protecting and defending citizens' rights. Paradoxically, it also conceives the state as the primary *threat* to citizens' rights. The very power vested in the state for preserving rights makes it a grave threat to them. In fact, most liberal theorists have worried little about the state's ability to protect individuals from one another, assuming that rational citizens would delegate sufficient powers to ensure that the job gets done. Instead, they worry almost exclusively about the state's potential for abusing its considerable power, detailing the limits on governments' powers and prerogatives.

This liberal model of natural rights informed the postwar human rights framework constructed through the UN. This is clear in the drafting and language of the UDHR and its related covenants,[6] as well as the later UN conventions and declarations, as I shall indicate below.

NSAs and the Inadequacy of the Liberal Paradigm

The roles played by NSAs in the violation of human rights as well as in their protection, promotion, and enforcement demonstrate the liberal paradigm's inadequacy for making sense of the real world of human rights practice. Let me first address NSAs as violators.

That states pose the primary threat to individuals' human rights no longer persuades. For women, the idea was never plausible; the physical and psychological violence directed against them by men "in private" amounts to a clear violation of their right to security and other basic liberties. To be sure, the state played a significant role in empowering men in their exercise of this power—through laws concerning marriage, couverture, property, inheritance, custodianship of children, and men's unrestricted right of sexual access to their wives' bodies, as well as through a general stance of "noninterference" in "private matters." Indeed, it is precisely because these violations occur on the "other" side of the public/private distinction that the state does not get involved; men's private "rights" are women's domestic wrongs.[7]

This brief illustration suggests two flaws with the liberal paradigm as it concerns NSAs and the violation of human rights. The first involves definitional problems: who counts as a "human" and how "human rights" are defined. If women are not considered human, or fully human in the manner of men and citizens, then obviously the liberal paradigm will not adequately protect their rights. This problem has been partially addressed through the feminist movement's successful struggle for woman suffrage and through efforts to eradicate legal distinctions between women's and men's rights, though more remains to be done.[8] Yet insofar as liberalism continues to insist on a rigid public/private distinction, women face gendered assumptions about the domestic division of labor and about their distinctive "nature" that too often translate into rights violations, in fact if not in law.

One of the central challenges for women's security is to win acceptance of men's violence against women as a human rights issue—or, of "women's human rights." This challenge demonstrates that definitions of rights refer primarily to the state and its interference in the activities of (male) citizens. Since men were citizens before women were, and *men's* rights qua husbands, fathers, and masters were upheld as *citizens'* rights by the state, the liberal definitions of human rights do not comprehend many wrongs done to women, children, and workers. These patriarchal assumptions anchor the liberal framework and are not easily eradicated.

This leads us directly into the second limitation of the liberal paradigm, a limitation with respect to its practical understanding of human rights. The assumption that human rights violations are committed by states, and states alone, radically restricts the functional meaning of human rights. Women should, of course, enjoy security from intimidation, physical abuse, and unwarranted detention at the hands of state authorities—as should men. But if the point of such a right is to protect the human dignity of women and men, say, or to ensure their autonomy, a narrowly constructed right against the state will fall unacceptably short and leave violations by NSAs unaddressed.

However, many NSAs also play vital parts in protecting and promoting human rights. NGOs like Amnesty International and Human Rights Watch, with more traditional relief agencies like Oxfam or the Red Cross/Red Crescent, are virtually synonymous with human rights today. These groups and others, which include countless individuals, monitor human rights locally and globally, pressure governments, provide aid and relief, raise awareness, and even participate in shaping human rights law and practice through UN conferences and other forums. Despite the limitations of some NGO-led approaches,[9] the human rights system could barely function without such groups.

It should be noted that while the UDHR and its associated covenants remain firmly rooted in the liberal tradition, subsequent instruments, such as the Convention on the Elimination of All Forms of Discrimination against Women (CEDAW) and General Recommendation 21 of the Committee on the Elimination of Discrimination Against Women (1994) begin to redress the shortcomings just canvased.[10] Moreover, the increasing *formalization* of NGOs' role throughout the system, coupled with mounting worries about terrorism, globalization, domestic violence, and other forms of "non-state" human rights violations, indicates that there is little dispute about the central role NSAs play in human rights practice today.

Theoretical Puzzles

The growing role of NSAs on the violations and enforcement sides of the liberal human rights paradigm, described above, demonstrates empirically its inadequacy for making sense of what I have been calling the real world of human rights practice. In this section I identify six theoretical puzzles occasioned by tensions between the liberal framework and the contemporary status of NSAs. These puzzles are theoretical in the sense that they address the conceptual framework of human rights; the puzzles speak to difficulties with which we must come to terms if we hope to make sense of NSAs and human rights.

Puzzle #1: What Is a Non-State Actor?

The variety of NSAs is impressive; the list includes corporations, organizations, individuals, and informal associations (see Arat, Chapter 1, and Spirer and Spirer, Chapter 3, in this volume). The first puzzle is that states are the only entities that are *not* NSAs. Superficially this is quite obvious, but putting it just this way brings the real problem into relief. *Non-state actor* is certainly a meaningful *label*, but it does not follow that it is a useful *concept*. What is the unifying characteristic—to use Wittgenstein's famous phrase, the "family resemblance"—among these diverse agents? What reasons might we have for thinking that there is some coherence among the members of this set given that it is defined negatively, in terms of what its members are not, rather than in terms of what they are? Supposing there is no such common characteristic, we might still sensibly be concerned with a neglected group of actors unified solely by their shared neglect. The challenge is to identify connections at the conceptual level as we consider the problems associated with specific NSAs in various contexts.

A subsidiary puzzle arises because the term *non-state actor* is more ambiguous than it might initially appear. A vast array of state-related actors, agencies, and organizations spans the spectrum from global to local. Some receive state funds and comprise states' representatives or officials; examples include IGOs, political parties, and many civic associations. Other NSAs carry out state-delegated functions in exchange for payment: relief agencies, contractors, hospitals, prison operators, and private security firms all fall into this category. Others, like terrorist cells and paramilitary outfits, may be sponsored covertly by states. Still others, such as TNCs and financial speculators, operate within a framework of rules for domestic and global trade and finance explicitly created by states through IGOs like the IMF and WTO. Does it help to conceive these actors as *non-state* actors? How much state involvement, and of what kind, makes an actor a *state* actor? What responsibility do states bear for the activities of such agencies, and how do we make that determination? State-related actors force us to question the neat dichotomy implied by the idea of NSAs.

Puzzle #2: What Is the Difference between a Crime and a Human Rights Violation?

In the liberal paradigm human rights violations are typically committed by states; the difference between crimes and human rights violations is mainly a question of the violator's identity. But this view has never been entirely satisfactory. To begin with, the state is "created" precisely to assure protection of individuals' rights against violations committed by other individuals. Even in the liberal paradigm, then, crimes and human rights violations are confounded and the identity of the violator does not explain everything. Confusion on this point is endemic. Among the earliest human rights instruments, the Genocide Convention explicitly incorporates private individuals, and early UN instruments recognize a duty of NSAs to respect and promote human rights. Still, the substantive Articles of those agreements are clearly framed with states in mind.

The distinction is also problematic because one aim of postwar human rights activism and jurisprudence has been to eliminate the distinction by securing the national and international criminalization of human rights violations. Still, we do not associate human rights violations with crimes in everyday parlance. Wrongs and injustices are considered human rights violations if they shock and outrage the conscience of humanity. On the other hand, as Jack Donnelly has argued, human rights are especially powerful precisely when positive law and policy fail to address grave moral wrongs and gross injustices in society.[11]

Although more recent human rights theory and practice have moved away from this early liberal focus on states as violators, the close association between states and human rights violations lingers.[12] Once we accept that NSAs are major violators of human rights, however, what remains of this liberal association is exploded. Even if we agree that the distinction between crimes and human rights violations seems worth rescuing, it is not clear how we can rescue it: How can we differentiate human rights violations from (other) crimes?[13] Is every murder, every rape, a human rights violation? Probably so—and there is little problem in thinking of them as such. What about assaults? Is a barroom brawl a violation of human rights? The probable answer here is, "it depends." But it is hard to see on what it depends. If the sharp distinction between human rights and more "pedestrian" wrongs blurs, will the moral and political power of human rights be seriously degraded?[14] Then again, we differentiate easily among crimes: jaywalking and kidnapping are both crimes, but we do not regard them as anything like equivalent wrongs. We need to weigh the value of preserving the distinction against the difficulty of maintaining it.

Puzzle #3: Protection, Promotion, and Enforcement of Human Rights

The third puzzle concerns the extent to which we want to move away from a state-centered view when it comes to the protection, promotion, and enforcement of human rights. For instance, one frequent criticism of corporate codes of conduct is the *lack of a state role* in enforcing them.

The reluctance to consider meaningful enforcement or compliance except under state auspices actually implies a much *greater* role for the state in human rights enforcement. If we expand the human rights framework to recognize NSAs as potential violators while insisting on a state role in enforcement, much more vigorous and intrusive state involvement in the activities of a very wide range of groups would become necessary. This prospect only grows when we consider monitoring functions. This puzzle is all the more puzzling because students of human rights are well aware of NGOs' crucial role in monitoring and promoting human rights—as well as their positive (if indirect) effect on enforcement through publicity and political pressure.

States have jealously guarded their exclusive control over their internal affairs,[15] often invoking sovereignty as a trump in response to sanctions or criticism of human rights abuses. This makes insistence on a state role in human rights enforcement even harder to comprehend, especially when we recall that much of the progress that has been made in protecting and enforcing human rights has come through attacking sovereign privilege. Perhaps it is because NGOs have become so widely accepted as part of the current (state-centric) system of human rights enforcement, and their contributions are so widely recognized, that so little attention is given to their role in enforcement. Of course, doubts about corporate codes of conduct arise in part from suspicions about the goals and motives of corporations, doubts that are in many instances warranted. Still, one can imagine a much greater role for community groups, universities, charitable organizations, and many other NSAs in the effective protection, promotion, and enforcement of human rights, and one can imagine a number of additional roles that traditional NGOs might take on in this process. Besides, it makes little sense to rule out solutions before we have fully defined the problem. Many potential efforts in the areas of protection, promotion, and enforcement—like human rights audits and impact assessments and citizen councils and juries—deserve serious consideration.

This puzzle is also significant because of the dual role of states as violators and protectors of human rights. While focusing on NSAs, we should not be blind to state's ongoing role as violators of human rights or to the correlation between intrusive state power and the frequency and severity of violations. Since states will play a crucial role in any expanded human rights regime, devising new and effective roles for NSAs in protection, promotion, and enforcement must be a priority.

Puzzle #4: Sovereignty and Human Rights

As we have seen, sovereign power in the liberal paradigm comes from individuals; it is power transferred from individuals to the state for the express purpose of protecting natural human rights. The contractually constituted state at the heart of the liberal paradigm is, considered externally, the sovereign state of international relations theory. In this external dimension the state's legitimacy has traditionally been taken for granted; it enjoys a presumptive moral and political legitimacy reflected in the UN Charter. Internally, the sovereign state derives its legitimacy from the consent of the people. Yet these de facto and de jure dimensions of state legitimacy remain strangely divorced in much international theory and practice.

The puzzle connected with sovereignty is twofold. One aspect concerns how we should think about the legitimacy of NSAs involved in the protection and enforcement of human rights; the other concerns what we should make of the widely lamented "decline" or "erosion" of sovereignty from a human rights perspective. NSAs' legitimacy problem is exemplified in complaints about the undemocratic nature of certain international human rights NGOs. Whence do such groups derive their authority? Unlike liberal (contractually constituted, sovereign) states, there is no presumption of consent and no corresponding element of control involved in their operations. Should we understand their authority or legitimacy as a function of the ends they seek? How can these be assessed, and by whom? In the liberal paradigm the right to participate in governance has been associated exclusively with the state (for reasons just described). Should that right now extend to participation in governing NSAs involved in human rights enforcement? How can we make sense of the role of "private" (non-state) actors in carrying out governance (state-like) functions?

With respect to the alleged decline of sovereignty often attributed to globalization and the concomitant expansion of private transnational economic "spaces" that purportedly lie beyond the jurisdiction of states, we must ruefully note that something best described as "state abdication" has been part and parcel of neo-liberal economic globalization for the past several decades. States use their still quite substantial resources and capacities to promote globalization and to create the transnational economic spaces they then complain they cannot control. To what extent the rhetoric of decline—and its associated professions of impotence—should be believed is difficult to judge.

If states are losing power and authority, their special role and obligations regarding human rights protection and enforcement come into question. In addition, some agents—NSAs or state-related actors—will have to take over their protection, promotion, and enforcement functions.[16] But as we have seen, the legitimacy of NSA action in such areas is open to grave doubts. What roles can NSAs play with respect to human rights in the international political economy? What roles should they play? How can these roles be justified or legitimated? What degree of state involvement is necessary in this process, and how can reluctant states be encouraged to maintain their involvement?

The decline in sovereignty represents remarkable opportunities for human rights as well. The same forces of globalization have helped develop and sustain a greater tolerance for multilateral intervention inside states—especially in cases where such intervention is designed to alleviate gross human rights abuses. Developments such as the arrest and detention of Augusto Pinochet and the development of the International Criminal Court similarly attest to the advantages of declining sovereignty. It is tricky to reinforce sovereignty without also reinforcing the immunity traditionally associated with, and trickier still to know what else we might work for in its place. Thus any efforts to bolster states against the threats posed by globalization should be pondered carefully by human rights advocates, lest we get what we wish for.

Puzzle #5: Where Do Human Rights Violations Happen?

In the liberal paradigm the creation of a "private" realm of state noninterference is an essential step in *preventing* states' violation of human rights. Human rights violations occur in relations between states and citizens—in public relationships—even though violations can include unwarranted state intrusion into the "private" sphere.

Like other aspects of the liberal paradigm we have considered, these distinctions are fraught with difficulties. First, the "private" realm of "noninterference" is in fact intensely regulated by the state. Laws regulating marriage, inheritance, welfare and pension provisions, women's employment prospects, procedures for the reporting and prosecution of domestic abuse (including the attitudes of prosecutors and judges toward such claims), and other factors all structure the domestic environment in ways that have a direct impact on the protection and promotion of women's right to security. The state quite literally creates the domestic sphere, right down to who counts as a husband and a wife (and who is not allowed to count as such). To then describe the family as a private sphere of noninterference defies all reason. The economic sphere is similarly structured by state regulation and oversight, though it too is defined as "private."

This umbrella of privacy shields wrongs done to women, children, and laborers from scrutiny within the liberal human rights framework. From its inception that framework saw the "private" domains as areas where citizens' interests dictated the regulatory substructure of relations while citizens' rights precluded certain kinds of state intervention. Contradiction was only avoided because of the limited extension of citizenship in early liberal societies. Now, as citizenship has expanded to include nearly all adults in many liberal societies, the contradictions are inescapable: protection of the rights of some citizens requires interference in what have traditionally been considered the "private" affairs of others.

The puzzles, then, concern *where* human rights violations occur and, concomitantly, where human rights protections obtain. The family, the economy (including those transnational economic spaces that supposedly escape states' reach), cyberspace—all are areas where privacy or sovereignty impedes states' traditional activities. Do we want to preserve a sphere of noninterference? How should it be defined? What kinds of authorities (states, NGOs, other kinds of NSAs) can legitimately operate within the various spheres? How do we decide? Should the same rights apply in all spheres?

Puzzle #6: NSAs and Defining Human Rights

Susan Moller Okin once remarked that rereading the classic texts of Western political thought and changing all of the pronouns along the way would not adequately remedy sex-based structures of exclusion and subjection built into those theories.[17] Our final puzzle stems from a related concern: how should we redefine human rights to bring NSAs into the framework? One solution would be simply to add NSAs into the liberal paradigm wherever we encountered the word or concept *state;* the logic of Okin's statement, however, suggests that this approach will be inadequate. In some cases merely changing the old definitions will not adequately protect individuals from violations committed by NSAs; in others, rights are defined in ways that make their relevance to NSAs unclear or troubling.

Let me give just two illustrations. Cases like women's right to security show how adding "NSAs" wherever "states" appear fails to provide adequate protection. As we have seen, the primary threats to women arise not from states but from men close to them. So adding in NSAs solves one part of the problem only if we consider abusive partners NSAs. But unless legal codes, social institutions (like police and courts), and societal attitudes and prejudices also change, redefinition of the right is not enough. Effecting these broader changes is no simple matter, practically or conceptually. For the second case, consider Article 16 (3) of the UDHR, which states that "the family is the natural and fundamental group unit of society and is entitled to protection by society and the State." Article 12 states that "no one shall be subjected to arbitrary or unlawful interference with his privacy, family, home, or correspondence, nor to unlawful attacks on his honour and reputation. Everyone has the right to the protection of the law against such interference or attacks." Let us consider two ways in which these rights become problematic once we incorporate NSAs into our analysis, both of which show the depth and complexity of our problem. First, protection of the family has historically shielded "private" activities and arrangements from state interference. For similar reasons, protecting the family can shield men's treatment of women from state scrutiny. Bluntly, wife-beating becomes an exercise of men's right to privacy. So the problem is that the greatest threats to women's (and probably children's) security arise within the home, with men. What gets protected by Articles 12 and 16 might well include violent patriarchal authority. Here the problem is not who or what agency threatens the family from the outside, but what injustices persist inside it.

We might reformulate these rights to specifically guarantee women's, children's, and the family's rights against NSAs like abusive or despotic husbands and fathers as well as against the state. Here, however, unless we further redefine the rights, we introduce problems bordering on the absurd. Should men and women engaged in extramarital affairs be considered violators of the rights of partners or families? Are children who run away from home or otherwise injure families guilty of human rights violations? The problem is not just who commits violations but also the *nature* of those violations. More generally, do we want to pursue rights like equality, due process, and nondiscrimination in the family? in the economy? in one but not the other? How far are we willing to go in authorizing the monitoring and enforcement of these rights? Where would such intervention leave the protection of intimate relations from state interference—which, despite its historical problems, has also been a crucial component of freedom? How much do we defer to individuals' beliefs about the proper structure of the family when these are in conflict with rights? Far from being rhetorical questions, these constitute very hard cases that arise when we try to incorporate NSAs into existing definitions of human rights.

Toward a New Human Rights Framework

In the limited space remaining I present four conjectures, based on our puzzles, about the broad outlines of an alternative human rights framework. These really are conjectures—propositions to be considered, revised, and refined in light of additional evidence and reflection.

Conjecture #1: We Should Abandon the State/Non-State Distinction

Similarities or differences among NSAs should not be the focus of our analytic approach. The category of NSAs is a useful label, directing our critical attention toward the roles played by numerous actors in the real world of human rights practice. Yet our concern is, I think, less who commits violations or undertakes protection and promotion functions than it is violations, protection, and enforcement themselves. Our heightened concern with actors' identities is probably an artifact of the liberal paradigm. I have emphasized that paradigm's empirical and conceptual poverty at some length. Abstracting from this backdrop, we might well describe our purpose as one of expanding our understanding of the range of actors and issues involved in the violation and the protection of human rights. Put this way, it becomes clear that the actors' identities are incidental, a function of their roles in human rights practices.

Accordingly, I propose a shift toward a functional understanding of human rights. On this view a "fundamental" human right is one necessary to the enjoyment of other rights; all such rights must be institutionalized and secured against standard threats.[18] Together, fundamental rights should comprise all the rights necessary to eliminate subjection. On this account, human rights are defined by what they do: guarantee freedom or emancipation. This functional definition highlights rights' indivisibility and interdependence; further, it resolves many problems concerning the definitions and the conceptual framework of human rights. By defining rights by what they do, we shift our focus from violators to violations, which can be identified by their effects. Thus, instead of changing pronouns, we can think in terms of eliminating them. That is, we can specify violations without worrying initially about who might be responsible for them. This specification would provide an analytic basis for defining and debating rights and for distinguishing between human rights violations and crimes (more below).

Conjecture #2: We Should Focus on Governance

A functional account of human rights begins by asking what they do rather than what they are and who violates them. One plausible view of their function is to promote emancipation, a state in which people are subject to no arbitrary or unaccountable authority.[19] In the language of political economics, human rights are concerned with *governance*. Governance refers to systems of rule "at all levels of human activity" entailing "the pursuit of goals through the exercise of control";[20]

by emphasizing that human rights apply wherever governance occurs we preserve the connection between human rights and the exercise of power and authority while extending the range of our concern beyond the power and authority of the *state*. A functional account thus emphasizes that all governance must be accountable and non-arbitrary—in common parlance, that everyone, insofar as possible, should be free.

This distinction permits us to consider the activities of NSAs insofar as they engage in governance, defined broadly. I am proposing simply that human rights should apply wherever governance occurs—though they need not apply in the same way.[21] By focusing on systems of rule at all levels and in all domains of life, we can theorize modes of realization and enforcement appropriate to each. This flexibility makes a more nuanced and comprehensive approach possible, allowing consideration of the wide range of actors and problems in the real world of human rights practice. A functionalist approach provides analytic criteria for identifying human rights and their violation. These criteria will of course be controversial, but I believe that they are likely to prove more susceptible of consensus than religious, cultural, or philosophical justifications of human rights.[22]

This approach also indicates how we might preserve the distinction between crimes and human rights violations. Governance, as its definition indicates, arises in ongoing patterns or systems of human relations; when the exercise of control within these patterns becomes arbitrary or hierarchical, domination and oppression emerge. It is precisely such developments that human rights are designed to preclude (again, with the aim of preserving freedom). In this view the distinction between human rights violations and crimes turns not on the definition of an act or on the identity of an actor but on whether it occurs within an established system of human relations and whether it generates an ongoing relation of subjection. However, this distinction is no cure-all. The functionalist approach cannot provide a bright-line determination in every instance; rather, the idea is to differentiate crimes from human rights violations according to the system of relations in which they occur. Only within ongoing systems of interaction can relations of domination and oppression be established; only such instances should count as human rights violations. This is not to say that crimes are not frequently awful or to deny that they can have devastating consequences; it is simply to allow us to distinguish human rights, a special set of considerations regarding subjection in systematic patterns of relations, from the wider universe of human wrongs individuals might experience.

Conjecture #3: The Functionalist Approach Requires Pragmatism and Participation

States' exclusive role in protecting, promoting, and enforcing human rights in the liberal framework reflects their sovereignty: all public or political power belongs to the state. Not only human rights enforcement, but all legitimate public power is ascribed to the state in liberal theory. Popular sovereignty at least conveyed a new form of legitimacy upon the exercise of state power, though it left the state's monopoly unchallenged. Today we can no longer plausibly view states as the sole executors of political power. The concern with governance underlying the functionalist approach recognizes that systems of rule abound in our world, encompassing many domains in which states' roles are minimal, obscure, or hidden.

This recognition implies a pragmatic approach to protection, promotion, and enforcement. We should favor what works, looking for creative ways to secure human rights. The variety of systems of governance in our world warrants a corresponding variety of regulatory approaches. An already overburdened state is unlikely to provide the best or most efficient platform for expanding the human rights regime, though it will undoubtedly play a central role in that regime. State-related agencies, IGOs, and NGOs will play a growing role. This development should be welcomed insofar as it introduces better protection and enforcement. The caveat is important, however; we need to consider what constitutes "better" in this instance. Obviously, effectiveness and efficiency are important considerations. But recall that among the justifications for states' exclusive role in protection and enforcement—at least after the advent of popular sovereignty—was the direct democratic legitimation of that role. This kept power accountable, providing a check on the state through participation and elections. In the functionalist paradigm advocated here, participation is a fundamental right and thus obtains within all systems of governance, not just within states. All actors involved in governance—especially those involved in protecting and enforcing human rights—are bound by the logic and strictures of human rights. This accountability can only be ensured through participatory institutions.[23] Participation is fundamental because it provides a mechanism for protecting other rights through political activity; it also helps to legitimize—democratize—the human rights regime.

Conjecture #4: The Functionalist Approach Gives Human Rights Cosmopolitan Scope

Sovereignty was never consistent with the universality of human rights, despite their problematic association in the liberal paradigm. Now, globalization and domestic deregulation indicate clearly that sovereignty no longer plausibly describes our world. As states' ability or willingness to act in certain domains decreases, and as new economic and electronic spaces emerge with rapid political and technological change, deference to sovereignty's territorial and conceptual exigencies cannot be justified. Brief consideration of the human rights challenges raised in the global political economy reveals the futility of such deference. The functionalist approach takes securing fundamental human rights as its primary aim, respecting no borders or boundaries except those internal to a particular system of governance. It can therefore deal with systems of governance (trade regimes, TNCs) that operate across, through, and outside of conventional political jurisdictions.

As this implies, the functionalist framework is cosmopolitan; it respects the universality of human rights without requiring the imposition of centralized global institutions for their protection, promotion, and enforcement.[24] The key, implicit in the focus on governance, is that different patterns of subjection operate at different levels and must be addressed accordingly. Crucially, the location of the actors involved in some system of governance—in this or that country, in the public or the private—drops out. We are concerned with governance functions wherever they occur.

These four conjectures do not constitute a fully articulated alternative to the liberal human rights paradigm. They are a tentative response to the theoretical puzzles that arise when we try to incorporate NSAs into our thinking about human rights (and thus into the liberal paradigm). They are offered in a suggestive and provisional spirit, as the beginning of an important and overdue discussion. I hope, nonetheless, that they prove useful in evaluating the specific problems raised by the other contributors.

NOTES

[1] For a good overview, see Richard Tuck, *Natural Rights Theories: Their Origin and Development* (Cambridge: Cambridge Univ. Press, 1979).

[2] See Carole Pateman, *The Sexual Contract* (Stanford, CA: Stanford Univ. Press, 1988); and Charles W. Mills, *The Racial Contract* (Ithaca, NY: Cornell Univ. Press, 1997).

[3] Kenneth Minogue, "The History of the Idea of Human Rights," in *The Human Rights Reader*, ed. Walter Laquer and Barry Rubin (New York: New Amsterdam Library, 1979).

[4] Robert E. Goodin, Carole Pateman, and Roy Pateman, "Simian Sovereignty," *Political Theory* 25, no. 6 (1997).

[5] The social contract is one part of a much more complex system of agreements that includes the sexual, racial, and wage-labor contracts. Pateman refers to this system as the "original contract" (Pateman, *The Sexual Contract*). The discussion that follows is deeply indebted to her path-breaking analysis.

[6] See Stephen P. Marks, "From the 'Single Confused Page' to the 'Decalogue for Six Billion Persons': The Roots of the Universal Declaration of Human Rights in the French Revolution," *Human Rights Quarterly* 20, no. 3 (1998).

[7] Catherine A. MacKinnon, "Crimes of War, Crimes of Peace," in *On Human Rights: The Oxford Amnesty Lectures 1993*, ed. Stephen Shute and Susan Hurley (New York: Basic Books, 1993).

[8] See Hilary Charlesworth, "What Are 'Women's International Human Rights'?," in *Human Rights of Women: National and International Perspectives*, ed. Rebecca J. Cook (Philadelphia: Univ. of Pennsylvania Press, 1994).

[9] David Rieff, "The Precarious Triumph of Human Rights," *The New York Times Magazine*, 8 August 1999.

[10] Although note that General Recommendation 21 lacks binding force and that among its central concerns is the large number of reservations to CEDAW that gut its provisions on meaningful equality for women. Still, at least here the status of women within the family is clearly and firmly addressed.

[11] See Jack Donnelly, *The Concept of Human Rights* (New York: St. Martin's Press, 1985); cf. Jack Donnelly, *Universal Human Rights in Theory and Practice* (Ithaca, NY: Cornell Univ. Press, 1989); and Susan Mendus, "Human Rights in Political Theory," *Political Studies* 48, special issue (1995).

[12] An insistence perhaps related to the bourgeois character of early rights doctrines and bourgeois worries about the states' power to "violate" the right to private property through taxation or confiscation.

[13] It is at least possible to conceive a system of law designed solely around the protection of human rights. Reckless driving or negligence might be criminalized as violations of the reasonable care that others' rights of life and security demand. Administrative and procedural requirements might be justified through their role in guaranteeing citizens' civil and political rights.

[14] I place the term pedestrian in quotes here to signal my recognition that many wrongs are no less awful for being more commonplace.

[15] Whether they have ever possessed such control is another matter entirely (see Stephen D. Krasner, *Sovereignty: Organized Hypocrisy* [Princeton, NJ: Princeton Univ. Press, 1999]).

[16] The opening "if" is crucial: it is open to question whether globalization creates an institutional incapacity or an ideological unwillingness to perform certain functions.

[17] Susan Moller Okin, "Gender, the Public, and the Private," in *Political Theory Today*, ed. David Held (Stanford, CA: Stanford Univ. Press, 1991).

[18] See Henry Shue, *Basic Rights: Subsistence, Affluence, and U.S. Foreign Policy* (Princeton, NJ: Princeton Univ. Press, 1996).

[19] This assertion must go unsubstantiated here—though I contend that it is historically conceptually defensible.

[20] James N. Rosenau, "Governance, Order, and Change in World Politics," in *Governance without Government: Order and Change in World Politics*, ed. James N. Rosenau and Ernst-Otto Czempiel (Cambridge: Cambridge Univ. Press, 1992), 15.

[21] For a "semi-contextualist" approach to justice similar to what I envision here, see Ian Shapiro, *Democratic Justice* (New Haven, CT: Yale Univ. Press, 1999).

[22] I prefer this approach to ones based on dignity or human needs/functions because interpretations of these concepts vary greatly. Subjection—which can be understood flexibly in different contexts—might put human rights on a less controversial foundation. This emphasis also highlights the often overlooked connection between democracy and human rights.

[23] Shue, *Basic Rights*, 84.

[24] See Thomas W. Pogge, "Cosmopolitanism and Sovereignty," *Ethics* 103, no. 1 (1992).

3

Accounting for Human Rights Violations by Non-State Actors

Herbert F. Spirer and Louise Spirer

INTRODUCTION

This chapter takes a prospective look at how we can quantify human rights violations by non-state actors of both civil and political, and economic, social, and cultural rights, in order to provide a basis for monitoring and accountability. Starting with a taxonomy of non-state actors, we discuss how the same methodology that measures violations by state actors can be applied to violations by non-state actors in order to create a credible and sustainable accounting of the actions of non-state perpetrators.

A state can be defined as an entity having the following properties:

1. a permanent population
2. stable boundaries or a defined territory
3. under control of its own government
4. engaged in or having the capacity to engage in formal relationships with other such entities[1]

Thus, a state actor is the state itself or organizations or persons directly connected or responsible to the state. The term *non-state actor* (NSA), therefore, implies an actor in the international environment that is *not* a state or a state actor as defined above. This includes a wide spectrum of such NSAs, and current usage reflects that generality. At one end of this spectrum are NSAs such as environmental NGOs (for example, Greenpeace International), researchers (for example, Landmine Monitor's researcher network), and standards groups (for example, the International Organisation for Standardisation) that are unlikely to violate human rights. At the other end are ethnic groups, religious fanatics, a number of multinational corporations, guerrilla groups, rebel organizations, narcotics traders, and other NSAs that can, and often do, perpetrate violations of human rights.[2]

This definition uses the same term (NSA) for all these diverse groups, ranging from those whose only actions involve nonviolent protest and lobbying, to those who lay land mines or destroy forests in the course of extracting natural resources to those that target innocent civilians, attack government institutions, or destroy homes, farms, and businesses.

For the purposes of this chapter we narrow our definition to those NSAs whose actions would be considered violations of human rights if they *were* state actors. Thus, we start with a base of "rebel groups, irregular armed groups, insurgents, dissident armed forces, guerrillas, liberation movements, and de facto territorial governing bodies."[3] To this, we can add corporations, government-sponsored militias, paramilitary death squads, ethnic groups acting in concert, and, in some cases, individuals. There are also examples that are outside the preceding categories, such as caste violence against India's "untouchables"[4] and the Tulsa race riot of 1921 in the United States.[5]

To avoid ambiguity we use the term *non-state perpetrator* (NSP) to refer to those NSAs whose actions result in violation of human rights. Although we include rebel groups and "liberation movements" as NSPs, we are not implying that they are, ipso facto, perpetrators of human rights violations. Many are protesting such violations. However, we do argue that summary killing, torture, slavery, and similar actions are human rights violations, no matter which entity perpetrates them.[6]

We do not deal with the legal and strategic issues of whether to make an international human rights claim against an NSP, where existing national or local laws cover the violations. Our concern is accounting for violations of human rights by NSPs, once advocates for the victims decide to make a claim under international human rights norms in any venue.[7]

WHAT IS A VIOLATION BY AN NSP?

Our answer to this question is that violations by NSPs are, in the first instance, the same as violations perpetrated by a state. For civil and political rights, these actions are those that violate the rights defined by the Universal Declaration of Human Rights (UDHR) and the International Covenant on Civil and Political Rights (ICCPR). For economic, social, and cultural rights, they are defined by the International Covenant on Economic, Social and Cultural Rights (ICESCR) and the many conventions and resolutions that form the body of international agreements that are generally accepted by the international community as defining human rights. By "accounting for violations of human rights" we mean furnishing an analysis of the actions of the perpetrators that violate the mandates of the agreements referred to in the previous paragraph.

To account for violations, first, we need clear and specific definitions of actions that constitute violations. Such a definition is the measurable conceptualization of a construct, an abstraction that forms the essence of the violation of a right specified by the governing documents. Only after the act of definition can we "account" for such violations by using the methodology of information systems and data analysis to collect, count, analyze, and describe such actions to create a sustainable record.

Civil and Political Rights

For a simple example of a measurable (and hence, countable) violation drawn from civil and political rights, we start with Article 3 of the UDHR, "Everyone has the right to life." The measurable violation corresponding to the right to life is death, which in the operation of "accounting" can be the identification of a cadaver or a report by an individual eyewitness to a killing. This is, unhappily, an accounting that is often "easy" to do in the sense of making a record of the act. (Even mass graves can yield useful estimates of the number of dead buried there.)

However, the context of measurement is of considerable importance in less clear-cut cases. By context, we refer to the totality of factors that affect the definition of a measurable violation. This includes, but is not limited to, the objectives of the organization seeking an accounting, its mandate, available resources, geographical location, cultural factors, capacities and personnel, and the ultimate uses for the accounting of violations (for example, a truth commission, tribunal, public accounting).

A good example of a more complex accounting arose in meeting the objectives of the Truth and Reconciliation Commission of South Africa (TRC), whose objectives, as set out in the Promotion of National Unity and Reconciliation Act, were defined as to "give as complete a picture of the gross violations of human rights that took place as a result of past conditions."[8] Without explicit reference to the UDHR, the TRC initially defined four major categories of violations in the Promotion of National Unity and Reconciliation Act as killing, abduction, torture, and severe ill-treatment.[9] The latter two categories can be related to the second half of Article 5 of the UDHR, "No one shall be subjected to . . . cruel, inhuman or degrading treatment or punishment." Of course, it would be naive to expect to create a definition that would be valid for every situation; the TRC term "severe ill-treatment" does not often appear in other contexts, and its definition is particular to the South African experience: "Severe ill-treatment covers all forms of inflicted suffering that did *not* happen in custody (for example: injury by a car bomb or beaten up at a rally)."[10] Working as a group and reasoning from the TRC context and purpose, its stakeholders and the analysts defined eight categories of human rights violations, which in turn were divided into a total of ninety *relevant* types of violations.[11] Few human rights projects will lead to this many types of violations, but this case is an excellent illustration of the nature of the problem of reducing human rights constructs to measurable elements in support of credible accounting.

Although most observers fault the apartheid government (a state actor) for human rights violations in South Africa, what must be recognized is that *NSA*s also perpetrated many of the violations recorded by the South African TRC. For example, the complete TRC statement given in *Making the Case* describes a gross violation of human rights committed by members of the Mandela United Football Club.[12] Such violations can be and have been defined, counted, or measured, and they are subject to the same analysis, using the same methodology.[13]

Economic, Social, and Cultural Rights

Evaluation of both state perpetrators and NSPs under the ICESCR presents more complex challenges. An important challenge stems from the expectation of the gradual realization of these rights. Thus, instead of applying a common standard, most of these rights must be evaluated with respect to norms that may be set on a country-by-country basis.[14]

However, the problem goes deeper, involving

> the different nature of economic, social, and cultural rights; the vagueness of many of the norms; the absence of national institutions specifically committed to the promotion of economic, social and cultural rights *qua* rights; and the range of information required in order to monitor compliance effectively all present challenges.[15]

The ICESCR provides in Article 2.1 that

> each State Party . . . undertakes to take steps. . . *to the maximum of its available resources, with a view to achieving progressively the full realization* of the rights recognized in the present Covenant by all appropriate means (emphasis added).

Thus, the ICESCR sets the stage for monitoring economic, social, and cultural rights through reporting by states on the "progressive realization" of rights to the extent that the state's "available resources" permit. This approach has many implementation problems and has been subject to a great deal of criticism. In a comprehensive analysis of the problems inherent in this approach, Audrey Chapman makes a strong argument that in 1993 there was a "current absence of effective monitoring."[16] She also notes that the Economic, Social, and Cultural Rights Commission itself fails to use this method consistently; if truly used to monitor rights, it would require extraordinary information-system capabilities from the data collection to the analyses that would constitute an effective accounting for lack of conformance.

Unhappily, our recent experience is that this situation continues, for the same reasons and with the same unsatisfactory results. Various bodies hold workshops, meetings, and seminars to draw conclusions and make recommendations—and nothing happens to change the deficiency in monitoring economic, social, and cultural rights through progressive realization. This is not surprising in view of the conceptual, methodological, and political problems. These problems are compounded by failure to apply the conceptual and methodological techniques of the relevant social science, the lack of information-system and data-analysis resources provided at the international level, and the limitations and lack of cooperation of the states that are party to the ICESCR.

Fortunately, other observers have made the case for the inadequacies of the use of progressive realization as a measure of economic, social, and cultural rights and argue for the use of a *violations-based* approach to monitoring economic, social, and cultural rights.[17] The use of such an approach is valuable because (1) one can use the established methods of the civil and political rights violations approach, and (2) a time series of violations provides the basic data for imposing the concept of progressive realization on an NSP. Conceptually, NSPs are not states, and hence not parties to the covenant.

It might make sense to judge a corporation by a progressive realization rationale, but most NGOs do not have the resources to deal with information systems and the analytical capacities necessary to monitor NSPs on an ongoing basis. In addition, there is no value in describing the victimization by ethnic or guerilla groups, or other organizations that may be practicing discrimination, in the language of progressive realization. The concept is almost totally without meaning in accounting for violations by NSAs. There is little leverage to be gained in trying to use progressive realization to reduce victimization with actors who lack obligations under the covenant.

We propose that the actual and potential actions by NSPs that negatively affect the economic, social, and cultural rights of individuals and groups be accounted for by a violations approach. To illustrate this approach with a specific readily defined right, we focus on Article 7 of the ICESCR. Article 7 starts with a statement "the States to the present Covenant recognize the right of everyone to the enjoyment of just and favourable conditions of work which ensure, in particular . . . " and provides a list of conditions, including "safe and healthy working conditions."[18] To account for the violations of this right by a corporation that has been flagged as an NSP by a grassroots NGO, we can follow a hierarchical structuring process leading to a controlled vocabulary and clear definition similar to that for the example described in the South African TRC, "severe ill-treatment" (see Table 3–1).

We have deliberately chosen a pair of similar civil and political rights and economic, social, and cultural rights violations to emphasize the parallelism of the process of categorization and structuring. However, a structuring can be used to define a violation that is less parallel to a violation of civil and political rights. Article 12 of the ICESCR specifies: "The States Parties to the present Covenant recognize the right of everyone to the enjoyment of the highest attainable standard of physical and mental health."

Table 3–1. Categorization and definition of a human rights violation

Domain	Civil and Political Rights Violation by State Actor	Economic, Social, and Cultural Rights Violation by Non-state Actor
Designation	Severe ill-treatment	Unsafe working conditions
Definition	Severe ill-treatment covers all forms of inflicted suffering that did *not* happen in custody (for example, injury by a car bomb or being beaten up at a rally).	A workplace environment in which workers incur physiological, psychological injury, or death due to circumstances out of their control, such as that resulting from defective machinery; other hostile workers, supervisory, or managerial employees; air quality; or contaminants, pollutants, poisons, or improperly designed ergonomic factors.
Types	Burning of building, severe beating, injury by burning, deprivation, injury in an explosion, incarceration, imprisonment or detention, psychological or mental ill-treatment, etc.	Severed body part, loss of sight, cancer, or loss of fertility, attributable to presence of hazardous materials in the workplace; threats by supervisors or other employees, etc.

As this right is stated, the state incurs an obligation and members of the population acquire the right to enjoy a high standard of health. To apply this to an NSP, we hold that a similar obligation falls on the NSP not to violate this right. For example, a corporation violates this right when it pollutes the water supply of a community to the extent that there is a measurable, verifiable reduction in health of people using that source.

There is a wide range of possible health effects that might result from "pollution." In some situations the effects of the pollutant may be known, and it may be possible to unequivocally establish the source of an individual's health problems. In a case with this symmetry of cause and effect, sound methods of data collection will assure a credible accounting.

An example is the December 3, 1984, leak of methyl isocyanate gas from a Union Carbide India Limited pesticide plant in Bhopal, India, just after midnight.[19] The initial two-hour release had immediate effects directly related to methyl isocyanate exposure when forty tons of methyl isocyanate poured out of the tank over a nearly two-hour period and escaped into the air, spreading within eight kilometers downwind, over the city of nearly 900,000. Thousands of people were killed (estimates range as high as 4,000) in their sleep or as they fled in terror, and hundreds of thousands remain injured or affected (estimates range as high as 400,000) to this day. The most seriously affected areas were the densely populated shanty towns immediately surrounding the plant—Jayaprakash Nagar, Kazi Camp, Chola Kenchi, and the Railway Colony. The victims were almost entirely the poorest members of the population.

This is not *one* NSP violation of human rights; hundreds of thousands of violations might immediately be counted, plus even more due to longer-term effects. Unfortunately, the accounting above is inadequate. It refers only to gross estimates ("thousands," "as high as," and so forth). Thus, the unfortunate (and perhaps unforgivable) sloppiness and incompleteness in accounting for these violations cannot be helpful in achieving redress for victims and their families.

Despite this criticism, and acknowledging the difficulties, the methods that were used by both state actors and NSAs illustrate the wide range of methods that may be used to determine the scope, timing, and number of violations by NSPs. In Bhopal the record shows the use of the following methods:

1. medical records of health centers treating persons in the area
2. passive epidemiological observations provided to national health system
3. medical studies by national governmental research organizations[20]
4. academic epidemiological studies[21]
5. studies by NGOs[22]
6. studies by students
7. door-to-door field surveys

Bhopal was a dramatic event with considerable economic impact. The stakes for the Indian government were considerable. It needed to have an accounting of the human problems (that we would call violations) to pursue redress to support some of the costs of caring for the survivors and to provide income for the government. The results of the procedures described above undoubtedly played a role in achieving the limited measure of redress that was obtained. Legal action against the corporation ensued, and fines were levied.[23]

Consider this example of a claim by an NGO that industrial mining operations are violating Article 11 of the ICESCR, which covers the right to an adequate standard of living. Community members in the community, close to the mine, reported that while the number of shops has increased since the opening of the mine, so has the number of alcohol outlets. In addition, the number of people coming into the town has increased with no migration control. Increased numbers of people have meant that the cost of housing has increased, which has forced poorer community members out of housing. The cost of building materials is more expensive, and obtaining manual labor for traditional agricultural work has become more difficult. New houses constructed for the community that was relocated were built in lines rather than in a traditional style around a central square. Additionally, the people were not given plots of land for growing crops or raising animals around the houses. House owners are still waiting to be given legal title to their new houses.

We show how this claim could have been made into a substantive accounting for violations by this industrial NSP. We do this not to criticize the work but to show readers how easily this accounting could be made credible and substantive, thus making a strong case for redress by the mining corporation (see Table 3–2).

As is clear from the methods used to account for the consequences, the Bhopal catastrophe called for credible and sustainable accounting for the violations by NSAs. Whether perpetrated by state actors or NSAs, the skills required are those provided by such professionals as epidemiologists, statisticians, public health experts, medical personnel, information systems specialists, management experts, and so forth. Most NGOs do not have such experts on their staff (Physicians for Human Rights and Médicins sans Frontières are notable exceptions). The NGO that wishes to account for violations effectively must recognize the need for this expertise early in its work and seek it through the use of consultants and profit and non-profit organizations that can provide such technical assistance.[24] Seeking expert advice and consultation is standard practice for organizations in areas other than human rights that are concerned with social policies.

In addition, NGOs seeking such expertise must recognize that, with few exceptions, this expertise comes at a price. When starting a project where experts are required, the NGO must budget realistically. Even if the experts volunteer their services, travel and other out-of-pocket expenses should be covered by the project. NGOs should seek sufficient

Table 3–2. Claims in the example with information needed to give substance and credibility

Claim	Information needed to give substance and credibility to the claim	
Community members in the community, close to the mine, reported that while the number of shops has increased since the opening of the mine, so has the number of alcohol outlets.	"close to the mine"	Within what radius, in kilometers?
	"number of shops has increased"	*From* how many *to* how many?
	"so has the number of alcohol outlets"	*From* how many *to* how many? What is the percentage norm for number of alcohol outlets?
	"since the opening of the mine"	How long has the mine been open, in appropriate time units?
"the numbers of people coming into the town has increased"	*From* how many *to* how many?	
"the cost of housing has increased"	The average cost of housing has increased *from* what *to* what? What is the norm for housing costs in the region?	

funds for these purposes. If the victims of the effects of these projects are to be redressed, their advocates must get reliable estimates and produce credible and sustainable accounting for the violations of economic, social, and cultural rights.

CONCLUSION

With respect to accounting for violations, we believe that the interests of the actual and potential victims of violations of human rights by NSAs are best served by the following guidelines:

1. Make a clear distinction between NSPs of human rights violations and other types of NSAs. But . . .
2. Recognize that the nature of violations of civil and political rights by NSPs are the same as those by state actors, except for the identity of the perpetrators.

3. Account for violations of civil and political rights by NSPs by defining them in hierarchical terms, as is done when accounting for violations by state actors.

4. Collect, count, and measure using the techniques of information systems, data-analysis and relevant social-science methods.

5. Account for economic, social, and cultural rights violations using the techniques described above, once countable and/or measurable violations have been defined. Use a violation-centered approach as opposed to the concept of progressive realization as proposed in the covenant. Define violations using relevant social-science methods to develop violation definitions from the general constructs of the covenant.

6. When accounting for both types of rights, use appropriate quantitative expressions rather than vague and imprecise statements whenever possible.

7. Use every possible source of expertise to provide sound, quantitative, and sustainable accounting of violations. In planning, and throughout the accounting process, enlist expert social scientists, statisticians, epidemiologists, and information-system specialists rather than trying to develop such skills in the NGOs. It is more important to educate NGOs to evaluate the need for such assistance and realistically to budget for it.

NOTES

[1] Paraphrased from Lori Damrosch et al., *International Law: Cases and Materials,* 4th ed. (St. Paul, MN: West Group, 2001), 250. As pointed out by John Gay of Sechaba Consultants, this definition illustrates the difficulty of drawing a precise boundary between state and non-state actors. Some internationally recognized African countries barely meet the requirement of being under control of the government.

[2] Of course, there is no limit to the types of such organizations. See Joyeeta Gupta, *On Behalf of My Delegation, A Survival Guide for Developing Country Negotiations* (Amsterdam, The Netherlands: Center for the Sustainable Development in the Americas and the International Institute for Sustainable Development, 2000), http://www.cckn.net/www/index.html (accessed 1 May 2005). See esp. "Part I: The Negotiating Context, 5. State and Non-State Actors." See also P. Sands, "International Law, the Practitioner and 'Non-State Actors,'" Rede Lecture, Cambridge, 22 October 1998, 3–4.

[3] The International Campaign to Ban Land Mines, Non-State Actors Working Group website, http://www.icbl.org/campaign/wg/nsa (accessed 1 May 2005).

[4] See, for example, Human Rights Watch, *Broken People: Caste Violence against India's "Untouchables"* (1999). Human Rights Watch website http://www.hrw.org/reports/1999/india/ (accessed 1 May 2005).

[5] See, for example, Scott Ellsworth, *Death in a Promised Land* (Baton Rouge: Louisiana State Univ. Press, 1982).

[6] This is a complex issue. For example, who is to be held accountable for violations of human rights by corporate NSPs? Should it be the corporation as a legal entity, officers, shareholders, individuals, or some combination?

[7] An interesting case in which a suit was initiated in a US federal court arguing that the University of Oklahoma had violated a patient's human rights under the Nuremberg Code is discussed in Eliot Marshall, "Cancer Study Lawsuit Dismissed in Oklahoma" *Science* 8, no. 295 (February 2002): 949–50.

[8] Patrick Ball, Herbert Spirer, and Louise Spirer, eds., *Making the Case: Investigating Large Scale Human Rights Violations Using Information Systems and Data Analysis* (Washington, DC: American Association for the Advancement of Science, 2000), 41, http://shr.aaas.org/mtc/ (accessed 1 May 2005).

[9] Ball et al., *Making the Case*, 43. The final set of human rights violations categories also included abduction, associated violence, other violations, and unknown violations.

[10] Ibid., 55.

[11] Ibid., 55–62.

[12] Ibid., 69–84.

[13] As in the case of a corporation, who is responsible? Is it the individuals, the club, its leadership, or some combination? How best to obtain redress—in this instance in the sense of closure—for the victims? This is a decision for the TRC.

[14] Audrey R. Chapman, "A 'Violations' Approach for Monitoring the International Covenant on Economic, Social and Cultural Rights," *Human Rights Quarterly* 18, no. 1 (1996): 29.

[15] Ibid., 30.

[16] Ibid., 24–36.

[17] For an argument that the violations approach is necessary but not sufficient, see Clarence J. Dias, "Towards Effective Monitoring of Compliance with Obligations and Progressive Realization of ESCR," paper presented at the Second Global Forum on Human Development, Candido Mendes University, Rio de Janeiro, Brazil, 9–10 October 2000, http://hdr.undp.org/docs/events/global_forum/2000/dias.pdf (accessed 1 May 2005).

[18] Of course, we should exercise good sense in monitoring these rights. "One should distinguish between employment which is inherently dangerous (for example, police officers) and employment that is inherently safe (for example, textile work) unless an NSP chooses to neglect protective measures." J. Gay, private communication by email, 6 February 2002.

[19] Our report is based on Case no. 233 of the American University Trade and Economic Database (TED), Bhopal Disaster, http://www.american.edu/TED/BHOPAL.HTM (accessed 1 May 2005). TED is a collection of American

University graduate student case studies. This case study used information gathered only from secondary sources, but citations and bibliography are included. As our purpose is limited to an example, we are not passing judgment on components of the case.

[20] In this case the organization was the Indian Council for Medical Research, New Delhi, India; it included twenty-five Bhopal studies in 1985.

[21] In this case the groups were the Jawaharlal Nehru University, New Delhi, and the London School of Hygiene and Tropical Medicine in 1989.

[22] For example, the study by Medico Friend Circle in March 1985, description available online, http://www.geocities.com/mfcircle/ (accessed 1 May 2005).

[23] Much controversy exists over the nature of the legal actions, the voluntary actions by the corporation, the role of the Indian and American governments, and the actual occurrences. We do not take a stand on these issues. We use this case only as an overall example of the nature of certain processes of accounting for NSP violations.

[24] Benetech, a venture-philanthropic organization, has created The Martus Project to provide information services to human rights organizations. Information is available online, http://www.benetech.org/projects/martus.shtml (accessed 1 May 2005).

Part II

The Role of Corporate Actors

4

Realizing Rights
in the Work Place

*Corporate Codes of Conduct
and Empowerment from Below*

Rainer Braun and Judy Gearhart

INTRODUCTION

Codes of conduct (CoC) for corporate responsibility have shown surprising staying power. They have evolved over the last ten years from ad hoc instances of damage control when corporations found themselves accused of exploitative working conditions to institutionalized multi-stakeholder initiatives for the promotion of labor rights. CoC are odd creatures; they are voluntary commitments to uphold rights as they define a company's level of accountability for working conditions in supplier factories. Not surprisingly, the verdict on codes is still out. Are they limited simply to being tools for corporate risk management, or do they have the potential of furthering the realization of human rights?

In this chapter we argue that CoC can make an important contribution to human rights, if, and only if, they focus on the participatory, or empowering, dimension of human rights. This requires making a distinction between a narrow or "regulatory" approach and a broader, "participatory" approach to the realization of human rights. We argue that the latter ought to be taken as seriously as the former and that a regulatory or law-centered approach has limited potential fundamentally to improve workers' access to their rights. Treating transnational corporations (TNCs) as a group of non-state actors (NSAs) with immediate human rights responsibilities, we then show some of the developments in the field of work-place CoC and discuss how these developments relate to the idea of worker empowerment "from below."

HUMAN RIGHTS AS A POLITICAL CONCEPT

The key idea of human rights is that power (rather than the state as a structure for power) is legitimized, and therefore we can broaden the definition of human rights to a set of rules that regulates the relationship between the powerful and the powerless. Following this explanation, human rights may be interpreted and instrumentalized in different ways. For our purposes, we can roughly distinguish between a narrow view of human rights, which focuses on improving legal systems to ensure rights by regulation, and a broader view of human rights which ensures rights in a political way by empowering vulnerable groups to participate in political decision making.

The narrow human rights approach—as it prevails in the context of the United Nations and other multilateral forums—concerns itself with improving systems of law and order. The goal is to bring national legislation into conformity with international human rights law. Domestic judicial systems are scrutinized, criticized, and advised as to how to uphold laws that respect human rights. The narrow approach considers the actual implementation of government policies often only in a second, almost remote step. The trajectory of how social change is brought about is "top down": from international organizations, to national governments, and eventually to the citizenry. The narrow approach, based on theories of international law, places the responsibility for human rights solely on sovereign nation states. From this point of view, it makes sense to focus on legal systems and regulatory structures. The state, as the ultimate power bearer in legal theory, holds ultimate responsibility for the realization of rights, and all stakeholders are subject to its oversight.

Within this theory, CoC are an uneasy fit, because they turn our attention away from the clearly defined obligations of the state and toward the voluntary interactions of the private sector. The inherent arbitrariness of voluntary interaction, and consequently that of codes, has caused a lot of suspicion within the human rights community—

and deservedly so. This redirection of responsibility risks undermining the major achievement of human rights as a coherent system, as it questions the state's inexhaustible accountability for the well-being of its subjects. Once we open Pandora's box of non-accountability, we are back on the path to discussing concepts of natural rights, which lack clear definitions of obligations and duty-holders.

Therefore, before challenging the narrow approach, we need to acknowledge it as a tremendous success, without which any discussions of human rights were largely meaningless. Yet, some of the strengths that allowed human rights to gain recognition in the first place severely confine them at the same time. For political reasons, human rights could only be codified and given the weight of international law as long as they respected the national sovereignty of each state. The human rights regime is based on the understanding that each nation decides whether it wants to obligate itself to the requirements of international treaties (covenants and conventions) and the concomitant scrutiny of the United Nations and/or regional intergovernmental organizations.

One of the great potentialities of human rights, however, is that they have an importance that transcends legal systems and affects people beyond the confines of national law. Thus a parallel, rather than a contrasting, broader approach—a more "politically charged" view—emphasizes human rights as a means for political empowerment. In the narrow understanding the *existence* of functional regulatory systems is of key importance. In the broader sense human rights are about the *change* of power structures, or at least about ensuring the potential for change, that is necessary to bring about the realization of rights. The latter understanding emphasizes the need for enabling socially disadvantaged strata of society to gain access to, and weight in, political and economic decision-making processes that affect their lives.

This view is supported by the International Bill of Rights directly, because the state is not separated from its subjects.[1] Citizens have the right "to take part in the conduct of public affairs" (ICCPR, Art. 25). The state's accountability is not limited to providing goods and services and overseeing public affairs; it extends to grant inclusion of its citizens ("without distinction of any kind"—ICCPR, Art. 2.1) into decision-making processes. Similarly, in the field of industrial relations, the International Bill of Rights (ICCPR, Art. 22.1; ICESCR, Art. 8.1) clearly states the right to form trade unions, the intent of which can be interpreted in the same inclusive spirit: to allow workers to gain a voice in corporate decision making.

Human rights serve an eminently political function in that their raison d'etre is borne out of the idea of limiting the power of the nation state over its citizens. Economically and politically vulnerable groups gain an important argument in their process of empowerment once they learn that they have universally acknowledged rights. The realization of human rights is not the result of charitable giving begetting gratitude, but the fulfillment of obligations that those in control are duty-bound to provide. As Jack Donnelly puts it, "Rights empower, not just benefit, those who hold them."[2] In this context it is of lesser importance whether a current government has allowed its country to become a signatory party to an international treaty because we can justifiably consider the declaration of a universal right to transcend boundaries. The sheer existence of the logic and language of rights, therefore, can serve as a "door opener" for change from below.

To apply our comparison of the broad and narrow human rights approaches to the effects of CoC on the factory floor, human rights monitors ought not limit their function to observing outcomes, but need to consider the processes that bring outcomes about.[3] The relation between wages and overtime, for example, is better assessed by allowing workers to decide for themselves what is acceptable and what is not rather than imposing standards from the outside. Essentially, in order for regulation to qualify as human rights compliant, it needs to be informed by participatory processes. And participatory processes can only be effective if workers understand their entitlements, to which CoC can make a crucial contribution.

NON-STATE ACTORS

Our distinction of approaches also allows us to consider the role of NSAs with regards to human rights. NSAs such as corporations are not treated as human rights violators within a narrow, state-centric human rights regime. Corporations may engage in illegal activities, civil or criminal, for example, by using child labor, discriminating against women, or suppressing trade unions. The human rights dimension of such misconduct sets in, however, when these violations become endemic to corporate practice and a government is unable or unwilling to prosecute these crimes. The state therefore needs to regulate and police private sector activities in order to ensure their human rights conformity.

Interpreting human rights from a narrow view forces us to limit serious human rights advocacy to governments. A broader approach that emphasizes the relationship between the powerful and the powerless allows us to regard corporate actors as being *directly* responsible for human rights. This view derives from the understanding that corporations have come to be global players with huge political influence and immense economic power that evade domestic regulatory regimes. The nation state, accordingly, is seen as increasingly losing its operational sovereignty,[4] which limits a government's ability to protect and fulfill human rights.

Even though many TNCs outsource production steps—and therefore evade direct accountability for how their goods and services are produced—they do hold enormous sway over the working conditions at their independent subcontractors and suppliers. They gain this asymmetrical leverage from their function as "gatekeepers" to the lucrative hard currency markets of a few industrialized countries, for which the rest of the world is competing. Developing countries fail to penetrate these markets for lack of skill (technology, marketing) or access (for example, trade barriers for agricultural and textile products). Governments in developing countries are therefore often hesitant to prosecute labor infractions in their jurisdictions, because they are desperate to promote export trade and attract investors.

Especially in the case of small developing nations, corporations have long been able to overwhelm governments in order to pursue their interests. If, then, corporations bear power similar to or even beyond that of governments, and human rights concern themselves with the relationship between the powerful and the powerless, corporations must bear some responsibility to foster respect for workers' rights. The shift in political power (from the nation state to TNCs) is bringing about a concurrent shift in responsibility for human rights.[5] This view is increasingly shared within the human rights community, as several established "traditional" human rights NGOs have begun to direct their advocacy at corporations.[6]

The framers of the International Bill of Rights foresaw the need to stretch the responsibility for human rights beyond governments. The preambles of both covenants state that "the individual . . . is under a responsibility to strive for the promotion and observance of the rights recognized." Thus, to the extent that corporations seek to make a bona fide effort to be law-abiding global citizens, they are under the obligation to regard human rights as a guide for their relations with workers and communities in which they operate. This obligation needs to be clearly defined in order to be meaningful. Human rights demand from states that they both regulate and let their citizens participate at the same time. In order for NSAs to respect the human rights of their stakeholders, the same must be true. It is this exigency for a participatory element that makes or breaks CoC as a tool for human rights. In other words, corporate attempts to fulfill their human rights obligations with a regulatory (top down) approach are simply not good enough. Regulating work-place conditions from corporate headquarters may bring important improvements, but such policies are in effect risk-management strategies—they do not qualify as a true human rights approach.

It needs to be clearly stated that a human rights understanding of CoC does not favor the privatization or minimization of regulation (which a corporate risk-management approach to CoC may). Instead, a human rights perspective obliges us to regard CoC as an entry point to reinvigorate public oversight over corporate governance. In view of this objective, a participatory approach to human rights becomes especially important, because it anchors the realization of rights with their holders (here: workers), who are then better able to press governments back into the game.

We are not arguing in this essay that the participatory approach is superior to the regulatory. The approaches are mutually reinforcing and contingent upon each other. We do argue, however, that the empowerment dimension of human rights that is brought about by participation has been underserved compared to the regulatory approach. And as we are leaving the realm of "pure" human rights, where nation states reign fully sovereign (here meaning being able to ensure human rights through domestic policy), we are necessarily broadening the concept of human rights. This reconsideration is justified by the forces of political reality. We all may prefer a world in which people successfully hold their governments accountable for the realization of human rights, but for the moment an analysis that lacks due consideration of corporate power seems sterile and bears the danger of becoming irrelevant.[7]

Codes of Conduct and Trade Unions

The empowerment dimension of human rights lends itself easily to a discussion of labor rights. The work of the International Labour Organization (ILO), the main norm setting body for international labor rights, was from the outset predicated on the understanding that both employers and workers should play an active role in its formulation.[8] This framework thus placed a premium on participation, with trade unions being the vehicle for worker representation.

The usually obvious power relationship between management and workers results in a clear objective for human rights work, at least from the trade union perspective: to involve workers in company policymaking through collective bargaining agreements. To that end, it is easy to develop criteria for judging progress (for example, ratio of organized workers, reduction of accidents, worker representatives on corporate boards). Trade unions are a proven instrument for a participatory approach to human rights, and their shortcomings (corruption, under-representation of women, internal democratic deficits, clientelistic politics, and so on) are similar to the challenges facing any democratic process. Yet, despite many a "bad apple" in parliamentary democratic systems, democracy remains the "least worst system" of politics and, by the same measure, free trade unionism remains the "least worst system" when it comes to worker representation. Unfortunately, though, the majority of codes were not supportive of trade unionism when they first came out. An ILO study of more than two hundred voluntary CoC found a "paucity of treatment" of the rights to freedom of association and collective bargaining, as only approximately 15 percent of codes contained references to these core labor rights.[9]

CoC continue to multiply and evolve, but we can roughly distinguish three phases in their development. The first phase, from the early to the mid 1990s, was characterized by TNCs beginning to recognize their influence and responsibility for working conditions in their suppliers' factories. Prior to the first codes, TNCs had argued that they had no complicity in these abuses and thus no role in solving them. The public was not much impressed by this strategy and brand-targeted consumer pressure led to a growing number of TNCs publishing CoC, thereby acknowledging their role in the campaign for better working conditions in their supply chains.

The next phase of corporate involvement through codes was marked by the understanding that a mere declaration of intent and a good-faith agreement that suppliers would adhere to stipulations in CoC were not sufficient. The developing of monitoring systems was primarily spurred by companies realizing they needed to do more than have suppliers sign an agreement to comply with the code. As consumer campaigns picked up in the mid to late 1990s, some codes even became something of a "public relations liability" when companies were taken to task in the press for the appearance of false promises.[10] The public demanded that TNCs recognize their (however indirect) responsibility for work-place abuses. It also became clear that an increasing number of companies were beginning to publish work-place codes, and many were trying to "get away with less" by "dumbing down" the standards.

These kinds of inconsistencies among codes and the lack of enforceable monitoring and inspection mechanisms were the impetus behind multi-stakeholder initiatives that set out to develop uniform codes and rigorous, standardized monitoring systems. The leading multi-stakeholder initiatives were thus formed from the mid to the late 1990s: Social Accountability International (SAI); the Fair Labor Association (FLA); and the European-based FairWear Foundation (FWF).[11] The Clean Clothes Campaign, a European network of consumer campaign groups, the UK-based Ethical Trading Initiative, and the US-based Workers' Rights Consortium are related initiatives that seek to secure business commitment to a set of work-place principles but do not have standardized monitoring and certification programs. Many other, often company-specific CoC systems exist, but these six distinguish themselves for having made the most earnest efforts with regard to the promotion of human rights, rather than corporate public relations. These initiatives come from heterogeneous topical backgrounds, but they have more similarities than differences; all of them see their work on CoC as part of the larger human rights debate. This implies that they intend to go beyond improving work places as a result of charitable goodwill and instead aim at systems of corporate accountability that will bring about entitlements to workers.

All six of the above-mentioned initiatives agree that the involvement of local actors in the implementation and critical analysis of their systems is key to their long-term success. The initiatives are trying to make participation for worker representatives in their own efforts a reality, but so far none has come up with a convincing way to ensure local involvement in a way that consistently puts developing-country organizations on an equal footing with the northern participants in the debate. Partnerships with local trade union organizations have been especially difficult because the different initiatives have varying affinities to the trade union movement. In many countries, cooperating with trade unions is impossible because they are either outlawed or severely repressed. In those countries where trade unions are able to operate, the relationship between a multi-stakeholder initiative and local unions can be tricky. First, due to their experience during the Cold War, trade unions in developing countries can be highly suspicious of outsider interference. Second, CoC may be viewed as competition rather than a complementary element of labor rights realization. Local trade unions will therefore participate in CoC initiatives only if they are included in the policymaking processes of the "code setters," that is, if they have some sense of ownership of the process, either directly or through international representatives. Recent efforts among the six groups to collaborate may help resolve this dilemma, as it would make it easier for trade unions to cooperate with several groups instead of having to pick among competing initiatives. A common understanding among the initiatives of how to incorporate trade unions (locally and internationally) will be a major stepping stone in consolidating a multi-stakeholder approach to private-sector labor rights enforcement.

A third stage of TNC involvement in work-place human rights is currently under way, if admittedly to a very limited extent. In this stage TNCs are recognizing the depth and the comprehensiveness of the problems at stake. A few corporations are realizing that in order to improve work-place conditions at their suppliers in a meaningful way (for whatever motivation), they need to persuade their business partners of the benefits of decent work-place conditions and help them in making the necessary changes. These companies are beginning to invest in training programs, at times agreeing to pay for factory improvements and verification audits. For example, Reebok representatives worked closely with local worker-rights NGOs and factory managers to enable workers to participate in democratic elections of their worker representatives in Kong Tai and Fu Luh, two of Reebok's supplier factories in China.[12] And in some cases TNCs are beginning to recognize the direct impact that their ordering procedures and production lead times are having on excessive overtime in factories.[13] In these cases, the corporate role is beginning to change from passive inspector to active promoter of better working conditions. These businesses are also beginning to understand that local worker-rights advocates may be valuable allies in this process.

Summing up, we see a tendency, however fledgling, of TNCs acknowledging first their role, then their indirect responsibility, and finally their direct responsibility for human rights in the production process.[14] A small but growing number of TNCs have moved from their initial disregard for the "business and human rights debate" to an increased acceptance of and constructive involvement in the nexus of human rights and business activities and the potentially constructive role local workers' advocates can play in this context. Some corporations are also more accepting of the role of trade unions (albeit this thinking is more prevalent in Europe than the United States).

Where Is the Debate Today?

More than analyzing the strong and weak points of the existing systems of corporate monitoring, what is critical to the discussion of how codes can contribute to the promotion of human rights is a brief look at some of the central points under debate. Some of the debates are rather technical (data disclosure/transparency, auditor capacity building), others systemic (supply chain depth, brand company certification *vs.* factory certification), and some highly political (living wage debate, monitoring freedom of association, financing the systems). The discussion of these issues can shed some light on concerns about the potentially negative and positive impacts of CoC. At the same time, these issues indicate that this is a field still very much in formation and without clear leadership and agreement about what the long-term goals are and how to reach them.

The following three specific debates are illustrations for assessing the empowerment focus of CoC and monitoring systems.

1. *How effective can a complaints and appeals procedure be?* In order for any labor monitoring system to be effective, workers must be able to challenge the findings of outside inspectors. The role of local workers' advocates is therefore critical, as workers will need a trustworthy local agent to channel their complaints. If advocates exist, local trade unions should be able to use them as a mechanism for educating and informing workers about how they can claim their rights. Open labor rights activism is often illegal, yet a functioning complaints and appeals procedure (demanded by an investor in order to comply with a CoC) might provide a first step toward an advocacy structure and human rights capacity building. The question of an exogenous push for human rights is a delicate one, as opinions differ passionately on the extent to which the international human rights systems should

be responsible for preparing local advocates. Even if workers are invited to participate in the implementation and monitoring of a code and the internal complaints system is effectively addressing workers' concerns, such a process can be dangerous, as it might (unwittingly) set up a "company union." The human rights intention for CoC is that a functioning complaints system will help open up organizing space for trade unions and serve as the starting ground for freedom of association and collective bargaining.

2. *What level of disclosure should be required of companies?* This question is linked to whether monitoring systems are viewed as a carrot or a stick for factory compliance. In 2003 the FLA started publishing audit report summaries and tracking charts that "detail the noncompliance findings of FLA-accredited independent monitors and track the progress of Participating Company remediation in these factories."[15] SAI only requires disclosure after a supplier has been certified, thus protecting unsuccessful attempts of compliance with the standard. Once a factory is certified, however, the name, location, and products of the supplier are published on the SAI website. SAI also publishes summary results of complaints investigations and resolutions. FWF, on the other hand, does not press member companies for supplier locations. FWF only requires its corporate members to post their name and brands, the number of suppliers and country locations, and the number of suppliers that have submitted to external audits.[16] Meanwhile, the Workers' Rights Consortium takes a different approach, publishing names and locations of participating brands' factories and working to build a network to support worker-initiated complaints instead of advocating a monitoring system per se.[17]

From a human rights point of view, the key question about disclosure is how much and in what form the audit information is most useful to the workers inside the factories. Disclosure is very important to activists and consumers in industrialized countries, but less so to the affected workers, who are well aware of work-place problems. The disclosure of labor rights violations can be nonetheless empowering to workers because it helps to build a support network of informed allies.

3. *How demanding is the content of the code?* There is less and less debate about the content of codes, as the different initiatives over the last years have converged toward the ILO's understanding of core labor rights and their interpretation. The Preamble to the ILO Constitution calls for "the provision of an adequate living wage," but even the

ILO has shied away from identifying universal standards for the crucial area of wages. In the world of CoC, disagreements persist over whether a so-called living wage clause is necessary or not. As with most rights, the right to a decent living poses definitional problems, and a living wage is nearly impossible to define accurately. It is equally difficult, however, to confirm whether overtime hours are being worked voluntarily, or due to the insufficiency of wage levels. For workers, the distinction is stark; a code with a living wage clause gives them the possibility to distinguish between voluntary overtime and "survival" overtime spurred by poverty wages.

Many TNCs hesitate to sign on to a code requiring that suppliers pay a wage that meets workers' basic needs. Even if companies are willing to agree to a living wage on principle, they are concerned about assuming a potentially unsustainable financial liability. Companies are concerned that volatile currency markets and hyperinflation in developing countries might overburden them if wage levels are fixed to cost-of-living requirements rather than the logic of labor supply. A global commitment to a living wage would also imply the obligation to pay a living wage in the United States, which poses a much bigger obstacle than in developing countries.[18] Meanwhile, many human rights groups have hesitated to push for a living wage requirement because of the definitional problems it creates.

Regardless of how much regulators need precise definitions, we need to be careful not to sacrifice a human right (such as the right to remuneration that provides for a decent living—ICESCR, Art. 7a) because we cannot set a regulatory benchmark for it. The alternative is a process-oriented participatory approach, which allows the rights holders to define whether a wage is a living wage or not.

Turning CoC into true human rights instruments requires a clear concept of what is intended in the long run: improved working conditions implemented by management and caused by external supervision (analogous to our regulatory understanding of human rights), or the creation of political space for workers to organize and to help themselves through internal pressure (analogous to the participatory approach), or both.[19] A clarification on final intent of the leading proponents for CoC will likely make the current debate more constructive and possibly allow for increased cooperation among initiatives, which would in turn boost the political momentum, clarify issues for consumers, and keep corporations from playing initiatives off of one another.

Work-place CoC as an Instrument for Empowerment

Human rights and corporate conduct are difficult to discuss together, because they operate under different parameters. Human rights have to be understood as a comprehensive system of entitlements that are interdependent and interrelated.

Business operations, in contrast, are necessarily focused singularly on optimized input-output ratios. Industrial success is based on an ever-increasing division of labor, and while such an arrangement makes for a highly complex economy, the individual firm is seeking to limit its operations for highest efficiency. This structure allows for a company to incorporate only very specific and narrowly defined social objectives into its operations. A company, for example, can easily avoid child labor by simply banning it. Businesses, however, are ill equipped to deal with the resulting social complexities of a ban,[20] such as children forced into worse situations of work or affected families moved from poverty-level incomes to indigence. The Convention on the Rights of the Child, for example, calls for the principle of the best interest of the child, yet to define this best interest goes far beyond the mandate of a private company.[21]

From a business point of view, it would make most sense to outsource human rights compliance and monitoring (that is, bring in the experts) rather than providing it internally, in case the market demands them. The problem is, human rights are not for sale. Monitoring alone is not the same as actually enjoying a right. Rights need to be realized by those who are entitled to them—and the right to something is not a tradable good.[22] It is very difficult, then, to find the intersection of what human rights demand and what corporations can be expected to provide—given their different modi operandi. That is why instead of limiting corporate human rights obligations to a checklist of work-place standards, we are suggesting a concept of participatory decision making and empowerment as an interpretative lens by which corporate human rights conformity may be assessed.

Going back to our distinction between a narrow and a broad approach to human rights, the central question in the debate on codes becomes that of their consequences. Will CoC result in change "from above" through management implementation, with possibly faster and farther reaching improvements, or will they bring change "from below" through collective bargaining, which might result in messy compromises and perhaps even injudicious decisions made by workers? If, for a micro example, workers favor marginal increases in pay over an improved air filtering system in their negotiations with management, their choice may be unwise with respect to their own health or with regard to environmental externalities. Some social justice activists might find such priorities outrageous. Yet, the consequence of an empowerment process will be that people make their own choices, and not the ones inferred by third parties. What might be easily forgotten in the discussion on CoC is that the goal of empowerment must reach workers first and not reside with third-party activists (especially those far away in industrialized countries).

In light of this distinction, the way CoC are framed to focus either on the achievement of objective/technical goals or on the participation of workers themselves in defining and prioritizing goals makes a crucial difference. The lack of worker participation in decision-making processes, often caused by outright hostility of governments and employers, is one of the main reasons why abusive working conditions exist in the first place. The decisive question for CoC then becomes to what degree they might be able to open doors for worker participation. This is not to say that a shortened working week in a *maquiladora,* fewer children forced into bonded labor in mines, and the use of less-harmful pesticides in fruit plantations are worthless achievements. CoC can, and have already, made improvements in selected circumstances that should not be discounted. But these achievements are of a somewhat technical nature (length of time, number of children employed, concentration of chemicals). They are, therefore, more in line with a legalistic understanding of human rights, where benchmarks are being defined, and noncompliance leads to remedial action. These achievements—especially in the case of export processing where the benchmark definition, the inspection, and the sanctions all are imposed from outsiders—are not sufficient on their own to ensure the political quality of empowerment so urgently needed to address the *cause* of work-place abuses.

As a growing number of companies begin to take a broader view of their responsibility, it will be important for the human rights community to emphasize the need for participatory elements in order to ensure the positive long-term impact of codes. A critical consideration for international and local human rights communities in this process is the delicate balance of working objectively with trade unions and NGOs at the same time. Central American NGOs engaged in labor rights monitoring, such as GMIES (the Independent Monitoring Group in El Salvador), have been criticized by companies for being pro-union and by unions for not sufficiently defending workers' interests.

Worker advocates in the field and the managers of monitoring systems need to ask themselves constantly whether they are creating a path that will enable worker organizing or that will become a substitute for workers' organizations. International monitoring systems will need to answer this challenge on a case-by-case basis. They are well advised to keep workers' organizations abreast of how their systems work and of new developments in the field. Trade unions, at the same time, need to play an active role by seeking to ensure their participation in the day-to-day implementation and monitoring of codes and by working with human rights advocates to use codes strategically to demand that both state actors and NSAs uphold—and even promote—human rights.

CONCLUSION

CoC can serve different purposes. If codes state a human rights intent, and aspire to be taken seriously, they will need to follow a clear concept of human rights. Otherwise, human rights risk being misappropriated, once taken out of a state-centered context. To avoid this outcome, we suggest a human rights approach based on participatory decision making and empowerment. An empowerment approach to human rights can serve as a test of whether CoC are helping to realize rights or whether they are limited to reducing corporate risk. CoC can be effective for ensuring workers' rights in the long term to the extent that they enable worker empowerment as opposed simply to providing a management tool for corporations. Ensuring worker empowerment as a central goal for codes will depend, in turn, on the extent to which trade unions are—and are willing to be—included as an integral partner in their development, implementation, and oversight.

Codes have already made a strong contribution in more firmly establishing the human rights accountability of companies. TNCs have a growing influence on the realization of rights, and their different nature from nation states requires us to reconsider avenues of advocacy and systems of enforcement. CoC are only one attempt to hold TNCs accountable. The verdict on codes is still out, but it is not too soon to define expectations and the measures by which we will assess their contribution.

NOTES

[1] The International Bill of Rights consists of the Universal Declaration of Human Rights (UDHR) and the two covenants that codified the declaration into international law, the International Covenant on Civil and Political Rights (ICCPR) and the International Covenant on Economic, Social and Cultural Rights (ICESCR).

[2] Jack Donnelly, *Universal Human Rights in Theory and Practice,* 2nd ed. (Ithaca, NY: Cornell Univ. Press, 2003), 8.

[3] The monitoring of processes is different from bringing about processes. This is a crucial distinction for the fine line between the mandate of human rights monitors and that of trade unions.

[4] Wolfgang H. Reinicke, "Global Public Policy," *Foreign Affairs* 76, no. 6 (November/December 1997).

[5] "The Maastricht Guidelines on Violations of Economic, Social and Cultural Rights" (in Stephen A. Hansen, *Thesaurus of Economic, Social, and Cultural Rights: Terminology and Potential Violations* [Washington, DC: American Association for the Advancement of Science, 2000], 265) take this power shift into account: "It is no longer taken for granted that the realization of economic, social and cultural rights depends significantly on action by the state, although, as a matter of international law, the state remains ultimately responsible for guaranteeing the realization of these rights."

[6] Amnesty International has been active in the diamonds campaign. See Amnesty International, *Human Rights—Is It Any of Your Business? A Management Primer for Companies* (London: AI, Prince of Wales Business Leaders Forum, 2002). The Lawyers' Committee for Human Rights and the Robert F. Kennedy Center are members of the Fair Labor Association (FLA), and Human Rights Watch has a separate advocacy focus on corporations and human rights. See http://www.hrw.org/corporations/ (accessed 31 August 2004).

[7] As Arvind Ganesan writes in a Human Rights Watch commentary: "While recognizing that corporations are not rights agencies, we believe that the corporate sector has a critical role to play in enhancing respect for universally recognized human rights." Arvind Ganesan, "Business and Human Rights—The Bottom Line," *Human Rights Watch Commentary,* www.hrw.org/corporations/commmentary (accessed 31 August 2004).

[8] For an in-depth discussion of the ILO's role in interplay of human rights and labor rights, see "Special Issue: Labour Rights, Human Rights," *International Labour Review* 137, no. 2 (1998).

[9] International Labour Office—Governing Body (Working Party on the Social Dimensions of the Liberalization of International Trade), *Overview of Global Developments and Office Activities concerning Codes of Conduct, Social Labeling and Other Private Sector Initiatives Addressing Labour Issues,* GB.273/WP/SDL/1 (Geneva: November 1998), 24.

[10] In an extreme case, the California State Supreme Court ruled in May 2002 that the footwear and apparel company Nike is subject to lawsuits (and potential liability) for claims it made about labor conditions at its suppliers abroad, under a law that protects customers from misleading product information. The case was settled in September 2003 in an appeals court. As part of the settlement Nike agreed to donate US$1.5 million to the Fair Labor Association, of which it is a founding member. This was referenced in an editorial titled "When Nike Speaks" in *The New York Times* on 10 December 2002. Another story, reported by Adam Liptak, titled "Nike Move Ends Case Over Firms' Free Speech," appeared in *The New York Times* on 13 September 2003.

[11] Detailed descriptions of these groups are available on their respective websites. The Maquila Solidarity Network (MSN) provides comparative analyses of the different initiatives efforts' in its *Codes Update,* available on its website.

[12] Doug Cahn, "Statement by Doug Cahn, Vice President of the Human Rights Programs, Reebok International Ltd.," before the Congressional Executive Commission on China, 28 April 2003, http://www.cecc.gov/pages/roundtables/042803/cahn.php (accessed 31 August 2004).

[13] Interview with Amy Hall, Social Accountability Representative, Eileen Fisher, Inc., 9 October 2003, New York.

[14] This three-step development brings to mind the three different types of states' obligations with regard to economic, social, and cultural rights violations as defined by the Maastricht guidelines. According to the Maastricht guidelines the state has the responsibility to respect, protect, and fulfill human rights. In other words, the state is obliged to not violate human rights itself (for example, forced arbitrary evictions), to protect its citizens from violations by third parties, and to create structures positively to realize rights, such as the creation of public health services. The three obligations are purposefully in a dynamic order, as not committing human rights violations by the state itself should be easy enough to achieve, and therefore addressed immediately. Likewise, TNCs first acknowledged their role, then set out to protect workers from their suppliers, and some now are trying actively to create structures of human rights realization, such as creating space for worker organizing or improving public sector accountability.

[15] FLA, "Transparency Project," http://www.fairlabor.org/all/transparency (accessed 31 August 2004).

[16] FWF, "Principles and Policies of the FairWear Foundation," http://www.fairwear.nl/engelsframe1.htm (accessed 31 August 2004).

[17] Workers Rights Consortium, "Factory Disclosure Database," http://www.workersrights.org/fdd_results.asp (accessed 31 August 2004).

[18] The Harvard Law School Human Rights Program presents divergent points of view on the living wage debate and on CoC in general. See Harvard Law School Human Rights Program, *Business and Human Rights: An Interdisciplinary Discussion Held at Harvard Law School in December 1997* (Cambridge, MA: Harvard Law School Human Rights Program, 1999).

[19] One example of such a bottom-up process was when workers at a Kenyan pineapple farm brought a complaint forward (with the help of Kenyan and Italian human rights groups) to SA8000–certified Coop Italia. Per its commitments to the SA8000 standard, Coop Italia pressed the Kenyan supplier (Cirio-DelMonte) to address the workers' complaints, which were finally resolved over a three-year process with the involvement of the farm's trade union.

[20] For a discussion of the potentially negative effects of banning child labor, see Zehra Arat, "Analyzing Child Labor as a Human Rights Issue: Its Causes, Aggravating Policies, and Alternative Proposals," *Human Rights Quarterly* 24, no. 1 (2002).

[21] For the scope of the complexities involved, see Philip Alston, ed., *The Best Interest of the Child: Reconciling Culture and Human Rights* (Oxford: Clarendon Press/UNICEF, 1994).

[22] In order to clarify this distinction: a worker may forego her participation in a union for extra compensation, but she still retains the right to join one. Human rights do not allow for the sale of rights.

5

Multinational Corporations as Non-State Actors in the Human Rights Arena

James L. Gunderson

INTRODUCTION

One type of non-actor in the international arena that has generated considerable concern with respect to human rights is the multinational corporation. The foreign affiliates of multinational corporations now employ about 54 million people and account for about one-tenth of world GDP.[1] The wisdom of leaving them largely on their own to oversee their conduct warrants continued debate, particularly as we watch the United States, one of the most influential opponents of the earlier UN project to regulate multinational corporations, respond to its own series of corporate governance scandals with extensive legislation to replace self-regulation.[2]

This chapter explores the responsibilities that the international human rights framework imposes on multinational corporations and their accountability under that framework, as well as the less formal

---

This essay presents the author's personal views, shaped by years of representing companies in their international businesses, and more recent experience promoting corporate social responsibility and corporate governance through nonprofit organizations.

oversight of NGOs. In this context, opportunities for multinational corporations to promote human rights are also examined.

THE POSTWAR DEBATE

In the late 1960s and early 1970s our state-centric human rights system tested its powers over multinational corporations. Developing countries passed legislation aimed at regulating multinational corporations, nationalized some of their assets, and increased controls on incoming investment. However, the system's weaknesses were more apparent than its strengths.

Countries became worried about the flexibility of companies to relocate operations and the potential leverage this gave them to avoid national initiatives to improve labor standards and promote other human rights priorities. In the mid-1970s the public also became aware of the extent to which some large multinational companies had been spending tens of millions of dollars bribing government officials in developing countries and meddling in their domestic politics. Confronted with the limitations of national governments vis-à-vis multinational corporations, the United Nations began exploring extra-national approaches to the issue with its Commission on Transnational Corporations, which began focusing on a UN Code of Conduct for Transnational Corporations in 1976.

National governments' attitudes toward business also changed dramatically during the 1980s and 1990s, and efforts shifted from controlling to attracting multinational companies. The era of deregulation and privatization brought widespread enactment of legislation to attract foreign direct investment, the adoption of hundreds of bilateral investment treaties, and the involvement of dozens of investment promotion agencies. Many forms of traditional development aid were discredited as economically destructive, while the image of business corporations shifted from exploitative to value-creating enterprises.

The United Nations shifted toward engaging multinationals in 1992, when the UN Code of Conduct for Transnational Corporations was abandoned and the newly formed Business Council for Sustainable Development, a coalition of international companies, was assigned the task of writing the recommendations on industry and sustainable development for the UN Conference on Environment and Development (the Earth Summit) held in Rio de Janeiro. The shift to engagement continued with the speech by Kofi Annan to the World Economic Forum in Davos in 1997 in which he stated, "Peace and prosperity cannot be achieved without partnerships involving the governments, international organizations, the business community and civil society."[3] The Global Compact proposed in early 1999 and launched at the United Nations in mid-2000 seemed to complete at least the formal shift to engagement.

As the UN shifted to engagement, an increasing number of NGOs adopted the oversight role that was once envisioned for the Commission on Transnational Corporations. Many of these NGOs have themselves become multinational organizations, beyond the power of individual countries to regulate, and have developed several methods for taking companies to task for activities of which the NGOs disapprove. Just as the limitations of the international human rights framework, reliant as it is on national governments, frustrates human rights advocates where multinational corporations are concerned, the absence of any formal oversight of NGOs raises concerns from the perspective of the multinational corporations that they seek to influence.

RESPONSIBILITIES OF MULTINATIONAL CORPORATIONS FOR RESPECTING HUMAN RIGHTS

The responsibilities of multinational corporations for human rights are not the product of a particular legal system or multilateral framework. The Universal Declaration of Human Rights (UDHR) was proclaimed as a common standard for all peoples, regardless of whether they are lucky enough to live in a community with functioning democratic institutions. The UDHR addresses itself to every individual and every organ of society.

The human rights responsibility of an organization is greatest in circumstances where its power over people is not effectively overseen and regulated by a legitimate governmental authority. Multinational corporations employing, operating near, or producing essential goods for people who are unprotected by a legitimate functioning government clearly have human rights responsibilities toward those people. If a multinational corporation assumes governmental roles, such as community health care, education, and security in a "company town," it assumes the human rights responsibilities associated with that role. The absence of any sovereign or democratic legitimacy to do so should not shield a multinational corporation from human rights responsibilities if it chooses to take on governmental roles.

If a multinational corporation so involves itself in the domestic politics of a country in which it operates that it acquires the power significantly to influence government policy, serious responsibilities accompany that power as well. Mining companies that worked with the South African Apartheid government to design discriminatory policies, and companies that advised the Nazi regime in Germany in developing the Nazi forced labor system and then actively recruited labor from that system, were jointly responsible with the governing regimes.

Some of the most alarming accusations of human rights violations by multinational corporations involve complicity in human rights abuses by governments or insurgents in communities that lack adequate institutional mechanisms to protect human rights. If a multinational corporation carries out activities that directly assist a government in perpetrating human rights abuses, it is guilty of complicity in those human rights violations, regardless of whether the company actually wanted those violations to take place. It is less obvious under the current principles of international human rights law whether a multinational corporation could be considered complicit in human rights violations if it accepts business benefits resulting from government activities that violate human rights, but some level of responsibility in that regard is emerging in practice.[4]

Respecting Human Rights in the Work Place

The most direct relationship multinational companies have with people is the employment relationship. The fundamental human rights associated with employment are those set forth in the ILO Declaration on Fundamental Principles and Rights at Work. The work-place responsibilities for multinational corporations that flow from these principles are well established.

Any direct employment of forced or child labor by a multinational corporation would be a human rights violation per se. Freedom of association, collective bargaining, and the elimination of discrimination require more analysis in their application. Fortunately, they are specifically addressed in the ILO's Tripartite Declaration. The OECD Guidelines for Multinational Enterprises also address collective bargaining and discrimination in the multinational company context. Those guidelines reflect a quarter century of revisions and coordinated input through advisory bodies representing business, labor, and civil society, giving them a balance similar to the ILO declaration.

Companies also have direct responsibility for occupational health and safety in their operations. Although specific standards vary from one industry to another, health and safety practices of companies are among the most widely operative company metrics after financial reporting, and industry associations often set the minimum relevant standards. A multinational corporation's responsibility for the health and safety of its employees while they are on its premises working for the company is not diminished simply because the environment away from company premises is unhealthy, dangerous, or without adequate healthcare services.

The work place is an important social setting where companies play a major role in the functioning of other civic freedoms besides assembly and association. Company policies affecting freedom of expression, freedom to practice religion, and privacy must not be arbitrary or repressive but reconcile needs of the business with the preservation of the rights of others. Not only must the policies be appropriate, but the disciplinary practices employed must be appropriate. Supervisors represent the company, thus they must be trained in how to deal with employees and understand that corporal punishment and physical coercion are not acceptable.

Respecting Human Rights of Others in the Community

The operations of a multinational corporation have an impact on many people besides its employees. Physical operations of a business can affect the community's health and safety, and local business practices can affect social and economic development in a community. The assimilation of responsibilities for these sorts of effects into the UN framework for human rights is more recent and less complete than responsibilities for employees. One must look beyond the International Bill of Rights for guidance.

Environment-related responsibilities for local operations are the most developed in the human rights field. In Resolution 45/94 of its 68th plenary meeting in 1990, the UN General Assembly formally recognized that all individuals are entitled to live in an environment adequate for their health and well-being. A company that knowingly releases toxic substances in a manner that is hazardous to people (for example, into their drinking water) bears responsibility for the resulting health conditions and human rights violations.

The nature of environmental harm is such that the usual attributes of responsibility for harm (that is, the duty to repair, remedy, or compensate) have given way to a doctrine of prevention. Environmental problems are extremely difficult to remedy, thus they must be prevented.

The OECD Guidelines for Multinational Enterprises include a chapter spelling out what a company must do to satisfy its responsibility to prevent serious environmental damage to the communities in which it operates. The key responsibility is to establish and maintain a system of environmental management appropriate to the enterprise, and the guidelines list the essentials for such a system. Environmental management is also the centerpiece of the Agenda 21 chapter on the role of business and industry.[5]

Setting up company facilities in a particular location also involves local property rights and possibly the rights of vulnerable groups requiring use of the land, such as indigenous peoples. In the absence of government institutions to protect affected people, multinational corporations must do everything required to ensure they are respecting such rights. Human rights responsibilities of multinational corporations that require extensive private security arrangements for their local operations can be particularly complex.

Respecting Human Rights of Consumers

In addition to their employees and the residents of the communities in which they operate, multinational corporations can have significant impact on the consumers of the products or services that they produce or contribute to. Food is particularly important in this respect.

The UN Committee on Economic, Social and Cultural Rights makes one of its most explicit statements about business responsibility for the right to adequate food in its General Comment on that part of the ICESCR: "All members of society—[including] the private business sector—have responsibilities in the realization of the right to adequate food. . . . The private business sector—national and transnational—should pursue its activities within the framework of a code of conduct conducive to respect of the right to adequate food, agreed upon jointly with the Government and civil society."[6] To be adequate, the food must be free of contamination or naturally occurring toxins. Adequacy also means in sufficient quantity, so that unfair business practices creating scarcity in order to boost prices could violate this human right if it deprived people of adequate food.

The OECD Guidelines for Multinational Enterprises also include a chapter spelling out what a company must do to satisfy its responsibility to consumers to use fair business, marketing, and advertising practices and to ensure the safety and quality of the goods and services it provides.

Responsibility for Human Rights across the Value Chain

Design, production, sales, integration, installation, and support are distinct activities in the value chain, which may be the responsibility of several independent business entities tied together with contracts. The multinational corporations may be positioned at different points in the chain, with different types of relationships with suppliers of raw materials, components, and services and with distributors of their products or services. The more power a particular company has along a value chain, the more responsibility it bears for the human rights implications of activities up the supply side of the chain or down the distribution side of the chain.

The OECD has recently focused attention on the application of its guidelines to the supply chain. Its Business and Industry Advisory Committee has pointed out that a firm's power over other entities in its supply chain will depend on the industry, the number of suppliers involved, the structure and complexity of the supply chain, and the firm's market position. Out of hundreds of suppliers that a multinational enterprise is likely to purchase from, it is unlikely to be able to dictate policy to more than a handful, and the costs of monitoring that limited number are going to be high.

A multinational company's ability to ensure respect for human rights through its distribution channels will also depend on a range of factors analogous to the supply chain factors, that is, the industry, the number of distribution channel alternatives involved, the structure and complexity of distribution, and the firm's market position. As a general rule, the party that owns the brand that primarily determines the customer's choice has the most relative power, and therefore the most assurance responsibility, along the distribution chain.

Accountability of Multinational Corporations for Human Rights Violations

The UN-sponsored international human rights framework is designed primarily to protect people from human rights violations by the military, the police, and other institutions of the state. Direct enforcement of these rules by international legal institutions is generally limited to the individuals responsible for the actions, rather than the corporations that they manage. They are also focused on activities that are so serious that they constitute international crimes, such as slavery, torture, genocide, war crimes, and crimes against humanity. For human rights issues below that very high threshold, national governments are the main source of oversight and enforcement under the framework.

The obligations of national governments under this system include preventing individuals, organizations, or enterprises from violating many of those rights, but this is an evolving and as yet incomplete area of international human rights law. Where the relevant UN body reviewing human rights complaints finds that a state has not met its responsibility, the remedy is to invite the state to supply information on the steps it has taken to give effect to that body's findings. This is not a system equipped to ensure vigorous enforcement of the human rights responsibilities of multinational corporations in places where the local authorities are not capable of, or interested in, doing so.

Enforcement in National Courts

In jurisdictions with human rights appropriately written into their domestic law and an independent, functioning judiciary that offers recourse to victims against the perpetrators of human rights violations, the system should generally work. Unfortunately, widespread cases of the worst sort of human rights abuses often take place in countries without adequate judicial institutions.

The United States has offered the possibility of jurisdiction in US district courts for "civil action by an alien for a tort only, committed in violation of the law of nations or a treaty of the United States" under the Alien Tort Claims Act (ACTA) (28 USC §1350), adopted in 1789. The ATCA became a basis for bringing suit against people who violate obligatory, internationally recognized human rights in other countries but can be served with process in this country, in a series of suits beginning in 1980. In 1991 the United States Congress passed the Torture Victim Prevention Act (28 USC §1350), which reinforces this possibility of suing in US courts for human rights abuses abroad.

Accountability to NGOs

Human rights cases against multinational corporations began appearing in US courts under the ATCA in the mid-1990s, and with increasing frequency since then. Many of these cases have been initiated by or strongly supported by NGOs hoping to stop activities that they disapprove of on human rights grounds. While the lawsuits can be costly for the companies concerned, and present the risk of damages claims if the plaintiffs prevail, they are employed by NGOs primarily as one of several ways to engage in media campaigns attacking the reputation of the multinational corporation. Damage to reputation rather than court-awarded damages is often the more serious threat to the company.

Another sanction employed by NGOs for human rights violations by multinational corporations is the consumer boycott, a potent weapon against multinational corporations with significant dependence on consumer sales. It might be a corporation selling directly to the consumer, such as a major supermarket chain. More likely it is a company with a single, all-important consumer brand, often corresponding to the name of the company itself, such as Del Monte for food products, or Nike for apparel. A company in a business that does not operate through major consumer brands, such as a mining company, a producer of industrial equipment, or a producer of generic commodity goods, is not going to be as vulnerable to a media campaign directed toward the general public as a company with a valuable consumer brand.

Although major consumer brand companies are just one part of the overall group of multinational companies, they are often the most powerful within their value chain. As discussed earlier in this chapter, they can often exercise more power to ensure compliance with human rights norms among the various companies in the supply and distribution chains that they purchase from and sell to than any other company involved.

Unlike in cases brought in national courts, NGOs using consumer boycotts are not compelled to follow the definition of responsibilities of multinational corporations provided by the international human rights framework described in the earlier part of this chapter. They are free to call an activity a human rights violation if they believe they can generate coverage in the media and a sense of outrage in the consumer. The standard to which they hold multinational corporations is a developed country standard, and in extreme cases the activity considered a human rights violation in the home country may be an activity that the "victims" depend upon for their livelihood and to which they have few, if any, alternatives.

The standard of evidence that NGOs must adhere to in these situations is often simply that of the media organizations that they seek coverage from, and in the case of some organizations and some target corporations, the accusation by itself may be considered newsworthy.[7] Multinational corporations may, and normally do, respond to accusations with their own media campaigns, but in doing so they risk increasing the publicity involved and appearing defensive, both of which could exacerbate the damage. On the other hand, consumer loyalty to established brands is often resilient and rapidly restored after a controversy loses coverage.

A brand is more about feelings than reality, and media campaigns directed at consumer loyalty must be very simplistic to succeed. Human rights situations, on the other hand, involve complex issues and often require difficult, multifaceted responses. For example, a company facing a boycott because it employs child labor may be tempted to immediately fire all of those child laborers so that it can quickly publicize the fact that it no longer employs them, rather than to develop a program to address the needs of those child laborers and their families. In those cases the human rights cause may be advanced at the expense of the people human rights are actually supposed to benefit.

Notwithstanding its limitations, the threat of consumer boycotts has broadened into the wider concept of reputation risk and has encouraged the most important consumer brand companies to invest significantly in improving their practices and monitoring the practices of their suppliers in order to avoid surprises. Concern over reputation risk has spread as a management best practice to companies that do not depend on consumer brands and has helped to make human rights litigation a more significant issue to management and to the boards of directors that oversee management.

The oil companies, pipelines, mining companies, and government contractors typically sued by NGOs have little dependence on consumer brand recognition, but they fear the effect that a negative reputation for human rights could have on campus recruiting and employee motivation, as well as the resulting uncertainty on the part of certain investors, and, in extreme cases, discomfort by business customers concerned about being associated with a company whose reputation is under attack.

Accountability to Stakeholders

The stakeholders of a multinational corporation are the various con-stituencies that directly contribute to, and depend on, their success. The dominant stakeholders for multinational corporations are nor-mally the shareholders. While the shareholders of a multinational cor-poration typically include governments, individuals, and any other entity with funds to invest, it is the institutional investors that largely represent the shareholders of most major multinational corporations.

From the typical institutional investor's viewpoint, the responsibil-ity of a corporation's management is to increase the value of share-holder investment in the corporation by making the corporation itself more valuable. The investor's concern for the impact a corporation's activities will have on human rights is related primarily to how human rights violations could hurt the value of the company either by reduc-ing its revenue (for example, through damage to brand or reputation) or increasing its costs (for example, through lawsuits). That concern on the part of investors could affect its decision to buy or sell the shares of the company concerned, or it could affect the investor's participa-tion, as a shareholder, in the governance of the corporation.

Decisions by investors to buy, continue to hold, or sell a listed company's shares naturally affect the company's share price, and so indirectly affect the company's cost of capital. The decision may also have an important impact on the company's incentive programs for its employees (for example, employee stock option programs). Social and ethical investment firms have come to represent a significant percent-age of the two largest equity capital markets, the United States and the UK, as well as certain other markets, including the Netherlands and Sweden. These firms generally use social and environmental criteria to exclude investments in companies that are found wanting in em-ployee relations, community involvement, environmental impact, hu-man rights, and product safety. Many of the firms contend that performance in these categories is a useful proxy for overall perfor-mance and that investment in firms that meet their criteria will there-fore outperform portfolios with investments in firms considered less socially responsible or ethical. They also attract funds from investors who believe it is more ethical to invest on that basis.

While some screens tend to be overly simplistic, many of these funds employ experienced research firms to investigate the qualifica-tions of companies and are under pressure to show investment returns.

However, since their reputations depend more on avoiding companies that prove "bad" than on sticking with companies that prove "good," a company facing an NGO's media campaign would normally have to prove its innocence categorically in order to avoid being treated as guilty. A tarnished human rights reputation could trigger disinvestment by a significant portion of the equity market. That is an important consideration for the rest of the equity market, since the value of its investment, too, is at stake. The rise of social and ethical investment institutions and the increasing sensitivity of the equity capital markets have combined to amplify the power of NGO media campaigns to affect multinational corporations.

Concern with the potential impact of a human rights violation on the value of a company can also prompt an investor to take action as a shareholder. Public pension funds, religious organization funds, and labor union investment funds increasingly use the proxy voting process for listed companies in the United States to submit shareholder proposals to companies regarding environmental and labor-related issues. Normally, these are precatory resolutions, which would not compel management to do anything even if they were passed by the requisite majority shareholder vote. On the other hand, they have significant symbolic importance as expressions of the will of the shareholders, and proponents often seek company concessions in exchange for withdrawing the proposals.

One shareholder resolution campaign by unions, public pension funds, social and ethical investment funds, and religious investors has produced dozens of proposals over the last several years calling for the corporations to adopt codes of conduct that include core human and labor rights standards, and several companies have responded by doing so. Other current examples are a campaign calling on US-based multinationals operating in sub-Saharan Africa to report on the effect of deadly diseases on their operations, another calling on pharmaceutical companies to "establish and implement standards of response to the health pandemic of HIV/AIDS, TB, and malaria in developing countries, particularly Africa," and a third calling for disclosed guidelines on clinical trials carried out abroad.

Proponents of shareholder resolutions promoting socially responsible conduct generally make some effort to associate their proposals with increasing shareholder value. However, they are often investing in the companies simply in order to qualify as shareholders in order to be able to make their proposals, and shareholder value is secondary to the political purpose of the campaign. The company proxy statements in which the shareholder proposals are published are widely distributed at the company's expense and are often considered newsworthy by the media. Consequently, a shareholder proposal can serve as another foundation for a media campaign to direct attention to the activities of multinational corporations.

While the primacy of national governments underlies the United Nations and its international framework defining human rights responsibilities, it is NGOs that are most active in the oversight of multinational corporations in that arena. The NGOs' primary means of holding companies accountable is the use of media campaigns to attack their reputations, an exercise entirely outside the formal human rights framework.

Opportunities for Multinational Corporations to Promote Human Rights

During the explosive growth of technology companies in the late 1990s, the ability to recruit talent and motivate and retain their highest performing employees began to be as important to those companies as reputation among consumers is for consumer brand companies. They also became preoccupied with the development of social and human capital within their organizations through investment in education and training, through developing a culture of teamwork and creating learning networks, and through promoting a working culture that emphasizes quality and merit. Third, many of these corporations have sought to be truly global organizations.

These three areas of initiative are very closely aligned with the priorities of development and human rights. The most sought-after graduates and the key technology employees tended to be concerned about human rights issues and often expressed concern about the possibility of working for a "bad" company. The human and social-capital-building initiatives embraced by technology companies are directly applicable to capacity building and encouraging entrepreneurship in developing economies. The best of these companies believe that their search for the best recruits should include every country where a company operates, that management systems should emphasize local decision making, that adaptation of products and services to local markets should take place locally, that local joint ventures should be run with the same corporate governance principles as govern the multinational organization as a whole, and that earning a local reputation as a force of good should be a goal pervading the organization. Just doing what is in the best interests of the organization can be beneficial for the communities in which they do business.

An example of a more direct attempt to enhance motivation, development, and presence in remote locations is SEED, an initiative by employees of Schlumberger Limited to connect underprivileged schools in developing countries to the Internet. It is difficult to see this initiative as a defensive reaction to outside pressure. Schlumberger already had globally consistent employment policies; health, safety and environmental policies; and strong diversity and local management development policies that were the envy of other multinational corporations. Although the company has operated for decades in some of the most difficult human rights environments in the world, it has never been the target of human rights litigation or any media campaigns regarding the human rights impact of its activities. Yet many of its employees in those dispersed locations felt a strong desire to make a difference in the communities where they were working. Since the company has been a leader in remote connectivity for decades, local managers and a head office executive came up with the idea of providing local employees with the wherewithal to arrange connections to the Internet for needy schools in those remote regions. Within two years it became an indispensable part of Schlumberger's employee motivation programs, involving hundreds of local volunteers and dozens of schools.

CONCLUSION

The UN-sponsored international human rights framework adequately defines the human rights responsibilities of multinational corporations. It does not provide an adequate system of oversight and accountability in the most vulnerable regions where functioning democratic governments or institutions are not available. However NGOs have taken on an oversight role to fill that gap and have used consumer boycotts, litigation in US courts, and associated media campaigns to attack the reputations of multinational corporations that they believe have been engaged in serious violations of human rights. Multinationals accused of human rights violations may also be excluded from the portfolios of social and ethical institutional investors.

These campaigns have focused the attention of many leading companies on their responsibilities in the human rights arena and represent a significant disincentive against being associated with suspect activities. The growing importance of reputation to a company's ability to recruit and motivate high-performing employees also creates positive incentives for business practices that enhance human rights and local development while addressing the social and human capital development goals of the corporations themselves.

NOTES

[1] United Nations Conference on Trade and Development, *World Investment Report 2002: Transnational Corporations and Export Competitiveness Overview* (New York: United Nations, 2002), 1.

[2] With the Sarbanes-Oxley Act, areas of US corporate governance that were previously covered by relatively simple state rules and customary best practices have been brought under detailed federal regulation in the most extensive corporate securities legislation since the 1930s.

[3] Secretary General Boutros Boutros-Ghali also made statements regarding the promotion of closer association between the United Nations and multinational corporations at the World Economic Forum in Davos in 1995.

[4] In addition to responsibility from aiding and abetting, the commentary accompanying Principle Two of the Global Compact describes "beneficial complicity" as a company benefiting directly from human rights abuses, and "silent complicity" as the failure to raise systematic or continuous human rights violations with the appropriate authorities.

[5] Para. 30.3, as adopted by the Plenary in Rio de Janeiro, on 14 June 1992, refers to environmental management "among the highest corporate priorities and as a key determinant to sustainable development."

[6] Committee on Economic, Social and Cultural Rights, General Comment 12, "The Right to Adequate Food (Art. 11)" (12 May 1999), contained in document E/C.12/1999/5, para. 20.

[7] Of course an NGO has an interest in protecting its credibility. The legitimacy of an NGO is an important factor in determining whether it will be able to obtain useful information and have significant influence. At a minimum, an effective organization would be expected to be accredited by the United Nations, which would require registration as a nonprofit institution in its home country, existence for at least two years, and the maintenance of a democratic decision-making structure. Accountability to its members and to the groups it purports to represent is also important, but more difficult to assess.

6

Royal Dutch Shell

How Deep the Changes?

J. Paul Martin

INTRODUCTION

Corporate social responsibility is a growing field of international concern. Debates in the media, the courts and public opinion on how to enforce that responsibility range from the relevance and effectiveness of various normative frameworks, such as codes and treaties, to assessments of the de facto impact of multi-national corporations (MNCs), on local communities around the world. Some MNCs, though non-state actors, have annual incomes far in excess of those of the majority of their host states. Some carry on activities such as water management and access to energy that impinge on basic human rights. But with the exception of the WTO, MNCs still largely escape the direct scrutiny of the international legal regime. Even domestic laws, especially with respect to corporate activities in non-industrialized countries, have had an inconsistent impact.

Modern approaches to corporate social responsibility seek to address these legal and moral ambiguities and lacunae. During the past decade the challenges to corporate social responsibility have been most visible in certain industries, notably apparel, toys, pharmaceuticals, and the extractive enterprises. In the oil industry, virtually all the major MNCs based in Europe and North America have come under scrutiny for their practices in developing countries, none more so than Royal Dutch Shell Group.

In 1995 Shell was suddenly confronted by two challenges to its long cherished image of corporate citizenship: its plans for the disposal of the Brent Spar drilling platform in the North Sea, and the execution of the Nigerian community activist Ken Saro-Wiwa by the Nigerian government. One was primarily an environmental issue and the other sociopolitical, thus very different solutions were required to address these challenges. The Brent Spar case could have been resolved by a management decision to meet societal demands and by adopting an alternative technology for disposing of the platform. Nigeria, however, was more complex. At issue were social and economic relationships with roots deep in Nigeria's colonial experience, the corporation's relationships with a national government known for corruption, and dissatisfied local ethnic communities threatening social disruption and even secession.[1] There were also serious environmental problems attributed to Shell's operations. Both the Brent Spar and Nigeria cases were covered extensively in the world press, and the latter has finished up in the courts. This chapter concentrates on the Nigerian case.

There are many human rights issues in the Nigerian case. The subject originally caught the headlines because of the arrest and speedy sentence of capital punishment to Ken Saro-Wiwa, the charismatic and activist leader from the Ogoni people in southeastern Nigeria. Shell appeared to stay neutral, if not silently supportive, as the government went ahead with the execution. International concern with Shell's role in this incident eventually led to a case being introduced in the US District Court, Southern District, in 1999. In this case (still undecided), the son and brother of Ken Saro-Wiwa have sued Shell and Brian Anderson, the chief Shell executive officer in Nigeria at the time of the execution, for damages.[2] Both Shell and Brian Anderson are charged with recruiting and arming Nigerian military and police and enabling them to suppress the movement led by Saro-Wiwa, in violation of international law. The plaintiffs also claim that Shell conspired with the Nigerian authorities to put Saro-Wiwa and another activist to death.

Further human rights complaints implicating Shell Nigeria were elaborated in a May 2002 communication from the African Human Rights Commission.[3] In that case the African Human Rights Commission found Nigeria, through its partnership with Shell, in violation of six Articles (2, 4, 14, 18(1), 21 and 24) of the African Charter on Human and People's Rights. These violations were described as the widespread contamination of soil, water, and air; the destruction of homes, the burning of crops and killing of farm animals; and the climate of terror that has been visited upon the Ogoni communities in violation of their rights to health, a healthy environment, housing, and food. The Nigerian Shell subsidiary, Shell Petroleum Development Corporation, is mentioned in the decision because it is the minority shareholder with the Nigerian National Petroleum Company (NNPC). Shell, moreover, operates all the facilities in question. The decision calls upon the Nigerian government to stop all attacks on the Ogoni, to investigate human rights violations, to compensate victims, to prepare environmental and social impact assessments, to inform people of health risks, and to provide remedies.[4] These recommendations are addressed to the government, not Shell Nigeria or its national partner, NNPC. The federal government was held responsible for not enforcing its laws. The Shell Company was criticized as the main operator in the region where it had already been forced to shut down its operations because of an extremely hostile community, namely the Ogoni.

Judging by a 2002 report by Human Rights Watch, the situation remained unchanged.[5] The cover of the report quotes a youth leader: "The solution to conflict is that there should not be double standards. What belongs to somebody should be given to him. People impacted by a project should benefit." The commissioner for the environment in Bayelsa State is reported by Human Rights Watch to have said that he sees "Shell as an active collaborator in the mindless assault on the minority by the majority tribes. . . . As far as relations with communities are concerned we have not seen any changes at all. The flow stations are protected by armed soldiers, they don't give any employment to the youth. As commissioner of the environment I have not seen any changes in corporate philosophy."[6] A development expert from an NGO is quoted in the same report as saying that "the Shell rethink has made no difference, though there has been some movement. . . . There are some people within Shell who have benefited from the cash economy, infrastructure projects, and so on. They won't let that go and put communities in the driving seat." What has been Shell's response to these criticisms?

SHELL'S RESPONSE

Founded in 1897, The Shell Transport and Trading Company quickly became a global player in an industry that, in terms of its range of products and geographical reach, arguably has influenced the past hundred years of world history more than any other single industry. Shell is especially proud of its own heritage, implied in its continued use of "Royal." Its officers have been imbued with a confident sense of social mission and just reward. As Henri Deterding, one of its first and most successful executives, said, "Profits in their true sense are simply the reward of foresight and courage—the foresight to see where opportunities exist to meet mankind's needs more adequately and more cheaply than before; and the courage to risk one's energies and one's savings in exploiting those opportunities." Today, Shell is one of the world's three largest private oil companies, with extensive upstream assets as well as substantial research, marketing, and refining activities.

Throughout its history Shell has portrayed itself as closely associated with technological and social progress, as well as committed to ethics and social responsibility. In his 1995 book, *A Century in Oil*, historian Stephen Howarth recounts how the 1897 fledgling Shell Transport and Trading Company grew into a giant modern non-state actor.[7] Even before the book appeared, the company became embroiled top to bottom in the two major crises discussed above: Nigeria and Brent Spar.

In its initial analysis of Brent Spar and its Nigeria problems, Shell acknowledged that its management and employees were too attuned to the company and its internal culture. Shell's response was to invite outsiders, opinion leaders from government, academia, the media, and NGOs, to speak frankly with Shell executives and middle management. Among the problems identified were "perceptions of Shell as 'Eurocentric,' arrogant, focused on short-term commercial goals, insufficiently interested in renewable sources of energy and adhering to outdated business principles which tolerated double standards."[8]

One of the first outcomes of the rethinking was a revision of the group's 1976 general principles. The revised 1997 principles state that the company recognizes five areas of responsibility:

- to protect shareholders' investment,
- to win and maintain customers,
- to respect the human rights of their employees,
- to seek mutually beneficial relationships with those with whom they do business, and
- "to conduct business as responsible corporate members of society, to observe the laws of the countries in which they operate, to express support for fundamental human rights in line with the

legitimate role of business and to give proper regard to health, safety and the environment."

It was the first time that Shell's principles included the words *human rights*. Annual reports were re-structured to give increasing attention to the social issues governed by the principles, ranging from health and gender balance among employees to the group's capacity to reach all stakeholders. More recent reports, such as that of 2003, have included feedback even from hostile stakeholders.[9] To match principles with practice, Shell recognized that it would have to look less passive in the face of social injustice, deciding, for example, to plead publicly with the government for the rights of other Ogoni who had been arrested by the Nigerian government. Shell also portrayed the classrooms and health services it was building as recognition that human rights is about more than people being held in detention.

In 1998, in the words of Philip Watts, then the group managing director, the issues raised by Nigeria and Brent Spar were problems of

> expanded expectations, and demands based on differing perceptions and values. . . . Nigeria shows the difficulties for a subsidiary within an international group of companies operating in a less developed country wracked with political and social tensions, and constantly in the international spotlight. The media linked the political and environmental issues, and the world expected the company to resolve them.[10]

For Watts, the solution was one of process, namely, the need for open and honest general debate about the role of multinationals; increasing clarity with regard to Shell's values, principles and practices; and credible implementation. "Shell companies are not just economic actors; nor can they be social activists, however. Their role lies somewhere in between, as responsible, efficient and acceptable business organizations acting on the changing world stage."[11]

Over the years Shell has developed new internal policy directives and management primers; it participates in international voluntary codes[12] and organizes social assessment programs within both external affairs and the production units of the company. It maintains regular dialogues within the company as well as with NGOs and universities in the UK and overseas. The chief executive in each country is required to submit an annual letter reporting on the unit's adherence to the principles. These letters provide the basis for a report by the Group Audit Committee, which, in turn, is subject to review by the group's external auditors. This emphasis on social accountability is said to have obliged Mark Moody-Stuart, Watts's predecessor, to defend his watch against accusations that Shell was more concerned about social issues than generating profits.[13]

Human rights have maintained a profile in all these activities. Among the most recent publications is *Human Rights Dilemmas*, a training manual to encourage management thinking on issues of religious freedom, freedom of association, employment conditions, discrimination, child labor, security and safety, community relations, partnerships, and the rights of indigenous communities.[14] Shell's website announces that it has worked with the Danish Institute for Human Rights to develop a Compliance Assessment Tool as a more systematic way for businesses to approach human rights issues.

Recognizing the challenge presented by its own corporate culture, Shell has sought to refine the thinking of its senior staff through the use of training scenarios and simulations. Through role playing and other techniques, it encourages its officers to think through problems from the perspective of others. These scenarios have examined the concepts of sustainable development, new energy technologies, the scarcity of one or more resources with potential social and political changes.[15]

Routine internal and external monitoring of human rights and social issues for Shell is managed by the London-based External Affairs unit under Robin Aram, who organizes special response teams from time to time. Aram's and his associates' strategy has emphasized engagement through being ready listeners and honest reporters. In 2000 one such stakeholder, the British NGO SustainAbility, was asked to prepare a detailed forty-seven-page report assessing the effectiveness of Shell's reporting on social issues. Aram has also turned to NGOs and others outside the group to help produce the primers used to guide managers on topics such as human rights, indigenous peoples, and sustainable development. However, there is still no real mechanism to ensure that ordinary Shell employees understand the importance of human rights in their work site. This is especially problematic in some developing countries where human rights are often seen as little more than the work of leftist NGOs protecting the rights of criminals.

The 2001 annual report noted that Shell had been studying how new energy scenarios will develop prior to 2050 and how to halt rising carbon dioxide emissions while still meeting the pressing need to improve living standards, especially in the developing world. Nigeria taught Shell that energy scenarios are no longer sufficient. It has to develop strategies to monitor and respond to the complex social environments in which it has to operate. This thinking has led to a more comprehensive and active vision, one that includes sustainable development and strategic social investment.

Sustainable Development

Being in the public spotlight with regard to its practices in Nigeria forced Shell to reexamine its economic and social relations with the communities that surround its facilities, especially poor communities. Shell first talked about sustainable development at the 1992 Earth Summit in Rio de Janeiro. After the Nigerian crisis the idea was studied further by a 1997 steering committee headed by group chairman Mark Moody-Stuart. Positive social performance and support for sustainable development began to be portrayed as just good business. In July 2002 Philip Watts, chairman of the Committee of Managing Directors, noted that sustainable development increased operational effectiveness, promoted innovation, and supported Shell's reputation.

Defined most frequently at the early stage as "meeting the needs of the present without compromising the ability of future generations to meet their own needs,"[16] the promotion of sustainable development became a long-term project, a concept to be embedded in all the group's business and management practices. Its three integral dimensions are economic, environmental, and social. Shell's booklet on sustainable development, entitled *There Is No Alternative*, produced for the 2002 Johannesburg World Summit, defined the concept as improving energy technologies and partnerships for self-development, biodiversity, and community development.[17] Integral to the strategy is "positive engagement with communities and national and local authorities."[18]

Contributing to Sustainable Development points out that Shell has long been committed to contributing to economic, environmental, and social progress, but that it is now also important to show that the group's business approach is not one of "profit at any cost." As its core business depletes the world's reserves of fossil fuels, Shell wants to offer a portfolio of energy solutions that will match aspirations for sustainable development. Initially, the strategy emphasized process rather than substance. The booklet, for example, suggests that sustainable development can best be achieved through "engagement," that is, "talking and listening to stakeholders, assessing what we've heard and how best we can respond. In other words, start with dialogue—decide—and then deliver."[19]

More recently the group has sought a more substantive approach to sustainable development. In 2001 Donal O'Neill of The Hague Office wrote:

> Companies operate in unsettled countries because they have natural resources, customers and employees, like everywhere else. For Shell operating ethically in such areas isn't just correct morally—it also makes sound economic sense. It gives the stability that is essential for the security of long-term investments. . . . Stability is a win-win situation for the country and the company. It also ensures the sustainability of the company itself as a creative vibrant, living entity, a valued corporate citizen in the host country, for which innovative, independent and committed people want to work. Such sustainability goes together with responsibility.[20]

With its favored long term in view, Shell believes that its "rich diversity" is a strength that "connects us to the cultures and aspirations of the people and countries where we operate. Strong relationships are critical to building trust and shared success."[21]

Sustainable Communities is the title of one of the three core programs of Shell's new philanthropic arm, the Shell Foundation. Created in June 2000, the foundation is designed to encourage cleaner energy, promote youth enterprise, and fund projects that help marginalized and disadvantaged communities to participate in and benefit from wider economic opportunities. The idea of the foundation is to move away from older styles of corporate philanthropy and community assistance to community development.

Some further insights into Shell's ideas and practices in regard to sustainable development are to be found in the Shell Foundation's 2000–2002 report *Spreading Success*. The report describes Shell's "business-based approaches to key sustainability issues," new public-private partnerships, and other ways of using the "power of the Shell Group to achieve lasting social benefits." The foundation works with a $250 million endowment. So far, the emphasis of the grant making has been on sustainable energy projects (more than forty), self-help business-principle-based projects in poor rural communities (ten), and youth enterprise activities (fourteen). Equally important has been the adoption of strategies that emphasize partnerships with and among civil society and government.

Assessing Shell's Response

One very positive result is that the records and reports of the Shell Group's more than two hundred wholly owned subsidiaries or companies' records are now more open to scrutiny. Shell's actions have also been the most normatively influential on other oil companies that are revising their corporate social practices. Its executives, not just external affairs, are accessible to the media, meet regularly with NGO leaders, often at the executive's invitation, and take part in international projects such as Global Compact and the drafting of the December 2000 Voluntary Principles on Human Rights and Security. The Shell Group maintains a website that not only sets out its principles and information on its practices but also welcomes public comments and makes its management handbooks available to the public. *People, Planet, and Profits: The Shell Report 2001* addresses Shell's commitment to high standards of business; economic, environmental, and social performance; and engagement with its stakeholders. Many of the pages in the forty-eight-page report include a "You told Shell" section that includes both favorable and critical comments. The report also includes a loose sheet prepaid mailer on which readers can submit further comments. Improved communication has other benefits as Shell's executives can rise in the morning with little fear of an unanticipated negative headline in the morning papers. Another important positive outcome is that Shell now acknowledges a wider range of social responsibilities.

A real challenge to the principles fleshed out in the documents is to make them operational in each country. The grassroots implementation of the new social policies is a particular challenge to Shell, as it is structured as a composite of wholly owned subsidiaries (independent companies). In their very different social and political contexts, executive officers of each company are free to make their own day-to-day decisions within general policy parameters. Accountability takes the form of their annual reports on financial and social performance. In the absence of sophisticated social-assessment mechanisms and indicators that permit outside scrutiny and year-to-year evaluation, these reports address only the more visible problems, with little long-term analysis. Senior corporate management is thus more likely to be made aware of human rights issues through third parties like the media or an NGO. All this leaves three important substantive questions to be addressed. The first concern is the adequacy of voluntary principles, as opposed to legal obligations. This raises the second question, namely, the degree to which MNCs are subject to international law. Finally, there is also the more general topic, namely, the fundamental ethical question concerning fairness in the distribution of the wealth that its operations generate. Should all the profit go the shareholders?

Distribution of the Wealth

Shell is a worldwide enterprise, operating in all the richest and many of the poorest countries. Looking at the corporation as a creator of wealth, the overall ethical query involves the principles and patterns that govern the distribution of that wealth. In its operating principles Shell recognizes five groups of beneficiaries or stakeholders: shareholders, customers, employees, those with whom they do business, and society. As do other corporations, Shell sees profitability as essential to staying in business. For Shell, shareholders are the primary beneficiaries. Its operating principles promise "to protect our shareholders' investment and provide an acceptable return." Shell generally maintains its commitment to high standards in its relations with customers and other businesses. Shell's treatment of its employees receives only modest criticisms, such as a lack of diversity—and Shell is now responding to that. The difficult, ill-defined stakeholder category is society.

Shell receives the greatest criticism for its relations with its host communities, most evidently in the form of lawsuits and street protests such as those staged by Nigerian women in 2005 against another international energy company operating in Nigeria. Communities in the Delta region of Nigeria accuse Shell of environmental abuse, and Shell accuses the villagers of sabotaging the pipelines that cause the pollution.

One problem is that while the corporation's commitment to all major stakeholders (shareholders, business partners, and so on) is regulated by generally accepted principles or established procedures (for example, market forces or commercial law), no such framework or regulatory system protects the local communities or indeed national communities, who are often victimized by the exploitation of their natural resources. In practice, the local community's share of the revenues depends on a given national government's ability both to negotiate a strong contract and then to ensure a fair and just distribution of the proceeds. As this is rarely the case, aggrieved local communities will increasingly bring the scope of Shell's social responsibility into question.

Thus, Shell not only has to avoid direct human rights violations, but it may also have to answer to local communities and monitors in the outside world for the use of the revenues it pays to the national government. This is a tall order in a well-wired world where local events quickly become world news. With the recent growth in the influence of civil society at the local level, Shell can expect to find itself embroiled more frequently in conflicts between central governments and local communities seeking a greater share of the revenues.

Social relations at the grassroots, including the distribution of benefits of the corporation's activities, are initially the purview of the country-based officers. Community relations and NGO relations pose a particular challenge. Moreover, human rights principles and practice alone are imperfect tools to assure distributive justice in the form of revenue sharing. At best, human rights principles help identify patterns of discrimination and advocate due process in a situation where oil companies and their host governments typically develop complex and often secret formulas of revenue distribution.[22] A large part of the revenue is often outside the control of the corporation.

According to Shell Nigeria, when the price of oil was around $19 a barrel, the Nigerian government received $13.92 and the oil companies $1.08, with the remainder going to operating costs and future investment. At that time the daily output was over 800,000 barrels. In December 2002, when the price was $30 a barrel, the government received more than $20 a barrel. When a barrel of oil sells for over $50, the share of revenue going to the central government compared with the relatively small amount that, even with recent national legislation mandating a 5 percent share for local communities, actually reaches those communities in the Delta region remains a serious problem for Shell. It has lobbied the government for appropriate legislative changes. In the meantime, the staff and facilities of the oil company become

accessible targets of local frustration, a situation that led to Shell's closing of its operations in Ogoniland, causing it to lose millions of dollars
a day. The distribution of wealth generated by its activities is thus
more than a philosophical question. It has a direct impact on the Shell
Group's income.

If human rights principles do not substantively define a fair sharing
of the wealth, they do offer principles that value the participation of
communities in the political and economic decisions that affect their
lives—consistent with the lessons Shell claims to have learned from
experience: (a) the early identification of the social and environmental issues and needs, (b) early sustained dialogue with all, including
local, stakeholders, (c) a fair and transparent process, (d) commitment
to the highest social and environmental standards, and (e) government
and NGO partnerships to ensure the delivery of schools, health, and
other social services, all of which are designed to build trust and credibility among the stakeholders. All of them are relevant to resolving
the situation in Nigeria. Few seem to have been operationalized in
Ogoniland.

In practice, for example in 2001, Shell Nigeria directed over $52
million to community development projects in the region, ranging from
microcredit ($2.9 million) to the support of hospitals ($4.9 million)
and education ($8.1 million) projects. This was a strategic social in-
vestment move made by Shell. The largest segment of the funds ($23
million) went to infrastructure—roads, bridges, and electrification. The
stated aim was to reduce poverty among the seven million inhabitants
of the Niger Delta, using partnerships and participatory approaches,
as well as advocating for the protection of human rights. Another goal
was to "secure license to operate for the company on a sustainable
basis." In other words, community development was part of the strategy to ensure that Shell would continue to operate in the region.

One of the hardest challenges in regards to social issues is defining
and implementing a corporation's relationship with government. In
July 2002 Philip Watts argued that "responsible investment is where
business can make the greatest contribution to sustainable economies and have the most impact on poverty. But governments must
accept their own responsibilities."[23] As bearers of legal obligations based
on domestic laws and constitutions as well as international treaties,
governments must address the human rights needs of their peoples.
It is thus also the legal responsibility of governments to make the
most of the contracts they sign with corporations seeking to exploit

their nonrenewable resources in order to ensure that all of their people benefit to the maximum. The record of the major petro-states is not stellar in this respect. Some corporations have introduced clauses into contracts to ensure that governments fulfill their social obligations in the communities around their proposed facilities.

Corporate social responsibility is severely tested when governments use oil revenues to fund a civil war or to persecute a segment of the population rather than alleviate social ills. This is the current problem in Sudan, and Shell is similarly accused because of its past activities in Nigeria. Such situations are even further complicated when the company relies on the same military to protect its facilities and personnel, and thus also its profits. Rethinking its position on these issues, Shell joined an international coalition of corporations, NGOs, and the US and UK governments to draft guidelines to govern the use of government and private security force by oil companies. Titled "Voluntary Principles on Security and Human Rights," this December 2000 document sets out best practices for extractive companies in regard to risk assessment and relations with state security services and private security agencies. Shell Nigeria brought its practices in line with the principles in 2001, but neither the UK nor the US government has followed through on its proposed role to enforce and report on compliance. Shell Nigeria, however, has found that its past practices (of ten years ago) are now being used as grounds for class action suits in US courts against its then CEO Brian Anderson and the parent Shell company.

Corporate social responsibility is also severely tested where the national government is known to allow the diversion of funds to illegal private purposes, when the same funds could have been used to alleviate abuses associated with the basic needs of its poor. The Human Rights Watch Report records another side of the coin. A development expert was concerned with the fact that

> anything that does not deliver instant cash, people are not interested. Someone paid 30,000 naira (US$230) a month does not want to do anything. We try to set up small-scale enterprises or other projects, they ask how much they earn, and then they're not interested. So they all depend on the oil companies. If we run a workshop nobody will come if they're not paid; when Shell pays a "seating allowance" they want to know why we don't.[24]

These conditions are very consistent with other research on the development problems of petro-states.[25] The generation of wealth, even when it reaches local communities, does not necessarily lead to social and economic development.

Judging by relative expenditures in the field and at the corporate level, Shell's commitment to human rights and social issues is definitely less than its commitment to environmental issues. In the Camisea project, a relatively small Brazilian NGO was used to advise on the social issues. And in Gabon, Shell is working with both the World Wildlife Fund and the Smithsonian to assure an environmentally friendly presence, but without a comparable social assessment and planning unit. Overall, sustainable development has been best fostered and supported financially in the company's environmental policies and practices. As the continued shutdown of Shell's operations in Ogoniland illustrates, societal sustainability is much more complex because it depends on choices of a political nature and on sensitive relations with both local and national public authorities—in other words, on factors largely outside the company's control. Criteria of progress in social accountability need further work. Moreover, there has been no assessment of what the corporate commitment to human rights means to its more than 100,000 employees.

The Adequacy of Voluntary Principles

Recent legal and human rights literature argues that corporations are legally subject to international human rights law.[26] This growing body of legal opinion states that a corporation can be held accountable for abuses within its realm of operations, such as religious, ethnic, and gender discrimination; slavery or forced labor; child labor; torture; and other restrictions of personal freedom and safety—as well as for inadequate housing, sustenance, health care, and education. Moreover a corporation can be held accountable not only for human rights violations of which its activities are a direct cause, but also such indirect violations as, for example, when income or logistical assistance received from the company is used by a government to suppress or discriminate against persons within its jurisdiction.

The Preamble of the UDHR delineates the promotion of human rights as fundamental to "freedom, justice and peace in the world" and as "a common standard of achievement for all people and all nations."

Human rights statutes are designed to define common values and transcend more particular corporate, ethnic and other views of peace and social justice. Human rights standards, according to the UDHR, hold that "all human beings are born free and equal in dignity and rights" (no. 1), and that human rights are the entitlement of every human being "without distinction of any kind, such as race, color, sex, language, religion, political or other opinion, national or social origin, property, birth or other status" (no. 2). Unlike voluntary principles, the human rights paradigm asserts that these rights also imply legal obligations. In the case of international human rights, these obligations fall specifically on the governments that host Shell and have signed the various treaties implementing the UDHR.

As distinct from Shell's own principles or other voluntary principles such as the UN Global Compact, international law and international human rights law provide greater definition and precision, as well as standards and institutions that enjoy broad acceptance on the part of the international community. The degree to which corporations can be held responsible in terms of international law either directly or indirectly, namely, through their host governments, is debated. But the legal system is now becoming more effective.[27]

One danger with the emphasis on corporate codes is that they distract from the treaty obligations on states. For their part, however, states should recognize that they can fulfill their own statutory obligations by imposing contractual obligations, such as employment standards, on companies within their jurisdiction.

Defining the Legal and Ethical Terrain

The dimensions of the legal and ethical terrain in human rights are extensive and difficult to define. The terrain is extensive in other ways as well. Energy and energy management have a huge impact on modern life. In Shell's management primers, human rights dilemmas are portrayed as self-contained dramas and questions of ethics, good training tools for management. Human rights and human rights violations are neither defined nor analyzed in terms of the broader and systemic context of globalization and the economic and social conditions of the countries in which most upstream operations exist. Shell's current social-assessment systems monitor only a few conditions, for example, workers' housing, within some host communities, while there is no overall research, planning, or sharing of experience as how best to re-invest in those communities. Choices are left to local managers, and there is no body of information on best practices.

Missing in these decisions and theories about sustainable develop-ment is a discussion of how the wealth is distributed among all the various stakeholders ranging from executives and shareholders to lo-cal communities. This wider framework extends to the complex regu-lations of the WTO that privilege the countries and corporations that can underwrite the cost of any required legal or diplomatic actions. Sustainable development aspirations will work best when they are based on an understanding of how these forces influence corporate strategic social investments that address or simply have an impact on surrounding ills such as poverty, HIV/AIDS, maternal and child health care, water systems, endemic diseases, and the use of drugs and alco-hol.

Every Shell employee in the field is potentially a witness to human rights abuses on the job and in the community. On the job, he or she might see discrimination, exploitation, and nepotism in recruitment, benefits, services, promotion, and choice of local suppliers; payoffs to local authorities and others; mistreatment of others by security per-sonnel; and health hazards. Shell's commitment to human rights will be in place only when every employee understands the relevance of human rights to his or her social situation and each employee feels that any response to abuse will find a support and a search for an effective remedy on the part of the corporation. Similarly, surround-ing communities need to feel the government's and Shell's commit-ments to address environmental hazards and predictable systemic human rights abuses associated with oil projects, such as the exploita-tion of migrant workers, trafficking and other patterns of mistreat-ment of women, HIV/AIDS-inducing behavior, suspect land and property arrangements, corrupt and ineffective criminal justice and security procedures, not to mention more general conditions of pov-erty, hunger, and lack of education and social services.

Shell's own concepts of sustainable development offer the principles to "do business differently" but not necessarily the strategies for every circumstance. Among critical elements in planning are early identifi-cation of the social and environmental issues and needs; early sus-tained dialogue with all, including local stakeholders; a fair and transparent process; commitment to the highest social and environ-mental standards; and government and NGO partnerships to ensure the delivery of schools, health, and other social services—all of which are designed to ensure trust and credibility among the stakeholders.

Integral to the model is building social capital, namely, the capacity of local institutions to assume ever more complex development and service tasks. For their part, human rights principles emphasize due process and legal obligations, the primacy of personal security and safety, and especially the importance of civil and political participation. The human rights perspective focuses the action on the community, its rights and its needs, as opposed to simply absolving Shell or a given government.

In the same positive vein Shell has recognized that strategic social investments linked to its business operations are more than just the financial transfers. In every field situation Shell personnel can bring substantial professional knowledge and expertise that could be incorporated into the local development forces without trespassing on the domain of local government. A simple example would be offering courses offered at local universities and colleges taught by its local or expatriate managers, engineers, and economists. In all such activities the social effectiveness that Shell seeks inevitably requires drawing a fine line between partnership and intrusion, between good citizenship and taking on the role of government. Ultimately, in addition to avoiding human rights problems, such activities improve the relationship between the corporation and its host communities. This can be achieved only by successful strategies that truly support sustainable political, economic, and environmental development of those communities.

In recent years, in the face of difficult local social circumstances associated with human rights abuses, Shell has always retained and even increased its investment rather than pulling back or withdrawing. In doing so it argues that it can convey a beneficial social message. Shell, for example, stayed in South Africa throughout apartheid. It increased investment in Nigeria immediately after the Ken Saro-Wiwa incident, and recently it has come close to agreeing to a partnership to develop a natural gas project in Western China, even though it means operating among a population already disgruntled with its treatment by Beijing, especially with the regime's policy of moving ethnic Chinese into the region and favoring them with the best jobs.

In all cases there were sound business reasons for its decisions, and Shell argued that it could contribute more by its presence than by leaving the projects to others. In the first two cases there were clear profits to be made. In the case of China, although profits would probably be marginal, Shell saw the project as a foothold in an important future national market and perhaps a stake in a project that would eventually link China, and perhaps the rest of the world, with the major reserves of oil and gas in Caucasus and Central Asia.

The de facto social outcomes of Shell's presence in these and other situations have yet to be independently assessed. In each, Shell's social involvement has been cautious, readily deferring to local culture (read: government), practices, and politics. Certainly Shell's commitment to social responsibilities has not yet imposed any obvious major financial losses upon its shareholders, even before comparing any such costs with prospective net earnings and strategic alliances.[28] On the contrary, the group has lost and continues to lose millions of dollars because of its failure to solve its social circumstances in Nigeria.

CONCLUSION: THE WAY AHEAD

In 1998 Chairman Watts claimed that Shell Nigeria "is being asked to find solutions to local political and societal problems although it has no political or social authority to do so."[29] The thrust of this chapter has been to suggest that human rights principles and Shell's own insights into sustainable development and strategic social investment now offer a more advanced but not yet adequate guide to finding solutions to local political and societal problems. I argue that Shell has put in place the scaffolding, that is, the principles, but not yet the building itself, that is, a human rights culture and practice among its employees throughout its worldwide group of companies. The acid test of these principles and experience is, of course, whether or not Shell will use them to reopen its facilities in Ogoni.

Implied in the human rights movement is the principle that many of the groups or individuals whose rights are being violated, such as slaves, prisoners in Dachau, or victims in the Rwanda genocide, need the assistance of third parties to help end their sufferings. A commitment to help others has always been a characteristic of the international human rights movement. The cases against Shell in the US District Court and against the Nigerian government at the African Human Rights Commission, for example, were all brought by civil society groups. Independent monitoring and advocacy therefore need to remain integral to promoting corporate responsibility.

Human rights, however, are slowly becoming part of international corporate culture, and Shell's corporate executives are aware of the challenges. The situation on the ground, however, is more uneven, with much depending on the attitude of each country CEO. At the moment, one suspects that most of these field executives tend to resist external scrutiny of their social performance. Also missing on the ground is an appreciation on the part of the individual employees that his or her participation in the company's commitment to corporate responsibility and human rights is integral to a stable business environment.

The promotion of human rights is a question of attitude as well as knowledge and skills. As in all engineering, successful social projects are more than a bright idea. They need *all* the pieces necessary, all the pieces *in good working order,* and all working *together.* None of Shell's training manuals, for example, yet deals with fostering good local government and good relations with local government. One result has been that, because of poor relations with the public officials concerned, its local philanthropic activities result in schools or health facilities dependent on Shell rather than on local resources. As elsewhere in the world, the state of human rights in the surrounding communities depends on the capacity of local public institutions and on local civil society. Without imposing their own agenda, Shell subsidiaries can engage both sectors by providing more technical assistance and capacity building. Well executed, the real benefit of outreach to local government would be trust building.

The official commitment to human rights and to sustainable development definitely provides a new strategic framework for Shell to think about its relationship with and obligations toward its host communities. It will require, however, more independent research on the ground to know the degree to which these human rights and other corporate responsibility policies and practices have become a normal part of being a Shell employee rather than just the responsibility of "external affairs."

NOTES

[1] Shell has been operating in Nigeria for over sixty years. It employs around four thousand full-time staff, 95 percent of whom are Nigerian. Its Nigerian operations are a joint venture with the Nigerian National Petroleum

Corporation (55 percent), Elf (10 percent), and Agip (5 percent). Shell owns 30 percent and is the project's operator.

[2] Case No. 96 Civ. 8386 (KMW), Judge Kimba M. Wood.

[3] African Human Rights Commission, October 2004 Communication 155/ 96, 30th Ordinary Session, http://www.achpr.org/francais/_doc_target/documentation (accessed 30 September 2004).

[4] African Human Rights Commission, Communication 155/96.

[5] Human Rights Watch, *The Niger Delta: No Democratic Dividend* (New York: Human Rights Watch, October 2002).

[6] Human Rights Watch, *The Price of Oil: Corporate Responsibility and Human Rights Violations in Nigeria's Oil Producing Communities* (New York: Human Rights Watch, January 1999).

[7] At the time of the events covered by this chapter, the Shell Group linked two separate public companies, Royal Dutch Petroleum Company and the Shell Transport and Trading Company, with 740,000 and 270,000 shareholders, respectively. The first is domiciled in the Netherlands and the second in the UK. In 2005 these two groups were merged into a single company, headquartered in the Hague.

[8] Lynne Sharpe Paine, *Royal Dutch/Shell in Transition (A)*, Harvard Business School Case Study #N9–300–039 (Cambridge: Resident and Fellows of Harvard College, 1999).

[9] These reports are available on the Shell website.

[10] Philip Watts, in *Companies in a World of Conflict: NGOs, Sanctions and Corporate Responsibility*, ed. John V. Mitchell, papers from a workshop in Oslo by the Royal Institute of International Affairs (London: RIIA, 1998), 25.

[11] Ibid.

[12] Notably the Global Sullivan Principles, The UN Global Compact, The Voluntary Principles on Security and Human Rights, the OECD Guidelines, and those of the International Chamber of Commerce.

[13] Paine, *Royal Dutch/Shell in Transition (A)*.

[14] These dilemmas were preceded by a human rights primer prepared in consultation both within and outside Shell, notably with Amnesty International in the Netherlands and Pax Christi. Available on CD-ROM, Governance in Shell, 4th ed. (2003).

[15] Philip Watts, *Doing Good Business: What Contributing to Sustainable Development Means and Why It Matters* (London: RIIA, 2002).

[16] H. Rouls, *Contributing to Sustainable Development—A Management Primer* (London, Shell, 2001), 5. Available on the Shell website.

[17] *There Is No Alternative* (London: Shell International Limited, 2002) contained brief descriptions of illustrative cases, largely from Africa.

[18] Rouls, *Contributing to Sustainable Development*, 23.

[19] Ibid., 10.

[20] Donal O'Neill, "Principles, Dilemmas, and Choices," privately circulated paper, quoted with author's permission, 22–23.

[21] Harry Roels, *People, Planet, and Profits: The Shell Report 2001* (The Hague: Shell International BV, 2001). Available on the Shell website.

[22] Terry Lynn Karl, "The Perils of the Petro-State: Reflections on the Paradox of Plenty," *Journal of International Affairs* 53, no. 1 (Fall 1999): 31–48.

[23] Watts, *Doing Good Business.*

[24] Human Rights Watch, *The Niger Delta.*

[25] Karl, "The Perils of the Petro-State."

[26] International Council for Human Rights Policy, *Beyond Voluntarism: Human Rights and the Developing International Legal Obligations of Companies* (Geneva: International Council on Human Rights Policy, 2002).

[27] Ibid.

[28] A case could be made that potential human rights problems at least partially motivated Shell to walk away from its $500 million investment in the Chad-Cameroon project. Shell's official story pointed to an overall reassessment of its worldwide investments that suggested that projects elsewhere offered better economic prospects.

[29] Watts, in Mitchell, *Companies in a World of Conflict.*

Part III

Non-State Actors in Conflict Situations

7

Global Civil Society Actors and 9/11

Richard Falk

INTRODUCTION

As the memory of 9/11 grows less traumatic with the passage of time, it becomes possible to assess some of its effects on world order with greater objectivity. In this chapter the focus is placed upon the extent to which the attacks altered the role, agenda, and impact of global civil society actors. The essential premise of the analysis is that the attacks unleashed a war of global scope that disclosed the potency of non-state, non-territorial "uncivil society" actors, especially when linked by way of transnational networks. This negative potency was earlier disclosed through the activities of transnational crime and drug networks, as well as the illicit activities of private sector arms dealers. But we should not overlook positive forms of potency that had flourished in the 1990s, taking shape as a transnational global justice movement. These initiatives persist in an array of formats in the first decade of the twenty-first century. The high visibility of the annual sessions of the World Social Forum has established a venue for the assertion and pursuit of a variety of global justice grievances and aspirations. Perhaps too hopefully, Jonathan Schell described the massive grassroots expressions of opposition to the Iraq War around the world as constituting "the world's other superpower."[1]

But it is the negative implications of non-state actors (NSAs) that challenge traditional ideas of world order most fundamentally, giving impetus on the part of the leading state actor, the United States, to a visionary and non-realist project for global security based on global empire. For most of the peoples of the world, neither the chaos of non-state political violence nor the imposed order of empire seems a beneficial solution to the problem of global security. To overcome this dilemma, several lines of action seem relevant, including seeking adherence to international law and respect for the UN, a shared commitment to humanitarian intervention as needed to protect vulnerable peoples around the world, and nonviolent resistance and rejection of both political violence directed against civilians (terrorism by both state and non-state actors) and to extreme forms of coercive action by the preeminent state actor that could at its worst eventuate in a new political phenomenon, namely, global fascism.[2] Two directions of emphasis seem responsive to these concerns: a politics of implosion within the United States that reorients the approach to global security in a dramatic fashion and the rise of a "new globalism" combining the activism of global civil society actors with the efforts of moderate state actors seeking to promote global democracy as integral to achieving global security in a tolerable form during this early part of the twenty-first century.

The post-Westphalian character of the "war" unleashed by 9/11 seems to be the appropriate starting point, both conceptually and politically. This first borderless war of global scope in human history instigated a fundamental change in conflictual behavior and the governance structure of world political life. In the war on terrorism neither principal antagonist is a "normal" sovereign state. Al Qaeda is a concealed network of still largely uncertain proportions and character operating in dozens of states to engage in violent anti-Americanism; the United States, as adversary and antagonist, has been operating as a global state, possessing military bases in some sixty countries, embarked on the weaponization of space, coercively implementing a discriminatory nonproliferation regime prohibiting the possession of weaponry of mass destruction, and claiming the right to disregard the sovereignty of other countries and the human rights of individuals while in pursuit of suspected terrorist enemies. In this period of confusion and turmoil, many leaders of important sovereign states are trying to balance their shared resistance to this broad tendency to subvert their territoriality and sense of national independence in the name of anti-terrorism against a prudential impulse to accommodate geo-political pressures being mounted by the United States to engage in a common struggle against the menace of fundamentalist violence.

The diplomatic struggle during 2002 and 2003 between the United States and some of its traditional European allies about how to resolve the Iraq crisis depicts the deep structural tension that is characteristic of the post-9/11 world order. The tension is essentially an encounter between sovereignty-oriented Europeans seeking to fashion global security policy on the basis of intergovernmental cooperation and law enforcement, and hegemonic Americans insisting that new realities require a global security regime administered from Washington. Those civil society actors seeking global justice are caught in the middle (as are most states) and need to reassess their global roles and priorities in light of these crosscurrents associated with crucial changes in the overall global setting. What seemed so path-breaking in the 1990s by way of promoting global justice and democracy, and thereby transforming economic globalization for the benefit of the entire human family, now appears to have become of secondary significance,[3] as the civil society efforts focus on preventing wars, meeting the challenge of uncivil political extremism, and avoiding an American-run global empire.

A new factor in the mix of elements on the global stage is the rise of what might be termed "uncivil society" actors. These actors operate clandestinely and in defiance of law and ethics, pursuing illicit commercial and political goals of a transnational character. The rise of uncivil society actors challenges the Westphalian framework, designed to regulate states in their transnational activities while entrusting territorial regulation to the governments of sovereign states. To some degree states have accommodated themselves to global civil society actors that were pursuing widely endorsed world-order values on matters associated with environment and human rights, as well as a broad range of humanitarian issues, although neo-conservatives are beginning to regard NGOs as antagonistic to their programs of social control.[4] Although there existed significant uncivil actors that engaged in a wide spectrum of profit-making criminal activities, and those composed a regulatory challenge, this was not a radical threat to the basic framework. But the 9/11 attacks, their magnitude and traumatic exposure of statist vulnerability, have had some contradictory structural impacts, at once emphasizing the outmoded character of a statist world order in the face of uncivil global political actors and the hardening of statist internal structures in an effort to prevent the penetration by these transnational political forces, or at least to limit their effectiveness to the extent possible. These new considerations also complicate the relations among the four sets of actors shaping world order at present: states, market forces, civil society forces, and uncivil society forces.

In the post-9/11 world, civil society forces have to oppose the encroachment on human security by the uncivil society without endorsing the encroachments by the state on human rights. It is important also not to lose sight of the degree to which neo-liberal market operations are aggravating the problems of the poor throughout the world as well as undermining some of the most important efforts to protect the environment. The anti-globalization movement that was born in the streets of Seattle in late 1999 as a demonstration against a ministerial meeting of the WTO gained momentum until 9/11 but then lost some of its salience because of a shift in political priorities in global civil society to antiwar and anti-imperial ends.

Into this new global setting, there is also a need to resituate the UN and international institutions. In general, the UN and other international institutions support the regulatory efforts to control the activities of uncivil actors, especially by way of state action and intergovernmental cooperation, but the UN failed to restrain the US enunciation of a preemptive war doctrine. Also, the UN has yet to do much to accommodate civil society actors pursuing constructive ends. At present, their participation is kept at the outer margins of the formal undertaking of these institutions, with scant opportunity for meaningful participation. Indeed, the earlier 1990s were more hospitable, allowing NGOs at UN world conferences on global issues to become lively arenas for the interplay between governments and the social forces of global civil society, and to function as occasions for the formation of global networks among representatives of these forces. Precisely, the momentum of this process induced a statist backlash later in the last decade of the twentieth century, major states opposing using UN resources to fund such conferences, at least temporarily. This dynamic has contributed to the development of receptive venues for NGO activity, the most spectacular of which to date has been the annual meetings of the World Social Forum, which drew some 100,000 global civil society militants at its 2003 meeting in Puerto Allegre.

So far, the most impressive setting for the synergistic blending of civil society, states, markets, and international institutions has been at the regional level, particularly within the confines of the European

Union, although the process has slowed due to the apparent impasse with respect to the adoption of a European Constitution. It may be that this arena of experimentation will generate a model for a post-Westphalian world order, initially for regional arrangements, but later transferred to the global level.

THE DECADE AFTER THE COLD WAR

With the fall of the Berlin Wall, new global agendas, arenas, and policy priorities emerged. The 1990s came as close to producing "a normative revolution" (moves toward global justice, the strengthening of international law, the rise of human rights, assertions of universal jurisdiction, and the acknowledgment and redress of unresolved historic grievances) as the world has ever known.[5] If such an array of positive initiatives had been sustained, it would possibly have led in a matter of decades to some form of humane global governance, providing the peoples of the world with a more peaceful, equitable, sustainable, democratic, and hopeful foundation for global security.[6]

Of course, such an optimistic picture of the future was never by any means assured, or widely shared. For example, early in the 1990s Samuel Huntington aroused anxieties around the world with his strident portrayal of "a clash of civilizations," premised on the contention that "civilizations" were resuming their pre-Westphalian dominance over the historical process and bloody warfare, based on inter-civilizational strife rather than familiar Westphalian patterns of rivalry among sovereign states, would intensify.[7] Although it originally received mixed reactions and substantial criticism, after 9/11 some hailed Huntington's voice as prophetic.

Another troubling image of the future was associated with corporate globalization in a predatory form theorized as neo-liberal ideology, also known as the Washington consensus.[8] Such a trend, seemingly dominant in the 1990s, gave a new non-Leninist spin to economistic forms of geo-politics in which the locus of global policymaking was moving beyond the control of sovereign territorial states.[9] The consolidation of a world market and the emancipation of capital flows from the control of states could render obsolete much of the traditional warfare between sovereign states.[10] But globalization also involved accentuating inequities between rich and poor throughout the world, as well as deteriorating environment and heightened risks of ecological collapse.[11]

There was also widespread suspicion that the United States was pursuing a global dominance project under the aegis of promoting economic globalization.[12] Washington was seen as setting the ideological and policy parameters for global economic policy via the IMF and World Bank, as well as disseminating a popular culture that was homogenizing the peoples of the world around American consumerism, its tastes and values, while standing guard over this unfolding process with the most formidable military capability that has ever existed. Favorable accounts of this dynamic of Americanization stressed America's unique global reach, its capacity to dominate by means of its control over "soft power," the attractiveness of its political economy, along with its singular ability to project its military power throughout the planet to destroy any state foolish enough to challenge such a world order.[13] Skepticism about such an optimistic hegemonic scenario resulted from anticipations about the future based on the spread and deepening of disorder. Failed states in Sub-Saharan Africa presented one version of this idea about the future, while the ethnic and religious strife in the Balkans gave grounds for another version.[14]

What is most interesting at this moment is that none of these lines of developments any longer seems adequate as explanation or prediction. Our understanding of global trends has been recast by 9/11, giving an emphasis to the subversive challenge posed by uncivil NSAs that rely on violence directed at soft targets, and an imperial response that claims to treat the world as a battlefield in which there are no neutral parties. At such a historical moment there is reduced space for civil society actors dedicated to global reform, human rights, and human security.

RESPONDING TO 9/11

The attacks of 9/11, combined with the recognition of a continuing capability and will of the al Qaeda network to inflict severe harm, refocused the attention of many governments on traditional problems of national security, but in light of new tactics and targets. The Westphalian era strategies that were preoccupied with war among states and involved seeking "balance," "containment," and "deterrence" started to be deemed irrelevant. To be sure, there was always a dimension of this statist world order that was concerned deeply with internal struggles for power and independence and was accompanied by forms of anti-state political violence now called terrorism.[15] But such struggles were essentially carried on within the domains of territorial sovereignty, even if occasionally spilling across nearby borders. These political activities have been understood in recent decades as claims associated with the right of self-determination. Such conflicts were essentially "internal wars" that did not raise doubts about the viability of the Westphalian world order. Also, this violence did not lead civil society actors to be perceived as challenging the basic contours of world politics.[16]

With 9/11 it became evident that a new mode of political violence, mega-terrorism, posed a fundamental security and *conceptual* challenge, giving non-state violence a capability comparable to that associated in the past with wars conducted by major states. Moreover, the espoused transnational goals of al Qaeda were unrelated to the dynamics of self-determination with respect to any particular state but could be better understood either as resistance to American encroachment on the Arab Islamic world or as an undertaking to reconstitute a post-Westphalian Islamic *umma*. Arguably, as well, the challenge of 9/11 was manipulated by the US government to enable the pursuit of certain previously formulated plans of Bush advisers to reconfigure world politics after the Cold War on the basis of American preeminence.[17] Such a conception of global security under the aegis of American military dominance has been most authoritatively formulated in the official document *National Security Strategy of the United States of America*, issued by the White House in September 2002. An antecedent report, "Repairing America's Defenses," published in 2000 by the Project for a New American Century, contains most of the elements that are featured in the *National Security Strategy of the United States of America*: the need to sustain American military dominance beyond challenge; the desirability of promoting regime change in countries opposing this approach to global security; and the emphasis on uses of force by the US government that could not be reconciled with independent readings of international law. This American grand strategy, with its call for increasing defense spending and a greater willingness to rely on the use of force as a foreign policy tool, with or without the backing of the UN, represented an intensification of the approach taken by prior American mainstream leaders.

In the process of advancing this ambitious geo-political agenda, the terrorist menace as understood during the 1990s was reformulated in crucial ways. This non-state transnational political violence, conducted by an enemy that lacked an address, that is, possessed no particular territorial base, was shifted from the category of international crime, which would call for energetic law enforcement, including international police cooperation, to the category of war. As war, it was possible to call for a dramatic mobilization of the resources of the organized world society to overwhelm this civil society. The magnitude of the challenge to the established order was fully acknowledged, and quite possibly exaggerated or misrepresented by the United States. Despite some worries, governments and world public opinion initially accepted the necessity of this expansive American response. An impassioned President Bush, however, articulated the American response in the language of a "global state" rather than as a normal sovereign state seeking to restore its security by working cooperatively, if urgently, with the established order. Just days after the 9/11 attacks, on September 20, 2001, Bush peremptorily told a joint session of Congress that "every nation . . . now has a decision to make. Either you are with us, or you are with the terrorists."[18] Later on, the initial consensus sympathetic to the defensive war against an outlaw Afghanistan regime dissipated, and the buildup preceding the Iraq war exposed deep cleavages among Western states that had been allied for decades. When recourse by the US government to the UN and NATO did not produce complete submission to its will, this same logic was relied upon by Washington to bully states in the setting of multilateral institutions: the Bush leadership insisted in September of 2002 that either the UN support the US-led war against Iraq or it would find itself irrelevant.[19] The US secretary of state, Colin Powell, further asserted that the United States was prepared to exercise "its sovereign right" to initiate war unilaterally against Iraq if deemed necessary for its security.[20] This claimed sovereign right is properly understood as a repudiation of the long effort by international law to inhibit the discretion of states to wage non-defensive wars.[21]

What has been exhibited in responding to the al Qaeda attacks is this admixture of Westphalian and post-Westphalian ideas and practices. The Westphalian resurgence involves the renewed centrality of security concerns of a war/peace character, combined with a claimed right to wage war without regard to preexisting international law or the UN as the main security mechanism for the world. Many states, but especially the United States and its coalition partners, have become more concerned with policing their borders, assessing the loyalties of resident Islamic male minorities, and mounting a draconian regulation of immigration. But there are present also post-Westphalian elements, especially the disregard of sovereign rights of those states that do not join actively in support of America's global strategy of response, including the imposition of regime change on a traditional territorial actor by recourse to war, as was done to Iraq. Here, the two approaches overlap, causing intense controversy. So long as the American response seemed rationally designed to cope with the distinctive challenge of mega-terrorism as the mode of violence used by uncivil NSAs, recourse to war was internationally accepted as a reasonable bending of legal constraints and sovereign rights, and the US government was given the benefit of the doubt in the UN and elsewhere. But when that same logic was extended to Iraq, which could neither be portrayed as an imminent threat nor as significantly linked with mega-terrorism, the assault on the Westphalian order became for many governments and civil society actors a transparent move toward American global dominance of an imperial character that has had, ironically, an aggravating impact on the menace of mega-terrorism.[22] In the UN, and other responsible arenas, the re-articulated challenge became one of separating out the genuine threat of mega-terrorism from the genuine threat of American global dominance (including the warpath that led from here to there). Increasingly, even in relation to Afghanistan, it appears that the 9/11 attacks would have been addressed more *effectively*, if that was the goal, by revamping international law enforcement through greatly augmented resources and cooperative procedures. That would have vindicated the viability of the statist framework of world order and its ability to meet the challenge mounted by a non-state network within the framework of international law, as adapted through agreement and cooperative action.

Without doubt, the world order that had seemed so simple during the Cold War was becoming ever more complex and contested. On one side, the potency of al Qaeda was providing the United States a rationale for global empire, another form of bypassing the plural order of late twentieth century world order that had been since 1990 increasingly attentive, if inconsistently, to the rule of law and an ethos of global cooperation at the intergovernmental level.[23] On a second side was the evolving debate about how to constitute a new security regime for the world that would be responsive to mega-terrorism and the dangers associated with the possession and proliferation of weaponry of mass destruction.

Also challenged were those civil society actors seeking deep global reform by way of democratization. How could such actors avoid a new circumstance of irrelevance? If the agenda of the North had shifted to global security, could not the agenda of the South continue with its preoccupation with the deficiencies of economic globalization, as well as with various aspects of human rights, including efforts to deal with abuses of women, of labor, and of indigenous peoples? Or should a unified set of transnational forces fashion a more encompassing agenda that combined antiwar resistance and empire-building with a menu of global justice concerns and goals? The massive antiwar demonstrations around the world in the period leading up to the Iraq war revealed a restive civil society and an antiwar majority in all established democratic states. This unprecedented display of the transnational character of NSAs and their networks climaxed on 15 February 2003, when as many as 10 million demonstrators in some fifty countries expressed their opposition to the Iraq war. Although it failed to prevent the war, or even to sustain its own opposition to American imperial policies, this global mobilization suggested a new type of global politics, which might yet crystalize in a more durable form in the years ahead.

One side effect was an apparent spontaneous agreement that the anti-globalization movement would be somewhat subordinated to the urgent antiwar efforts. Of course, for most activists the two goals are intertwined to such an extent that there is no need to suggest a dilemma. Opposing a war against Iraq successfully creates an atmosphere in which attention can be again focused effectively on the deprivations, inequities, and wastes of economic globalization, as well as the suffering resulting from poverty, chaos, and environmental decay. At the same time, so long as the war fever rages, it must be treated by the political therapy of populist outrage, relying on the lawmaking successes of the 1990s that saw emerge "a new globalism," the coalition initiatives of civil society actors linked to the efforts of moderate governments. Such collaborations, "the next new thing" in global lawmaking, produced such notable outcomes as the anti-personnel land-mines treaty and the Rome Treaty establishing the International Criminal Court, as well as the climate of opinion that produced the Kyoto Protocol dealing with the emission of greenhouse gases.

RETHINKING THE FUTURE OF GLOBAL CIVIL SOCIETY

The above-mentioned developments involved factors that work for and against the influence of various global civil society actors. In general, the renewed emphasis on the security mandate of the state, combined with the realization that society is acutely vulnerable to concealed uncivil forces in its midst, has had a constraining effect on civil society actors. At the same time, the al Qaeda attacks confirmed the rather revolutionary view that non-state political networks could be more formidable adversaries in the twenty-first century than most states. As well, it became apparent that while governments were incapable of checking the American disposition to wage "wars of choice" to achieve regime change in unfriendly states, civil society could exhibit an intense antiwar commitment. Despite the failure of antiwar demonstrations in preventing the war, the failing occupation policy in Iraq may generate a new tidal wave of global opposition to the militaristic geopolitics, or might lead American policymakers to scale back their imperial plans. The effects on uncivil networks are more difficult to discern, as their lawlessness and secret modes of operation tend to conceal their activities. The priority accorded to anti-terrorist law enforcement and regime change may indirectly strengthen in some settings transnational drug networks and arms sales by shifting policy priorities among statist enforcement agencies. Drug production in Afghanistan already is many orders of magnitude greater than it was during the latter years of Taliban rule.

Assertions about the role of civil society actors in light of the global setting produced by 9/11 and the US response can be numerous, reflecting differences of geographical, political, and civilizational space. However, there are at least four domains of policy in which civil society pressures could play a creative role, either in the form of direct action or by reinforcing the constructive Westphalian capacity to fashion cooperative intergovernmental responses to the twin challenges of terrorism and imperialism.

Supporting Adherence to International Law and Respect for the Independent Authority of the UN

At a time when American power is unchecked in the world by countervailing state forces and American vulnerability to mega-terrorist attacks creates unprecedented anxieties, particular importance should be accorded to *both* adapting international law to the new necessities of the al Qaeda threat and respecting that part of international law designed to restrain war-making among states. It needs to be reaffirmed that the primary responsibility of the UN is to operate as a war-prevention institution. Those in civil society have a co-responsibility to understand the contradictory play of forces, so that they neither adhere rigidly to a self-defeating legalism nor somehow give indirect blessing to the geo-political nihilism, which capitalizes on 9/11 as a justification to abandon the tradition of restraint in using force to settle disputes among sovereign states. Although some stretching of international law to encompass the imminent threat of further non-state mega-terrorist aggression seemed reasonable to validate recourse to war against the Taliban at the time,[24] in retrospect, in light of a resurgent resistance, even the Afghanistan war seems a mistake. But however viewed, the Iraq war was in no way reconcilable with international law, nor could it be qualified as a principled exception. The US government deliberately tried to throw the mantle of anti-terrorism upon its move toward war against Iraq, but without any convincing proof that such a war was either necessary or effective with respect to the al Qaeda threat, or with regard to the alleged menace of Iraqi weapons of mass destruction.

Similarly, the debate in the UN associated with the implementation of Security Council Resolution 1441 on inspection and disarmament in Iraq (as applied to weapons of mass destruction) has been widely interpreted as supportive of allowing the UN to operate within the frame of its charter rather than serving as an agent of American-led geo-politics.[25] The Bush administration's implication that a failure to authorize war against Iraq would underscore the *irrelevance* of the UN denies the organization its role as "the legitimate authority" exclusively competent to mandate a war that falls outside the scope of self-defense as defined in Article 51, and would lead the UN to follow the ill-fated League of Nations down the path of idealistic futility. Such allegations seem so wide of the mark that peace organizations and proponents of a lawful foreign policy should insist on the importance of adhering to international law and working within the framework of the UN to resolve international disputes, especially when the adversary is a state rather than an un-civil society actor, such as al Qaeda. If the UN is allowed to become "irrelevant" in the manner meant by the Bush administration, it will because its authority is defied or evaded and there is no opposition to a major aggressive war launched by its leading member. The organization has also eroded its legitimacy to some extent by seemingly ratifying the legality of the American occupation of Iraq.

Civil society organizations, such as the Nuclear Age Peace Foundation, the Fellowship of Reconciliation, and the Lawyers Committee on Nuclear Weapons Policy, need to take the lead in clarifying the relevance of international law to uses of force in the relations among sovereign states and in exerting as much influence on the public and the media as possible to enhance the relevance of the UN in the spirit intended when founded in World War II. As such, the Security Council should be encouraged to reaffirm the UN Charter's insistence that recourse to force is an absolute last resort, and then only with an explicit authorization by the UN. If the Security Council fails to discharge this primary responsibility, then the residual authority to act should be given to the General Assembly, as it was in the early 1950s, through the adoption of the Uniting for Peace Resolution. Beyond the immediacies of the current debate, it would be an appropriate time to limit or eliminate the use of the veto and to endow the UN itself with the mission to provide enforcement capabilities with respect to obligations imposed on member states. Now that the International Criminal Court is established, civil society activists can push the international community to define "aggressive war," so that crimes against the peace could be authoritatively delimited, and the perpetrators made subject to criminal indictment and prosecution.[26] To the extent that formal institutions fail to implement these fundamental restraints on the use of force, there is a role for civil society to organize tribunals that address such issues as "aggressive war" in the setting of the Iraq war and fill the institutional gap.

It may also be helpful for public intellectuals with transnational visibility to encourage discussion of "just war" thinking in relation to mega-terrorism and to the discourse of war in the period after 9/11.[27] The assertion of transnational claims to use force preemptively cannot be unconditionally ruled out if the evidence overcomes a burden of persuasion with respect to establishing necessity, imminence, and reasonableness of such a claim. That is, the use of proportionate force against discrete terrorist targets could be seen as "just" only if no alternative was available, a failure to act is highly likely to produce severe harm in the target areas of the terrorist network at any time, and it is reasonable to suppose that force has a good prospect of eliminating or diminishing the threat if used preemptively and proportionately. Just-war thinking is a discourse whose attractiveness relates to its flexibility and potential universality, which are also its weaknesses, enabling varying and contradictory lines of policy to argue that a particular line of action is consistent with the doctrine.[28] Such weaknesses cannot be denied, making just-war thinking part of a deliberative process that at least acknowledges as indispensable the validity of limits on war-making, but can do no more than hope to situate those limits in the marketplace of ideas. In this regard there exists an intimate connection between *substantive* democracy and the revitalization of the just-war doctrine that bears directly on efforts to oppose America's global dominance project. If Congress continues to be unwilling to exercise its role as a check on presidential war-making, then it falls to civil society, first of all, the national citizenry, but subsequently, the membership of the UN and an activated world public conscience, to assume this responsibility. Such a mobilization, nationally and globally, is a test of whether such limits on war-making can be imposed from below, that is, by grassroots expressions of militant yet nonviolent public opinion.[29] Relying on a just-war framework, similarly to invoking international law, is helpful as a way of avoiding the impression that objections to a given policy are purely subjective matters of disagreement. Also, such reliance invites response and conversation, even debate, and in this respect restores some confidence in the capacities of political democracy to benefit the peoples of the world, despite the decline by atrophy of representative democracy in several leading countries and in the face of a compliant, self-censoring media.

But civil society could provide an even bigger contribution by clarifying the potential utility of a law-enforcement approach to global security in the face of threatened mega-terrorism. The severe difficulties associated with hostile occupations of Afghanistan and Iraq allow civil society actors to call for reliance on law enforcement, rather than a war approach. In the 1990s the law enforcement response to mega-terrorism seemed aimless and uncoordinated, giving rise to a widespread impression that law enforcement was futile and that something more coercive was needed, namely, war. But in reality, the law-enforcement model had not been used in a systematic and engaged manner. In the aftermath of 9/11 the degree of solidarity with US goals was so deep and widely shared around the world that there existed a revolutionary opportunity to fashion a formidable law-enforcement dimension to global governance, including the establishment of a volunteer UN enforcement capability. Such an emphasis remains timely.

FINDING COMMON GROUND
WITH INTERVENTIONARY GOALS?

Heeding the lessons of the Cold War, some intellectuals on the left have been urging a repositioning of progressive politics in an intermediate zone that shares America's alleged anti-authoritarian goals while opposing the reliance on war and militarism as the means to achieve human rights and regime change. In the 1980s Mary Kaldor advocated "détente from below" by exhibiting solidarity with the movements of opposition in Eastern Europe and the Soviet Union, and at the same time, opposed the provocative Pershing missile deployments in Europe being advocated by the hard-line Reagan presidency in the United States.[30] Writing at the time of the impending war against Iraq, Kaldor argued on behalf of regime change for Iraq without the devastation and danger of war, by proposing permanent monitoring for weapons of mass destruction, the establishment of an ad hoc international criminal court to indict Saddam Hussein and his main accomplices, and a variety of UN and grassroots pressures to exert democratizing external pressure on Iraq. Kaldor argued that "in the very different but comparable case of Iraq, I am concerned that the peace movement has not taken on the lessons of the 1980s peace movement about the importance of human rights."[31]

Of course, it is important to find an identity for the peace movement that is not just reactive, and it may be that in some settings the conditions exist for the sort of "dual strategy" that Kaldor proposed for Iraq, but the context must be carefully evaluated. It is also important to be cautionary about the 1980s, and even about the post–Cold War identity of the East European democracies. It is quite likely that a dangerous blood bath, possibly leading us back to the brink of World War III, would have occurred if Moscow had handled the rising tide of societal opposition in the manner of China at Tiananmen Square in 1989; in other words, the unexpectedly soft leadership of Gorbachev certainly facilitated, and was possibly indispensable to, the remarkably peaceful transformation of the Soviet "empire."

The question that civil society actors preoccupied with war/peace issues need to reflect upon is what in each given context can serve best to promote the well-being of the peoples of the world; whatever the "answer," it needs to be attentive to goals associated with both human rights and peace. But in the context of Iraq, the avoidance of war and military intrusions into Iraq were without doubt at the time of impending war, and since, the proper focus for peace politics. Even the UN's unqualified endorsement of coercive inspection was risky and unwarranted, eventually producing conditions that led to a tacit acquiescence in an illegal war, endorsing a set of false premises that Iraq poses distinctive dangers unless "disarmed," when a more sober assessment of threats in light of 9/11 would suggest a much higher level of concern about a dozen or so other countries, starting with Pakistan. The UN can be commended for not bending entirely to US imperial goals, but it also warrants criticism for seeming to go along with much of the American argument that could never be squared with either the UN Charter or international law and for not offering Iraq as a sovereign state any protection from aggressive threats and intentions.

Of course, progressive civil society forces should not forget their own positive agenda in the excitement of mounting huge antiwar demonstrations around the world. At times, it may become important to support even imperial policies as the lesser of evils, as initially seemed the case with recourse to war against Afghanistan.[32] It was not helpful in the immediate aftermath of 9/11 for the hard left in the United States and elsewhere to oppose a defensive response by Washington that was directed at reducing a continuing deadly threat posed by the al Qaeda network. The empty call then for a continued reliance on "law enforcement" in the 1990s mode to deal with mega-terrorism was ill-conceived and shallow, given the tactical ingenuity and visionary commitments of Osama Bin Laden, the legions of concealed terrorists that his genocidal ideas and training camps had produced, and the basic uncertainties relating to future attacks.

In essence, to pursue the sort of dual strategy that Mary Kaldor proposes in the present global setting requires a nuanced sense of context and cannot be lifted mechanically from the dramatically differing circumstances and opportunities of the latter stages of the Cold War as played out in Europe.

Reviving the Normative Revolution of the 1990s

Many hopeful developments occurred in the 1990s, as mentioned earlier, and civil society actors need to retain their focus on humane global governance and human rights while simultaneously resisting moves toward illegal and unjust wars, imperial geo-politics, and predatory globalization. I would argue on behalf of this sort of dual strategy for the early twenty-first century. Although the antiwar cause seems presently paramount, at least in the North, it is essential that issues including global warming, the regulation of global market forces, the protection of vulnerable peoples suffering from containable diseases and poverty, accountability of political and military leaders who commit crimes of state, and the redress of historic grievance (associated with slavery, dispossession and extermination of indigenous people, survivors of holocausts) continue to gain support from pressures mounted by global civil society. Carrying on this normative revolution is connected, as well, with sustaining hope in a dark time.[33] There are many opportunities for action along these lines, including innovative steps that contribute to a more effective governance structure for the world. I highlight three as suggestive.

1. *Establishing a global peoples assembly:*[34] Governmental representation has proven inadequate as a means of achieving substantive democracy in formulating global policy or of assuring meaningful participation by the peoples of the world in decisions and policies that affect their well-being. The intergovernmental debates of the UN, especially the Security Council, offer a highly significant forum for clarifying tensions among leading states and, under some circumstances, for moderating geo-political manipulations of world politics. But such debates often overlook democratic sentiments and priorities. The debate around the Iraq crisis was indicative. The UN unanimously endorsed a framework that presupposed the validity of coercive inspection and approved the option of war should inspection fail, but the peoples of the world were overwhelmingly opposed to war in relation to Iraq, regardless of what the inspectors found or didn't find and quite independent of their government's geo-political alignment. A global peoples assembly would enlarge the debate on such crucial global policy issues, overcoming some of the myopic closure that is brought about by the submission of worldwide media to a blend of geo-political and global market forces. Allowing civil society representatives to have an official voice in matters bearing on global policy would exert a potentially democratizing influence on the way politics proceed throughout the world.

2. *Abolish weapons of mass destruction:* Both the Iraq crisis and the failure of the nuclear weapons states to heed the 1996 Advisory Opinion of the International Court of Justice as to their obligation to pursue in good faith nuclear disarmament in accordance with Article VI

of the Treaty on the Non-Proliferation of Nuclear Weapons suggest a priority for civil society: exert pressure to establish an effective regime by stages for the abolition of *all* weapons of mass destruction, chemical, biological, radiological, and nuclear. There exist important building blocks, including widely ratified treaties creating regimes of prohibition with respect to chemical and biological weaponry, but lacking fully reliable forms of verification procedures. With respect to nuclear weaponry the drift of recent developments creates a genuine urgency: a selectively enforced nonproliferation policy linked suspiciously to the geo-political antagonisms and affinities of the United States; war dangers associated with the implementation of this regime; declared tendencies by the US government to hold open its option to introduce nuclear weapons into combat and to develop new types of weaponry more adapted to battlefield roles; the prospect of further efforts to achieve nuclear weapons status following the examples of Israel, India, and Pakistan. The civil society networks around the world, in collaboration with sympathetic governments, should re-launch an abolition campaign based on these considerations. Abolition 2000 was illustrative of such an initiative. The work of the Nuclear Age Peace Foundation over the past twenty years has been devoted to attaining these goals in a staged, responsible manner.

3. *Encouraging the International Criminal Court (ICC):* The most revolutionary innovation of the 1990s was the steps leading to the establishment of the ICC in mid-2002. The ideal of holding those with power individually responsible according to legal standards administered with an impressive commitment to the rights of the accused would go a long way toward avoiding the worst features of Westphalian sovereignty, with its premise that those who act for the state are immune internally and externally from legal accountability. Now that the ICC exists, it is important that its potential be realized to the greatest extent possible. It is up to civil society actors to avoid allowing the ICC to be subordinated to geo-politics in the manner of the nonproliferation treaty or to become an atrophied institution that exists but is never used; that is, either a two-tier structure in which the strong continue to enjoy the fruits of non-accountability while the weak are hauled before the court in a spectacle of self-righteous legalism, or a stillborn innovation that is never allowed to function as intended. One short-term antidote would be to build on the experience of the Permanent Peoples Court, which has functioned for the past thirty years, with its

base in Rome, to bring to world attention those violations of human rights and international law that are overlooked by the UN and traditional forms of diplomacy. Such a building process might include the establishment of a parallel civic institution that administers trials of individuals who are not properly apprehended by the ICC (or by national courts acting under claims of universal jurisdiction in the spirit of the Belgian national courts before the substantial repeal of the Belgian law due to intense intergovernmental pressure).[35]

Resisting the Drift toward Global Fascism

Perhaps the most disturbing challenge directed at civil society arises from deeper tendencies associated with the consolidation of economic and military power under the aegis of a rightist ideology that resembles fascism. These ideas are often hidden beneath claims of democratization and modernization, goals that may be genuinely affirmed by those who are seeking to construct the first global security system administered from one center of power; in practice, this would almost certainly turn into an oppressive variant of world order, best identified as a new political creature, namely, global fascism. Why fascist? Because it combines a visionary conception of the right to rule with a view that those who mount resistance must be destroyed by will and an iron fist. The more explicit formulations of such a global strategy do not acknowledge such designs, except indirectly.[36] Such a strategy is currently being implemented via the conduct of preemptive warfare, the establishment of a network of military bases in all critical areas of the world as supplemented by the militarization of space and the deployment of naval forces on the main oceans of the world, and approaches to the UN and other international institutions that offer the choice of subordination or irrelevance. Without being alarmist, it seems important to call attention to this fascist disposition on the world stage. It is also correlated with a concentration of vast and new powers in the US government designed to quell resistance at home—the Patriot Act and the Homeland Security Department—enacted with little organized opposition, given the climate of acquiescence and patriotic deference that has followed 9/11. Civil society actors are in a position to articulate the danger, and possibly activate more influential forces in the United States and elsewhere, which are currently dormant or seem attentive only to the short-run challenges of preventing imprudent war-making.

CONCLUSION

In this period, when the capacity of ordinary states acting in the manner of traditional diplomacy seems unable to control adverse global trends, it is vital to comprehend the changing context of world order. In this regard, civil society and global market forces must be taken into account. The rising resistance to predatory globalization that seemed such a defining reality at the end of the last century has now been eclipsed, at least temporarily, by a renewed emphasis on global security and a war/peace agenda. The al Qaeda network, its potency and extremism, demonstrated the vulnerability of the Westphalian framework, organized around outmoded notions of boundaries and territorial supremacy. At the same time, the moves of response led by the US government disclosed a frightening design to overwhelm the state structure of world order from above, imposing global dominance, by fascist means if necessary. The peoples of the world are now in the process of awakening to this second threat, but it is crucial that the progressive civil society actors of the world not overlook the persistence of the first threat. The alternative to global dominance under US control is not a revival of the Westphalian framework but a concerted process of movement toward the establishment of humane global governance that merges the goals of global and regional democracy, human rights, human security, global justice, the rule of law, and environmental sustainability. The magnitude of such an undertaking challenges civil society in a manner that is as much spiritual as it is humanistic, hopefully enlisting the positive energies of world religions as well as transnational social forces organized to pursue civil society goals. The role of states that share concern about the dilemma posed by the seeming alternatives of mega-terrorism and global imperialism is also crucial, creating the political space for civil society actors to operate. The Internet could play an empowering role, both by disseminating information and mobilizing grassroots forces around the world. To regenerate hope in the future depends on releasing the political and moral imagination of global civil society actors and those activists who combine their traditional citizenship in a given country with a sense of human solidarity that gives rise to a realistic overlapping "world citizenship."

NOTES

[1] Jonathan Schell, "The World's Other Superpower," *The Nation*, 14 April 2003, 11–12.

[2] See Richard Falk, "Will the Empire Be Fascist?" *Global Dialogue* 5, no. 1–2 (2003): 22–31.

[3] Daniele Archibugi, David Held, and Martin Köhler, eds., *Re-imagining Political Community: Studies in Cosmopolitan Democracy* (Cambridge, UK: Polity Press, 1998).

[4] The American Enterprise Institute has established a website to monitor the hostile activities of civil society actors, http://www.ngowatch.org (accessed 31 August 2004).

[5] See Richard Falk, "The First Normative Global Revolution: The Uncertain Future of Globalization," in *Globalization and Civilizations,* ed. Mehdi Mozaffari, 51–76 (London: Routledge, 2002); and idem, "Reviving the 1990s Trend toward Transnational Justice: Innovations and Institutions," *Journal of Human Development* 3, no. 2 (2002): 167–90.

[6] See Richard Falk, "Revisiting Westphalia, Discovering Post-Westphalia," *Journal of Ethics* 6 (2002): 311–51; and Ken Booth, "Human Wrongs and International Relations," *International Affairs* 71 (1995): 103–26. For an overview of the Westphalian era, see Charles W. Kegley, Jr., and Gregory A. Raymond, *Exorcising the Ghost of Westphalia: Building World Order in the New Millennium* (Upper Saddle River, NJ: Prentice-Hall, 2002).

[7] Samuel P. Huntington, "The Clash of Civilization?" *Foreign Affairs* 72, no. 3 (1993): 22–28, modified in *The Clash of Civilizations and the Remaking of World Order* (New York: Simon and Schuster, 1996).

[8] Richard Falk, *Predatory Globalization: A Critique* (Cambridge, UK: Polity Press, 1999); also, Michael Hardt and Antonio Negri, *Empire* (Cambridge, MA: Harvard Univ. Press, 2000).

[9] For a range of views along these lines, see Deepak Nayyar, ed., *Governing Globalization: Issues and Institutions* (Oxford: Oxford Univ. Press, 2002).

[10] This was well argued under the plausible circumstances of the prior decade by Richard N. Rosecrance, *Rise of the Virtual State: Wealth and Power in the Coming Century* (New York: Basic Books, 1999).

[11] George Soros, *On Globalization* (New York: Oxford Univ. Press, 2002); John Gray, *False Dawn: The Delusions of Global Capitalism* (New York: New Press, 1998); William Grieder, *One World, Ready or Not: The Manic Logic of Global Capitalism* (New York: Simon and Schuster, 1997); and Joseph Stiglitz, *Globalization and Its Discontents* (New York: Norton, 2002).

[12] There are by now many arguments to this effect. See, for example, Chandra Muzaffar, *Human Rights and the New World Order* (Penang, Malaysia: Just World Trust, 1993); and Yoshikazu Sakamoto, ed., *Global Transformation: Challenges to the State System* (Tokyo: UNU Press, 1994). This line of analysis has been confirmed since 9/11 by the White House document *Na-*

tional Security Strategy of the United States of America (Washington, DC: The White House, September 2002), http://www.whitehouse.gov/nsc/nss.html (accessed 31 August 2004). See also Andrew J. Bacevich, *American Empire: The Realities and Consequences of U.S. Diplomacy* (Cambridge, MA: Harvard Univ. Press, 2002).

[13] Among others, see Francis Fukuyama, *The End of History and the Last Man* (New York: Free Press, 1999); and Thomas Friedman, *The Lexus and the Olive Tree* (New York: Farrar, Straus and Giroux, 1999).

[14] Mary Kaldor, *New and Old Wars: Organized Violence in a Global Era* (Cambridge, UK: Polity Press, 1999); and Chris Hedges, *War Is a Force That Gives Us Meaning* (New York: Public Affairs, 2002).

[15] See Alexander George, ed., *Western State Terrorism* (London: Routledge, 1991); Mark Selden and Alvin Y. So, eds., *War and State Terrorism: The United States, Japan, and the Asia-Pacific in the Long Twentieth Century* (Lanham, MD: Rowman and Littlefield, 2004); and Richard Falk, *Revolutionaries and Functionaries: The Dual Face of Terrorism* (New York: E. P. Dutton, 1988).

[16] The pre-Westphalian form of world order was not centered on territorial entities. A variety of commentators has seen the rise of civil society actors as positing an emergent neo-medieval world order, although not previously with respect to war/peace. See Hedley Bull, *The Anarchical Society: A Study of Order in World Politics* (New York: Columbia Univ. Press, 1977).

[17] See the pre-Bush study by the Project for the New American Century, "Rebuilding America's Defense: Strategy, Forces and Resources For a New Century" (September 2000), newamericancentury.org website (accessed 31 August 2004); Jan Lodal, *The Price of Dominance: The New Weapons of Mass Destruction and Their Challenge to American Leadership* (New York: Council on Foreign Relations, 2001); and G. John Ikenberry, ed., *America Unrivaled: The Future of the Balance of Power* (Ithaca, NY: Cornell Univ. Press, 2002).

[18] George W. Bush, Address to Joint Session of Congress (20 September 2001), whitehouse.gov website (accessed 31 August 2004).

[19] George W. Bush, Address to the UN General Assembly, 12 October 2002, whitehouse.gov website (accessed 31 August 2004).

[20] Secretary of State Colin Powell's statement prior to the Iraq war, reported by Jeffrey Simpson, "Why Canada Gets No Respect in Washington," *The Globe and Mail*, 29 January 2003, A15 (accessed 31 August 2004).

[21] See views contained in "Agora: Future Implications of the Iraq Conflict," *American Journal of International Law* 97, no. 3 (July 2003); for skepticism about the relevance of international law to uses of international force, see Michael J. Glennon, *The Limits of Law, Prerogatives of Power* (New York: Palgrave, 2001).

[22] Bacevich, *American Empire*; Philip Bobbitt, *The Shield of Achilles: War, Peace, and the Course of History* (New York: Knopf, 2002); and Michael Ignatieff, "The Burden," *New York Times Magazine*, 5 January 2003.

[23] See Robert Jackson, *The Global Covenant: Human Conduct in a World of States* (New York: Oxford Univ. Press, 2000).

[24] See Richard Falk, *The Great Terror War* (Northampton, MA: Olive Branch Press, 2003); and idem, "What Future for the UN Charter System of War Prevention?" *American Journal of International Law* 97, no. 3 (July 2003): 590–98.

[25] For a range of views, see *American Journal of International Law* 97, no. 3 (July 2003).

[26] See Statute and Nuremberg Principles.

[27] See the remarks of Jürgen Habermas and Jacques Derrida in Giovanna Borradori, *Philosophy in a Time of Terror: Dialogues with Jürgen Habermas and Jacques Derrida* (Chicago: Univ. of Chicago Press, 2003), esp. 53–58, 73.

[28] Cf. Jean Bethke Elshtein, *The Just War against Terror: The Burden of American Power in a Violent World* (New York: Basic Books, 2003), and Falk, "What Future for the UN Charter System of War Prevention?"

[29] It is relevant that Archbishop Desmond Tutu, speaking at the antiwar rally in New York City on 15 February 2003, emphasized the absence of a just-war rationale for Washington's contention of a national prerogative to initiate war against Iraq.

[30] Mary Kaldor, Richard Falk, and Gerald Holden, eds., *The New Détente: Rethinking East-West Relations* (London: Verso, 1989).

[31] Mary Kaldor, "In Place of War, Open up Iraq," *The Nation* (2 February 2003), 1–6. I remain skeptical of this approach because it seems to endorse the goals of the United States based on its threats of aggressive war, itself a crime against peace on the basis of the Nuremberg tradition. To endorse Kaldor's approach would be to align civil society with the geo-political designs of the Bush administration, although that was certainly not her intention.

[32] I supported the Afghanistan war (see Falk, *The Great Terror War*, 61–72), but on further reflection I regard my position to have been in error, overlooking the prospects in the post-9/11 atmosphere for robust international law enforcement and unduly failing to note the dysfunctional approach of the US government to war and occupation.

[33] David Krieger, ed., *Hope in a Dark Time: Reflections on Humanity's Future* (Santa Barbara, CA: Cara Press, 2003).

[34] See Richard Falk and Andrew Strauss, "Toward Global Parliament," *Foreign Affairs* 80, no. 1 (2001): 212–20.

[35] For a discussion of universal jurisdiction, see Princeton Project on Universal Jurisdiction, *The Princeton Principles on Universal Jurisdiction* (Princeton, NJ: Program in Law and Public Affairs, Princeton Univ., 2001), law.uc.edu website (accessed 31 August 2004).

[36] There is no specific blueprint for global dominance aside from American preeminence depicted by the Project for the New American Century, "Rebuilding America's Defense"; and The White House, *National Security Strategy for the United States of America*. For a general perspective of the neo-conservative world view, see Robert Kagen and William Kristol, eds., *Present Dangers: Crisis and Opportunity in American Foreign and Defense Policy* (San Francisco: Encounter Books, 2000).

8

On the Accountability
of
Non-State Armed Groups

George J. Andreopoulos

INTRODUCTION

In recent years non-state actors (NSAs), and in particular non-state armed groups,[1] have come under increasing scrutiny, largely due to the alarming increase in the abusive conduct exhibited in contemporary armed conflicts, most of which are "internal."[2] These intra-state conflicts, which involve both state actors and NSAs, have brought into question some of the basic premises of the Westphalian order and have posed a serious challenge to the normative framework set by the Geneva Conventions. A major feature of this changing landscape of violence is the deliberate targeting of civilians, who often constitute the principal aim rather than the unintended consequence of otherwise legitimate military operations. In his first report to the Security Council on the protection of civilians in armed conflict, the UN secretary-general noted that the "deliberate targeting of non-combatants" is a key characteristic

Earlier versions of this chapter were presented at the CISS/ISA Conference, Heidelberg, June 26–28, 2001, and at the Columbia University Seminar on Human Rights in April 2002. I would like to thank the participants in these sessions for their useful comments.

of internal conflicts, which results in "civilian casualties and the destruction of civilian infrastructure." Among the perpetrators of this violence are "non-state actors, including irregular forces and privately financed militias."[3]

The perpetrators cannot be confined to armed groups. In Sierra Leone and Angola, for example, foreign businesses in the diamond industry have contributed to the prolongation and, in many instances, intensification of the conflict, as well as to the creation of arrangements indistinguishable from protection rackets. In the case of Sierra Leone, the involvement of small mining firms such as DiamondWorks, and its apparent connection with Executive Outcomes and Sandline, two major international security firms, raised critical questions about the protection arrangements entered into by weak governments in developing countries in order to ensure their survival. More than anything else, such developments point to a netherworld of shady interactions among business interests, security firms, governments, and paramilitary groups that could undermine a country's prospects for reconstruction and development.[4] In his second report on the protection of civilians in armed conflict, the secretary-general highlighted the need to "promote the exercise of responsible investment in crisis areas,"[5] indicating a recognition of the variety of NSAs that can affect the civilian welfare in conflict situations, as well as during the post-conflict, peacebuilding stage.

This chapter focuses on the challenges posed by armed groups and the need to adopt practices for engagement consistent with human rights and humanitarian law norms. While engagement practices can cover a wide spectrum of activities, including constructive dialogue, adoption of codes of conduct, shaming through media attention, sanctions, accountability mechanisms, and UN Security Council–authorized enforcement measures, the emphasis here is on legal accountability and its limitations.[6] In this context, the chapter examines (1) key provisions of international human rights law (IHRL) and international humanitarian law (IHL), and the importance of their growing convergence; (2) some recent promising developments; and (3) remaining legal uncertainties and the quest for alternative strategies. In the concluding section a few brief remarks are offered on the impact of the so-called war on terrorism in promoting accountability among armed groups.

THE NORMATIVE FRAMEWORK: IHRL AND IHL

These two bodies of law entail some important differences. Traditionally, IHL has been concerned with the treatment of combatants and noncombatants by their opponents in wartime (including the means and methods of warfare), while IHRL has dealt with the relationship between states and their own nationals in peacetime and in cases of public emergency. Moreover, IHRL is premised on near zero tolerance for the loss of human life,[7] while IHL operates within the context of conflict situations, that is, situations in which the loss of (combatant) life is taken for granted, and allowance is made for civilian casualties of lawful collateral damage.

The differences also extend to the work of activist organizations in the two fields. In general, human rights organizations are characterized by a commitment to campaigning and active denunciations of abusive conduct. On the other hand, humanitarian organizations, committed to the principles of neutrality and impartiality, emphasize service over exposure and shaming.[8] There are also differences in how these organizations relate to their respective bodies of law. For human rights organizations, IHRL provides an indispensable framework for their work, and government performance is analyzed and assessed on the basis of its relevant legal principles. For humanitarian organizations, IHL principles are assessed on the basis of their usefulness in ensuring access to those in need of assistance, rather than as defining benchmarks. Overall, their approach tends to be characterized by greater pragmatism than that of their human rights counterparts.[9]

Yet, even in earlier times, IHL and IHRL shared a fundamental normative concern: a commitment to human dignity and welfare irrespective of the status of the person (combatant or noncombatant) and of the situations in which the person's rights and responsibilities were to be exercised (peace, public emergency, war).[10] Despite this shared commitment, the division between the areas of applicability of IHRL and IHL has generated serious concern over possible legal uncertainties and ambiguities in connection with the protection of fundamental rights in situations of internal violence. While this is a multifaceted question, including issues of derogation from internationally guaranteed rights, lack of specificity of existing rules, and ratification of the relevant instruments, it is the accountability of NSAs that has posed one of the critical and least examined challenges to the protective frame-work.[11]

The focus of IHRL is the protection of the individual who holds rights against the arbitrary exercise of state power. The state must en-sure, by means of a series of negative (constraints on state power) and positive (intervention) acts, adherence to the relevant human rights norms. Yet language pertaining to the duties of individuals to promote respect and observance of human rights is included in the Interna-tional Bill of Rights, as well as in the 1948 Convention on the Preven-tion and Punishment of the Crime of Genocide, which calls for the criminal accountability of "private individuals" in addition to that of "constitutionally responsible rulers" and "public officials" (Art. IV).

If IHRL's emphasis on constraining the state was indicative of state-centrism, IHL exhibited a different form of the same preoccupation. As one analyst put it, IHL "was paradigmatically inter-state law, driven by reciprocity";[12] in such a framework, the emphasis was placed on state interests both during and after war, as opposed to the rights of individuals and populations.

The shift in favor of the rights of individuals in IHL instruments began with common Article 3 of the 1949 Geneva Conventions, which addressed for the first time the plight of people in non-international conflicts. Article 3, which incorporates a set of minimum standards of humane treatment, reflects the influence of the human rights discourse that gained momentum with the adoption of the Universal Declara-tion of Human Rights (UDHR) only a year earlier (1948). The notion of humane treatment without distinction in Article 3 echoes Article 2 of the UDHR; the references to the prohibition of cruel treatment and torture echo Article 5 of the UDHR; and the references to indispens-able judicial guarantees echo Article 10 and Article 11.1 of the UDHR. These intersections were further reflected in the provisions concern-ing the suppression of grave breaches and the universal jurisdiction approach.[13] Such developments, in conjunction with the aforemen-tioned Genocide Convention, which is the first UN-sponsored human rights treaty, signaled the progressive "humanization" of IHL.[14] In particular, these developments *deterritorialized criminal jurisdiction (the promotion of the principle of universality) and internationalized the criminalization of the most heinous of crimes against humanity regard-less of the situational context.*

Despite this promising trend, problems in the area of protection per-sist. In the context of IHRL the key issue remains the accountability of NSAs for the commission of human rights abuses. While numerous instruments (treaties, declarations, and resolutions) acknowledge the important role of individuals, groups, and associations in promoting respect for human rights and fundamental freedoms,[15] the extent to which failure to do so would attract international criminal responsibility, save for the commission of the most serious and systematic violations, remains unclear. In addition, most of the provisions included in these instruments are addressed to states and the extent to which they generate substantive obligations for NSAs, and the concomitant ability to monitor their compliance effectively, is indeed questionable.[16]

Here, a useful distinction can be drawn between armed groups, which effectively control part of the territory and its people and hence constitute de facto governments, and groups that do not meet these criteria. However, even if proper accountability mechanisms could be established for the former, they could hardly address the challenges posed by the latter, which are becoming increasingly visible in modern-day conflicts and operate in a gray zone between politics and criminality. In a contribution on armed-group adherence to international standards, the ICRC noted:

> Amongst armed groups, the distinction between politically-motivated action and organized crime is fading away. All too often, the political objectives are unclear, if not subsidiary to the crimes perpetrated while allegedly waging one's struggle. . . . Are we dealing with a liberation army resorting to terrorist acts, or with a criminal ring that tries to give itself political credibility? . . . No matter how one chooses to classify such armed groups, their *lack of discipline and structured command*, their unpredictability, their lack of interest in achieving external recognition . . . constitute additional obstacles to their observance of international standards.[17]

The issue of external recognition is of particular relevance here, especially when contrasted with armed-group activity of an earlier era. The 1977 adaptation of the Geneva Conventions was—among other things—dictated by the challenges posed by the actions of national liberation movements. While many of these movements engaged in terrorist-related activities, these activities were controlled by a political agenda aimed at international recognition. Thus, "the prospects of becoming a legitimate member of the international community acted as a constraining factor that sought to ensure the ultimate primacy of politics over pure violence"[18] and outright banditry. The problem here, as the ICRC indicates, is that international legitimacy, one of the main incentives for inducing compliance with international standards, carries very little weight.

Moreover, any meaningful proposals for creating obligations (and rights) for armed groups through enforceable legal instruments would definitely meet the resistance of many states, fearful of the repercussions of recognition implicit in such initiatives. This concern is one of the reasons for the routine demonization of armed groups by state actors and their characterization as outlaws, bandits, or criminals.

In the context of IHL, there are several critical challenges, two of which will be highlighted here. The first has to do with the threshold of applicability of IHL. The 1977 Geneva Protocol II, which developed and supplemented common Article 3 of the 1949 conventions, is applicable in non-international conflicts that reach a certain level of intensity. Excluded from the protocol's provisions are "situations of internal disturbances and tensions, such as riots, isolated and sporadic acts of violence and other acts of a similar nature."[19] Considering the reluctance of governments to admit to the applicability of Protocol II in situations of internal conflict, since such a move would be tantamount to an admission of failure to exercise control over part of their territory, the adherence to humanitarian standards in lower intensity situations is highly unlikely. This, however, and given the record of low government compliance, can also be an argument against further codification.

The second is related to the first. Protocol II applies to the armed forces of the state, in whose territory the conflict takes place, "and to the dissident armed forces or other organized armed groups which, under responsible command, exercise such control over a part of its territory as to enable them to carry out sustained and concerted military operations and to implement this Protocol."[20] Thus, the very characteristics that dissident armed groups must possess for the applicability of the protocol render the legitimacy of the government questionable (hence the aforementioned reluctance of governments to admit to its relevance).

From the perspective of civilian protection, this situation poses a set of critical questions. First, what are the applicable standards in low intensity situations? One possible answer here is that in such situations accountability of armed groups would be ensured by the application of domestic law. This, however, assumes that the government has the capacity and the willingness to enforce the law. What if this is not the case? What are the standards in situations in which the government is fighting against groups that do not meet the criteria established in Protocol II? Under these circumstances, what is the accountability of transient armed groups that engage in sporadic attacks, do not control any territory, and, most likely, are unable to meet some of the obligations outlined in Protocol II (such as the protection of the wounded, sick, and shipwrecked [Art. 7], due process [Art. 6], and the rights of those interned or detained [Art. 5])? Finally, what are the standards in situations in which none of the parties is a state, and the conflict is between two or more non-state armed groups?[21]

This discussion does not exhaust all pertinent concerns, but it is indicative of the range of issues that needs to be addressed.[22]

Recent Developments

A series of recent developments have led to a reexamination of the key facets of the protective framework and in the process have contributed to the gradual consolidation of the aforementioned paradigmatic shift. At the more general level, the last decade has witnessed an emerging global ethos of accountability manifested through the dynamic interplay of international and national justice options. From the ad hoc tribunals for the former Yugoslavia and Rwanda to the Special Court for Sierra Leone, from the arrest of former Chilean dictator Pinochet in England on charges of torture, hostage-taking, and murder, to the arrest of H. Habre (former dictator of Chad) on torture charges in Senegal, from the Mexican government's decision to extradite to Spain an Argentinean naval officer wanted for torture, to the trial and conviction of the "Rwanda four" in Brussels,[23] the underlying theme is one of intolerance for immunity and impunity and of support for transparency and accountability.[24] This theme is strengthened by the proliferation of nonjudicial accountability mechanisms, in particular truth and reconciliation commissions, which have contributed to the rising societal expectations of critical confrontations with their abusive past.[25]

Within this general trend the statutes of the two ad hoc tribunals, as well as their evolving jurisprudence, have contributed to the clarification of key concepts and to the growing influence of IHRL upon IHL. Among the most prominent examples is the delinking of the concept of crimes against humanity from the war nexus requirement of the Nuremberg Charter (which had basically confined crimes against humanity to wartime atrocities). As the Appeals Chamber of the International Criminal Tribunal for the former Yugoslavia (ICTY) ruled in the Tadic case, "It is by now a settled rule of customary international law that crimes against humanity do not require a connection to international armed conflict. Indeed, as the Prosecutor points out, customary international law may not require a connection between crimes against humanity and any conflict at all."[26] More recently, the Appeals Chamber upheld the Trial Chamber's finding that Article 4 of Geneva Convention IV was applicable in the context of the conflict in Bosnia Herzegovina, and hence the Bosnian Serbs detained in the Celebici camp should be regarded as "having been in the hands of a party to the conflict...of which they were not nationals," and, therefore, as protected persons.[27] This ruling is significant for confirming the necessity of applying more flexibly the requirements of nationality as determinative of the protected status of persons. In this context, the Appeals Chamber agreed with the prosecution that "depriving victims, who arguably are of the same nationality under domestic law as their captors, of the Protection of the Geneva Conventions solely based on that national law would not be consistent with the object and purpose of the Conventions."[28] Thus, the Appeals Chamber relied on a broad and purposive interpretation of the Geneva Conventions consistent with the tenor of the ICRC's commentary that "the Conventions have been drawn up first and foremost to protect individuals, and not to serve State Interests."[29]

The progressive emphasis on the rights of individuals and collectivities, as opposed to rights of states, is indicative of the international community's attempts to respond to the challenge of enhancing civilian protection to the maximum extent possible irrespective of the context. In a similar vein the 1998 Rome Statute of the International Criminal Court not only confirms the delinking of crimes against humanity from any type of conflict situation,[30] but also the expansion of the overall protective regime in accordance with the spirit of the Geneva Conventions.[31] More specifically, and in connection with non-state armed groups, the Rome Statute goes beyond the provisions of Protocol II. Although its "threshold" language is nearly identical to that of Protocol II,[32] the paragraph on armed groups effectively lowers the threshold for the existence of a non-international conflict. Article 8.2(f) refers to the applicability of the relevant provisions even in situations where there are no governmental authorities involved and the conflict is purely between organized armed groups. There is also no requirement for the organized group to be under responsible command or to exercise control over part of the territory.[33]

Another important development in the ICC statute lies in the definition of enforced disappearances and torture. Departing from the definitions provided for in the Declaration on the Protection of all Persons from Enforced Disappearance and the Convention against Torture,[34] the statute considers them as crimes against humanity that can also be committed by groups, thus delinking these offenses from official action.

Finally, during the last decade the UN Security Council has adopted numerous resolutions identifying the effects of internal crises as constitutive of threats to international peace and security. It also called upon non-state armed groups either to cease military activities or to adhere to internationally recognized standards during situations of internal conflict. For example, it imposed on UNITA an embargo on arms and related material for the continuation of military activities that contributed to "the further deterioration of an already grave humanitarian situation," a situation that—according to the Security Council—constituted a threat to international peace and security.[35] It called upon the "Kosovar Albanian leadership to condemn all terrorist action," and emphasized "that all elements in the Kosovar Albanian community should pursue their goal by peaceful means only."[36] Likewise, in 1998 the Security Council demanded "that all parties, groups, and individuals immediately cease hostilities and maintain a ceasefire in Kosovo."[37]

More recently, the Security Council has condemned all acts of violence that have occurred during the ongoing crisis in the Darfur region of Sudan. Placing a particular emphasis on violations committed by the Janjaweed militia, which have included "indiscriminate attacks on civilians, rapes, forced displacements and acts of violence especially those with an ethnic dimension," the Security Council resolution imposed an arms embargo "on all non-governmental entities and individuals, including the Janjaweed" and demanded that the government of Sudan disarm the militias responsible for these atrocities.[38] While the government of Sudan denied having any role in the recruitment and training of militias, reports from human rights groups have portrayed a different picture, indicating the existence of "a government policy of militia recruitment, support and impunity."[39]

While progress on the accountability front is at best episodic, these developments should not be underestimated. By directly calling upon armed groups under the auspices of Chapter VII, the Security Council has signaled its intention to consider inhumane conduct perpetrated by NSAs as a threat to international peace and security, regardless of its cross-border implications. Such a perspective opens the prospects for sanctioning measures (as was the case with UNITA), including, as a last resort, the use of force. While UN-authorized action has yet to materialize in such a context, the Security Council's growing involvement in this area cannot but sustain the emerging ethos of accountability.

But UN activity on this front has not been confined to the Security Council. On 22 April 1998 the Commission on Human Rights adopted a resolution condemning the abduction, forceful recruitment, torture, killing, enslavement, and rape of children by the Lord's Resistance Army (LRA) in Northern Uganda. The resolution called for the release and safe return of children and for all relevant actors to "exert all possible pressure" on the LRA "to release the children immediately."[40] It was the first time in the commission's history that a resolution calling upon a NSA to refrain from a certain type of abusive conduct was adopted.

Remaining Uncertainties and the Quest for Alternative Strategies

Despite these promising developments, the protective regime is far from comprehensive. There is a gray area between peace (where IHRL can apply under certain circumstances) and conflict that meets the intensity threshold of Protocol II, where it is not clear what the applicable standards of protection are. This uncertainty is compounded by the variety of non-state armed groups that renders accountability elusive.

While on the normative sphere progress has been substantial, on the operational sphere the abusive conduct persists, even in cases of groups that—due to their overall organizational capacity—clearly fall under the provisions of already existing rules.[41] This has led several analysts to question whether, in light of the appalling record of compliance with already existing rules, the emphasis should be on additional standard setting, as opposed to strategies for more precise identification of the said rules and promotion of compliance.

Several recent initiatives seem to be moving in the latter direction, and a few of them should be highlighted. First, in connection with the applicability of IHRL in situations of public emergency, General Comment 29 on Article 4 of the ICCPR, issued by the Human Rights Committee, constitutes an authoritative interpretation of the protective regime in these situations.[42] It has contributed to the clarification and restriction of permissible derogations by states from their obligations under the covenant. Particularly noteworthy are the identification of additional elements as non-derogable due to their character as norms of general international law,[43] the affirmation of the interdependence between derogable and non-derogable provisions, and the importance of obligations under other bodies of international law in restricting derogation powers under the ICCPR.[44] Concerning the latter, GC 29 has highlighted the importance of obligations under IHL (for example, on the right to fair trial) as critical safeguards relating to derogation.[45]

Second, there has been a clear evolution in the discussion over the drafting and adoption of a "minimum humanitarian standards" document, which has been renamed "fundamental standards of humanity."[46] The original purpose of this initiative was to create a document that would strengthen protection of all persons in all situations by closing the "gap" in cases of internal conflicts that fall below the Protocol II threshold, and are insufficiently covered by the pertinent IHRL norms. This effort, which has been on the agenda of the Commission on Human Rights since 1994, has generated, from 1998 to 2004, six reports by the secretary-general and a series of expert meetings to assess the merits and the strategy of this undertaking. The issue of NSA accountability has been identified as a critical one in this process.[47] The report of the most recent expert meeting stated that the endeavor should be seen less as standard setting and more as a "practical and concise set of basic principles restating applicable standards," that "could carry political/moral force when undertaking dialogue with armed groups and could be a useful tool in a wider approach involving different forms of incentives and disincentives."

In a similar vein, the secretary-general in his second report on the protection of civilians in armed conflict stressed the importance of a document that would facilitate constructive dialogue, with a special emphasis on the indispensability of "a structured dialogue with armed groups" as a means of protecting vulnerable populations. He expressed his intention to ask the Inter-Agency Standing Committee (ISAC) "to develop a manual of best practices for engagement with armed groups," which would "give guidance on how to promote a better understanding of the principles and operational requirements of humanitarian activities in such circumstances." The first draft of suggested contents for a manual on engagement with armed groups was prepared and was discussed at an informal meeting held in March 2002 in Geneva. The meeting included representatives of the Secretariat, UN agencies, and the ICRC (as observers) and focused on the outline of the guidance document intended to facilitate the agencies' engagement with these groups "to ensure adequate assistance to and protection of civilians in conflict areas."[48] In the most recent draft there has been a shift in the focus from "best practices" to "field practices," in order to incorporate the mistakes as well as the successes. Moreover, this draft emphasized that the manual is intended mainly for the UN personnel (resident/humanitarian coordinators, UN country teams, and field staff of UN humanitarian agencies) and not the wider humanitarian community; according to the reference group, this decision reflects the fact that UN staff "remain constrained by the potential impact of their actions on the sovereignty and the territorial integrity of Member States" and "subject to administrative procedures and security regulations which are different from the ones of other humanitarian partners."[49]

Finally, the ICRC has recently completed a major study on the customary rules of IHL in an attempt to provide an authoritative and comprehensive list of fundamental norms of humane conduct that would be applicable in all conflicts. The study is in two parts. The first part consists of a compilation of all the customary rules of IHL, and the second part consists of the practice on which the already identified rules are based.[50] An ICRC progress report noted that "perhaps the most striking result of the study" is "the number of rules . . . that are today customary in non-international armed conflict," and that "the principle of distinction, the definition of military objectives, the prohibition of indiscriminate attacks, the principle of proportionality and the duty to take precautions in attack are all part of customary international law, regardless of the type of armed conflict involved."[51]

One common theme of these initiatives is the *need to emphasize guidance over standard setting, or, to phrase it differently, the operationalization of already authoritatively determined standards as opposed to the further development of human rights/humanitarian law norms.* If this trend persists, the resulting document(s) should not take the form of a treaty text to be signed and ratified by member states, but the form of a guidance document(s) to be discussed and revised after extensive consultations among state actors and relevant NSAs.

There are several reasons why a legally binding document would be counterproductive. First, it would not overcome the problem of the legal responsibility of NSAs because only states would sign and ratify this instrument. Second, and probably more important, a legally binding instrument would meet the resistance of many states. Here, I return to the point made earlier in this essay. At a time when many developing countries are expressing serious concern over the recent trends in the doctrine of humanitarian intervention, the notion of armed groups as rights holders and thus entitled, in certain circumstances, to self-determination, is increasingly perceived as a vehicle for interventionary activities. An examination of the records of the General Assembly debate in the fall of 1999 that followed (what were perceived by many as) the secretary-general's "controversial comments" on sovereignty and intervention is a testimony to such a growing concern. Responding primarily to the questionable legal basis of Operation Allied Force, several delegates strongly objected to the proliferation of "humanitarian triggers" for enforcement action and the concomitant challenges to sovereignty.[52]

Last, but not least, an emphasis on standard setting would detract from efforts needed to devise strategies of constructive engagement with armed groups. The call for a "constructive dialogue" reflects a growing awareness of the need to think creatively on ways to reduce or end human rights abuses committed by armed groups. It is premised on the idea that labeling these groups as criminal or terrorist (even if many of their activities point in that direction) prevents, as one recent study on the subject has indicated, "forms of action that, even in extreme conditions, can help to protect civilians and reduce abuses."[53]

What forms may such actions take? Two examples relating to key issue areas of human rights/humanitarian law may provide useful insights. The first relates to child abduction in situations of armed conflict, and the second to the elimination of anti-personnel land mines. It is worth noting that in both issue areas legal instruments have recently entered into force; the most recent, the Optional Protocol to the Convention on the Rights of the Child on the involvement of children in armed conflict creates distinct obligations for non-state armed groups.[54]

The first example draws from the Ugandan experience. While the use of child soldiers has been a longstanding characteristic of the conflict, massive child abduction for military purposes is a rather recent phenomenon. According to a study on the LRA, beginning in 1994 the group stepped up its child abduction practices in order to build up its fighting forces.[55] This "new" form of abusive conduct marked the LRA as something different and provided a useful entry point to a whole array of human rights and humanitarian actors, including community-based associations of parents and relatives of abducted children, IGOs (like UNICEF), and international NGOs (like HRW), to sensitize domestic and international public opinion on the nature and extent of the problem. Part of this strategy involved direct appeals to the Kacoke Madit, a forum created by Acholi in the diaspora to facilitate dialogue in response to the escalation of the war.[56] According to some sources, the LRA leadership became deeply concerned over the possible alienation of diaspora Acholi that it decided to respond by—among other things—appointing a London-based exile as secretary for human rights.[57] While the experiment proved to be short-lived, it indicated that the LRA was not as impervious to the adverse impact of human rights/humanitarian campaigns on its public image as was originally thought. The critical issue was and remains the identification of the appropriate entry point.

The second example involves the 1997 Ottawa Convention on the Prohibition of the Use, Stockpiling, Production, and Transfer of Anti-Personnel Mines and on their Destruction.[58] While the convention applies to internal conflicts, it does not create any distinct obligations for non-state armed groups. To address the need for a mechanism that would draw armed groups "into a humanitarian solution to the landmine crisis," the International Campaign to Ban Landmines sponsored a conference entitled "Engaging Non-State Actors in a Landmine Ban." The conference, held on 24–25 March 2000 in Geneva, provided a forum for launching such a process of engagement.[59] It brought together representatives of armed groups, land-mine-ban campaigners, government representatives, and IHL experts. Armed-group representation included delegations from the Polisario (Western Sahara), the Moro Islamic Liberation Front (MILF-Philippines), the Kurdish Workers' Party (PKK), and the Sudan People's Liberation Army (SPLA). The presence of these groups was indicative of the concerns that the use of anti-personnel mines raise. These groups often control mined territory and, in their dual capacity as users and victims, have a stake in the renunciation of mines.[60]

One of the most important outcomes of this conference was the establishment of Geneva Call, an NGO that would act as the recipient of "deeds" of ban commitment by NSAs. The chancellery of the State of Geneva has agreed to act as a repository for the deeds signed by individual armed groups.[61] According to its December 2003 report, the organization had secured ban commitments by twenty-five NSAs "while others have issued public statements against the use of landmines and support mine action in areas under their control."[62] While the jury is still out, especially on the issue of implementation and its monitoring,[63] this initiative, seeking to parallel state action in situations of depositing instruments of ratification, has potentially far-reaching implications. In addition to affecting the legal profile of armed groups, it can provide a blueprint for the promotion of non-state armed-group accountability in other critical issue areas, such as the use of child soldiers, civilian-targeted bombings, torture, and hostage-taking.[64] Concerning the latter, such a development can partially address the concerns raised in the context of the aforementioned argument on the legal responsibility of NSAs.

It is important to stress at this point that these examples share a perspective of viewing engagement as part of an ongoing process seeking to identify appropriate entry points for the promotion of human rights/humanitarian norms. While such a strategy is not risk free, as it could give the impression that "abuses not being raised are somehow acceptable (or at any rate less objectionable),"[65] the very nature of this dialogic process would seek to ensure that sooner or later no aspect of abusive conduct would be immune from scrutiny.

A Brief Note on the "War on Terrorism"

Before we conclude, some brief remarks on the so-called war on terrorism are in order.[66] The terrorist attacks against the United States and the ensuing military campaign have cast a long shadow on initiatives in a whole set of critical issue areas. More specifically, the war on terrorism has added another layer of complexity to accountability-related projects that focus on engagement practices vis-à-vis armed groups.

The reasons are obvious. The international campaign against terrorism has reinforced the perennial reluctance of many governments to engage with armed opposition groups, routinely characterized as "beyond the pale," by endorsing the indiscriminate use of a vague label, a label that ipso facto delegitimizes certain opposition activities. In the post-9/11 period, the eagerness with which governments around the world have adopted "security" measures that can render them less accountable to their own people, and have used international institutions and procedures to seek approval of domestic legislation seeking to restrict dissent, is indeed troubling.[67]

These developments pose particular challenges to the human rights and humanitarian communities. The human rights approach can best operate in an environment where institutions "have careful regard for the law," and for the integrity of procedures.[68] In an environment in which terms such as *terrorist* or *war* can be used in an imprecise or loose manner, the risk of rendering a large number of people vulnerable increases, and the protective capacities of human rights organizations are thereby diminished.

The humanitarian approach can best operate in an environment receptive to its focus on access to individuals and groups in need of assistance. In this context it is the enormity of human suffering per se that, first and foremost, should shape the protection agenda. The campaign against terrorism raises several problems for the humanitarian task, two of which are of particular relevance here: (1) the prioritization of humanitarian action on the basis of its central/peripheral relation to the anti-terrorist campaign;[69] and (2) the emphasis on eliminating "terrorist groups" rather than on ensuring the safety of those living in areas under their control.

The potentially adverse impact of the war on terrorism on such initiatives is clearly acknowledged by the United Nations secretary-general in his third report on civilian protection: "The efforts of the United Nations to ensure access to vulnerable populations and to structure appropriate contact with armed actors for this purpose will be vastly more complicated if those armed actors are engaged in terrorist activities or are seen as being so involved.... The United Nations will need to formulate clear guidelines for its future work on the protection of civilians in armed conflicts where terrorist organizations are active."[70]

While the acknowledgment of the problem is important, statements should be followed by action. Unfortunately, the most recent draft of the manual on humanitarian negotiation with armed groups not only omits any discussion of this issue, but by referring to the constraints under which the UN agencies operate, it seems to lay the groundwork for bypassing rather than addressing it.[71]

CONCLUSION

Non-legally binding (guidance) documents are likely to constitute the most appropriate vehicle for enhancing accountability at this stage.

While the international campaign against terrorism has complicated this task by reinforcing some of the perennial state-centric arguments against such initiatives, the emphasis on operationalization rather than standard setting can mitigate some of its adverse effects. Given the nature of such documents, they would be more consistent with the paradigmatic shift from the rights of states to the rights of individuals and groups; they could neutralize the potential opposition of many states concerned with the perceived proliferation of humanitarian triggers for enforcement action. Last, but not least, these documents would signal the critical importance of an ongoing process of engagement, a long overdue complement to the existing strategies of promotion and protection.

NOTES

[1] In this essay "non-state armed groups" refers to groups that take up arms in a challenge to governmental authority or in situations of near or total anarchy resulting from the weakening or collapse of state institutions. Their goals can include the replacement of the previous government, secession, autonomy, or simply freedom to engage in outright criminal activities including theft, kidnappings, and other forms of banditry.

[2] There has been a plethora of terms to describe intra-state fighting and violence. The Geneva Conventions and the Additional Protocols refer to *non-international armed conflicts*. Due to disagreements over thresholds of applicability for humanitarian norms, the Secretary-General has used the term *internal violence* to "describe situations where fighting and conflict, of whatever intensity, is taking place inside countries" (Commission on Human Rights, Report of the Sub-Commission on Prevention of Discrimination and Protection of Minorities, *Minimum Humanitarian Standards: Analytical Report of the Secretary-General submitted pursuant to Commission on Human Rights resolution 1997/21,* 5 January 1998, E/CN.4/1998/87).

[3] "Report of the Secretary-General of the United Nations to the Security Council on the Protection of Civilians in Armed Conflict," 8 September 1999, S/1999/957.

[4] Ian Smillie, Lansana Gberie, and Ralph Hazleton, *The Heart of the Matter: Sierra Leone, Diamonds and Human Security* (Ottawa: Partnership Africa Canada, 2000), 6–7.

[5] "Report of the Secretary-General to the Security Council on the Protection of Civilians in Armed Conflict," 30 March 2001, S/2001/331.

[6] A good survey of possible actions for influencing armed groups is included in International Council on Human Rights Policy, "Ends and Means: Human Rights Approaches to Armed Groups" (Geneva: International Council on Human Rights Policy, 2000), 39–58.

[7] Even in the case of the death penalty, the consensus in the human rights community is to work toward its eventual abolition. Article 6.2 of the International Covenant on Civil and Political Rights (ICCPR) states that in countries that have not yet abolished the death penalty, the "sentence of death may be imposed only for the most serious crimes." Likewise, Article 6.6 affirms that nothing in the said Article "shall be invoked to delay or prevent the abolition of capital punishment." Several international and regional human rights instruments have already reinforced this trend. For example, the European Union has become a death penalty–free zone.

[8] Some humanitarian organizations, however, like the Médecins Sans Frontières, have recently adopted a human rights–oriented approach (International Council on Human Rights Policy, "Ends and Means," 13).

[9] Once again, there are no absolute rules. ICRC, a humanitarian organization, stresses the paramount importance of the relevant legal framework, which in this case is IHL (see International Council on Human Rights Policy, *Human Rights Crises: NGO Responses to Military Interventions* [Geneva: International Council on Human Rights Policy, 2002], 21).

[10] This shared commitment to a fundamental baseline of human welfare was most famously encapsulated in the Martens Clause, which appeared in the Preamble to the 1899 Hague Convention II and was later reaffirmed in the 1949 Geneva Conventions and in the 1977 Additional Protocols. See Article 63 (Geneva I), Article 62 (Geneva II), Article 142 (Geneva III), Article 158 (Geneva IV), Article 1 (Protocol I), and Preamble (Protocol II). On the Martens Clause, see James Brown Scott, ed., *The Hague Conventions and Declarations of 1899 and 1907,* 3rd ed. (New York: Oxford Univ. Press, 1918), 101–2; George Andreopoulos, "Offenses against the Laws of Humanity: International Action," *International Encyclopedia of the Social and Behavioral Sciences* (Oxford, UK: Pergamon, 2001).

[11] "Report of the Expert Meeting on Fundamental Standards of Humanity," Stockholm, 22–24 February 2000 (on file with the author); and Asbjorn Eide, Allan Rosas, and Theodor Meron, "Combating Lawlessness in Gray Zone Conflicts through Minimum Humanitarian Standards," *American Journal of International Law* 89, no. 215 (1995): 215–23. Recent developments on the issue of derogation, relating to the issuing of General Comment 29 by the Human Rights Committee, are discussed below.

[12] Theodor Meron, "The Humanization of Humanitarian Law," *American Journal of International Law* 94, no. 239 (2000).

[13] Articles 49/50 (Geneva Convention I), 50/51 (Geneva Convention II), 129/130 (Geneva Convention III), and 146/147 (Geneva Convention IV).

[14] Meron, "The Humanization of Humanitarian Law."

[15] See, for example, United Nations General Assembly Resolution 53/144, which in Article 10 stipulates that "no one shall participate, by act or by failure to act where required, in violating human rights and fundamental freedoms" (*Declaration on the Right and Responsibility of Individuals, Groups, and*

Organs of Society to Promote and Protect Universally Recognized Human Rights and Fundamental Freedoms, 8 March 1999, A/RES/53/144).

[16] Here a brief remark on state responsibility is in order. Several analysts have pointed out that regardless of whatever mechanisms are devised to promote armed-group adherence to human rights norms, the state does bear responsibility under international law for human rights violations in its territory, irrespective of the source of the problem. See the ruling of the Inter-American Court of Human Rights that involved the involuntary disappearance of an individual in Honduras (Inter-American Court of Human Rights, *Velasquez Rodrigues v. Honduras,* Judgment of July 29,1988 (Ser. C) No. 4. (1988), para 172 and 177, umn.edu website (accessed 31 August 2004). Although progressive, this cannot be a viable approach in cases of weakened or failed states.

[17] ICRC, *Holding Armed Groups to International Standards: An ICRC View* (Geneva: ICRC, 1999), 2.

[18] See George Andreopoulos, "A Half Century after the Universal Declaration," in *Concepts and Strategies in International Human Rights,* ed. George Andreopoulos (New York: Peter Lang, 2002), 9.

[19] Protocol Additional to the Geneva Conventions of 12 August 1949, and Relating to the Protection of Victims of Non-International Armed Conflicts Protocol II, Article 1.2.

[20] Ibid., Article 1.1.

[21] Presumably, in this case, the minimum standards of common Article 3 would apply, which are clearly necessary but not sufficient.

[22] For example, another critical issue is the overall relative weakness of the protective regime of Protocol II as compared to that of Protocol I, which covers international conflicts.

[23] The "Rwanda four" are two Benedictine nuns, a businessman, and a physics professor who were convicted by a Brussels jury in June 2001 on charges stemming from killings during the 1994 genocide. This trial was held on the basis of a 1993 Belgian law that provides for jurisdiction over crimes against humanity.

[24] Among recent works on the need for accountability, see Carlos Nino, *Radical Evil on Trial* (New Haven, CT: Yale Univ. Press, 1996); Carla Hesse and Robert Post, eds., *Human Rights in Political Transitions: Gettysburg to Bosnia* (New York: Zone Books, 1999); Martha Minow, *Between Vengeance and Forgiveness: Facing History after Genocide and Mass Violence* (Boston: Beacon Press, 1998); Stephen Macedo, ed., *Universal Jurisdiction: National Courts and the Prosecution of Serious Crimes under International Law* (Philadelphia: Univ. of Pennsylvania Press, 2003); and Ramesh Thakur and Peter Malcontent, eds., *From Sovereign Impunity to International Accountability: The Search for Justice in a World of States* (Tokyo: United Nations Univ. Press, 2004).

[25] Alex Boraine, *A Country Unmasked: Inside South Africa's Truth and Reconciliation* (New York: Oxford Univ. Press, 2001); and Priscilla Hayner,

Unspeakable Truths: Confronting State Terror and Atrocity (New York: Routledge, 2001).

[26] *Prosecutor v. Tadic* (IT-94-1), Appeals Chamber. Decision on the Defense Motion for Interlocutory Appeal on Jurisdiction, 2 October 1995, para. 141, un.org website (accessed 31 August 2004).

[27] *Prosecutor v. Zejnil Delalic, Zdravko Mucic, Hajim Delic, and Esad Landzo* (Celebici Case), (IT-96-21-A), Appeals Chamber Judgment, 20 February 2001, para. 106, un.org website (accessed 31 August 2004).

[28] Appeals Judgment, para. 81.

[29] Appeals Judgment, quoted in para. 96.; see also remarks by Meron, "The Humanization of Humanitarian Law."

[30] Article 7.1 of the Rome Statute.

[31] Articles 7 and 8 contain much broader definitions of crimes against humanity and war crimes than the respective statutes of the two ad hoc tribunals.

[32] Protocol II does not apply to "situations of internal disturbances and tensions," which are separate and distinct from non-international armed conflicts.

[33] While on one level these provisions may appear as instances of the progressive humanization of standards, on another level the lowering of the threshold for the existence of a non-international armed conflict has introduced a certain confusion concerning the relevant benchmarks of organizational capacity. If responsible command and control of territory are no longer relevant, on what criteria would the organizational capacity of an armed group be assessed? And, on a related matter, where should the line between non-international armed conflicts and situations of civil unrest be drawn? In addressing this issue the jurisprudence of the ICTY has suggested that a key criterion in making this distinction is the protracted nature of the armed violence between these groups (*Prosecutor v. Tadic*, para. 70).

[34] *Declaration on the Protection of All Persons from Enforced Disappearance,* General Assembly Resolution 47/133, 18 December 1992; and *Convention against Torture and Other Cruel, Inhuman, or Degrading Treatment or Punishment,* General Assembly Resolution 39/46, 10 December 1984.

[35] United Nations Security Council Resolution 864, 15 September 1993, S/RES/864 (1993).

[36] United Nations Security Council Resolution 1160, 31 March 1998, S/RES/1160 (1998).

[37] United Nations Security Council Resolution 1199, 23 September 1998, S/RES/1199 (1998).

[38] United Nations Security Council Resolution 1556, 30 July 2004, S/RES/1556 (2004).

[39] Human Rights Watch, "Darfur Documents Confirm Government Policy of Militia Support," a Human Rights Watch Briefing Paper (20 July 2004), hrw.org website (accessed 31 August 2004).

[40] Commission on Human Rights Resolution 1998/75, "The Abduction of Children from Northern Uganda"; see Andrew Mawson, *Peace at Any Price?*

A Discussion of Efforts to Influence the Lord's Resistance Army of Northern Uganda (Geneva: The International Council on Human Rights Policy, August 1999), 44.

[41] For example, the Taliban, when they constituted the de facto government in Afghanistan; the FARC in Colombia; and the SPLA in Sudan.

[42] United Nations, ICCPR, *General Comment No. 29. States of Emergency (Article 4)*, CCPR/C/21/Rev. 1/Add. 11, 31 August 2001.

[43] Additional to the ones listed in Articles 4.2 and 4.13.

[44] United Nations, ICCPR, *General Comment No. 29,* para. 15 and para. 16.

[45] Ibid., para. 16.

[46] For an overview of the different phases of this project, see David Petrasek, "Moving Forward on the Development of Minimum Humanitarian Standards," *American Journal of International Law* 92, no. 557 (1998).

[47] For example, the 2004 report highlights the importance of codes of conduct and memoranda of understanding concluded in the field among humanitarian agencies, state entities, and non-state entities in the promotion of fundamental principles of IHRL and IHL. See United Nations Economic and Social Council, Commission on Human Rights, Promotion, and Protection of Human Rights, *Fundamental Standards of Humanity: Report of the Secretary-General,* 25 February 2004, E/CN.4/2004/90: 14–15.

[48] IASC, Workplan 2002, Draft, 4 March 2002; Telephone conversation with Tania Karanasios, Policy Division, OCHA, 8 April 2002.

[49] *Manual on Field Practices in Humanitarian Negotiations with Armed Groups: Background for Collection of Field Practices* (no date; on file with the author). I would like to thank Mr. Manuel Bessler of OCHA and Mr. Piero Calvi-Parisetti of Gignos for providing me with a copy of this draft. The reference group, set up by ISAC to oversee the development of this manual, is composed of OCHA, OHCHR, UNHCR, UNICEF, UNDP, WHO, and WFP.

[50] Jean-Marie Henckaerts and Louise Doswald-Peck, eds. *Customary International Humanitarian Law*, vol. 1, *Rules*, vol. 2, *Practice* (Cambridge: Cambridge Univ. Press, 2005).

[51] ICRC, Customary International Humanitarian Law, 28th International Conference of the Red Cross and Red Crescent, 2–6 December 2003, 03/IC/14, Geneva, 2003 (on file with the author). I would like to thank Mr. Daniel Helle, deputy head of the ICRC delegation to the United Nations for providing me with a copy of the report.

[52] On the proliferation of humanitarian triggers, see George Andreopoulos, "Violations of Human Rights and Humanitarian Law and Threats to International Peace and Security," in Thakur and Malcontent, *From Sovereign Impunity to International Accountability,* 84–92.

[53] International Council on Human Rights Policy, "Ends and Means," 4.

[54] Article 4.1 of the Protocol (entered into force on 12 February 2002) stipulates that "armed groups that are distinct from the armed forces of a state should not, under any circumstances, recruit or use in hostilities person under the age of 18 years," unhchr.ch website (accessed 31 August 2004).

[55] Here I follow Mawson, *Peace at Any Price?*

[56] Ibid.

[57] Ibid.

[58] For the text of the Ottawa treaty, entered into force on 1 March 1999, see Adam Roberts and Richard Guelff, eds., *Documents on the Laws of War,* 3rd ed. (New York: Oxford Univ. Press, 2000), 648–66.

[59] International Campaign to Ban Landmines, *Armed Groups Asked to Commit to Landmine Ban* (31 March 2000), reliefweb.int website (accessed 12 April 2002).

[60] Ibid.

[61] Statement by Elizabeth Reusse-Decrey, president of Geneva Call, "Geneva Call: A Call for Humanity," *Geneva Call Magazine* 3, geneva.ch website.

[62] Geneva Call, *Annual Report 2003* (Geneva: Geneva Call, 2004), 6.

[63] See the sympathetic but critical reflections of Soliman M. Santos, Jr., Geneva Call's regional director for Asia, in "A Critical Reflection on the Geneva Call Instrument and Approach in Engaging Armed Groups on Humanitarian Norms: A Southern Perspective," paper presented at the Armed Groups Project Conference "Curbing Human Rights Violations by Non-State Armed Groups," 13–15 November 2003, Vancouver, British Columbia.

[64] The Deed of Commitment makes it expressly clear that this is the beginning of a broader commitment "to the ideal of humanitarian norms" and to the goal of contributing "to their respect in field practice as well as to the further development of humanitarian norms for armed conflicts."

[65] International Council on Human Rights Policy, "Ends and Means," 48.

[66] The scope of this essay and space limitations do not allow for a detailed discussion of this critical issue. I have addressed it in greater detail in George Andreopoulos, "The Impact of the War on Terror on the Accountability of Armed Groups," paper presented at the CISS/ISA Conference, Salzburg, 7–8 July 2004.

[67] Human rights organizations, like Amnesty International, have provided numerous examples of laws, official statements, and practices in many countries in the post–9/11 period that indicate the makings of a disturbing trend. See, for example, Amnesty International, *Annual Report 2002* (London: Amnesty International, 2002). On the use of international institutions and procedures, the best example is the reporting procedure envisaged by United Nations Security Council Resolution 1373, which has enabled many governments with well-documented records of massive and systematic repression (like Uzbekistan) to submit to the Counter-Terrorism Committee (CTC) reports cataloguing their concerted efforts to combat terrorism; for the CTC mandate and country reports, see Counter Terrorism Committee, "Mandate," un.org website (accessed 31 August 2004). Some of the human rights concerns relating to the legislation adopted by member states and the role of the CTC were raised by members of the Human Rights Committee during their briefing by the Legal Expert for the CTC ("Human Rights Committee Briefed on Work of Counter-Terrorism Committee," press release, 27 March 2003), HR/CT/630.

[68] International Council on Human Rights Policy, *Human Rights after September 11* (Geneva: International Council on Human Rights Policy, 2002), 39.

[69] See Nicholas de Torrente, "Challenges to Humanitarian Action," *Ethics and International Affairs* 16, no. 2 (2002): 7.

[70] "Report of the Secretary-General to the Security Council on the Protection of Civilians in Armed Conflict," 26 November 2002, S/2002/1300, 15–16.

[71] See *Manual on Field Practices in Humanitarian Negotiations with Armed Groups.* Needless to say, this is a preliminary assessment, since the manual is still a work in progress.

IV

Bio-ethics, Medicine, and Human Rights

9

The Genetic Revolution and Human Rights

Brave New World Revisited?

Peter Juviler

INTRODUCTION

Genetic engineering is the application of molecular biology through genetic testing and changes of "the inherited characteristics of an organism in a predetermined way by altering its genetic materials."[1] The genetic revolution in question here is the application of genetic engineering to human genetic testing, therapy, and enhancement. Gene research leaped forward after the discovery by James Watson and Francis Crick in 1953 of the double helixes of DNA (deoxyribonucleic acid), which structure genes. Techniques of recombinant DNA technology, or gene splicing, began in 1973 through altering genes of bacteria to produce beneficial substances such as insulin, human growth hormone, and vaccines.

Thanks to the National Science Foundation for its start-up funding of an interdisciplinary course on science and public policy devoted to the genetic revolution at Barnard College, Columbia University; to Prof. Timothy Halpin-Healy for setting up the course; to my co-teaching colleagues Philip Ammirato, who administered it, and Sanjay Reddy, Brian Morton, and Theresa Rogers for their part in the course; to Barnard Librarian Cynthia Johnson; to students Sarah Geiger and Meridith Villa; and to colleagues of the Columbia University Seminar on Human Rights for their comments on an earlier draft.

The human genome project has sought "to describe the sequence of all the DNA in the nucleus of a human cell—that is, to work out the order of the chemical 'letters' which carry the genetic message" in some thirty thousand genes, forming twenty-three pairs of chromosomes that shape human beings' makeup.[2] A preliminary map appeared in 2000 (simultaneously with that of the private company Celera Genomics), and a virtually complete one in 2003.[3]

Barbara R. Jasny and Donald Kennedy write: "The knowledge that all of the genetic components of any process can be identified will give extraordinary new power to scientists."[4] Similarly, Sociologist Toby Huff notes that humans are "now poised to alter the human genetic endowment—once thought to be irrevocably given by nature or by God." These alterations are intended for purposes of both therapy—the prediction, prevention and cure of diseases, and "'trait enhancement'—build, tint, intelligence, talent, temperament perhaps."[5] Scientists are not, or at least not yet, state-controlled managers of a totalitarian eugenics such as Aldous Huxley foresaw in his 1932 dystopia, Brave New World,[6] although government funding inevitably influences their work. Scientists' work is also shaped by a host of other significant non-state actors (NSAs): health insurers, corporations, bioethicists, religious associations, patients, parents, and latter-day Ponce de Leons in search of the fountain of youth.

This essay addresses the extent and limits of human rights guidelines for genetic engineering; the prominence of NSAs in the devising and uses of gene testing, therapy, and research involving such human rights as privacy, safety, access, and nondiscrimination; the question of conflicting rights to life of embryos and of beneficiaries of stem cell research; an emerging new consumer eugenics, along with issues of genetic enhancement and cloning; and the impact of commercial considerations and influences.

SEEKING HUMAN RIGHTS GUIDELINES

In genetics, "the whole bundle of rights that accompany both human beings and private property are now in doubt," as Huff has pointed out.[7] Society is heaving up ethical issues and conflicts over genetic engineering faster than international human rights treaty-making and governmental regulation can resolve them. So far, international norm-making has produced one pioneering but non-binding declaration.

At its 1992 session, the UN Subcommission on the Prevention of Discrimination and Protection of Minorities voted to consider implications for human rights standards of science's potential impact on human genetic structures.[8] A year later the UN World Conference on Human Rights noted "that certain advances, notably in the biomedical and life sciences, as well as in information technology, may have potentially adverse consequences for the integrity, dignity, and human rights of the individual."[9] On 11 November 1997 the UN Economic, Social and Cultural Organization (UNESCO) passed the Universal Declaration on the Human Genome and Human Rights. It received the UN General Assembly's approval on 10 March 1998 in a resolution that invoked principles proclaimed in the International Bill of Rights. It endorsed the purpose "to promote scientific and technical progress in the fields of biology and genetics in a manner respectful of fundamental rights and for the benefit of all."[10] The two basic questions suggested by developments in genetic engineering are, first, whether a common understanding of fundamental rights is possible, and second, whether inequalities of income and wealth can be overcome so as to make the genetic revolution indeed serve "for the benefit of all."

GENE TESTING, THERAPY, AND RESEARCH

Genetic knowledge is important because genes instruct cells to produce the proteins that shape the development of the embryo and fetus, and play a part in determining the development and health of the child and adult after birth. Gene testing takes patients and the medical profession into the realm of rights issues posed not by some totalitarian state eugenics but by NSAs' discoveries, technology, and choices. Just consider the tangle of issues inherent in gene testing, counseling, limits of patient privacy, medical experimentation, and, as we will take up shortly, genetic discrimination. Genetic testing is the search in a patient's or unborn child's DNA for genetic defects that predispose to disabilities or illnesses such as breast or colon cancer, muscular dystrophy, Alzheimer's, Huntington's disease, Tay-Sachs syndrome, cystic fibrosis, and many others. Gene therapy is the correcting of such threats to health posed by the defective genes.

Improved predictive capabilities through diagnostic testing have outstripped techniques of both follow-up prevention and individually tailored treatment regimens for those who have already developed disease symptoms. Hence, the need for more counseling as to whether to be tested at all, and as to how to cope with the "genetic hypochondria" that can come with awaiting the possible or certain onset of a genetically related illness or disability.[11] In fact, the Universal Declaration on the Human Genome and Human Rights asserts in Article 5(c) "the right of each individual to decide whether or not to be informed of the results of genetic examination and the resulting consequences."

Confidentiality and Rights of Access

"Research, treatment or diagnosis affecting an individual's genome," says the declaration, should require patients' "prior and free and informed consent," as well as "rigorous and prior assessment of the potential risks and benefits involved, and in accordance with "national law" (Art. 5[a]). Patients shall receive "just reparations for any damage sustained as a . . . result of an intervention affecting his or her genome" (Art. 8). Where the individual lacks the capacity to give consent, then "consent shall be obtained in the manner prescribed by law, guided by the person's best interest" (Art. 5[a][b]).

Article 7 of the declaration proclaims a patient's rights of confidentiality: "Genetic data associated with an identifiable person and stored or processed for the purpose of research or any other purpose must be held confidential in the conditions foreseen and set by law." Issues of privacy and confidentiality connect with possibilities of divulging testing results to third parties, including employers and insurance companies.[12] A widespread pattern of discrimination by insurance companies and employers against those who test positively for possible or confirmed genetic health disability has been already noted.[13]

In his plea for "strong federal laws against genetic discrimination," then Senator Daschle evoked the Universal Declaration of the Human Genome and Human Rights, indicating, "No one shall be subjected to discrimination based on genetic characteristics that is intended to infringe or has the effect of infringing human rights, fundamental freedoms and human dignity." In addition to the firm prohibition of employment and health discrimination "on the basis of predictive genetic information," he urged lawmakers to consult at least "scientists, geneticists, ethicists, consumers, employers, employee and employer groups, and insurers."[14] "Misuse of genetic information," Senators Jeffords and Daschle argued, "could create a new underclass, the genetically less fortunate."[15]

Perils and Protection in the Quest for Cures

Scientists are turning to humans as subjects in tests of cures for genetically linked ailments.[16] And the declaration on the human genome adapts human rights standards to the particulars of experimentation, gene therapy, and related procedures. It proclaims rights of researchers to states' educational, funding, and other support for human rights (Arts. 14, 20–25). But it leaves it up to states and non-state professionals to implement those standards, meticulously and with "intellectual honesty and integrity . . . because of its ethical and social implications" (Arts. 13, 15–19).

Clinical tests of new treatments for auto-immune deficiency involve supplying non-defective genes to immune-deficient patients using "retroviruses as carriers, through recombinant DNA therapy." Such gene therapy has its perils for patients volunteering as subjects in experiments, as in the case of eighteen-year-old Jesse Gelsinger, who was undergoing gene therapy for a metabolic disorder, but died in 1999 after recombinant DNA treatment, which involved the use of a modified cold virus to deliver healthy DNA.[17] Deaths and new illnesses that occurred as a result of other treatments, such as inserting corrective genes into bone marrow stem cells of babies with severe combined immunity deficiency, led the officials in the United States and France to suspend a set of experiments using recombinant DNA therapy in treating a fatal immune deficiency.[18]

Genetic Discrimination

In those countries permitting abortions at parents' discretion, international human rights norms leave freedom of choice to NSAs—religious authorities, parents, and counselors. The declaration on the human genome states in its preamble that "research on the human genome and the resulting applications open up vast prospects for progress in improving the health of individuals and of humankind as a whole," but emphasizes "that such research should fully respect human dignity, freedom and human rights, as well as the prohibition of all forms of discrimination based on genetic characteristics." Article 6 repeats that admonition: "No one shall be subjected to discrimination based on genetic characteristics, that is intended to infringe or has the effect of infringing on human rights, fundamental freedoms, and human dignity."

But is an embryo or a fetus also entitled to protection? States with freedom of choice generally leave decisions on whether to abort a fetus up to parents and related social mores to determine. Human rights norms? They give no clear guidelines. The ICCPR leaves the reach of the right to life to regional or national laws to define: "Every human being has the inherent right to life. The right shall be protected by law. No one shall be arbitrarily deprived of his life" (Art. 6.1). But when does being a "human being" begin? The rights of the fetus to life and to nondiscrimination are not recognized in the UDHR, where rights begin at birth: "All human beings are born free and equal in dignity and rights" (Art. 1). Hence, the rejection by the declaration on the human genome of "discrimination based on genetic characteristics" might plausibly be confined to discrimination after birth. Champions of parental autonomy and free choice certainly agree.

But parental choices may well reflect societal preconceptions in the United States and elsewhere concerning persons with disabilities (physical disabilities or genetic predispositions to fatal illness such as cystic fibrosis). The disabled are seen widely as more or less helpless and doomed to an unhappy life. On the other hand, Adrienne Asch holds that the benefits of bearing a child despite prenatally detected disabilities outweigh any costs to family, the disabled, and society, and she deplores the absence of prenatal counseling for parents facing the prospect of a child with disabilities.[19]

Whose Right to Life? Stem Cells, Embryos, and Repairing the Ailing

Right-to-life ethicists associated with various religions seek to ban laboratory techniques such as those using embryos discarded in fertility clinics to extract stem cells that can potentially develop into any cell in the body.[20] Using stem cells to replace missing human body cells points to possible cures for diabetes, Parkinson, and other diseases associated with cell decomposition.[21]

Neither international human rights law nor the declaration on the human genome specifically bans the use of discarded embryos. In August 2000, under the Clinton administration, the National Institutes of Health (NIH) issued new guidelines. The guidelines allowed public funding of research using human stem cells while denying funding for the extraction of those stem cells—mainly from discarded embryos stored in fertility clinics.[22] Opponents of stem-cell research argue that any tampering with genes in germ-cells is a violation of God's creation, involves the taking of innocent life, or both. Some oppose stem-cell research in the belief that evolution is an expression of the grand order of things, which unfolds according to a logic of natural selection. That logic is violated by human intrusion to reshape evolution beyond selective animal and plant breeding (already a problem for diversity, some argue).[23] Others oppose stem-cell research as a violation of the right to life of the embryos destroyed to obtain those cells.

In 2000 the Bush administration suspended the Clinton guidelines and decreed new guidelines, prefaced with a summation of the controversy and an invocation of Huxley's *Brave New World:*

> As the discoveries of modern science create tremendous hope, they also lay vast ethical minefields. . . . We have arrived at that brave new world that seemed so distant in 1932 when Aldous Huxley wrote about human beings created in test tubes in what he called a hatchery.[24]

Bush's order limited federal funding of stem cell research to that using only the sixty or so stem cell lines existing as of the date of his order. He depicted this as a way of opening up research to further possible therapeutic benefits of stem-cell research "without crossing a fundamental moral line by providing tax-payer funding that would sanction or encourage further destruction of human embryos that have at least a potential for life." But numerous articles or declarations by scientists complain that such limits greatly hamper research, setting it back years, especially since only some of the sixty lines have so far usable stem cells and access to those can be difficult.

Disagreements surface in the European Union (EU) between countries supporting EU funding of embryonic stem-cell extracting and research, and those supporting funding only on a basis similar to that decreed by President Bush—only on lines created before 27 June 2002. This dispute, originating in the public advocacy of each country, has tied up EU funding of embryonic stem-cell research for therapeutic purposes.[25] Facing a similar block in the United States individual states there are beginning to set up their own public funding of stem-cell research.[26]

One should not expect such limits as the funding ban to hold. Science is competitive. Funding limits impose a price on affected researchers. Before scientists engineered therapeutic or eugenic changes in human genes, they had developed techniques for conceiving a child *in vitro* and then bringing it to term in the womb of expectant mothers or surrogate mothers. The issues of rights to life, human identity, and genetic diversity trace back to those manipulations of reproduction.[27] In fact, during the 1970s NIH was not allowed to fund *in vitro* research on artificial insemination until an advisory commission could be formed to consider the issue. In the meantime, such research made rapid progress in the UK, where the first "test tube baby" was born in 1978, three years before such a baby was born in the Unites States. By the mid 1990s such advances in biotechnology, outside of genetic engineering, had already stirred attention and debate and nurtured a growing sub-field of bioethics. The advances led to innovations such as surrogate motherhood and *in vitro* fertilization, and to concerns over safeguarding human dignity and the rights of both donor and recipient.[28] Innovations in reproductive technology such as artificial insemination meant that parents could seek donors of eggs or sperms advertised as "superior" in looks or intelligence. According to Glenn McGee, those innovations introduced a form of *making* rather than *having* children, a form of eugenics.

Eugenics Past and Present

This emerging new eugenics through biomedicine, including an advanced part of it, genetic engineering, differs from the government-encouraged eugenics movement in the United States following the late-nineteenth-century wave of immigration and related social turmoil. Supporters of a public eugenics—the improvement of human heredity—permeated US elites, Congress, and a majority among microbiologists by the early twentieth century. Theodore Roosevelt endorsed eugenics by curtailing reproduction of allegedly defective persons:

> The great problem of civilization is to secure a relative increase of the valuable as compared with the less valuable or noxious elements of the population. Criminals should be sterilized and feeble-minded persons forbidden to leave offspring behind them. . . . The emphasis should be laid on getting desirable people to breed.

In the same passage, he noted that "the problem cannot be met unless we give full consideration to the immense influence of heredity."[29]

Unlike the partially state-sponsored eugenics of Theodore Roosevelt and his contemporaries, of the Nazis, or of the controllers and their hatcheries in the fictional *Brave New World,* the eugenics in prospect now is a new eugenics of individual choices and social fashions. It is engendered by advances in genetic engineering that are bringing what Roger Gosden terms a "new era of eugenic consumerism."

> Today we are more concerned about the abuse of reproductive freedom than about the vividness of *Brave New World.* Rather than being the cruel instrument of totalitarian government, eugenics has become transformed as people seek to fulfill their ambition to have the most treasured object— a healthy child. . . . If the twentieth century was notable for fertility control, in the twenty-first the emphasis of research will switch to producing a baby that is free of defects and attractive and arrives with perfect timing. . . . We are now invited as individuals to pick and choose from what is on offer in the reproductive marketplace, according to personal tastes and circumstances. This is the new era of eugenic consumerism.[30]

Genetic Enhancement

But what principles should guide eugenic consumers? Professional attitudes toward genetic engineering and its limits, says bioethicist Arthur Caplan, divide between utilitarianism, which emphasizes the benefits of extending and enhancing life, and the critics who point to its costs in "the loss of our humanity, the value of life, and the meaning of human experience."[31] The dawning era of gene enhancement gives utilitarians and their opponents much to argue about.

The declaration on the human genome lends normative support to those who oppose carrying genetic engineering of humans beyond therapy, to trait enhancement, as meddling with the evolutionary "heritage of humanity." Article 1 states that "the Human genome underlies the fundamental unity of all members of the human family, as well as the recognition of their inherent dignity and diversity. In a symbolic sense, it is the heritage of humanity." And Article 2 elaborates further on the incompatibility of human dignity with reducing "individuals to their genetic characteristics," stating that all people have "a right to respect for their dignity and for their rights regardless of their genetic characteristics. That dignity makes it imperative not to reduce individuals to their genetic characteristics and to respect their uniqueness and diversity."

Genetic enhancement through modifying genes before birth for the sake of an offspring's health is one thing. But the sentiment of the declaration echoes in the opposition to prospective attempts to impart predetermined characteristics such as athleticism, tallness, a high IQ, and so on.[32] In the early 1990s the bioethicist Duane Elgin wondered whether genetically enhanced individuals would still be human.[33] As the debate picked up, David Shenk asked: "What sort of boundaries should we set for ourselves? . . . Should any couple have the right to choose the blond-haired embryo over the brown-haired embryo? Homosexuality over heterosexuality? Should we try to 'fix' . . . congenital deafness? Baldness? . . . Consider the prospect of a pop-genetics culture in which millions choose the same desirable genes."[34] Cloning, the reproduction of genetically identical embryos or offspring, is even more controversial than gene enhancement by itself.

Cloning

The cloning of Dolly the sheep in 1996 stirred debate over the possibilities of human therapeutic and reproductive cloning. Therapeutic cloning features the cloning of stem cells, that is, stem cells with DNA identical to their potential ailing recipient's DNA. This would minimize chances of their rejection by the donor's immune system. In February 2004, Woo-Suk Hwang of Seoul National University reported cloning a line of embryonic human stem cells, ES cells, for therapeutic not reproductive purposes, and in 2005, eleven such lines by a more efficient method. But by November 2005 Hwang had admitted to unethical practices in paying the many women egg donors involved and pressuring two junior associates to supply eggs. In December a Seoul National University committee reported the 2005 experiment to be fraudulent. In January 2006 the committee reported that the 2004 results also were faked. The debacle damaged Korean national pride but had a bright side for some Korean scientists. Troubled young scientists had initiated the questioning in the first place. And the resulting disclosures gave impetus to increased vigilance on the part of research and scientific journals and the state.[35]

The declaration on the human genome reserves its strongest disapproval for reproductive cloning:

Practices which are contrary to human dignity, such as reproductive cloning of human beings, shall not be permitted.
States and competent international organizations are invited
to co-operate in identifying such practices and in taking, at
national or international level, the measures necessary to
ensure that the principles set out in this declaration are respected. (Art. 11)

Reproductive cloning, even if safe, say its opponents, violates a child's
right to an "open-ended future"; creates a burden for the child to live
up to parents' expectations; tampers with and alters human nature,
the natural order, the legacy of an evolutionary process;[36] and violates
the uniqueness of each human being as God's creation.[37] Absent universal and extraordinarily comprehensive health insurance, the high
cost of cloning humans will only further aggravate issues of discrimination and unequal access.[38]

In the United States the President's Council on Bioethics, which
met from April to July in 2002, advised a ban on reproductive cloning
and a four-year moratorium on therapeutic cloning; on 31 July 2002
the US House of Representatives voted 265–162 to ban all human cloning—reproductive or therapeutic.[39] Leon Kass, chair of the President's
Council on Bioethics, had testified[40] that therapeutic cloning opens up
a slippery slope toward reproductive cloning, which threatens a child
with ill health or malformation. It jeopardizes a child's identity and
individuality and parent-child relations in a process "further degraded
by Commodification."[41] It would start the country down "the path to
the Brave New World, a path made possible by the genetic control of
future generations. This is not an issue of pro-life versus pro-choice.
. . . It is only . . . about baby design and manufacture: the opening skir-
mish of a long battle against eugenics and against a post-human future."[42] On 21 February 2003 the House again voted to ban cloning.

The Senate remained deadlocked between supporters of a total ban
and advocates of a ban only on reproductive cloning. The latter group
included Leon Kass and the quadriplegic actor Christopher Reeve, who
testified that stem cells, particularly cloned stem cells, are the best hope,
maybe the only hope, for the 100 million Americans who are victims
of incurable diseases and the fifty-four million disabled.[43] That dead-
lock carries over internationally. In the UN debates over the drafting
of international rules regulating cloning, thirty-seven countries, including the United States and Spain, rejected the proposal, sponsored

by German and France along with twenty other countries, to ban *only* reproductive cloning.[44] They continue to uphold the argument that cloning and gene enhancement "touch the very essence of being 'human,' of the dignity and integrity of the human person," and the person's autonomy.[45]

But despite international and local objections, human cloning is likely to proceed—and if therapeutic, to be widely accepted.[46] Reproductive cloning will probably occur despite wide bans. Such is the power of science and technology joined with public demand. Rick Weiss cites examples of parents who are seeking to use reproductive cloning to have a child or to replace a deceased child or to produce a child that is the genetically corrected clone of an existing immune-deficient child in order to inject bone marrow cells from it into their sickly child and thus to correct its genetic deficiency.[47]

The speed and direction of advances in consumer eugenics will depend on a market shaped by social fashions and choices, but also their influencing by merchandisers of eugenics, and by public access to the treatment involved. Whatever our predispositions, we should not ignore the linkup between science and commerce, which includes another set of powerful NSAs.

Contradictions of Commerce

Eric Grace concludes that benefits from biotechnology far outweigh apparent negative effects. But when it comes to "the social aspect of biotechnology," Grace finds the evidence to be "more equivocal." Although biotechnology grew initially out of scientific curiosity about nature, Grace notes that

> the context in which most biotechnology research is conducted, however, is very different. Biotechnology is first and foremost a commercial activity—a reality that largely determines the priorities and goals of what is investigated and how it is applied. While the world may lack adequate vaccines, food, and pollution control, the focus of biotechnology companies is profit, not philanthropy.[48]

Pharmaceutical and gentech companies second the conclusion of *The Economist* that "science and profit have mixed very productively. . . . It is a happy marriage," as profits fund future research and development.[49] But what about access to the results of that research and development?

According to the declaration on the human genome, "Benefits from advances in biology, genetics and medicine, concerning the human genome, shall be made available to all, with due regard to the dignity and human rights of each individual" (Art. 12[a]). Yet the genetic revolution involves a basic contradiction between rights to intellectual property of researchers and genocorporations, and the public's rights to health benefits.[50] The ICESCR contains similar language: "The States Parties to the present Covenant recognize the right of everyone . . . to enjoy the benefits of scientific progress and its applications," but also "to benefit from the protection of the moral and material interests resulting from any scientific, literary, or artistic production of which he is the author" (Art. 15).

Intellectual property rights of scientists, laboratories, and gentech corporations, and state protection of those rights, could well price biotech products and treatments so high that only the affluent will be able to afford them, wherever comprehensive health insurance is lacking, internationally or locally.[51] A case can be made for Andrew Shapiro's vision of a "control revolution" bringing about "a massive transfer of power from state bureaucracies to individuals and corporations," and the separation of humans into separate castes or even species:

> The unpleasant extremes of this climate are not very difficult to imagine: an over-class buying itself genetic immunity—the development of a free-market eugenic meritocracy—or, to coin a term, biocapitalism. . . . We will compete for a better code. Such a eugenic culture, even one grounded in a democracy, will inevitably lead to the intensified recognition and exaggeration of certain differences. In a newly human-driven evolution, the differences could become so great that humans will be literally transformed into more than one species.[52]

Tom Athanasiou and Marcy Damovsky, taking a scary quote from molecular biologist Lee Silver about transformations into new castes such as "Genrich" and "Naturals" (as in the film "Gattaca," 1997), write: "The tension between personal liberty and social justice is a necessary one," and they "should not be collapsed into uncritical support for individual (or corporate!) rights."[53] But that may happen eventually. Ideals of each human's dignity and uniqueness and diversity will have to contend with the approach of a "reprogenetic" new age such as espied by Lee M. Silver, "an age in which we as humans will gain the ability to change the nature of our species."[54] Then, warn critics, human intrusion will divert evolution, reduce human genetic diversity, and thus destroy prospects of species' natural evolution and long-term survival.[55]

CONCLUSION

Progress in deciphering the rosetta stone of the human genome has prompted international quests for a human rights framework to guide state actors and NSAs involved. The achievements of scientists and the health benefits are unquestionable. Yet, even at this early stage, genoscience's discoveries and applications push beyond existing human rights frameworks. NSAs respond with heated debate over ethical questions relating to human identity, evolution, diversity, and prospects of a "posthuman future." Economically developed societies appear to be heading toward a non-state, consumer eugenics rather than, as some see it, an imminent Huxlian *Brave New World,* where NSAs—science and society—are subordinated to the eugenic state and its "controllers" in the name of a world without conflict and war.

The dawning revolution in human genetic research and development carries both promises for health and human rights, and, critics argue, possible threats to human rights through genetic discrimination in reproductive choices, inequality of access to "the benefits of science," and loss of human diversity, dignity, identity. If progress in the genetic revolution brings deepening inequality in access to its benefits, that will intensify issues of nondiscrimination spelled out in human rights covenants and the declaration on the human genome. Whether or not the genetic revolution reaches the point of dividing society into castes or even species of humans, contradictions of commerce are already further dividing societies—and parts of the world—as regards access to the benefits of genetic engineering.

A student suggested to our class on science and public policy that human technological "trespasses" on evolution and changes in human identity and diversity were part of the evolutionary scheme itself. Even if that is so, the genetic revolution can and should conform with human rights through proper safeguards of privacy, counseling, universality of access despite the contradictions of commerce, and the minimizing of genetic discrimination associated with genetic testing. However this all turns out, it will be mainly the work of persons and groups outside governments, thus further pointing to the inadequacy of near-exclusive international legal emphasis on state accountability for human rights observance.

NOTES

[1] Janusz Symonides, "New Human Rights Dimensions, Obstacles and Challenges: Introductory Remarks," in *Human Rights: New Dimensions and Challenges,* ed. Janusz Symonides (Brookfield, VT: UNESCO/Ashgate Dartmouth Publishing, 1998).

[2] Svante Pääbo, "The Human Genome and Our View of Ourselves," *Science* 291 (18 February 2001): 1219–20; John Maynard Smith, "The Cheshire Cat's DNA," *The New York Review of Books* 21 (December 2000), 43–46.

[3] DOEgenomes, "Timeline: Major Events in the U.S. Human Genome Project," ornl.gov website (accessed 31 August 2004); Merrill Goozner, "Patenting Life," *The American Prospect* (18 December 2000), 23–25; Eric S. Grace, *Biotechnology Unzipped: Promises and Realities* (Washington, DC: Joseph Henry Press, 1997), 69.

[4] Barbara R. Jasny and Donald Kennedy, "The Human Genome," *Science* 291 (18 February 2001): 1153.

[5] Toby E. Huff, "The Fourth Scientific Revolution," *Society* 33, no. 4 (May–June 1996): 9–10; Peter Juviler, "Clearing a Path to the International Bill of Rights," in *International Human Rights and Responsibilities,* ed. Kenneth W. Hunter and Timothy E. Mack (Westport, CT: Praeger, 1996), 61.

[6] Aldous Huxley, *Brave New World* and *Brave New World Revisited* (New York: Harper Colophon, 1965).

[7] Huff, "The Fourth Scientific Revolution," 10.

[8] Edward Lawson, ed., *Encyclopedia of Human Rights,* 2nd ed. (Washington, DC: Taylor and Francis, 1996), 144.

[9] United Nations, *World Conference on Human Rights: The Vienna Declaration and Program of Action, June 1993* (New York: UN, 1993), 1.11.

[10] Resolution of the UN General Assembly, "The Human Genome and Human Rights," 10 March 1999, A/RES/53/152; "Universal Declaration on the Human Genome and Human Rights," UNESCO resolution of 11 November 1997, portal.unesco.org website (accessed 31 August 2004).

[11] Mary Murray, "Nancy Wexler," *The New York Times Magazine* (13 February 1994).

[12] Jessica G. Davis, "The Impact of Genetic Research on Women's Health," in *Textbook of Women's Health*, ed. L. A. Wallis (Philadelphia: Lippincott-Raven Publishers, 1998), 989.

[13] Jeremy Rifkin, *The Biotech Century: Harnessing the Gene and Remaking the World* (New York: Penguin Putnam, 1998), 3, 160–69; Pääbo, "The Human Genome and Our View of Ourselves," 1220.

[14] James M. Jeffords and Tom Daschle, "Political Issues in the Genetic Era," *Science* 291 (18 February 2001): 1250.

[15] Ibid.

[16] Michael G. Lemonick, "Monkey Business," *Time* (22 January 2001), 40–42.

[17] Tricia Gura, "After a Setback, Gene Therapy Progresses . . . Gingerly," *Science* 292 (2 March 2001): 1692–97; Cheryl Gay Stolberg, "Tribute and Apologies in Gene Therapy and Death," *The New York Times,* 10 December 1999.

[18] Cheryl Gay Stolberg, "Trials Are Halted on a Gene Therapy," *The New York Times*, 4 October 2002; Eliot Marshall, "Gene Therapy a Suspect in Leukemia-Like Disease," *Science* 298 (4 October 2002): 34–35; Jocelyn Kaiser, "Seeking the Cause of Induced Leukemias in X-SKID Trial," *Science* (24 January 2003): 495.

[19] Adrienne Asch, "Public Health Matters: Prenatal Diagnosis and Selective Abortion: A Challenge to Practice and Policy," *American Journal of Public Health* 89, no. 11 (November 1999): 1649–57. C. Everett Koop, US surgeon general from 1981 to 1989, has depicted prenatal testing as potential "search and destroy missions."

[20] Gretchen Vogel, "Court Asked to Declare NIH Guidelines Legal," *Science* 292 (25 May 2001): 1463.

[21] Nicholas Wade, "Scientists Report Two Major Advances in Stem-Cell Research," *The New York Times,* 27 April 2001. Researchers have found a way to produce insulin-making cells from mouse embryonic stem cells (see Gretchen Vogel, "Stem Cells Are Coaxed to Produce Insulin," *Science* 192 [27 April 2001]: 615–16).

[22] Vogel, "Court Asked to Declare NIH Guidelines Legal," 1463.

[23] Glenn McGee, *The Perfect Baby: Parents in the Brave New World of Cloning and Genetics*, 2nd ed. (Lanham, MD: Rowman and Littlefield, 2000), 40, 48–50, 58–59.

[24] "Bush's Address on Federal Financing for Research with Embryonic Stem Cells," *The New York Times,* 10 August 2001.

[25] Gretchen Vogel, "At Odds Again over Stem Cells," *Science* (18 July 2003): 289; idem, "EU Stem Cell Debate Ends in a Draw," *Science* (12 December 2003): 1872–73.

[26] Ron Scherer, "States Race to Lead Stem-Cell Research," *Christian Science Monitor,* 25 February 2004; B. A. Robinson, "Stem Cell Research: All Sides to the Dispute," religioustolerance.org website (accessed 31 August 2004).

[27] Symonides, "New Human Rights Dimensions, Obstacles and Challenges," 18; McGee, *The Perfect Baby*; C. G. Weeramantry, "Human Rights and Scientific and Technological Progress," in Symonides, *Human Rights*, 243–64.

[28] Symonides, "New Human Rights Dimensions, Obstacles and Challenges," 18.

[29] Theodore Roosevelt, quoted in Rifkin, *The Biotech Century*, 117.

[30] Roger Gosden, *Designing Babies: The Brave New World of Reproductive Technology* (New York: W. H. Freeman, 1999), 5.

[31] Arthur Caplan, "Is Biomedical Research Too Dangerous to Pursue?" *Science* 303 (20 February 2004): 1142; A Report of the President's Council on Bioethics, *Beyond Therapy: Biotechnology and the Pursuit of Happiness* (Washington, DC, October 2003), bioethics.gov website (accessed 31 August 2004); Nicholas Wade, "Should We Improve Our Genome?" *The New York Times,* 11 November 2003.

[32] "Perfect?" *The Economist*, 14 April 2001, 15–16.

[33] Duane Elgin, *Awakening Earth: Exploring the Evolution of Human Culture and Consciousness* (New York: William Morrow, 1993).

[34] David Shenk, "Biocapitalism: What Price the Genetic Revolution?" *Harper's Magazine* (December 1997), 40.

[35] "Korean Cloner Admits Lying About Oocyte Donations," *Science* 310 (2 December 2005): 1402–4; "How Young Korean Researchers Helped Unearth a Scandal," *Science* 311 (6 January 2006): 22–25; "South Korean Team's Remaining Human Stem Cell Claim Demolished," *Science* 311 (13 January 2006): 156–57; Donald Kirk, "What's Next for Korea's Stem-cell Research?" *The Christian Science Monitor* (1 January 2006), 7.

[36] Francis Fukuyama, "In Defense of Nature, Human and Non-Human," *World Watch* (July/August 2002): 1–2; idem, *Our Posthuman Future: Consequences of the Biotechnology Revolution* (New York: Farrar, Straus and Giroux, 2002); Gina Kolata, "Researchers Find Big Risk of Defect in Cloning Animals: Random Genetic Errors," *The New York Times,* 15 March 2001, 1, 14.

[37] Pope John Paul II, speaking in Cracow, Poland, on 18 August 2002, lamented: "Modern civilization wishes to determine life through genetic manipulation and to establish the limit of death" (in Frank Bruni, "Pope Says Modern Mankind Is Usurping 'God's Place.'" *The New York Times,* 19 August 2002).

[38] Maxwell J. Mehlman and Jeffrey R. Botkin, *Access to the Genome: The Challenge to Equality* (Washington, DC: Georgetown Univ. Press, 1998).

[39] Stephen S. Hall, "President's Council on Bioethics Delivers," *Science* (19 July 2002): 297, 322–24; Cheryl Gay Stolberg "House Backs Ban on Human Cloning for Any Objective," *The New York Times*, 1 August 2002.

[40] Leon Kass, "Prepared Testimony before the House Judiciary Subcommittee on Crime," 7 June 2001, taken from Lexis-Nexis, 11 June 2002; see also Leon Kass, *Life, Liberty, and the Defense of Dignity: The Challenge for Bioethics* (San Francisco: Encounter Books, 2002), 130.

[41] Kass, "Prepared Testimony," 9.

[42] Ibid., 15.

[43] United States Senate Committee on Judiciary, "Drawing the Line between Ethical Regenerative Medicine and Immoral Human Reproductive Cloning," testimony of Dr. Leon Kass, 19 March 2003, judiciary.senate.gov website (accessed 31 August 2004).

[44] Germany bans all cloning but did not advocate that in the UN because it seemed unrealistic politically. See Gretchen Vogel, "UN Split over Full or Partial Cloning Ban," *Science* 298 (15 November 2002): 1316–17; Kirk Semple, "UN to Consider Whether to Ban Some, or All, Forms of Cloning of Human Embryos," *The New York Times*, 3 November 2003.

[45] E. B. Brody, *Biomedical Technology and Human Rights* (Paris: UNESCO; Cambridge: Dartmouth Publishing, 1993), 109, cited in Symonides, "New Human Rights Dimensions," 18; Meridith Villa, "Biotechnology and the Rights of the Unborn," undergraduate honors thesis, 8 May 2000, Barnard College, Columbia University.

[46] Wade, "Human Cloning Marches on without U.S. Help.

[47] Rick Weiss, "A Uniquely Human Debate: As Science Advances, Some Are Stating Their Cases for Freedom to Be Cloned," *The Washington Post National Weekly Edition*, 3–9 June 2002.

[48] Grace, *Biotechnology Unzipped,* 227–28.

[49] "Science and Profit," *The Economist,* 17 February 2001, 21–22.

[50] Richard Pierre Claude, "Human Rights in the Lab: The Science Provisions of the ESC Covenant," presentation to the Columbia University Seminar on Human Rights, 12 April 1999.

[51] Merrill Goozner, "Patenting Life," *The American Prospect,* 18 December 2000, 23–25; Rifkin, *The Biotech Century,* 41–45; Jerome Groopmen, "Who Wants to Live Forever?" *The New York Times*, 20 December 1999.

[52] Andrew Shapiro, quoted in Shenk, "Biocapitalism," 45; see also, Lee M. Silver, *Remaking Eden: Cloning and Beyond in a Brave New World* (New York: Avon Books, 1998), 294–308.

[53] Tom Athanasiou and Marcy Damovsky, "The Genome as Commons," *World Watch* (July/August 2002), 35.

[54] Silver, *Remaking Eden.*

[55] Wade, "Should We Improve Our Genome?"

10

Affordable and Accessible Drugs for Developing Countries

Recent Developments

Ruth Macklin

INTRODUCTION

Scholars in human rights and public health have identified several different provisions in human rights instruments as a basis for the claim that there exists a right to health care as well as the more difficult to attain "right to health."[1] Principal among these is Article 25 of the Universal Declaration of Human Rights (UDHR), which explicitly recognizes a claim to health: "Everyone has the right to a standard of living adequate for the health and well-being of himself and his family, including food, clothing, housing and medical care and necessary social services, and the right to security in the event of unemployment, sickness, disability, widowhood, old age or other lack of livelihood in circumstances beyond his control." Article 27 of the UDHR identifies another pathway to a right to health: "Everyone has the right freely . . . to share in scientific advancement and its benefits." To share in the benefits of scientific advancement "underscores the rights of the general public"[2] and can be interpreted to mean that the fruits of biomedical research must be made available to everyone who needs information or products developed in such research.

Portions of this chapter are published in Ruth Macklin, *Double Standards in Medical Research in Developing Countries* (Cambridge Univ. Press, 2004).

The ICESCR addresses "the right of everyone to the highest attainable standard of physical and mental health," requiring states to take certain defined steps, including "the prevention, treatment and control of epidemic, endemic, occupational and other diseases" and "the creation of conditions which would assure to all medical service and medical attention in the event of sickness" (Art. 12). The wording of the Article recalls the preamble of the 1946 constitution of WHO: "The enjoyment of the highest attainable standard of health is one of the fundamental rights of every human being without distinction of race, religion, political belief, economic or social conditions."[3]

How can these fundamental human rights claims regarding health care and health be realized in the poorest countries in the world today, given the prevalence of diseases that are difficult to prevent and costly to treat? And which actors should play a role in the progressive realization of these rights? Before turning to these questions, let me provide a brief reminder of some basic facts about biomedical research and its aftermath in developing countries.

RESEARCH IN DEVELOPING COUNTRIES
CONDUCTED BY INDUSTRIALIZED SPONSORS

Despite longstanding and widespread knowledge of the devastating toll diseases continue to take on populations in the developing world, industrialized nations have largely avoided playing an active role in seeking to improve the health status of people in poor countries. Although it is true that the United States and European countries have for many years conducted or sponsored biomedical research in developing countries, once the research was concluded, the sponsors— wealthy countries as well as industry—considered their work done. An awakening in recent years began with a recognition that "safari research," as it has been critically termed, comes close to being a form of exploitation of poor countries and their populations, from which research subjects are recruited. Researchers and sponsors have now recognized an obligation to "leave something behind" when the research is completed. The chief means for implementing this obligation has taken the form of helping developing countries build their own capacity to conduct research independently. Elements of capacity building include training scientists and other research personnel, contributing to the research and health-care infrastructure in the community or country, and most recently, providing training for scientific and ethical review of research. Although establishing and strengthening scientific and technological capacity in developing countries was stated as an obligation in a United Nations declaration more than a quarter of a century ago,[4] only recently has this obligation been affirmed and taken seriously by governmental and industrial sponsors of research in developing countries.

As beneficial as capacity building is for poor countries, it is far from a sufficient means of ameliorating the conditions created by historically prevalent diseases, such as malaria and tuberculosis, and in the past two decades, the HIV/AIDS pandemic. African nations have been hardest hit by AIDS, with an estimated more than 4 million HIV-infected individuals currently living in South Africa. The next area predicted to experience an explosion of the epidemic is Asia, with the huge populations of China and India at risk of spread from relatively small numbers currently infected to the general population. It is abundantly clear that as important as are education and behavioral interventions to prevent the spread of HIV infection, they have not been successful in containing the disease. Antiretroviral therapy, now reasonably effective in prolonging the lives of HIV-infected people in most industrialized countries, has so far been available only to a tiny minority of wealthy individuals in all developing countries except Brazil. Since 1997 the Brazilian government has been providing free antiretrovirals to the general population. In 1998 Brazil began to make copies of brand-name drugs to treat AIDS that are protected by patents in the United States but not in Brazil. However, the domestic capacity to manufacture antiretroviral drugs does not exist in most countries in Africa and Asia and is unlikely to be developed in the foreseeable future.

Thus, what are the ethically desirable options, and what steps have already been taken to make drugs affordable and accessible to developing countries? Alice Page in this volume describes the rather new development of negotiating prior agreements before initiating sponsored research in developing countries. In this chapter I outline four other recent developments that involve both governments and non-state actors: (1) the decision by some large pharmaceutical manufacturers to donate drugs free of cost or to reduce the price of anti-AIDS drugs; (2) differential pricing of drugs by manufacturers; (3) public-private partnerships; and (4) a (partial) retreat by the pharmaceutical industry from its earlier firm stance on patent protections.

Donation of Drugs by Pharmaceutical Industry

Several pharmaceutical companies have made outright donations of free drugs, primarily for medications to treat or reduce the incidence of HIV. Boehringer-Ingelheim offered to provide Nevirapene, a relatively inexpensive drug demonstrated to be effective in reducing maternal-to-child HIV infection; and Pfizer agreed to provide a drug in South Africa to AIDS patients affected by cryptococcal meningitis.[5] While these companies can be commended for their charitable acts, as "they represent an assumption of moral agency and moral responsibility by corporations," a critical view holds that "dependence on charity morally degrades the individual, by fostering dependence, promoting an attitude of humility toward the giver, and relieving the recipient of the ability to set terms and negotiate the terms of receipt."[6] Despite the apparent good will demonstrated by these charitable acts, this approach cannot possibly meet the needs of the populations in resource-poor countries.

Differential Pricing

Differential pricing (also called equity pricing or preferential pricing) is defined as "setting the price of essential drugs in a way that reflects countries' ability to pay, as measured by their level of income."[7] This concept must be distinguished from that in which different countries charge different prices for the same drugs—a variation that results from differences in government policies on the regulation of the drug market, tax policies, import duties, wholesale and retails markups, and so on. Different prices for drugs in various countries are typically not the result of a deliberate and systematic international policy, whereas differential pricing has precisely that structure. The aim of a policy of differential pricing is *to enable low-income countries to gain access to essential drugs for their populations.*[8] In low-income countries both the government and the majority of the population are unable to afford drugs that are needed for a variety of treatable conditions.

According to WHO, "Essential drugs are those drugs that satisfy the health care needs of the majority of the population, they should therefore be available at all times in adequate amounts, and in the appropriate dosage forms, and at a price that individuals and the community can afford."[9] WHO contends that public budgets for essential drugs could be increased, as governments of developing countries are responsible for the performance and regulation of the health system. However, prices are set by manufacturers, based largely on what the market will bear, especially when pharmaceutical products are under patent protection for a defined period during which there is little or no competition and prices are higher. Moreover, companies make most of their money from selling their drugs in high-income countries, and this has led to much less investment in research and development for products that would primarily be used in developing countries, such as much-needed anti-malarial drugs.

One need not be a thoroughgoing critic of the capitalist system to question whether there ought to be some exceptions to the rule that everything has a price, and the price ought to be set by the free-market economy. The sale and purchase of some things is altogether prohibited: human babies, for one example, and one's vote (at least in non-corrupt, democratic countries), for another. Until the accelerating trend in the 1990s toward privatization, European countries considered the health-care system to be exempt from the free-market system that operated for other commercial products. The US government has continued to treat health care as a commodity, with the exception of the two government-financed programs, Medicare for the elderly, and Medicaid for the poor.

Early efforts to reduce the high price of AIDS drugs were made by the Joint United Nations Programme on HIV/AIDS (UNAIDS). In 1997 UNAIDS began a collaborative effort that involved three pharmaceutical companies and health officials in Chile, Côte d'Ivoire, Uganda, and Vietnam. Despite this initiative, prices for antiretroviral drugs remained too high for most people in these countries. This marked the beginning of a trend, however, with manufacturers of antiretrovirals beginning successive lowering of prices.

It is hard to pinpoint the exact moment when the campaign began to convince drug companies to reduce the price of life-prolonging, health-preserving AIDS drugs for poor countries. In February 2001 Oxfam, a charity based in Oxford, England, began a campaign to force multinational drug companies to cut prices in poor countries. The charity did not limit its appeal to HIV/AIDS but included other drugs such as powerful antibiotics. In addition, Oxfam attacked the patent laws that have not permitted poor countries to import cheap, generic drugs from other countries without fear of retaliation.[10]

In early March 2001, Merck, one of the largest pharmaceutical companies, offered to sell two of its AIDS drugs to developing countries at much lower prices; it offered to sell Crixivan for $600 per patient per year and Stocrin for $500 per patient per year, while the prices in the United States were $6,000 and $4,700, respectively. Shortly thereafter, Merck agreed to cut the prices in Brazil, but not as much as in other developing countries ($1,029 for Crixivan and $920 for Stocrin); it claimed that its decision on which countries would qualify for its lowest price was based on the United Nations Human Development Index. The company's decision for Brazil was described as "bowing to pressure from that country's government, which was threatening to develop generic copies of one of the drugs." The Brazilian government also exerted pressure on Hoffmann-La Roche, a manufacturer of another AIDS drug, to lower its price.[11]

Altogether, between March and May 2001, the companies that agreed to sell their AIDS drugs at significantly reduced prices in developing countries were Merck, GlaxoSmithKline, Bristol-Myers Squibb, and Abbott Laboratories. In May 2001 Novartis, a Swiss drug company, agreed to cut the price of Riamet, a powerful medicine to treat malaria, for sale to WHO. Priced at about twelve dollars in industrialized countries, Novartis agreed to sell the drug to WHO for two dollars for a full treatment.[12]

It is natural to be skeptical—or even cynical—about the motivation of drug companies in reducing their prices or even giving away anti-AIDS drugs for free. However, recalling John Stuart Mill's words that—"utilitarian moralists have gone beyond almost all others in affirming that the motive has nothing to do with the morality of the action, though much with the worth of the agent"[13]—one can assert that reducing the prices of the drugs they manufacture can succeed in making beneficial treatments affordable and accessible to the world's poor, then it matters little if industry's CEOs made such decisions in order to enhance their image and prestige, or whether they did so from unalloyed altruism.

However, the approach of reducing prices can be faulted for some of the same reasons that donations of free drugs are ethically problematic: "Such offers are fraught with conditions, time and quantity based limitations and a continuing dependence of developing country's health care planning on the good-will of commercial organizations."[14] Ethical criticism aside, this piecemeal approach is hardly sufficient to meet the demand for drugs in the many developing countries. Big, international pharmaceutical companies are significant actors in the field of medicine and health, but acting alone they cannot realistically be expected to shoulder the burden.

Nevertheless, differential pricing is a big step. Yet, many questions are unanswered and details need to be addressed: How should priorities be set, both for health problems and particular products? Which countries should benefit from the scheme? What should be the role of international agreements? Who would be responsible for financing differentially priced drugs? How can developed countries be persuaded not to demand the same low prices?[15] In addition to these questions related to equity pricing, fighting the global burden of disease would require other simultaneous efforts.

Public-Private Partnerships

The 1990s witnessed a large growth in the formation of public-private partnerships, including the Global Alliance for Vaccines and Immunization (GAVI), the International AIDS Vaccine Initiative, and the Global Fund to Fight AIDS, Tuberculosis and Malaria. These and similar organizations operate by using funds to support research directed at products. They work more like investments than like grants, the projects being managed much as they would be in an industrial portfolio. The industrial partners in these ventures benefit by using patents that result from their collaboration to develop products that they can sell more profitably in industrialized countries. The commitment they make by entering into the partnership is to provide products to developing countries at reasonable prices. The establishment of these partnerships is a response to the failure of reliance on industry and market forces to bring health benefits in the form of drugs, vaccines and other medical products to poor people in developing countries. A related factor contributing to the establishment of public-private partnerships has been the restrictions posed by intellectual property rights.[16]

The failure of market forces to meet the needs of developing countries is illustrated by the lack of availability of vaccines for children in resource-poor countries. This failure is especially noteworthy since vaccines have traditionally been cheaper to manufacture and distribute than most other medications. One report notes that the pharmaceutical industry has had little interest in vaccines, despite their great public health value. As of 2000, vaccine sales constitute only 4 percent of the more than $400 billion per year pharmaceutical market.[17] According to WHO, in 1998 one in four children throughout the world did not receive routine immunization with the six basic vaccines against polio, diphtheria, whooping cough, tetanus, measles, and tuberculosis.

The proportion of children immunized each year against these six diseases declined between 1990 and 1998.[18]

In 1999 GAVI was established to ensure the protection of children against diseases that can be prevented by vaccines. GAVI promotes new vaccine development, coordinates existing immunization programs, and works at international, regional, and national levels with a special concern over accelerating research and development of vaccines for developing countries. According to GAVI, three widening gaps need to be addressed:

- the children who are still not receiving the "basic six" immunizations as compared to those who are reached through the polio-eradication initiative;
- the growing disparity in the number of vaccines available to children in industrialized and developing countries;
- the lack of investment in vaccine research and development for diseases that are prevalent in poorer countries.

GAVI has succeeded in attracting numerous public and private partners for this effort, including the United Nations agencies, WHO, the World Bank, and UNICEF; private foundations, the Bill and Melinda Gates Children's Vaccine Program, and the Rockefeller Foundation; the industry group, International Federation of Pharmaceutical Manufacturers Association; as well as public health and research institutions and national governments. One of the mechanisms GAVI has established is the Vaccine Fund, which provides direct support to countries in two forms. The first is provision of new and under-used vaccines, accompanied by safe immunization equipment; the second is in the form of funds to assist governments in strengthening their immunization services.[19] GAVI is a good illustration of a successful alliance among public and private partners that has already demonstrated the ability to raise funds and provide them directly for necessary vaccine products and services.

An equally promising newer development in forging public-private partnerships is the initiative taken by several United Nations agencies and the establishment of the Global Fund to Fight AIDS, Tuberculosis and Malaria. The call for creation of a huge fund to combat diseases that kill or disable millions of people in poor countries came from both Gro Harlem Brundtland, then the director general of WHO, and Kofi Annan, the secretary-general of the United Nations. Both leaders envisaged the need for commitments from government in rich and poor countries alike, as well as from private foundations, nongovernmental agencies, and the private sector to mount this effort. The effort would require funds not only for the purchase of drugs from manufacturers, but also to mount better education and prevention programs, build new clinics or enhance existing ones, train health care workers, and strengthen the infrastructure in other ways.[20]

Secretary-General Kofi Annan called for the establishment of a global fund on AIDS and health at the Organization of African Unity summit in Abuja in April 2001 and urged greater coordination among nations and a strong political and financial commitment to support efforts to combat AIDS.[21] A United Nations General Assembly Special Session on HIV/AIDS took place in New York in June 2001, and the UN adopted a declaration of commitment that set out clear goals for a global battle against HIV/AIDS. As of September 2004, pledges to the Global Health Fund have totaled more than $5.6 billion, the majority being from governments, including rather poor African countries such as Uganda, Rwanda, and Zimbabwe. Other donors included the European Commission, corporations, private individuals, and the Bill and Melinda Gates Foundation, which contributed $150,000,000.[22]

In May 2000, WHO and UNAIDS together launched a program called the Accelerated Access Initiative, which called for improved access to antiretroviral drugs to treat HIV/AIDS. Several major companies responded to this call, providing evidence that industry appears ready to lower prices to ensure equity pricing, as well as to collaborate with other partners to increase availability of their products. International public-private partnerships have also resulted in companies making drug donations to poor countries for such conditions as African sleeping sickness, malaria, and leprosy.[23]

The Commission on Macroeconomics and Health proposes as the next step forward a joint agreement among pharmaceutical companies and low-income countries, in collaboration with WHO, to set guidelines for pricing and licensing of production of drugs for the low-income countries. These guidelines would "provide for transparent mechanisms of differential pricing that would target low-income countries . . . and identify a designated set of essential medicines . . . at the lowest viable commercial prices."[24] Although the proposed arrangements would be voluntary, they would need to be backed up by safeguards in order to ensure implementation. The only safeguard currently in place is the mechanism of "compulsory licensing" specified in the world trade system as part of the Trade-Related Aspects of Intellectual Property Rights (TRIPS) agreement.

WTO, TRIPS, and Patents

The TRIPS agreement of the WTO requires all member countries to respect the patents held by pharmaceutical and biotechnology companies and to pass laws respecting medical patents. However, there is one provision than enables countries to make an exception to this rule. That provision permits countries to manufacture copies of patented drugs in case of a "national emergency." The mechanism for this is to obtain a "compulsory license" to make a generic copy of a drug; the patent holder is paid a reasonable royalty under this arrangement. Somewhat less certain under this provision has been the ability of a country to import a generic copy of a patented drug. An obvious question is what constitutes a national emergency. Arguably, the AIDS epidemic in countries with a high prevalence rate would qualify. Does the same hold for countries with a high incidence and prevalence of malaria and tuberculosis?

Drug companies and their international umbrella organization, the International Federation of Pharmaceutical Manufacturers Associations, have long resisted efforts to invoke the provision that would allow countries to make or import generic copies of patented drugs under the compulsory licensing clause. Over a four-year period the United States has come to soften its initial strong opposition to allowing South Africa (and by implication, other countries) from seeking compulsory licensing for AIDS drugs. In 1997 South Africa amended its laws to allow compulsory licensing, and an array of pharmaceutical companies brought suit against the country. The Clinton administration exerted pressure on the South African government to withdraw or modify this law.[25] As a result of bad publicity, the Clinton administration eventually withdrew its opposition, but the pharmaceutical manufacturers' lawsuit continued.

Despite expectations, the pro-business Bush administration did not reverse the softened US stance with respect to South Africa, and the thirty-nine drug multinational companies that had brought suit against South Africa began to negotiate to settle the lawsuit, especially after the European Union, WHO, and the National AIDS Council in France publicly supported South Africa's position.[26] In April 2001 the companies withdrew their suit, thus allowing South Africa to import cheaper anti-AIDS drugs and other medications.

This move did not end other ongoing battles, however. Since 1998 Brazil had already been a major challenger to the international pharmaceutical industry by copying and manufacturing AIDS drugs. State-owned laboratories in that country have produced generic copies of several patented AIDS drugs. In India, private companies, including Cipla, Ltd., are engaged in manufacturing generic drugs. In May 2001 the Bush administration threatened trade sanctions against Brazil, but the head of the Brazilian HIV/AIDS program called the US position "unacceptable."[27]

With the annual, controversy-provoking Ministerial Conference of the WTO due to take place in November 2001, the expectation was that the WTO would reiterate its firm stance on the TRIPS agreement, thereby continuing to make it extremely difficult for countries to obtain compulsory licenses to manufacture or import needed drugs for which patents are held by industry. Unexpectedly, however, the anthrax scare in the United States in October prompted a rethinking of the existing structure of patent protections. Although the United States resisted overriding the patent for an anti-anthrax drug, Cipro, held by Bayer, A.G., the Canadian government did just that by ordering a million tablets of a generic version of the drug from a Canadian company on the grounds that "these are extraordinary and unusual times. Canadians expect and demand that their government will take all steps necessary to protect their health and safety." Bayer, the manufacturer of Cipro, condemned Canada's action.[28]

With these developments as a backdrop, it was natural to wonder what would transpire at the WTO meeting in November 2001. Advocates of compulsory licensing have argued that this is the best alternative among efforts designed to provide essential drugs to developing countries, especially for AIDS. The authors of one article argue that "making use of the . . . TRIPS provision or even breaking international trade agreements might be a given developing country's most effective means of providing life-saving medication time-efficiently to its people."[29] Bio-ethicist Dan Brock concurs:

> When developing countries choose not to respect product patents as their only effective means of making available pharmaceuticals necessary to save lives and protect the

health of their citizens, doing so is arguably a step forward
to greater justice between the developed and developing
world; this may be a case where two wrongs make a right,
that is where existing global injustices make not respecting
product patents, which in the absence of those injustices
would be wrong, all things considered, morally justified.[30]

Others have leveled strong criticism at the United States for supporting the WTO agreement and imposing or threatening to impose
trade sanctions on developing countries that have sought to produce
or import inexpensive generic copies of drugs. Oxfam International
issued a briefing paper early in November 2001, entitled "Eight Broken Promises: Why the WTO Isn't Working for the World's Poor."[31]
Broken promise 6—"Global patent rules that safeguard public health
in poor countries"—charges the United States and other industrialized countries not only with threatening the health of vulnerable communities in developing countries but also of "extreme double
standards," because "the U.S. and Canadian governments have shown
themselves willing to threaten to override patents at home when faced
with bio-terrorist threats to their own citizens. Although no compulsory licenses for patented antibiotics were eventually issued, the threat
of purchasing low-cost generics was successfully used to bargain down
prices." The Oxfam paper recommended that the social and develop-
mental objectives of TRIPS should be paramount; health obligations
should take precedence over intellectual property rights; and governments should have an absolute right to introduce compulsory licenses
in order to meet pressing public-health needs, and to import patented
drugs from the cheapest source.

The Declaration on the TRIPS Agreement and Public Health, issued at the WTO Ministerial Conference on 14 November 2001, was
not the best that might have been achieved. Nevertheless, it is an improvement over the previous situation, which left much uncertainty, if
not a presumption against the right of developing countries to gain
access to much-needed drugs. Paragraph 4 of the declaration states:

We agree that the TRIPS Agreement does not and should
not prevent Members from taking measures to protect public health. Accordingly, while reiterating our commitment
to the TRIPS Agreement, we affirm that the Agreement can
and should be interpreted and implemented in a manner

supportive of WTO Members' right to protect public health and, in particular to promote access to medicines for all.[32]

Paragraph 5 specifies that "each Member has the right to grant compulsory licenses and the freedom to determine the grounds upon which such licenses are granted" and "each Member has the right to determine what constitutes a national emergency or other circumstances of extreme urgency, it being understood that public health crises, including those relating to HIV/AIDS, tuberculosis, malaria and other epidemics, can represent a national emergency or other circumstances of extreme urgency." These statements make it explicit that the developing countries themselves are the ones to make determinations regarding compulsory licensing and national emergencies, surely an improvement over the previous situation. What, then, are the shortcomings of the declaration on the TRIPS agreement?

The declaration does not go far enough, as it still contains a prohibition against importing inexpensive, generic drugs from countries that have the capability of manufacturing them. Paragraph 6 states:

> We recognize that WTO members with insufficient or no manufacturing capacities in the pharmaceutical sector could face difficulties in making effective use of compulsory licensing under the TRIPS Agreement. We instruct the Council for TRIPS to find an expeditious solution to this problem and to report to the General Council before the end of 2002.

In effect, the Ministerial Conference sent this important issue back to committee. The net effect is that India and Brazil, probably also Thailand and China, and possibly a very few other developing countries will be able to manufacture affordable generic medications for their own populations. It remains uncertain just what will happen if these countries seek to export the generic drugs to the much larger number of developing countries (which are also much poorer). An executive of India's largest pharmaceutical company was said to have predicted that multinational drug companies would strongly resist any attempt on the part of generic drug makers like those in India to export their copies of drugs for which the big manufacturers in the West hold patents.[33]

Even more dismaying is the fact that the poorest countries would not be able to afford even these much less expensive drugs. In a poor country such as Uganda—where the per capita governmental expenditure on health care is estimated at US$8–12 per year—the new declaration on TRIPS, the Global Health Fund, and the charitable donations or price reductions by multinational drug companies, taken all together, will not be able to meet the needs.

HUMAN RIGHTS AND ACCESS TO DRUGS

How far do these recent developments go in fulfilling the UDHR claims that "everyone has the right freely . . . to share in scientific advancement and its benefits" and "the right of everyone to the highest attainable standard of physical and mental health." It is evident that the actions of pharmaceutical companies in giving away free drugs and lowering the prices of some drugs, however commendable, are insufficient to provide necessary medications for "everyone" in developing countries. These actions by drug companies are only a small step toward what George Andreopoulos calls the "progressive realization of everyone's right to enjoy the benefits of scientific progress and its applications."[34]

Applying the human rights responsibilities set forth by Andreopoulos would help in assessing the adequacy of the other initiatives:

a) governments of developing countries incur responsibilities under human rights instruments for the progressive realization of everyone's right to enjoy the benefits of scientific progress and its applications;

b) the realization of this right exists independently of the increase in resources; it requires effective use of available resources;

c) the international community incurs certain responsibilities to provide—through international cooperation and assistance—resources enabling developing countries to fulfill their obligations under the relevant human rights instruments;

d) the above-mentioned responsibilities include the more equitable distribution of the benefits of science;

e) the responsibilities of host country governments and those of the international community are clearly interrelated; and

f) non-state agents (for example, non-state sponsoring agencies) incur certain responsibilities under existing international human rights instruments.[35]

The establishment of the Global Health Fund to fight AIDS, Tuberculosis and Malaria is a much larger step in fulfilling several of the
responsibilities noted by Andreopoulos's item (a), but even Uganda
and Zimbabwe contributed to the fund; as specified in (c), many industrialized countries have contributed to the fund, as have international organizations; and as for item (f), private foundations and a few
corporations were among the contributors.

The WTO declaration of 14 November 2001 is certainly an improvement over the previous version of the TRIPS agreement. However, the
restrictions stated in paragraph 6, which limits the ability of developing countries without their own manufacturing capabilities to import
generic drugs manufactured in other countries, fails to meet a human
rights test on two counts. First, it fails in the necessary steps for the
progressive realization of everyone's right to enjoy the benefits of scientific progress, as stipulated by Andreopoulos (a), since it undermines
the "effective use of available resources" (b) in industrial countries.

The second count of failure in the recent declaration pertains to
"the right of everyone to the highest attainable standard of physical
and mental health." If the opportunity to import cheaper medications
is disallowed, developing countries cannot fulfill their own human
rights responsibility.

Moreover, conceptual, ethical, and policy questions remain to be
resolved, and require further study and discussion. How can it be determined when the highest attainable standard of health has been
reached? Against which measures is "highest attainable" to be defined?
How should priorities be set among the competing health-related needs
in developing countries, and what role, if any, should donor nations
and international organizations play in promoting some priorities over
others in working with ministries of health in developing countries?
Making drugs more affordable to the populations in developing countries is only a first step toward realization of the human right to health,
but it is a giant step.

Numerous factors besides lack of money hinder access to drugs in
many developing countries, although poverty is the single most important reason why people in developing countries cannot obtain the drugs
they need.[36] These other factors include inefficiency and waste in health

care delivery systems, inadequate systems for distribution of drugs within a country, lack of reliable scientific information and appropriate education and training of health-care personnel, and local perceptions and beliefs about illness and medicine. The relatively poor health-care infrastructure in many developing countries is a leading factor that inhibits access to drugs by large numbers of people. These diverse barriers to adequate access to much-needed drugs cannot readily be removed, even if cheaper medications are made available and the Global Fund provides financing for drugs to treat AIDS, malaria, and tuberculosis.

These background conditions underscore the salient responsibility of industrialized countries to contribute to capacity building in developing countries. As noted earlier, the UN Declaration on the Use of Scientific and Technological Progress includes a provision that states the responsibility of governments to "co-operate in the establishment, strengthening and development of the scientific and technological capacity of developing countries with a view to accelerating the realization of the social and economic rights of the peoples of those countries."[37] Moreover, this responsibility is not confined to governments. The huge pharmaceutical companies that conduct drug trials in developing countries (and reap the financial rewards) have the same responsibility, as do individual biomedical researchers from industrialized countries, whether sponsored by the public or private sector.

NOTES

[1] Jonathan M. Mann, "Medicine and Public Health, Ethics and Human Rights," *Hastings Center Report* 27, no. 3 (1997); Lawrence O. Gostin and Zita Lazzarini, *Human Rights and Public Health in the AIDS Pandemic* (New York: Oxford Univ. Press, 1997); George Andreopoulos, "Declarations and Covenants of Human Rights and International Codes of Research Ethics," in *Biomedical Research Ethics: Updating International Guidelines,* ed. Robert Levine and Samuel Gorovitz with James Gallagher (Geneva: Council for International Organizations of Medical Sciences, 2001).

[2] Andreopoulos, "Declarations and Covenants," 191.

[3] In Gostin and Lazzarini, *Human Rights and Public Health,* 5.

[4] UN Declaration on the Use of Scientific and Technological Progress, cited in Andreopoulos, "Declarations and Covenants," 193.

[5] Udo Schüklenk and Richard E. Ashcroft, "Affordable Access to Essential Medication in Developing Countries: Conflicts between Ethical and Eco-

nomic Imperatives," *Journal of Medicine and Philosophy* 27, no. 2 (2002): 179–95.

[6] Ibid., 186–87.

[7] WHO Secretariat, "More Equitable Pricing for Essential Drugs: What Do We Mean and What Are the Issues?" background paper for WHO-WTO secretariat workshop on differential pricing and financing of essential drugs, Hosbjor, Norway, 8–11 April 2001 (paper dated 30 March 2001).

[8] Ibid.

[9] WHO, "The Use of Essential Drugs," WHO Technical Report Series 895 (Geneva: WHO, 2000).

[10] Donald G. McNeil, Jr., "Oxfam Joins Campaign to Cut Drug Prices for Poor Nations," *The New York Times*, 13 February 2001, A6.

[11] Melody Petersen and Larry Rohter, "Maker Agrees to Cut Price of Two AIDS Drugs in Brazil," *The New York Times*, 31 March 2001, A4.

[12] Melody Petersen, "Novartis Agrees to Lower Price of a Medicine Used in Africa," *The New York Times*, 3 May 2001, C1.

[13] John Stuart Mill, *Utilitarianism* (1863; Indianapolis: The Liberal Arts Press, 1957), 23–24.

[14] Schüklenk and Ashcroft, "Affordable Access to Essential Medication in Developing Countries," 186.

[15] These and other questions, with some proposed answers, are provided in WHO Secretariat, "More Equitable Pricing for Essential Drugs." The report concludes that the most feasible approach would be having two broad price bands—one for low-income countries, the other for the rest of world.

[16] Gordon Conway, "Biotechnology and the War on Poverty," in *Biotechnology and Sustainable Development: Voices of the South and North,* ed. Ismail Serageldin and G. J. Persley (Wallingford, Oxford: CABI Publishers, 2003).

[17] Ibid., 18.

[18] WHO, *WHO Vaccine Preventable Diseases Monitoring System, 1999 Global Summary* (Geneva: WHO, 2000).

[19] For more information, see the GAVI website, www.vaccinealliance.org.

[20] Barbara Crossette, "A Wider War on AIDS in Africa and Asia," *The New York Times*, 30 April 2001, A6.

[21] Joint United Nations Programme on HIV/AIDS (UNAIDS), www.aegis.com/news/unaids/2001/UN010625.html.

[22] For the pledges and contributions, see the theglobalfund.org website (accessed 31 August 2004).

[23] Commission on Macroeconomics and Health, *Macroeconomics and Health: Investing in Health for Economic Development* (Geneva: WHO, 2004), www.un.org/esa/coordination/ecosoc/docs/RT.K.MacroeconomicsHealth.pdf (accessed 31 August 2004).

[24] Ibid., 89.

[25] Tina Rosenberg, "Look at Brazil," *The New York Times Magazine*, 28 January 2001.

[26] Rachel L. Swarns, "Companies Begin Talks with South Africa on Drug Suit," *The New York Times*, 18 April 2001, A3.

[27] Barbara Crossette, "Brazil's AIDS Chief Denounces Bush Position on Drug Patents," *The New York Times*, 3 May 2001, A5.

[28] Amy Harmon and Robert Pear, "Canada Overrides Patent for Cipro to Treat Anthrax," *The New York Times*, 10 October 2001, A1.

[29] Schüklenk and Ashcroft, "Affordable Access to Essential Medication in Developing Countries," 191.

[30] Dan Brock, "Some Questions about the Moral Responsibilities of Drug Companies," *Developing World Bioethics* 1 (2001): 33–37.

[31] Oxfam, "Eight Broken Promises: Why the WTO Isn't Working for the World's Poor?" (Oxford: Oxfam, 2001), www.oxfam.org.uk/what_we_do/issues/trade/bp09_8broken.htm (accessed 31 August 2004).

[32] WTO, Declaration on the TRIPS Agreement and Public Health, Ministerial Conference, 14 November 2001, WT/MIN(01/DEC/W/2).

[33] Celia W. Dugger, "A Catch-22 on Drugs for the World's Poor," *The New York Times*, 16 November 2001, W1, 7.

[34] Andreopoulos, "Declarations and Covenants," 196.

[35] Ibid.

[36] Richard Laing, "Improving Access to Essential Drugs," talk presented to The World Bank on 28 February 2000.

[37] Cited in Andreopoulos, "Declarations and Covenants," 193.

11

Prior Agreements in International Clinical Trials

Ensuring the Benefits of Research to Developing Countries

Alice Page

INTRODUCTION

This chapter examines the use of prior agreements in international clinical trials as a way to promote the human right to health by ensuring the provision of drugs and other research benefits to developing countries where research is conducted. Post-trial access to the benefits of research is an issue that has not yet had the benefit of careful study and public discussion. Agreements on making research benefits available to host countries after a study is completed have begun to surface

This paper was originally prepared as a commissioned paper for the National Bioethics Advisory Commission (NBAC). Substantial portions of the paper were adopted by the commission and appear in either identical or similar form in its report (NBAC, *Ethical and Policy Issues in International Research: Clinical Trials in Developing Countries* [Bethesda, MD: NBAC, 2001]). A revised and expanded version of the paper was published in *Yale Journal of Health Policy, Law, and Ethics* 3 (December 2002), 35. Finally, the paper was revised in conjunction with the author's presentation at the Columbia University Seminar on Human Rights in December 2001. The views expressed herein are solely those of the author.

in international clinical trials only recently, and thus they are limited in number.

The chapter rests upon two closely related assumptions that are well documented in international research ethics guidelines. First, clinical research conducted by an industrialized country in a developing country should be responsive to the health needs and priorities of the population on which it is carried out.[1] The research should aim, in other words, to improve the health of the population from which the research participants are drawn. Second, the developing host country, not just the research participants, should benefit from the research.[2] This obligation can be characterized as a means of applying or implementing the first premise. Unless there is a reasonable likelihood that the intervention proven effective in a particular study will be made available to the population on which it was tested in the foreseeable future, research cannot be responsive to the health needs of that population or be expected to improve its health.[3]

Both of these assumptions are grounded in distributive justice, an important ethical principle that, in the research context, demands that no one group or class of persons assume the risks and inconveniences of research if that group or class is unlikely to benefit in the future from the fruits of that research. However, these assumptions can also be linked to two separate but closely related human rights: the right to health and the right of all people to share in the benefits of scientific advancement. Both rights are firmly established in the Universal Declaration of Human Rights (UDHR) and the International Covenant on Economic, Social, and Cultural Rights (ICESCR) (see Chapter 9 in this volume). The individual right to health is dependent upon the right of all people to share in the benefits of scientific advancement. Clinical research involving human participants can improve human health and welfare by advancing scientific knowledge and understanding of disease. It then follows that individuals are entitled to enjoy the benefits of clinical research, and that, more specifically, successful interventions and other research benefits must be made widely available to those who need them.

Access to health care plays an important role in the human right to health. In the developing world, however, extreme poverty and a disproportionately high burden of disease impede access to health care. Given the limited individual capacity for realization of the right to health, participation in research may be the only means by which the poor in developing countries can obtain medical care. Research conducted in developing countries by researchers and sponsors from the industrialized world often occurs "under conditions of unequal bargaining power, information, and human need."[4] Many interventions are well beyond the economic reach of both individuals and their governments, and there is a growing concern about the need to protect developing countries from exploitation by ensuring that they receive a more equitable share of the benefits of research. Yet, one of the most difficult challenges in research conducted in the developing world is crafting practical and economically feasible solutions that promote human rights.

The principal focus of international human rights instruments is the relationship between the state and the individual. However, a variety of actors incur human rights obligations when research is conducted in the developing world. The governments of developing countries have a responsibility to act in ways that will enable their populations to share in the benefits of research while, at the same time, the international community has a duty to help those governments fulfill their obligations. Human rights obligations are also imposed upon non-state actors in research. For example, a pharmaceutical company or an international health organization may influence the capacity for realization of individual human rights, and it too incurs responsibilities for the benefit of developing country populations.[5]

HOW PRIOR AGREEMENTS CAN BE USED TO MAKE RESEARCH BENEFITS AVAILABLE

The term *prior agreements,* or alternatively, *community benefit agreements,* generally refers to the arrangements made before the research begins and that lay out a realistic plan for making effective interventions or other research benefits available to the host country after the study is completed. The use of the term *agreement* generally is not meant to have any legal connotation, although some of these agreements may be legally binding instruments. It is difficult to formulate general rules regarding the nature and scope of prior agreements. Every study conducted is unique, and the needs and circumstances of developing countries vary greatly and can be expected to change and evolve over time.

The parties to these agreements usually include some combination of producers, research sponsors, and potential users of effective interventions or other research benefits. Industry, academia, and organizations of various kinds are frequently producers and sponsors in these arrangements, while developing country governments and nonprofit health organizations are most likely to be users. Since researchers are not directly responsible for providing effective interventions to host countries (they neither control research funds nor are they policymakers), they may not be parties to these agreements. However, researchers from both industrialized and developing countries still have an important role as advocates to ensure that issues pertaining to post-trial obligations are fully considered as part of protocol development and review.

Questions related to the representation of the study population in the negotiation process also need to be addressed. Researchers serve in this capacity by advocating for the use of the study intervention in the host country after the study is completed. Yet, in almost all cases, the study population is represented at the national level, generally by a Ministry of Health, which issues the permission for the study to be conducted. Often a local governmental body is involved as well. But unless the national government is both willing and able to act, interventions are not likely to be widely available in the country after the study is completed. Because resources are so scarce, it is important, yet extremely difficult, for developing countries to establish priorities for health-care research, and even when the commitment is there, many simply cannot make interventions available without external funding.

Prior agreements can be used to provide the benefits of research to populations from which study participants are drawn in at least two ways. One way is to design prior agreements so that the intervention, if proven effective, will be made available to the host country at a cost it can afford. This could be accomplished, for example, by providing the intervention to the class of individuals represented by the participants in a clinical trial for a specified period of time at a specified cost. Or if the country's need for a particular drug can be adequately quantified and the shelf-life of the drug and other factors render it appropriate to do so, the country could make bulk purchases of the drug at a subsidized price.

Prior agreements can also be designed to provide benefits derived from research other than the effective intervention. Where the benefit involves technology transfer, a pharmaceutical company could agree to grant to the government a free or low-cost license to manufacture a drug in exchange of a commitment from the government to manufacture and distribute the drug to its population. Capacity building is another type of derivative research benefit, whereby researchers and sponsors help build the capacity of the host country for designing and conducting clinical trials, for scientific and ethical review of proposed research, and for implementing the results of the research after the trial is completed. These efforts, which find some support in international documents,[6] are aimed at reducing the imbalance between the high burden of disease in developing countries and their lack of technical capacity to make use of existing knowledge or generate new knowledge to address health problems. Developing countries consider capacity building to be an extremely important research benefit.[7] Another derivative research benefit is the provision of various forms of health care. For instance, the post-trial maintenance of a primary care clinic established in conjunction to a study might be extremely beneficial to the host community. Researchers' commitment to continue to work with the host country to solve a particular health problem constitutes another type of benefit.

Capacity building and researcher commitments can be particularly important benefits to the country, especially if the research does not result in an effective intervention for a number of years or the experimental intervention proves not to be effective.

The negotiation of the benefits depends on a number of factors. The health problem being addressed is one such factor. Will there be a need for the intervention once the study is completed? Can the health problem be cured, or is it a chronic or terminal condition? What will be the cost of the intervention or other benefits? The nature and number of sponsors that would be responsible for providing the intervention are also relevant. Is the sponsor, for example, an NGO or a pharmaceutical company? Likewise, the conditions in the host country, as well as its capabilities, influence this process. One of the most important considerations would be the country's health-care system. In poorer developing countries, incorporating a provision of an effective intervention may be most appropriate. The suitability of providing a benefit other than effective intervention would depend upon the nature of the benefit and the economic and technological development levels of the country. Technology transfer, for example, makes good sense for countries with strong local pharmaceutical industries (or those in the process of developing them), while assistance in building research capacity or obtaining researcher commitments would help practically all developing countries.

HUMAN RIGHTS AND RESEARCH
CONDUCTED IN
DEVELOPING COUNTRIES

According to Harold Varmus and David Satcher, "one of the great challenges in medical research is to conduct clinical trials in developing countries that will lead to therapies that benefit the citizens of these countries."[8] It has been argued that, in order to be ethically acceptable, research must "offer the potential of actual benefit to the inhabitants"[9] of a developing country. This argument is equally applicable in the human rights arena as it is to the principle of distributive justice in research ethics. In both contexts it is not enough that the study intervention is provided to the participants in a trial. Without a guarantee of affordable access to the intervention by the population from which the participants are drawn, the developing country receives little benefit. If the knowledge gained from the research is used primarily for the benefit of the industrialized world, the research may be rightly characterized as exploitative, unethical[10] and in violation of human rights. Glantz and his co-authors adds that it is not enough to make an effective intervention available to a developing country by removing the financial barrier to access, if there is no means of getting the intervention to the population that needs it "in the absence of a plan to improve the country's health care delivery capabilities."[11]

Of course, one may ask why research is conducted in developing countries. There are two good reasons. First, no known effective intervention exists for a serious health problem in most developing countries. Second, lacking the necessary resources, developing countries cannot purchase the existing effective interventions, and some may not be able to provide even the most rudimentary health care. Under these circumstances many experimental interventions should be tested precisely because they offer the promise of an affordable alternative, which might provide some, but not the most effective, benefit. Thus, the question of whether an effective intervention will be affordable in the host country is extremely important in both instances. If the intervention proves to be too expensive, its effectiveness becomes irrelevant. In other words, if the research will not benefit the developing country, it should not be done.[12]

Why Prior Agreements Should Be Used in International Clinical Trials

Most stakeholders in the research enterprise probably would agree that, at least in principle, the use of prior agreements is desirable and should be encouraged in international clinical trials. Prior agreements can assist researchers, sponsors, ethics review committees, developing country governments, and other involved parties to focus on whether the host country will truly benefit from the proposed research. Others would contend, however, that it simply is not feasible to use prior agreements to ensure post-trial availability of effective interventions and other research benefits to developing countries. They oppose prior agreements for several reasons, including the following:

- It would serve only to delay or prevent new drug research in developing countries.
- There are financial, logistical, and other formidable obstacles to the use of prior agreements.
- It is not the prevailing international standard.
- It would go far beyond the influence one can reasonably expect researchers to have to affect changes in a country's health policy.[13]

Delaying or Preventing Research

Objections to prior agreements on the grounds that negotiations would serve only to delay or prevent new drug research in developing countries,[14] are dismissed by the advocates who argue that even if the claim is true, the population has lost nothing because the benefits of the research would not be available to them anyway.[15] They add that blocking the research would protect the host country from being exploited by the industrialized world, which is the main beneficiary of research. However, prior agreements do not need to deter research sponsors from investing, because sharing the benefits may not be as costly as it has been assumed.

First, the assumption that effective interventions will simply be distributed to developing countries free of charge is erroneous. While it is true that a few countries cannot afford to buy interventions even at a subsidized cost, others are able to buy interventions as long as they are not expected to do so at industrialized world prices.[16] Still others can be licensed to produce interventions. And, over time, as both their economic and technological capabilities improve, interventions should become more accessible to developing countries.

Second, while research sponsors will play a primary role in providing effective interventions in many instances, this will not always be the case. Creative funding arrangements may need to be devised in order to provide incentives for private industry to undertake research on neglected diseases occurring primarily in the developing world. And, where research sponsors from both the public and the private sectors are either unwilling or unable to bear the cost of making interventions available, the actual or perceived barrier to research imposed by prior agreements can be reduced through the use of creative arrangements designed to more widely distribute any financial burdens of fulfilling post-trial obligations to developing countries.

There Are Formidable Financial, Logistical, and Other Obstacles to Prior Agreements

A second criticism is that, in practice, many aspects of prior agreements can be extremely problematic.[17] In addition to availability, affordability, and distribution, issues involving technology and intellectual property must be considered prior to conducting research.[18] It may be difficult to determine how to define the class to which the benefit will apply. How and by whom should that determination be made? Do the people of the host country constitute the class? What if the research participants represent populations that are not confined by national borders? Does the obligation to provide the benefit extend to participants from earlier trials? Difficulties could also arise with respect to the provision of intervention. Who should be responsible for providing it? What does making the intervention "available" mean in a particular situation? For some designated period of time? For as long as the intervention is needed? Will the intervention be provided free of charge, or will there be some nominal cost associated with it? If the latter, how will that cost be determined?

It is easy for some to dismiss the use of prior agreements because of these difficult questions. However, the difficulties inherent in the negotiation and implementation of prior agreements do not outweigh the moral imperative to secure them. The resolution of critical health problems always requires that parties grapple with complex and challenging issues, and it is readily acknowledged that the concerted efforts and talents of multiple partners from diverse environments and

disciplines are often needed. Collaborative efforts are routinely employed to address problems concerning the funding and/or distribution of drugs in developing countries in a non-research context, and
there is no good reason to believe that these same types of problems
cannot be resolved in international clinical trials.

The process of negotiating prior agreements would require the parties to examine the expected benefits of the proposed research carefully and also help to ensure that there would be no delays in availability.
There is no reason to believe that these types of issues cannot be effectively addressed before the research begins or that it is somehow easier
to address them after the study is finished. Ultimately, the parties involved need to reach an understanding about how the country will
actually benefit from the proposed research before it begins. This does
not mean that the entire population must benefit immediately, but
rather that the parties should be convinced that sufficient numbers of
individuals will benefit over a reasonable period of time so that a meaningful contribution to the overall welfare of the country is evident.

Not the Prevailing International Standard

Another objection to requiring prior agreements in international clinical trials relies on the fact that the obligation to make effective interventions and other research benefits available to host communities is
not the prevailing international standard either in research ethics or
in human rights.[19] One response to this argument is that morality—no
matter what the context—is not about "what is," but rather, "what
ought to be."[20] The applicable provisions of the UDHR and the ICESCR
can reasonably be interpreted to mean that such an obligation should
be adopted in order that research conducted in developing countries
serves to promote the human right to health in those countries.

Moreover, an ethical obligation to make effective interventions avail-
able to host countries can be traced as far back as 1979 to the *Belmont
Report*.[21] Today, such support is found in several international docu-
ments: the CIOMS *International Ethical Guidelines;* the *World Medical
Association Declaration of Helsinki*; the UNAIDS *Guidance Document;*
the WHO's *Operational Guidelines for Ethics Committees that Review
Biomedical Research*; and the Ethics Committee of the Human Genome
Organisation (HUGO) *Statement on Benefit-Sharing*.[22]

Support for an ethical obligation to make effective interventions
available after a study is over has manifested itself in two ways. First,

the documents listed above all encompass the notion that the ethical acceptability of the proposed research, including issues related to product availability and benefit sharing, should be determined before research is under way. Second, a more limited number of them[23] impose an affirmative obligation to provide effective interventions to the host community or country. The UNAIDS *Guidance Document* deserves special mention as it was the first document of its kind to focus explicitly on resolving drug access problems as part of international clinical trials.

Various provisions relating to post-trial benefits have also begun to appear in the ethics guidelines of a few industrialized and developing countries. The guidelines promulgated by the United Kingdom,[24] Canada,[25] and Nepal[26] simply indicate that access issues should be dealt with prior to the start of research and do not impose any affirmative obligation to make effective interventions available once a trial is completed. In contrast, Uganda[27] and Brazil[28] require more than just discussions in advance of research about making effective interventions available.

Influence by Researchers on Health Policy Is Unrealistic

Requiring prior agreements is also objected to by those who argue that the requirements "would go far beyond the influence one can reasonably expect of researchers concerning changes in a country's health policy."[29] In other words, what is the likelihood that government policy in a developing country will change as a result of conducting the study so that the effective intervention will get to the people who need it?[30] The answer to this question is "sometimes." One example, which illustrates the limited influence of researchers to make effective interventions available, is the iodination of salt to combat goiter in Nigeria. In that case it took the Ministry of Health fifteen years to act. However, another example involving the use of nevirapine to reduce mother-to-child transmission of HIV in Uganda is indicative of a study that successfully influenced national health policy.[31]

The problem, in most instances, is neither the inability of researchers to influence national health policy, nor the imposition of prior agreements on reluctant developing countries. Rather, the access to effective interventions goes far beyond affordability; it is a health-related issue that has received insufficient attention from both the international research and human rights communities. As noted, "Research considerations cannot be divorced from considerations of health, and health cannot be divorced from the economic and political considerations that affect health."[32]

Sometimes one or more of these parties may not be willing to make a firm commitment to making an effective intervention available until after the conclusion of a clinical trial. An international health researcher who testified before the NBAC addressed this point:

> In a vaccine study in another African country . . . the Health Ministry resented the requirement that some commitment be made up front feeling that that was a patronizing requirement and that they would be able to make a commitment when they saw the results of the study and could do an appropriate analysis of cost and benefit. And that gets to some of the perceived paternalism and rigidity of the current [ethics] guidelines.[33]

Moreover, the results of the trial may strengthen the position of the host country in negotiating with sponsors, manufacturers, and others.

However, in the complex and uncertain environment in which research is conducted, what is important is to include the input of the host country, and if the host country wants to ensure that post-trial benefits are made available to its population, a prior agreement can only help.

Prior Agreements in Use in International Clinical Trials Today

Globalization and the AIDS epidemic have made the industrialized world more acutely aware of the magnitude of health problems in developing countries and the imbalance in the global burden of disease. These factors have highlighted the need for moral progress and a reform of the existing system that keeps the developing world in poor health and poverty and that impedes every aspect of its advancement. This new awareness should lead to the conclusion that we must entertain unique and untested approaches in research to narrow the gap between the industrialized and the developing worlds by promoting awareness of the human right to health. Increasingly, efforts are being undertaken in advance of research to make effective interventions and other research benefits widely available in communities where research is conducted. The different types of agreements that have been employed by WHO, the International AIDS Vaccine Initiative (IAVI), and VaxGen are discussed below.

The World Health Organization

WHO, the leading international health organization in the world, collaborates with pharmaceutical and biotech companies as well as manufacturers of health-related instruments and equipment in order to promote the research and development of new health-related products and technologies. An essential element in these dozen or so collaborations is the negotiation of agreements prior to the commencement of research to ensure that final products will be made widely available to developing countries at low cost.[34]

Generally, WHO collaborates with industry in two ways. First, it may design, conduct, and fund studies, trials, and other development work on proprietary industry products in which WHO expresses an interest and/or is invited to collaborate. Second, it may license certain intellectual property that WHO owns to industry for further development into a final product. Industry then licenses and manufactures such products.

Prior agreements between WHO and its industrial partners are mindful of the organization's interest in ensuring that successful products are made available to the public, and to the public sector of developing countries in particular, on preferential terms, and of industry's interest in obtaining a reasonable return on its investment.[35] The legally binding agreements follow standard WHO principles and are negotiated on a case-by-case basis.[36] As a result, final terms and conditions may differ depending on a variety of factors, such as the ownership of the intellectual property rights in question, the stage of the product's development at the time of negotiations, and the past and expected future contributions to the collaboration by the parties.

In all of its collaborations, WHO seeks to ensure that its public-sector objectives are achieved by requiring that prior agreements provide that products and technologies developed with WHO support will be made generally available both to the public and to public-sector agencies either by the industry partner or through a license to WHO, if the industry partner decides to abandon the project. The industry partner must further agree to make the product available to public-sector agencies for distribution in such countries "in sufficient quantities to meet the needs of such agencies."[37]

In addition to commitments relative to quantity, commitments are also sought relative to pricing. Pricing commitments obtained from industry partners may differ depending on whether or not the product will be distributed through the private sector. If it is to be distributed through both the private and public sectors, the price at which the product is made available to public-sector agencies "shall be (i) preferential compared to the Private Sector price, and (ii) set at the lowest possible level permitting a commercially reasonable return on combined worldwide sales of the Compound for Distribution in both Public and Private Sectors."[38] The product can be sold in the private sector at whatever price the industry partner chooses. Pricing commitments from industry partners can also take the form of "cost, plus a modest mark-up" or of a maximum price, depending on the circumstances.[39] Cost, plus a modest mark-up can be used at any stage of the collaboration, provided the terms can be defined and agreed upon. In contrast, a maximum price commitment can only be used if the development work is at such a point that the parties are able to determine what it will cost to make the product.[40] If the product will not be distributed through the private sector, availability to public-sector agencies shall be "at the lowest possible, commercially reasonable price."[41] Bulk purchase is another mechanism used to ensure availability of products at the lowest cost possible.[42]

A final item of negotiation involves the time period during which product availability is ensured. Although there is no fixed time, "at the end of the agreed period of time the company must agree to provide technology transfer to enable the country or countries concerned to continue either to manufacture the product themselves or through a sublicensing agreement to have somebody else manufacture it for them."[43]

The International AIDS Vaccine Initiative

The IAVI is an international scientific nonprofit organization founded in 1996 with the single aim of accelerating the development of safe, effective, accessible HIV vaccines for global use through the investment of what it calls social venture capital. The organization's work is driven by the belief that a vaccine represents the world's best hope to end the AIDS epidemic. IAVI links promising vaccine approaches with countries in which to test them and seeks to accelerate product development and clinical trials through public-private partnerships among vaccine developers, manufacturers, and those who will test the vaccines. Most of IAVI's efforts are focused in developing countries where the epidemic is most severe, and it seeks to ensure that people in developing countries for whom particular vaccines are designed benefit from those vaccines once they are developed.

To date, IAVI has invested $20 million to create six vaccine development partnerships with individuals and entities from both industrialized and developing countries. It also contributes expertise "as needed, in areas ranging from project management to regulatory affairs and infrastructure for clinical trials."[44] IAVI's focus on encouraging industrial participation in AIDS vaccine development is based on the belief that private-sector involvement and ingenuity in this process are crucial. A successful AIDS vaccine will necessarily rely on technologies covered by new and existing patents. Realistically, however, prospects for the development of an AIDS vaccine by the pharmaceutical and biotechnology industries alone are unlikely for several reasons.[45] IAVI's prior agreements with its industrial partners call for reasonable pricing policies for the public sector in developing countries. In return for financing early vaccine development, companies agree to make the vaccine available to the public sector in developing countries in quantities reasonable to demand and at the cost of manufacturing plus a reasonable profit, which is defined. IAVI retains certain rights if companies do not, or are unable to, meet their contractual obligations.[46]

IAVI has also developed "a strategy for addressing the many economic, political, and logistical obstacles to immediate and widescale access in the developing world."[47] Most recently, IAVI created a "virtual vaccine company model" designed to achieve its 2002–2004 research agenda.[48] This model consists of vaccine development partners, centralized laboratories and reagent production, large-scale development and manufacturing partnerships, partnerships for Phase 3 clinical trials in developing countries, and core regulatory dossier design.[49]

VaxGen

VaxGen, a California-based biotechnology company, developed the first AIDS vaccine candidate in the world to enter Phase 3 efficacy studies. The company raised money to finance its own trials in an effort to get the vaccine tested as quickly as possible.[50] Two trials are being conducted. The first trial is being conducted in the United States, where the participants are mostly homosexual men. Thailand is the site of the second trial, where participants are all intravenous drug users at high risk of becoming HIV-infected.[51]

Thailand has one of the fastest growing rates of HIV infection in the world, and the government has made the development of an AIDS vaccine a health priority.[52] As a condition, the Thai government required that the country receive research benefits in two forms, the product itself and capacity building.[53] VaxGen offered an informal agreement to the Thai Ministry of Public Health specifying that, should there be a licensed product, the country would receive special treatment from the company in making the product available in Thailand, and it agreed to make a concerted effort to decrease the cost of the vaccine for the country; arrangements could be made for a bulk shipment of the product with filling and finishing in Thailand.[54] The benefits involve capacity building, and the Thai researchers view the transfer of knowledge and technology as extremely important. VaxGen has already transferred its data management capabilities in Thailand. The company has developed a repository of laboratory specimens, and technical know-how is being provided to the Thais about how to store, track, locate, and connect data to specimens. VaxGen is also training the Thai researchers to conduct Phase 3 trials; previously the Thais' experience was limited to Phase 1 and 2 trials.[55]

However, Mary Pat Flaherty and Doug Struck report that VaxGen would not agree to provide the post-trial benefits sought by the Thais.[56] First, VaxGen refused to pledge care for research participants who became HIV-infected during the trial. Thai health authorities finally agreed to provide the best local therapy, described as "years behind what an American could expect." Second, VaxGen refused to guarantee that the vaccine, if proven effective, would be sold to the Thais at a reduced price. Finally, VaxGen rejected the Thai requests for profit-sharing and for a manufacturing plant to be located in the country. They note, however, that VaxGen has invested almost $600,000 in equipment and facilities that will remain in Bangkok when the study is over.[57]

CONCLUSION

Many opportunities and challenges remain in pursuing the use of prior agreements in international clinical trials. Some agreements, such as those employed by WHO, have proved successful. Agreements forged by other entities, such as IAVI and VaxGen, remain to be tested. Since the examples are limited with regard to their numbers, and the specific and detailed information about the agreements and the negotiation processes is not available, it is difficult to extract a set of general principles concerning the use of prior agreements in international clinical trials. However, a few observations are in order.

It may be important to distinguish, at least in some cases, between those situations where a developing host country is a party to a prior agreement and those where a developing country (or countries), although not a party to an agreement, is its ultimate intended beneficiary. Out of necessity, industry is very likely to play a prominent role in most, if not all, of these arrangements. However, the presence of a third party with strong ties to the industrialized world acting on behalf of, or in conjunction with, a developing country, may be critical to the successful negotiation of benefits. Organizations, such as WHO and IAVI, are more experienced than many developing-country governments in negotiating agreements to develop and distribute health care goods and services collaboratively. In addition to economic resources, they possess (or are able to purchase) the scientific, medical, technological, business, and legal know-how that developing countries tend to lack. These organizations can also utilize legally enforceable contracts in their collaborative partnerships.

In contrast, some developing countries are not even aware that they can obtain post-trial benefits through the negotiation of a prior agreement. Others that are engaged in negotiating prior agreements are severely disadvantaged by the inequities in bargaining power between them and their industrialized world partners, which is most problematic if the developing country attempts to negotiate without the assistance of a third party.

The importance of securing the benefit of building research capacity as part of a prior agreement should not be underestimated. Although the provision of successful interventions to developing countries may help them address particular health problems in the short term, by building their capacity to conduct research, developing countries will be better situated over time to solve their own health problems independently.

By helping to ensure that effective interventions and other research benefits will be made widely available in the countries in which they are tested, the use of prior agreements in international clinical trials shows great promise as a way to promote the individual human right to health in developing countries. They are far from solving the problems, but, as is always the case, solutions to difficult and complex problems must begin somewhere.

NOTES

[1] See Council for International Organizations of Medical Sciences (CIOMS), *International Ethical Guidelines for Biomedical Research Involving Human Subjects* (Geneva: CIOMS, 2002). Guideline 10 reads: "Before undertaking research in a population or community with limited resources, the sponsor and the investigator must make every effort to ensure that the research is responsive to the health needs and the priorities of the population or community in which it is to be carried out."

[2] See World Medical Association (WMA), *World Medical Association Declaration of Helsinki: Ethical Principles for Medical Research Involving Human Subjects* (Ferney-Voltaire, France: WMA, 1964); Amended: 29th World Medical Assembly, Tokyo, Japan, October 1975; 35th World Medical Assembly, Venice, Italy, October 1983; 41st World Medical Assembly, Hong Kong, September 1989; 48th General Assembly, Somerset West, Republic of South Africa, October 1996; and 52nd General Assembly, Edinburgh, Scotland, October 2000. Principle 19 reads: "Medical research is only appropriate if there is a reasonable likelihood that the populations in which the research is carried out stand to benefit from the results of the research." See also Leonard H. Glantz, George J. Annas, Michael A. Grodin and Wendy K. Mariner, "Research in Developing Countries: Taking 'Benefit' Seriously," *Hastings Center Report* 28, no. 6 (1998): 38–42; and Robert Crouch and John Arras, "AZT Trials and Tribulations," *Hastings Center Report* 28, no. 6 (1998): 26–34.

[3] CIOMS, *International Ethical Guidelines,* Guideline 10.

[4] Madison Powers, "Theories of Justice in the Context of Research," in *Beyond Consent: Seeking Justice in Research*, ed. Jeffrey P. Kahn, Anna C. Mastroianni, and Jeremy Sugarman (New York: Oxford Univ. Press, 1998): 147–65.

[5] George Andreopoulos, "Declarations and Covenants of Human Rights and International Codes of Research Ethics," in *Biomedical Research Ethics: Updating International Guidelines,* ed. Robert Levine and Samuel Gorovitz with James Gallagher, 181–203 (Geneva: CIOMS, 2000).

[6] See, for example, CIOMS, *International Ethical Guidelines,* Guideline 20. See also Guidance Point 3 of UNAIDS, "Joint United Nations Programme on HIV/AIDS," *Ethical Considerations in HIV Preventive Vaccine Research: UNAIDS Guidance Document* (Geneva: UNAIDS, 2000).

[7] Karen Hofman, "The Global Forum for Bioethics in Research: Report of a Meeting, November 1999," *Journal of Law, Medicine, and Ethics* 28 (2000): 174–75.

[8] Harold Varmus and David Satcher, "Ethical Complexities of Conducting Research in Developing Countries," *New England Journal of Medicine* 337, no. 14 (1997): 1003.

[9] Glantz et al., "Research in Developing Countries," 39.

[10] Ibid. See also Carlos del Rio, "Is Ethical Research Feasible in Developed and Developing Countries?" *Bioethics* 12, no. 4 (1998): 328–30; and Crouch and Arras, "AZT Trials and Tribulations."

[11] Glantz et al., "Research in Developing Countries," 41. See also CIOMS, *International Ethical Guidelines,* Guideline 21.

[12] Leonard H. Glantz, testimony before the NBAC, Washington, DC, 13 January 2000, in meeting transcript, 140–96.

[13] Two other objections to requiring prior agreements are (1) it would create a double standard with regard to research conducted in the United States and other industrialized countries; and (2) prior agreements can always be breached. See Alice Page, "Prior Agreements in International Clinical Trials: Ensuring the Benefits of Research to Developing Countries," *Yale Journal of Health Policy, Law, and Ethics* 3 (2002), 35.

[14] Reidar Lie, "Justice and International Research," in Levine, Gorovitz, and Gallagher, *Biomedical Research Ethics*, 27–40; Glantz et al., "Research in Developing Countries."

[15] Glantz et al., "Research in Developing Countries."

[16] The pharmaceutical industry routinely claims that high drug prices are required to finance the high cost of research and development as well as to compensate for research failures and the large number of drugs that are never profitable. See Pharmaceutical Research and Manufacturers Association of America (PhRMA), *1999 Pharmaceutical Industry Profile* (Washington, DC: PhRMA, 1999). However, some experts argue that the industry devotes most of its revenues to marketing research, marketing, and paying CEO salaries and shareholder dividends rather than to research and development. See Donald Drake and Marian Uhlman, *Making Medicine, Making Money* (Kansas City, MO: Andrews and McMeel, 1993); Alan Sager and Deborah Socolar, "Affordable Medications for Americans; Problems, Causes, and Solutions," paper presented to the Prescription Drug Task Force, United States House of Representatives, Washington, DC, 27 July 1999. Moreover, the US government plays a significant role in the research and development of drugs from which industry ultimately profits, including several antiretroviral drugs used to treat AIDS. See Patrick Bond, "Globalization, Pharmaceutical Pricing, and South African Health Policy: Managing Confrontation with U.S. Firms and Politicians," *International Journal of Health Services* 29, no. 4 (1999): 765–92; Margaret Duckett, "Compulsory Licensing and Parallel Importing," Background Paper, International Council of AIDS Service Organizations, 1999, http://www.icaso.org/docs/compulsoryenglish.htm (accessed 31 August 2004); and Mary Griffin, "AIDS Drugs and the Pharmaceutical Industry: A Need to Reform," *American Journal of Law and Medicine* 17, no. 4 (1991): 363–410.

[17] Lie, "Justice and International Research."

[18] See, for example, UNAIDS, "Joint United Nations Programme on HIV/AIDS," Guidance Point 2.

[19] See, for example, Lie, "Justice and International Research."

[20] See, for example, Ruth Macklin, "After Helsinki: Unresolved Issues in International Research," *Kennedy Institute of Ethics Journal* 11, no. 1 (2001): 17–36; Solomon Benatar, "Justice and International Research: A Response to Reidar K. Lie," in Levine, Gorovitz, and Gallagher, *Biomedical Research Ethics*, 41–50.

[21] In reference to the principle of justice and the distribution of the burdens and benefits of research, the National Commission indirectly addresses the issue of making effective interventions available to the populations used for testing. It states that "whenever research supported by public funds leads to the development of therapeutic devices and procedures, justice demands that these not provide advantages only to those who can afford them and that such research should not unduly involve persons from groups unlikely to be among the beneficiaries of subsequent applications of the research." See National Commission for the Protection of Human Subjects of Biomedical and Behavioral Research, *The Belmont Report: Ethical Principles and Guidelines in the Protection of Human Subjects* (Washington, DC: Department of Health, Education, and Welfare, 1979), 5.

[22] See CIOMS, *International Ethical Guidelines;* WMA, *World Medical Association Declaration of Helsinki,* as amended in 2000. The latest revision of the *Declaration of Helsinki* contains a new provision concerning the need for the accrual of some potential benefit to host countries; UNAIDS, "Joint United Nations Programme on HIV/AIDS"; WHO, *Operational Guidelines for Ethics Committees that Review Biomedical Research* (Geneva: WHO, 2000); and HUGO Ethics Committee, *Statement on Benefit-Sharing* (London: HUGO, 2000).

[23] CIOMS, *International Ethical Guidelines*; UNAIDS, "Joint United Nations Programme on HIV/AIDS"; WMA, *World Medical Association Declaration of Helsinki,* as amended in 2000.

[24] Medical Research Council of the United Kingdom (MRC-UK), *Medical Research Council Interim Guidelines for Research Involving Human Participants in Developing Societies: Ethical Guidelines of MRC-Sponsored Studies* (London: MRC, 1999).

[25] Medical Research Council of Canada (MRC-CA); Natural Sciences and Engineering Research Council of Canada (NSERC); Social Sciences and Humanities Research Council of Canada (SSHRC), *Canadian Tri-Council Policy Statement, Ethical Conduct for Research Involving Humans* (Ottawa: Public Works and Government Services, 1998).

[26] Nepalese Health Research Council, *Guidelines for Health Research in Nepal,* rev. draft (Nepal: NHRC, 2000).

[27] National Consensus Conference, *Guidelines for the Conduct of Health Research Involving Human Subjects in Uganda* (Kampala, Uganda: NCC, 1997).

[28] National Health Council (NHC), Resolution No. 196/96 on Research Involving Human Subjects (Brazil: NHC, 1996). Addition: 1997, Resolution No. 251 (Brazil: NHC, 1997).

[29] Lie, "Justice and International Research," 29.

[30] Alfred Sommer, testimony before the NBAC, Arlington, VA, 16 September 1999, in meeting transcript, 147–210.

[31] Nuffield Council on Bioethics, *The Ethics of Research Related to Healthcare in Developing Countries* (London: Nuffield Council on Bioethics, 2002).

[32] Benatar, "Justice and International Research," 41.

[33] Jack Killen, testimony before the NBAC, Arlington, VA, 16 September 1999, in meeting transcript, 120.

[34] P. Griffin, e-mail communication to Alice Page (18 July 2000).

[35] WHO, *Policy on Patents: Information Paper on WHO Patents Policy* (Geneva: WHO, 1985).

[36] WHO, *WHO Guidelines on Interaction with Commercial Enterprises,* preliminary version (Geneva: WHO, 1999); WHO, Draft Memorandum of Understanding (Geneva: WHO, 1999); WHO, *Policy on Patents.*

[37] WHO, Draft Memorandum of Understanding, 3.

[38] Ibid.

[39] P. Griffin, e-mail communication to Alice Page (11 February 2000).

[40] Griffin, e-mail (18 July 2000).

[41] WHO, Draft Memorandum of Understanding, 3.

[42] P. Griffin, testimony before the NBAC, Washington, DC, 13 January 2000, in meeting transcript, 104–38.

[43] Ibid., 144.

[44] IAVI, "Call for Nominations: IAVI Policy Advisory Committee," 20 June 2002, iavi.org website (accessed 31 August 2004).

[45] Thomas Nchinda, "Initiatives in Health Research," in *The 10/90 Report on Health Research 1999,* ed. Sheila Davey, 99–124 (Geneva: Global Forum for Health Research, 1999).

[46] IAVI, "Call for Nominations"; see also IAVI, Draft Industrial Collaborative Agreement (New York: IAVI, 1999), 5–7.

[47] IAVI, "IAVI Releases Blueprints for Speeding Vaccine Development," *IAVI Report* 5, no. 4 (2000): 9; IAVI, *AIDS Vaccines for the World: Preparing Now to Assure Access* (New York: IAVI, 2000).

[48] IAVI, "The IAVI Research and Development Agenda 2002–2004," http://www.iavi.org/vaccinedev/agenda.asp (accessed 31 August 2004).

[49] IAVI, "IAVI's Virtual Company Model," http://www.iavi.org/vaccinedev/vdp.asp (accessed 31 August 2004).

[50] Bill Snow, "VaxGen: Pushing the Envelope," in *HIV Vaccine Handbook: Community Perspectives on Participating in Research, Advocacy, and Progress,* ed. Bill Snow (Washington, DC: AIDS Vaccine Advocacy Coalition, 1999), 195–99.

[51] "VaxGen Announces Results of Its Phase III HIV Vaccine Trial in Thailand: Vaccine Fails to Meet Endpoints," *PR Newswire Association,* 12 November 2003.

[52] Jose Esparza, "AIDS Vaccine Research in Asia: Needs and Opportunities, Report from a UNAIDS/WHO/NIID Meeting, Tokyo, 28–30 October 1998," *AIDS* 13, no. 11 (1999): 1–13.

[53] Marlene Chernow, e-mail communication to Alice Page (1 May 2000).

[54] Donald Francis, e-mail communication to Alice Page (17 November 1999).

[55] Esparza, "AIDS Vaccine Research in Asia."

[56] Mary Pat Flaherty and Doug Struck, "Life by Luck of the Draw," *Washington Post*, 22 December 2000.

[57] Ibid.

V

Cultural Forces, Practices, and Institutional Challenges

12

The News Media
in the Arena of Human Rights

Anne Nelson

INTRODUCTION

When the United States invaded Afghanistan and Iraq in the after-math of the 9/11 attacks, the actions reopened old debates over the role of the US news media. Many argued that news organizations should be evolving into truly independent non-state actors in times of con-flict, acting as arbiters in policy debates between political parties and disagreeing nations. But others point to a growing popular revival of the notion that the news media, and television broadcasters in particu-lar, should serve the interests of patriotism—a path that would nudge them into the narrower role of quasi-state propagandist.

If one examines the arc of twentieth century media coverage of con-flict, one can only conclude that there has been no common norm of propriety. In the periods building up to the First and Second World Wars, the US print media took part in a vigorous debate as to whether the country should go to war. Once the United States declared war, public questioning of policy by news organizations was usually re-garded as aiding the enemy. The war in Vietnam was entered through the back door, without a declaration of war that could be clearly de-bated. Reporters questioned the conduct of the war and then, increas-ingly, the premise of the war itself. This skepticism was reinforced over the Reagan era, with the brushfire conflicts that marked the final grim chapter of the Cold War. Massive slaughters took place under

Communist regimes in Cambodia and Afghanistan, but the US news media also doggedly reported abuses committed by US client states in other parts of the world, often documenting passive or active US support. This news coverage, in which the actions of US proxies were judged independently as well as in terms of their utility to US policy, served as a pillar of the evolving human rights policy infrastructure.

The attacks of 9/11 marked a departure from the immediate post–Cold War era in countless ways, beginning with the idea that the United States was directly involved, both as the subject of an attack and as a party in a declared war. At the same time, coverage was dramatically affected by parallel shifts in the US media industry. Commercial television networks, under fierce financial pressure to rebuild flagging audiences, competed with reality-based entertainment programs by bringing real-time reports from journalists "embedded" with the troops. While the embedded journalists undoubtedly provided a more detailed and emotive coverage of US troops in the field, some of the space and attention they consumed might usefully have been redeployed to cover missing diplomatic, political, cultural, and economic dimensions of the international story. Nationalist imagery emerged in news broadcasting, with yellow ribbons and flag motifs overtaking the once-neutral set designs.

Technology was also altering the landscape, internationally and at home. Arabic-language satellite broadcasters—most notably Al-Jazeera—stirred emotions in Arab and Muslim populations by broadcasting tape loops of bloody imagery of civilians killed by US bombing campaigns. In the meantime, US television news executives were told that their advertisers, and much of the public, considered reporting on civilian casualties of US bombing to be "unpatriotric." Viewers threatened to boycott programs; sponsors threatened to cancel ads.

The issue of news content was hardly less conflicted. Pre-war Afghanistan and Iraq were unquestionably human rights disasters. But to what extent could Afghanistan's tragedies be blamed on the Taliban, and what was the legacy of the 1979 Soviet invasion? Where did the ravages of Saddam Hussein's cruelty end, and the devastating impact of the US-backed international embargo start? US news media coverage of both situations had been erratic in the decade leading up to the conflict. To what extent was that gap due to the two countries' censorship practices and hostility toward the foreign press—and to what extent was it the result of the US news media's lack of interest in crises with limited entertainment value?

These questions were merely the latest versions of an ongoing debate in the news media: when should news organizations serve the narrow and immediate interests of the "national interest" as defined by popular opinion or the current administration, and when should they aspire to more universal values? This chapter considers some aspects of the historical evolution of the news media as a moral force in human rights and humanitarian debates.

THE AMBIVALENT "ACTOR"

The news media has an immense impact on the development and implementation of human rights policy in current world affairs. But a paradox lies at the heart of this fact. Many journalists who work for the most influential news media in the United States (the country that is the primary focus of this chapter) reject the notion that the news media should be an "actor" at all. They see their function as descriptive, with the expectation that policymakers and the public will utilize the information they provide for the benefit of a democratic decision-making process. The modern US model of print journalism calls for descriptive reporting on the news pages, with prescriptive recommendations limited to the editorial pages. Some journalists are wary of being considered "activist" and even argue that conscientious journalists should not exercise their right as citizens to vote. (This differs from practices in most of Europe, where publications tend to have ties to political parties, and where reporters are often encouraged to take a stand and project an editorial "voice" in their news stories.)

The independent model has been a significant strain in US journalism since its earliest days. The independent spirit runs contrary to the officialist model that predated the existence of the independent press but is still actively practiced in the United States and elsewhere. The officialist model serves to publicize government policies and actions without critical reporting or examination from an opposing viewpoint. The independent model has been particularly important in the development of coverage of human rights issues throughout US history. In many cases, if the government or other powerful institutions determine that given practices are in the national interest, only independent news organizations can bring them to light for public debate.

But there are also at least three distinct strains within the independent news media. The first strain, the commercial news media, operates only from a profit motive. In general, these media outlets devote little attention to human rights issues of any kind and will not be covered here (without denying that they do occupy a large portion of the news marketplace and exert a strong influence on mass culture). Entertainment and consumer publications, supermarket tabloids, and much of commercial broadcasting falls into this genre.

Another category is often called the mainstream news media. These are news organizations (of varying size and quality) that function as businesses but still purport to serve the public interest. They include quality metropolitan newspapers, news and literary magazines, and the three major network news divisions, plus CNN. Over time, these outlets have increased the attention they give to reporting that addresses themes and use sources related to the human rights community. But quite often these news organizations are not "actors" as much as they are "acted upon"—that is, they are reluctant to present information that challenges conventional notions of the public interest or the immediate interests of their readership. If the official or the public climate starts to shift, these news outlets may serve as catalysts to speed change. Reporters in these news organizations often must withhold information they believe to be true and pertinent until the public climate is ready for it—or find an alternate venue for publication.[1]

At certain crucial moments in history, mainstream news organizations may choose to occupy moral ground and document abuses in a way that challenges policy and public opinion. One example of this is a handful of Southern newspapers, such as Mississippi's *Delta Democrat-Times*, which took courageous stands in support of the Civil Rights movement in the 1960s. These are the opportunities for news organizations to make history, win prizes—and, at times, to sacrifice readership, lose advertising, and court bankruptcy.

A third category is "journalism of conscience." This represents news organizations that do not have profit as their primary goal; they are often subsidized by religious or public institutions, foundations, or other nonprofit entities. They have a more strongly defined public service mission and are more likely to risk unpopular perspectives. They also may be identified with causes or partisanships.

Mainstream journalists dread the label "advocacy journalist." This is usually not a problem for journalists who publish in magazines of opinion, such as *The Nation, The New Republic*, or *The National Review*, or for commentators on the increasingly popular "crossfire" format television programs. The "advocacy" designation is usually not appropriate for the news pages and programming of other organizations that combine traditional reporting techniques, a high degree of professionalism, a public service mandate, and a nonprofit structure. This category includes the *Christian Science Monitor*, National Public Radio, and PBS's news and documentary programming. The news organizations "of conscience" have been highly influential in advancing human rights reporting before a climate of broad public interest and acceptance has been achieved. They have also contributed to a "trickle up" phenomenon, in which their innovative reports find their ways to the pages of mainstream publications.[2]

SOME PARAMETERS
FOR INDEPENDENT HUMAN RIGHTS REPORTING

For the purposes of this paper, human rights (and their humanitarian corollaries) are assumed to be a set of humane values that stands independent of the interests of the state and the national economy.

Let us assume that it is natural for every nation to pursue its own short-term interests in expanding its political and economic power. Let us also assume that the national news media, under usual circumstances, would be inclined to sympathize with the pursuit of these interests. Human rights reporting comes into play most emphatically when journalists witness, record, and report actions that run counter to state policies or propaganda. One example might occur in reporting an act that might be helpful to a short-term military goal, such as bombing a hospital filled with slightly wounded soldiers who will soon return to the front, that is contrary to international law and a humanitarian ideal.

When and how should the news media "undermine the national interest" in the name of a broader humanity? When and how should the news media reduce an economic advantage, such as cheap goods produced abroad by forced labor, in the name of promoting universal labor standards? One can argue that humane standards are in the long-term national interest, but history demonstrates that nations in hot pursuit of a military objective or a trade advantage will discard this notion as a luxury.

Nonetheless, over the past generation, the amount and the quality of human rights and humanitarian coverage in the US news media has increased dramatically. I would like to trace these themes historically and discuss how they play out in the current environment.

Definitions

The first problem we face in addressing the news media's role in the area of human rights is one of definitions. *News media, journalism,* and *reporting* are terms that cover an immensely broad and varied terrain, both in style and substance—even if we were going to limit the discussion to forms present in the United States in the early years of the twenty-first century. The *New York Review of Books* falls under the category of journalism; so does the *National Enquirer.* Broadcast news includes shouting matches on the Fox Network, full of insults and devoid of facts, as well as the content-rich "Newshour" on PBS. These programs share the same technological means of production and dissemination, and each must answer to the same imperatives of audience, market, and state influence, but they do so in distinct and sometimes surprisingly different ways.

Technology and Journalism's Varied Reasons for Existence

What is journalism for? A list of motivations could include the following:

1. To promulgate official information.
2. To promote an interpretation of a broader social good. This can be the function of a religious or reformist entity or movement.
3. To advance the agenda of a political opposition that seeks to expand influence and, in many cases, control of the state's power.
4. To entertain or otherwise engage an audience, often in pursuit of profit.

One should bear in mind that these four functions are by no means mutually exclusive.

Journalistic Origins

Journalism can be defined as the reproduction of information, conducted on a regular basis, to be distributed to an audience of multiple individuals. The earliest forms of *journalism* in this sense were court publications, whether in Rome or Beijing. These early societies shared a centralized power structure, limited technology and means of distribution (both of which were essentially controlled by the centralized power structure), limited literacy (the power structure largely defined who had access to education in the written word), and harsh retaliation toward dissent. There was little room for separate strains to promote religious, reformist, or political counter-currents. In medieval Europe the authority of the church dominated many forms of education and the dissemination of information, especially the written word, and the use of Latin was an effective barrier to limit unauthorized access to the "information industries" of the day.

The modern paradigm of *news* must begin with the "Big Bang" of the 1600s. The Reformation shattered the authority of the Catholic Church and was promulgated as a reformist, moral response to corruptions and abuses committed within the Catholic Church and by the regimes that supported it. The Reformation was undoubtedly fueled by Gutenberg's invention of the printing press sometime in the fifteenth century, which made the written word accessible to new populations. The Bible and other crucial texts were soon published in the vernacular, as well as Latin, contributing to the rise of localized sectarian movements throughout northern Europe. This gave local populations a greater sense of collective identity based on a common language and encouraged the movements that led to the concept of the rights of the individual—an important precursor to the concept of human rights.

It is hard to overstate the extent of the social and political upheaval that followed these developments. Europe's bloody wars and purges created generations of religious refugees who flooded the new North American colonies. The British Protestants who settled New England shared characteristics that would have a great influence on the development of journalism in North America:

1. A distrust of a strong centralized state. In their experience, the state could be changeable, brutal, and arbitrary.
2. An emphasis on individual interpretation of the text or the "word." This was accompanied by a belief in the importance of individual conscience, often in defiance of human authority, and a commitment to literacy.
3. A middle-class orientation, with a strong representation in the merchant class and trades and an affinity for new technology.

The first century of Western newspapers, in both Europe and North America, saw many new publications founded, using the new technology in competing spirits—some to promote the new Reformation practices of exposing abuse and challenging authority, and others in the old tradition of publishing imperial court records and maintaining the status quo.

Obviously, providing a chronicle of official events is a necessary function of the news media. It is also important to remember that many of the first newspapers of North America were born as subsidiary operations of printers' shops to realize income from commercial announcements; the news content, or journalism, was an afterthought. Nonetheless, the social context led the public to seek independent news sources to explain the developments that were going on around them. The press in Boston became a crucial "non-state actor" in deploring the stamp tax (which hindered newspaper finances), the Boston Massacre, and other actions of the Crown. Revolutionary-era newspapers were forerunners to a polarized, partisan press and were often blatant vehicles for propaganda. They frequently reported alarmist and outright false information. But these publications were also instrumental in defining the rights of British citizens in opposition to the British state (and the economic interests of the mother country), laying the groundwork for both national independence and for a journalism of conscience.

Slavery as a Paradigm for Human Rights Reporting

It was one thing to remonstrate about the "rights of man" as expressed in the experience of one's friends and neighbors. Slavery presented an entirely different challenge to American journalism. Slaves were defined as a population apart, both alien and inferior, and in some cases, subhuman.

Slavery was introduced to the North American colonies in 1619, after it had taken root as a solution to the Spanish colonists' labor shortage in the Caribbean. Some religious leaders in the Northern colonies formally denounced the practice by the late 1600s, and their opposition grew over the next century.[3] The framers of the Constitution were bitterly divided over the question and compromised by defining slaves as "three-fifths" of a person for census purposes.

Over the last decade of the eighteenth century a slave revolt swept through the prosperous Caribbean French colony of Saint-Dominque. In 1804 the colony won independence and the new name of Haiti, presenting the white populations of North America with a new set of disturbing questions. Both French expeditionary forces and the black insurgents committed atrocities. French refugees poured into Southern ports, and newspapers in Virginia and Carolina published their testimonies as warnings of the dire consequences of unleashing a slave population. But for anti-slavery publications of the North, the pertinent abuse was slavery itself. The *New England Palladium* of Boston predicted that those "oppress'd with slavery's galling chain" would bring about "Virginia's dreadful doom."[4]

Once again, a confluence of technology, political tension, and shifts in theological and moral philosophy ushered in a new phase of journalism, this time driven by the issue of slavery. The anti-slavery press gained momentum in the 1830s. William Lloyd Garrison founded the abolitionist newspaper *The Liberator* in 1831. The American Anti-Slavery Society was launched two years later and established its own weekly, *The Emancipator*. In 1835 the American Anti-Slavery Society launched the biggest direct-mail campaign up to that date in US history, aided by advances in transportation and reductions in the price of printing. It flooded the United States with over a million pieces of anti-slavery literature, astonishing and outraging slave-holding recipients in the South (and anticipating decades of human rights direct mailings of the future).

The publications engendered by the anti-slavery movement marked a significant departure for US journalism. William Lloyd Garrison was a professional journalist who had run local newspapers in New England before *The Liberator*, and he prided himself on his loyalty to an uncompromising "Truth" while keeping his pages open to the broadest possible range of opinion. *The Liberator* and other anti-slavery publications were models of "associational journalism," financially supported by contributors who shared the cause. Neither Garrison nor his counterparts would consider changing the content or the position of the newspaper to gain new subscribers or increase revenues. These publications were early prototypes of public service journalism, or journalism of conscience, motivated by conviction and negligent of profits. These enterprises were also circumscribed by their cause; Garrison closed *The Liberator* in 1865, once emancipation had been achieved.

Reporting on Humanitarian Issues in Historical Context

By the early 1830s the United States had become the world's leading consumer of news, with some nine hundred newspapers—about double the number of those in Great Britain, its closest rival.[5] Advances in the technology of production allowed publishers to create the "penny press"—cheap, mass circulation newspapers.

Slavery and its intense regional tensions defined much of the political and journalistic discourse in the United States in the following years, culminating in the Civil War—which gave newspapers a boost in readership and influence. The treatment of civilians and prisoners of war and other humanitarian concerns were covered by newspapers on both sides, but often in misleading, slanted, and propagandistic fashions. The press on both sides was heavily censored, and criticism of the war effort was considered "unpatriotic."

But the bulk of the journalistic criticism that the Union and the Confederacy considered objectionable was aimed at their treatment of their own troops—faulty supplies, miserable or nonexistent medical treatment, and worse. The rights of enemy civilians and soldiers were not clearly defined. When Sherman's army burned its way through Georgia, it was considered a travesty by the South and a military necessity by the North. The Union judged the conditions at Andersonville, the notorious Confederate prison camp, to be murderous and executed the commander at the end of the war, while Confederates claimed that their own wartime privations made it impossible to provide for the Union prisoners. (Evidence was presented after the war that prison officials had turned away local citizens offering food for the prisoners.) In other words, "rights" were largely reserved for those on the same side.

Nonetheless, the period did mark at least one significant humanitarian breakthrough. A Washington government clerk named Clara Barton was stricken by the sight of wounded Union troops lacking in care and medicine. She took on the role of collecting medical supplies and delivering them to the battlefield, making no distinction between Union and Confederate wounded. She established contacts with the newly founded Red Cross in Switzerland and later founded the American branch of the organization. Barton campaigned relentlessly for the United States to sign the first Geneva Conventions of 1864, which addressed the rights of wounded combatants, the debut of international humanitarian law. The United States finally signed the Conventions in 1882, and they would begin to serve as a benchmark for journalists, as well as many other purposes.

The Spanish-American War of 1898 was the first international conflict fought by the United States to be provoked by arguments based on international human rights. The news media played a central role in instigating the conflict. There had been a long-simmering independence movement in Cuba, which had spent centuries under Spanish colonial rule. Spanish abuses of the Cuban civilian population were covered extensively and dramatically by US metropolitan dailies. While Spain's counter-insurgency tactics were indeed brutal, there were many cases in which US newspapers grossly exaggerated, and even invented, Spanish misdeeds, in the interest of their own circulation wars.

Abuses of the civilian population were usually the centerpiece of the story. When Cuban insurgents attacked sugar plantations and melted back into the population, Spanish General Valeriano Weyler herded civilians together into concentration camps, where one-third of them died of hunger and disease. US newspapers ran vivid accounts of "Butcher" Weyler and romanticized accounts of Cuban revolutionaries and their sympathizers. Once the United States entered the war against the Spanish, it completed invasions of Cuba and Puerto Rico expeditiously and with relatively few casualties. But—as usual—there were complications. The United States replaced Spain as a colonial power, for the short term in Cuba and over the long term in Puerto Rico. Worse, it replaced Spain as the antagonist against the nationalist forces in the Philippines. A second war took place from 1899 to 1902, which was a humanitarian disaster. It is estimated that nearly 5,000 US soldiers died in the conflict—along with 20,000 Filipino soldiers and 200,000 Filipino civilians.

US press coverage of the conflict in the Philippines included highly critical reports of US military conduct, especially considering the euphoric accounts of the Caribbean invasions.[6] The US troops, many of them inexperienced young farm boys from newly settled Western states, compared shooting dark-skinned Filipinos to hunting rabbits. Many writers, politicians, and reformers reacted in dismay and organized opposition to the war in the form of the Anti-Imperialist League. Some, like Mark Twain, published a steady stream of articles in *Harper's* and other popular outlets, drawing attention to US mistreatment of Filipino civilians and questioning US military policy. But it is important to note that most of the intellectual energy of this movement came from individuals who made their reputation in other fields and used the platform to take a critical position—not from the professional journalists.

World War I advanced the mechanization of modern warfare and the infliction of casualties on an unprecedented scale. US troops, entering the conflict late and in relatively small numbers, were spared the worst of the war; the US civilian population was certainly shielded from the full measure of the European experience. Furthermore, war correspondents still traveled under military protection and control. Stylistically, their prose tended to alternate between praise for the gallantry of their own troops and epithets applied to the enemy.

The atrocities of the Second World War defy description. Nonetheless, I attempt to make several points here, in the brief space available. First, US press coverage of Europe in the years leading up to the conflict tended to be highly politicized and unsystematic, rendering it incapable of reporting the escalating human rights abuses and restrictions of civil liberties that were predictive of the conflicts to come. One reason for this was the United States's own political polarization, as the country was shaken by labor disputes and battered by the depression. For example, Walter Duranty, the *New York Times* correspondent in the Soviet Union, was dismissive of the importance of Stalin's purges.

US reporters based in Germany differed in their reactions to Hitler's rise. Journalists like William Shirer (of Universal Service, then CBS) and Sigrid Schultz of the *Chicago Tribune* were resident correspondents in Berlin and provided a steady stream of reports that warned of the mounting danger of the Nazi regime. They chronicled Hitler's systematic elimination of dissent and civil society—the closing of opposition newspapers, the purge of the Reichstag, the arrest of dissenting intellectuals—even as they themselves faced mounting censorship in the years leading up to the war.[7]

But without a public or policy context that emphasized human rights in the United States, these stories had little impact. In fact, Hitler's early actions against leftists and trade unions were praised by many in the United States. Hitler's initial measures to deprive Jews of civil rights in the early 1930s must be regarded in the context of the flagrant anti-Semitism that was practiced in the United States at the time. This is to say nothing of the institution of racial apartheid in some Southern states and the widespread practice of lynching, in which the rule of law was trampled, usually with impunity. Furthermore, as evidence of the Jewish Holocaust in Europe mounted, editors at *The New York Times* downplayed the information out of fear of fueling resistance to US involvement in the war by anti-Semitic sectors.[8]

In other words, the United States may have been a constitutional democracy at the time, but it did not have a prevailing culture of human rights that systematically placed civil rights and civil liberties above regional practices and political concerns. International reporters found it impossible to hold other countries systematically to standards that were not met—or even attempted—at home.

Over the war years, the US government encouraged the news media to cover Nazi abuses. In general, the US press emphasized Nazi atrocities in Western Europe more than abuses committed in Eastern Europe or Japanese atrocities in Asia (other than those committed against Allied troops). All US war correspondence was subject to heavy military censorship, mainly concerned with projecting a positive public image of the success of the war effort.

If Axis abuses were reported on an uneven basis, violations of Geneva Conventions by Allied troops were essentially taboo. The 13 February 1945 firebombing of Dresden is a prime example. According to British historian Philip Knightley, the city's primary function was to receive refugees from Silesia, fleeing the Russian advance. The city contained no major military targets, yet the British RAF dropped three-quarters of a million incendiary bombs, killing an estimated 100,000–130,000 German civilians, far outstripping the number of casualties from the atomic bomb in Hiroshima or the combined British casualties in the Blitz. The following week, the Associated Press reported, "Allied Air Chiefs have made the long-awaited decision to adopt deliberate terror bombings of German population centers as a ruthless expedient of hastening Hitler's doom." (The British had excluded war correspondents from the bombing mission and banned publication of the AP report.) The policy to direct bombings against civilians had actually been adopted several years earlier.[9]

Allied military authorities also tried to prevent press coverage of the use of the atomic bomb at Hiroshima on 6 August 1945. As Knightley points out, "By the first week in September, three weeks after Japan had surrendered and nearly a month after Hiroshima, there still had been no account by a Western correspondent of the effects of the atom bomb on the two Japanese cities. General MacArthur had placed all southern Japan 'off-limits' to the press, and instead of ending censorship, had tightened it."[10]

British reporter Wilfred Burchett managed to get to Hiroshima for a firsthand report. He broke the initial story in the *London Daily Express* on September 5. A year later John Hersey's sweeping account of the bomb's devastation of the civilian population ran in *The New Yorker* magazine. The use of the atomic bomb is still hotly debated. And as we have seen in Afghanistan and Iraq, many still question the patriotism of journalists who publish reports of civilian suffering inflicted by their own country's armed forces.

The Second World War was undoubtedly unleashed by the actions of the German government, which committed human rights violations of unthinkable proportions. The Nazis destroyed the independent German news media in the 1930s, to the extent that nothing resembling our notion of authentic journalism was available to the German public on civil rights issues, humanitarian concerns, or most other areas of interest to this chapter. But the Allies' news media had some lapses as well. Even in the aftermath of the war, many stories went untold: mistreatment and intentional starvation of German POWs; widespread extrajudicial killings of ethnic German civilians in former occupied territories of Eastern Europe and in the former Soviet Union; the creation of vast numbers of refugees from the same region in measures that paralleled "ethnic cleansing" in later eras. Some of the refugees were complicit in the crimes of the Nazi Occupation, others had been merely passive beneficiaries, and still others' only crime had been to be German-speaking or descended from Germans. But in many regions the entire ethnic German population was held accountable under the "principle of collective blame" based on their cultural identity, not their specific acts.[11] Just as the internment of innocent US citizens of Japanese extraction went largely unquestioned by news outlets during the war, the US news media had little interest in the rights of German and ethnic German populations.

The period following World War II established the groundwork for the modern conception of human rights. The Tokyo and Nuremburg Trials; the Universal Declaration of Human Rights; and the establishment of the United Nations system were all phenomena that helped to redefine the duties of modern states toward their citizens, as well as the role of the international community.

But even though the concepts of international law and international government were evolving, newspapers and broadcasters were still national news media—and subject to a nationalist perspective. Furthermore, the Cold War led to a propaganda war, in which news reporting was a weapon of choice for all sides. Among the conventions of this conflict were exaggerations, fabrications, and the use of a journalistic cover for purposes of espionage—a damaging practice for legitimate journalism. The Soviet bloc's press was so heavily censored that reports relating to human rights issues there were limited to the sporadic, fragmented accounts of the underground press.

But the US news media also still struggled for independence from official policy. One famous example is Seymour Hersh's account of the My Lai massacre in Vietnam. The story—detailing the killing of over 100 unarmed civilians by US troops on 16 March 1968—was originally circulated in Washington by a soldier who had heard about it in Vietnam. The army was pressed into conducting a court martial, but the investigation was given little attention in the news media. It took the efforts of Hersh, a young free-lance journalist—and many rejections from major news organizations—before the story ran. My Lai changed the course of reporting on the war.

Many government and military officials believed that US press coverage of Vietnamese civilian casualties undermined public support for the war and was to blame for its loss. Many US journalists hold that the era of critical reporting on Vietnam and the Watergate scandal represents their profession's finest hour. One could also argue that it was this period, and not the immediate postwar years, that set the stage for the modern form of human rights and humanitarian reporting.

Vietnam was the first war in US history in which crucial reporters and editors at leading national news organizations came to assume an outright adversarial position toward the government regarding an ongoing war. For some journalists, the cumulative evidence of the abuse of the human rights of Vietnamese civilians became more compelling than the definition of US national interests in the war as articulated by the Nixon administration. As part of this process, journalists adopted new methods of documentation, such as extensive interviews with hostile or potentially hostile populations. A few journalists, notably Harrison Salisbury of *The New York Times,* traveled to Hanoi to report on civilian bombing casualties there. This action would have been unthinkable in World War II Tokyo or Berlin, and furthermore, it would have been considered irrelevant.

Human Rights and Humanitarian Reporting in the Reagan Era and Beyond

Journalists were even freer to pursue such independence in the proxy wars that followed Vietnam, in which US interests were only vaguely defined and indirectly pursued. In the Cold War conflicts of Africa, the Southern Cone, and Central America, the United States had client states on hand to blame for human rights violations, even if the violations were receiving US approval or support. But the proxy wars also advanced the development of human rights–oriented journalism in the US press. Under the Reagan administration journalists who reported on human rights violations by client states were sometimes called Communist dupes, but it was difficult to define them as traitors, given that their own country was not an official party to the conflict.

In some ways the most conspicuous human rights failure of US press of the period was the inability or unwillingness to publicize fully the magnitude of the humanitarian catastrophes in Cambodia in the late 1970s and Afghanistan in the early 1980s. Both areas were sealed off from foreigners, and their own news media were eliminated. It is extremely difficult to piece together detailed, accurate stories from the fragmentary evidence that can be mined by refugee testimony and similar sources, though some news organizations tried. Nonetheless, the world was largely able to go about its business without too much thought about the two to three million Cambodians and over a million Afghanis who were being massacred. The US news media were caught up in their own issues, which included detailed attention to US client states—which was appropriate, but not to the extent that it should have worked against energetic coverage of the larger calamities.

This chapter of history illustrates a characteristic and systematic weakness in US human rights reporting that persists this day: it is ethnocentric. The easiest story to publish is the story of an abuse committed against one's own citizens. The second easiest is the abuse committed by one's government or one's government's enemy. The most difficult story to publish is the abuse committed by unfamiliar parties against unfamiliar parties—even if they occur on an immensely larger scale. Our inability to create an early warning system for human rights and humanitarian crises in places that "don't involve us"—such as Afghanistan and Iraq in the late twentieth century—increases our chances of our becoming tragically involved at a later and more difficult stage.

The Human Rights Bureaucracy

In the late 1970s human rights reporting in the news media began to benefit from the institutionalization of a human rights bureaucracy in the United States. One important step in this process was the Carter administration's establishment of the post of Assistant Secretary of State for Human Rights (now Assistant Secretary of State for Democracy, Human Rights, and Labor). The post has taken on different coloration from administration to administration, but its creation marked a moment in which human rights were declared to be an explicit component of US foreign policy. The State Department gradually took on increasingly professionalized human rights reportage functions, and many individuals within the bureaucracy became both knowledgeable about and committed to the principles of human rights. Over time, this helped to make human rights a permissible, and even a required, topic for international coverage. The State Department's annual country reports on human rights have become a respected and reliable yardstick, with strong research presented in a remarkably even-handed fashion.

There was even more rapid development among NGOs. Amnesty International, born in the UK in the 1960s, underwent a period of rapid growth in the United States in the late 1970s and 1980s. Outreach and education of the news media were an Amnesty concern from the beginning. Terminology grounded in human rights concepts and international law began to enter the newsrooms, initially in the UK, and subsequently in the United States and elsewhere. Likewise, Helsinki Watch, which gradually mushroomed into Human Rights Watch, began to take shape in the late 1970s and promoted the idea of nonideological standards for human rights records. As far as journalists were concerned, the time was right. Many journalists who had grown up in the skeptical environment of the Vietnam era wanted to move beyond the politicized standards of the Cold War.

The new human rights NGO establishment worked hard, with increasing sophistication, to cultivate the news media. Some of the common strategies were:

- First, to produce a formidable stream of opinion (or op ed) articles in their areas of expertise for both first- and second-tier newspapers;
- Second, to cultivate individual reporters who covered related beats, and to learn how their editorial process functioned;
- Third, to generate vast quantities of scrupulously documented field research that provided extensive, verifiable raw material for stories, and to expend energy in placing them in the hands of those in the editorial food chain most likely to utilize them.

It is useful to consider the reasons why an organization like Human Rights Watch, for example, was so successful in bringing its case to the news media. One was the scope of its research. The organization was scrupulously active in researching abuses by both left-wing and right-wing regimes, which distinguished it in an era when debates were highly charged and ideologically colored. It had an advantage over Amnesty International in the 1980s in that Amnesty's mandate limited its critiques to governments, while Human Rights Watch had fewer restrictions. In the postwar world insurgencies were an urgent reality, and documenting and denouncing abuses by guerrilla organizations, as well as governments, gave the research an air of reality. Human Rights Watch also covered a vast amount of ground with an emphasis on accuracy. Researchers participated in seminars on documentation and research methodology, reports were extensively footnoted, and there were relatively few errors.

It has been argued, with justification, that the West's response to the crisis in the former Yugoslavia was deeply flawed and that its inaction in Rwanda was calamitous. But this was not for lack of information. In fact, in both areas the immediacy and the detail of the reporting on the unfolding disasters represented a quantum leap from the information available from the regions in earlier crises. In both cases the scope of reporting available in the United States owed a demonstrable debt to groundwork human rights organizations had laid earlier.

The human rights disasters of the 1990s illustrated that the reporting and documentation function of human rights groups was becoming even more influential due to the cutbacks occurring at US news organizations on overseas staff. Again, this was particularly brutal at the big three US networks. News divisions that used to boast of field reports from a host of foreign bureaus began to close them, compromising their news content in the process. In the current era, reporters in New York do voice-overs in the studio for videotaped stories shot by video wire-service reporters for television syndicates—many of them British. A network will cover Latin America out of Miami or Atlanta, while all of Europe is explained from an office suite in London. The number of overseas bureaus has held steady or increased over the past decade at very few organizations, such as the Associated Press and Bloomberg News, and major papers like *The New York Times* and the *Washington Post*. But many second-tier markets, like Chicago and San Francisco, have had to compromise by cutting back on their foreign news staffs.

Human rights organizations learned that once they established a reputation for credibility and thoroughness, they could originate and place a major story with a degree of success that once belonged only to government institutions. Over the past decade the division of labor between human rights organizations and journalists has become blurred. A symbiotic relationship has evolved: human rights reports refer to leading US newspapers extensively. The same newspapers will run stories on reports released by the organizations, and their reporters will use staff members as sources.

Is this problematic? Not necessarily. Journalism, by its very nature, involves the brokerage of information, and journalists depend on their sense of judgment and professionalism to know which information is reliable, which should be countered with an opposing source, and which to discard. Human rights organizations must be evaluated individually and weighed like any other source, and even individuals within them must be judged according to their level of competence and expertise. Each organization—governmental or nongovernmental—has agendas, explicit and tacit, and a journalist must take this into account as well.

But the best of the human rights NGOs have raised the standards of objectivity of international reporting through clearly stated standards and rigorous research. Over the past two decades journalists have observed the merits of an approach based on the standards of law. This appreciation has made its way into an increasing amount of international coverage.[12]

But it bears repeating that most of the above comments apply chiefly to one narrow band of the US news media: the quality metropolitan daily. It is easy to find a large number of original news stories with human rights orientations in *The New York Times*, the *Washington Post*, the *Los Angeles Times*, the *Wall Street Journal*, and (occupying a somewhat different niche) the *Christian Science Monitor*. It should be noted that each of the first four publications has a circulation in the rough neighborhood of a million. The combined circulation of these newspapers is some five million in a country of 270 million people. They influence a narrow elite, but they extend that influence through the other news organizations that run their wire services or otherwise pick up their stories.

Another tier of worthwhile coverage exists in regional newspapers like the *Miami Herald*, *Newsday*, and the *San Francisco Chronicle*. Quality regional papers will often run excellent pieces of international coverage based on the interests of their local readership and local ethnical communities. Some of the most extensive coverage of Africa in the

United States appears in newspapers that serve heavily African American communities like Chicago, Cleveland, and Washington, DC. Several California dailies have exceptional reporting on Asian issues, and border newspapers in the Southwest often break important stories on Latin America.

Certain magazines, including the leading news magazines and literary magazines, publish analytical essays and include a human rights perspective in their international stories.[13] National Public Radio offers strong human rights reporting as an intrinsic part of its extensive international coverage. US television is a more difficult proposition. Individual programs like CBS's "60 Minutes," ABC's "Nightline," and PBS' "Frontline," routinely cover human rights–related stories with sophistication. But overall, coverage of international news on television has been shrinking, making it more difficult to find any thematic development to stories, and making breaking international news more episodic and remote. CNN held a certain promise under Ted Turner's outspoken tenure, but since its acquisition by Time Warner, it has been cutting back on international content and staff. The advent of cable television has brought BBC World Service television into many US homes, but its degree of influence is unclear.

The larger issue is that Americans appear to be less interested in in-depth international coverage on television, their medium of choice. The traditional network news programming has suffered from new competition. At the height of the war in Iraq in the spring of 2003, the combined audience for the half-hour evening news broadcasts of ABC, CBS, and NBC was twenty-nine million, as reported by the Associated Press. The February "sweeps" rating for Fox's entertainment program "Joe Millionaire" was, by comparison, forty million, also reported by the Associated Press. Increasingly, the relevant question may be not what form of news Americans absorb, but whether they are consuming any real news at all.

CONCLUSION

It is an open secret that American democracy depends on policies formulated and disseminated by various elites. At best, an informed electorate approves these policies through participatory democracy. At worst, a distracted and disengaged electorate allows the advancement of policies whose consequences come as an unpleasant surprise.

In the current era, thanks to the Internet, the engaged consumer of news has access to more information—and more information of quality—than earlier generations could imagine. Among leading news organizations, human rights and humanitarian reporting has grown in scope and influence over time and is now in another period of dynamic growth.

On the other hand, the episodic and entertainment driven side of the news business has created new, and sometimes destructive, pressures. Diplomats now talk about the "CNN effect," in which persistent, one-dimensional coverage of an international crisis can create overwhelming public pressure for intervention—even if no one can formulate an approach to intervention that actually improves the circumstances.

In the journalistic food chain not all journalists and news organizations should be judged by the same standards. Some of them, such as journals and magazines of opinion, have the primary function of advancing the debate. Reporters for newspapers of record must remain in dialogue with the policy community and the public, especially when views diverge, and use the responsible accumulation of evidence to suggest cases for change in policy. The role of the broadest commercial media may be, at best, simply to explain the bare outlines of such change to a mass public once it has already taken place.

But the challenge for all journalists, no matter which medium they serve, is to sustain a universal perspective. They must view an innocent civilian of any nationality as possessing the same rights to security as a compatriot; they must acknowledge the same fundamental right to a safe work environment for workers on the other side of the world as for workers across the street. It will always be logistically impossible to document the workings of the world, and its abuses, in a comprehensive fashion. But journalists and their managers should continue to incorporate the notion of universal values into their picture of the world. This is necessary—if not sufficient—for the creation of the informed citizenry that is required for a fully functional democracy.

NOTES

[1] See the passage on Vietnam in this chapter; see also Chris Hedges, "A Gaza Diary," *Harper's* (October 2001): 59–71.

[2] See Alan Nairn, "Our Payroll, Haitian Hit," *Nation* (9 October 1995): 36–39.

[3] Sydney Ahlstrom, *A Religious History of the American People* (New Haven, CT: Yale Univ. Press, 1993), 650.

[4] Alfred N. Hunt, *Haiti's Influence on AnteBellum America: Slumbering Volcano in the Caribbean* (Baton Rouge, LA: Louisiana State Univ. Press, 1988), 118.

[5] In David Paul Nord, *Communities of Journalism: A History of American Newpapers and Their Readers* (Urbana: Univ. of Illinois Press, 2001), 94.

[6] See David Haward Bain, *Sitting in Darkness: Americans in Philippines* (Boston: Houghton Mifflin Company, 1984); and Stuart Creighton Miller, *Benevolent Assimilation: The American Conquest of the Philippines, 1899–1903* (New Haven, CT: Yale Univ. Press, 1982).

[7] See William Shirer, *Berlin Diary: The Journal of a Foreign Correspondent, 1934–1941* (Baltimore: Johns Hopkins Univ. Press).

[8] See Lucy Davidowicz, *War against the Jews* (New York: Bantam Books, 1986).

[9] Philip Knightley, *The First Casualty* (Baltimore: Johns Hopkins Univ. Press), 314.

[10] Ibid., 300.

[11] For the case of ethnic Germans in Czechoslovakia, see Center for Economic Research and Graduate Education (CERGE), *Czech Republic 1998: Facing Reality*, 1999, www.cerge-ei.cz/publications/books/contents_98_pdf.asp (accessed 31 August 2004).

[12] For David Rohde's approach to forensic investigation and testimony, see David Rohde, "The Rohde to Srebrenica," http://www.columbia.edu/itc/journalism/nelson/rohde/ (accessed 31 August 2004).

[13] The most notable of this group would be *The Economist*, *The New Yorker*, the *New York Review of Books*, *Harper's*, and *Mother Jones*, all of which have contributed greatly to the field. Others, with more specialized or marginal coverage, include *Time*, and *Newsweek* and *Businessweek* for stories on international labor rights.

13

No Empty Vessel

Media Roles in Human Rights

Thomas R. Lansner

INTRODUCTION

The media's position in the human rights firmament is complex and at times highly problematical. Media freedom itself is an essential human right. And absent freedom of expression, few other rights can be fully enjoyed. Yet that freedom may be misused to incite abuses. And a free marketplace of ideas and ideologies, with open access to and easy ability to exchange and publish information, will sometimes introduce new tensions by increasing heterogeneity and fomenting often well-justified demands for change.

Media are a crucial mobilizing tool that helps turn ideas into action. Mass media are the primary conduit for information through which people are informed of and understand the wider world. Media outlets are owned by governments, political parties, religious institutions, and secular groups with varied agendas, and by commercial groups whose primary motive is profit. The media's moral and professional responsibilities in reporting human rights are vigorously debated. An "active open media"[1] can promote human rights, development, and democracy by informing people of their rights, by encouraging participatory governance, and by increasing transparency and demanding accountability of the broadest range of societal actors. But by commission or omission, media can also help subvert basic liberties by encouraging acquiescence to or active support for human rights violations.[2]

Reporting on human rights and humanitarian issues also faces structural obstacles inherent in the style of most news reporting. News reports, especially in the dominant short-form journalism of television, radio, and daily newspapers, nearly always emphasize events over process, description over explanation, and post facto analysis over prediction and early warning. The sources used to comment on events and the language of discourse and description can also condition audience perceptions and reactions.[3]

Whatever the content, emerging technologies and globalization of public, private, commercial, and personal communications networks are creating enormous changes in how people gather information and to whom they disseminate it. National and cultural sovereignty is increasingly challenged by the organic growth of virtually linked affinity groups that identify by affiliations other than kith and kin. Thicker horizontal linkages and disintermediation allow greater voice to marginalized groups—those typically most subject to the most persistent and egregious human rights violations. Activists demanding respect for human rights and humanitarian law are increasingly adept at using tools of modern mass media to move their message, from community radio stations that raise local awareness, to global advocacy networks, to sophisticated websites that mainstream information from traditionally excluded communities.

Human rights and social justice advocates operate in a crowded marketplace of ideas and products, of course. They sometimes compete with one another for attention and funding, and almost always against governments and other interests whose resources usually far outstrip those of even the most prominent human rights groups. Powerful institutions will often deploy disinformation and lies to discredit criticism, and they sometimes resort to legalized suppression, intimidation, or physical attacks against rights advocates and media if their perceived vital, or simply vested, interests are threatened. Some authoritarian regimes claim that media coverage of human rights violations are attempts to impose "Western" standards on other societies and that denunciations of human rights abuses often reflect tactical alliances among Western activists, media, and out-of-power Asian elites vying to depict a false image of governmental repression.[4]

Human rights advocates also face increasing obstacles from concentrated commercial mass media whose pursuit of profit often precludes serious coverage of social justice issues. Yet the gradual gathering of popular support for the core values of human rights and humanitarian law, which by no coincidence has grown with the reach of the mass media, is an increasingly powerful foundation for a global movement that rejects abuses. Media can help lead this struggle by battling for their own freedom, by exposing abuses, demanding accountability, explaining rights, and by giving voice for all sectors of society.

This chapter surveys the issues above, first via a brief historical tour of how media and communications have served as an actor in the rising struggle to establish and promote respect for the rule of law, human rights, and humanitarian law. It then discusses modern media roles: reporting on human rights; advocacy and "peace media"; and "hate media" incitements to human rights abuses. The impact of emerging information and communications technologies in helping to create universal constituencies for universal rights, and to empower new actors to reach wider audiences directly as well as through conventional and community media, is then assessed. How the human rights message might best be mainstreamed into mass media not only to influence opinion but to change values and to avoid "the indifference of eternal vigilance" is addressed. Finally, some suggestions regarding how to encourage an active open media that approaches human rights coverage as a core professional responsibility are offered.

SOVEREIGNTY
AND PERMEABLE INFORMATION FRONTIERS

Media systems and media freedom have typically been assessed within individual nations, usually in reference to the press. Now, national "sovereignty" over any communications or cultural production is steadily dissipating. Local and national struggles are ever more transparent to the outside world. The growing permeability of information frontiers offers new possibilities of learning, cooperation, and advocacy.

Historically, the extent of sovereignty was measured by the area over which a particular ruler or group exercised physical control. And this rarely extended any further than command over lines of physical communication by land or water. Sovereignty over territory also presumed the power of exclusion—of people, of goods, of information. Sovereign power to exclude or contain information, however, has eroded at a quickening pace since the development of long-distance telecommunications, beginning with the telegraph in the mid-nineteenth century.

While globalized media in some forms have long existed, high entry costs meant that their direct availability and impact have mostly been at the elite levels of societies. New technologies offer local, national, and regional human rights advocates far greater and cheaper access to global networks of resources and influence. To use them well, however, they must master media techniques to deliver their advocacy messages effectively, as will be discussed below.

BABYLON TO THE CRIMEA, STELLAE TO NEWSPRINT

One of the earliest known recorded elaborations of legal practice is found in the code of Hammurabi, laws proclaimed by that Babylonian king in his eighteenth century BC empire. Among its wide-ranging provisions were details regarding the treatment of prisoners of war, perhaps the first written example of humanitarian law. The code was in many aspects far from humane, incorporating the death penalty, severe corporal retribution, and formal distinctions in rights and penalties according to rank, age, and gender. Yet it does represent consistency and uniformity of rights and responsibilities throughout Hammurabi's realm. And it was literally written in stone, the medium through which the code was proclaimed. Stellae on which the laws were engraved were relatively immutable. The literate, at least, could consult a plainly stated code of justice not subject to the potentially capricious whims of the powerful.

In the ancient world news and ideas traveled slowly. Oral storytelling was the principal way that knowledge was conveyed among peoples, across cultures, and through generations. Change was most often incremental, and Hammurabi's code was certainly the cumulative expression of centuries of experience. The provisions regarding prisoners of war reflect times in which battle and conquest were common enough that Babylon's rulers believed behaviors during conflict should in some measure be regulated.

About two millennia later wartime suffering rose to become the subject of public concern in a far different setting. For British soldiers fighting against Russia in the Crimean War (1853–56), the dangers of battle were compounded by poor nutrition and abysmal medical care. This has often been the lot of the common soldier, and in some conflicts today still is. But in Britain in the 1850s these conditions were for the first time reported by independent correspondents writing for a free media. Competitive, mass-produced newspapers vied for market share among a growing literate public eager for news. The train, and then the telegraph, increased the speed with which word of faraway events could reach other countries. Dispatches by the (London) *Times* Constantinople correspondent Thomas Chenery describing horrific military hospital conditions inspired Florence Nightingale to take ship with a band of nurses and nuns to care for wounded soldiers, and to later carry on with a movement that changed the face of medical care in Britain.[5]

Edwin Laurence Godkin, one of the first professional war correspondents, believed that the press, and the public opinion of its readers, could influence those in power. He was reporting at a time when several factors in the evolution of technology and governance converged to allow this possibility. Beginning in the mid-1800s the telegraph allowed the first electronic transmission of news and other information. Steam engines, and later electric power, allowed mass printing and circulation of British newspapers that were distributed by railways throughout the country. Godkin was writing for a relatively free, independent, and active press, which did not face suppression for contradicting the current regime. And of highest importance was the existence of an elected government, which (despite serious limitations on franchise that tempered its legitimacy) had to answer to Parliament and the voters.

The presence of these three conditions—media freedom and independence, wide dissemination of and access to media content, and official accountability—today remain the most accurate measures of the media's potential to influence opinion and policy. Yet, as will be discussed later, this does not guarantee that human rights or humanitarian issues will be covered, promoted, or respected.

GADFLIES AND CRUSADERS

In the United States press freedom was considered so crucial to a free people that the right was enshrined in the first amendment to the US Constitution in 1789. A defining test of the press's ability to challenge government in America had played out over a century before while New York was a British colony. John Peter Zenger, a German immigrant newspaperman living in lower Manhattan, published scathing criticisms of then-governor William Cosby. In 1733, Cosby jailed Zenger, shuttered his *Weekly Journal*, and ordered issues containing satirical cartoons to be burned "by the hands of the common hangman or whipper," for, in part, "tending . . . to bring His Majesty's government into contempt."[6]

The law favored Governor Cosby, but Zenger had the right to trial by jury. And his fellow New Yorkers refused to convict him of any crime, on the simple basis that what he published was in fact true.[7]

Four decades later, both open and underground newspapers and pamphlets were important tools for American revolutionaries, as they have continued to be for activists in scores of countries over more than two centuries since. After independence was won, the free press became a crucial tool in the struggle to abolish slavery, both in Britain and the United States. Beginning in the 1820s dozens of anti-slavery newspapers were launched in the United States. Many received support, including printing presses, from chapters of the American Anti-Slavery Society, which was founded in 1831 and, with its British predecessor, can be counted as among the first human rights NGOs.[8]

Abolitionist newspapers, including a number published by former slaves, certainly helped turn Northern public opinion against slavery, although they faced stiff competition from pro-slavery newspapers (and it is interesting to note that the Anti-Slavery Society was driven by the issue of whether it should also support equal rights for women, of any color). When the American Civil War erupted in 1861, the Confederate government, mindful of the power of media to influence British public opinion, secretly bought newspapers in Britain that were used to expound the rebel cause and encourage British aid to the Confederacy.

Their mission accomplished, most of the crusading anti-slavery newspapers wrapped up publication by the end of the Civil War. Yet the efforts of the "muckraking" press to expose malfeasance were highlighted again in the 1880s, when *Harper's Weekly* published scathing articles and Thomas Nast's cartoons lampooning governmental corruption in New York City.[9] Political boss William Tweed, who was eventually jailed for corruption, reportedly complained to the *Harper's Weekly* editor, "I don't care a straw for your newspaper articles, my constituents don't know how to read, but they can't help seeing them damned pictures."[10] Tweed's comment speaks to the influence of a "watchdog" media and also to the importance of fashioning messages that audiences can easily understand.

ACCESS, COMPLEXITY, DIVERSITY

Who can access information offered by even active open media is also a crucial issue. The impact of any mass media is in the first instance limited to those can see or hear the message. Absent broad access, the media's power to inform, to shape agendas, and to provide a civic forum, is severely restricted. Distribution, literacy, availability of vernacular media, and consumer costs all affect access. Emerging information and communications technologies (ICTs), including the Internet and satellite broadcasting, are reaching new and diverse audiences, enabling "many-to-many" communications and redrawing established hierarchies of communications.

Media that allow voice must also be diverse and inclusive. Even many moderate critiques of existing media structures in the most democratic societies urge much greater popular participation in generating media content and decentralization of its means of dissemination.[11] It can be argued that in many developing countries domestic media are usually even more demonstrably beholden to the state or elite interests through official control or the narrow economic base of most private media enterprises. In many cases mass media consent is merely mandated rather than even manufactured. Media ownership always matters; its importance is encapsulated in A. J. Liebling's aphorism, "Freedom of the press is guaranteed only to those who own one."[12]

Blatant bias is often seen in state media that are controlled by those in power, with human rights abuses unreported or denied and regime preservation too often masquerading as "nation building." However, much information in private media is also less than balanced and fair, sometimes by partisan design, sometimes because of poor reporting standards. Private media are often utilized as just one means to pursue the grand prize of power.

INTERNET AND EMERGING ICTS

Today, new ICTs are very rapidly changing how people access and exchange information.[13] Satellite broadcasting, Internet access, and other new or expanding ICTs reduce the power of single sources of information. Hierarchical forms of information distribution from governments, powerful societal institutions, and established mass media outlets are being supplemented, if not supplanted. While this growing "disintermediation" of data flows expands the pool of individuals and groups able to transmit and access information, it may be very difficult to gauge the integrity and reliability of the information product.

The effect on efficiency for mobilization is clearer: cheaper and faster communications allow much greater contact, networking, and information sharing even among civil society groups with few resources.[14] "Digital divide" concerns address important matters of access and appropriate content, but there is no doubt that however unevenly distributed to date, new ICTs are broadening debate and building new communities around the globe. Except in a few of the world's most reclusive and repressive lands, excluding information is increasingly impossible. Open access to information is the prerequisite, and not a perquisite, of modern economies. High levels of information access are the oxygen of economic growth for countries that wish to join the global knowledge-based economy. Without it, inbound investment is inhibited and domestic innovation stifled. But increased information provided by an open and accessible media inevitably spurs political debate as well as economic development. Restrictions on media and other information flows by regimes seeking to suppress political discussion, "ideological impurity," or "cultural contamination" are not only increasingly ineffective but also negatively affect economic prospects.

MEDIA RIGHTS, MEDIA RESPONSIBILITIES

The global standard for media freedom is utterly unambiguous. Article 19 of the UDHR states succinctly that "freedom of expression" includes the right "to seek, receive and impart information and ideas of all kinds, regardless of frontiers, either orally, in writing, or in print, in the form of art, or through any other media."

Like many other rights, though, this one is far from universally honored. The Freedom House Press Freedom Survey for 2002 describes 75 of the 187 countries or territories assessed as "free," 51 as partly free, and 61 as not free.[15] It is of little surprise to note that the 17 countries with top ratings are mostly developed democracies, and that among the two dozen lowest-ranking nations are most of the world's worst abusers of human rights overall.

The direction of causality is not discussed, and often press freedom is one of many basic rights denied. But absent an active open media, it is most likely impossible to build a culture of human rights, which requires that people understand the fundamental freedoms that are their irrevocable birthright. Yet many people whose rights are not respected often have little awareness or limited understanding of those rights and their government's responsibilities to protect and promote them.

Media can play crucial roles in developing this awareness. Freedom of expression—if respected as guaranteed by Article 19 of the UDHR—opens the way for the spread of information, education, and debate. Quick advantage should be taken of any window of opportunity to explain and encourage respect for human rights. Even renewed repression is never as effective once people have learned of their rights.

Most media practitioners in emerging democracies lack sufficient educational background or life experience to relate human rights information to their audiences directly or as an important component shaping their reporting. Seminars on the reporting of human rights, the rule of law, and electoral processes can help bridge this gap between the *de jure* existence of these rights and the ability of media to communicate their meaning to the public.

Even in more mature democratic states that may enjoy broad prosperity and strong traditions of rule of law, media's watchdog role is crucial to balancing the tremendous power that inheres in government, is amassed by businesses, and is sometimes accorded to other societal actors. Presenting the views and concerns of the public is another central role. Active open media serve to inform, articulate, and report public opinion, to the edification of policymakers, opinion leaders, and the public itself.

To many advocates of media freedom, especially in the United States, these are the only roles media should be expected to play: the nominally objective "reporter" of events, and the provider of "disinterested" analysis upon which an engaged citizenry can base its informed participation in the political process. In this, many media practitioners protest too much, and it is utterly disingenuous to deny the degree to which news selection helps shape public perceptions and the policy agenda.

Journalists, editors, publishers, and other media practitioners in both developed and developing countries should be encouraged and assisted to create strategies to disseminate this human rights information and incorporate it into their overall reporting on events in their countries and elsewhere. Offering primers in fundamental freedoms is an important step in promoting more and better human rights coverage.[16]

This is no overnight task. Global networking and support should be emphasized to help dispel the isolation that advocates of fundamental freedoms, including media practitioners, often suffer in less than free societies. Contact and cooperation with international governmental organizations and NGOs on the national, regional, and international level should be encouraged and assisted.

Another key area for countries in transition is the understanding and reporting of electoral processes. Decades of electoral charades, reported by a tightly controlled press, have left many media practitioners ill equipped to report on open elections. The need to assess the entire electoral landscape, including electoral law, election commissions, voters' lists, and opposition and nonpartisan participation—as well as the more obvious questions of freedom of expression and association—is often little appreciated.

Accepting that media can play an important human rights and pro-democracy political role is not to demand that all media be nonpartisan. Private media, beyond the boundaries of reasonable regulation of incitement and libel in the context of guarantees of free expression, should bear no such responsibility. Political parties, advocacy groups, religious organizations, and purely commercial interests operate media for what may be their own very parochial purposes. And programming decisions driven by self-censorship and even free editorial choices may produce information no less skewed than official propaganda. For-profit media worldwide largely operate on the lowest-common denominator principle, seeking broad commercial appeal to maximize profit. The trend toward sensationalism and exploitative coverage is clear. It is essential to acknowledge that the marketplace's demands may in effect be no less insidious than a government's dictates.

PROMOTING RIGHTS, ADDRESSING CONFLICT

The informational role for media in developing democracies is more complex than in mature democracies. The structures and processes of new or newly empowered institutions, of the roles of the judiciary, of legislatures, of governmental bodies, require explanation. Awareness of rights must be widespread if they are to be asserted and respected.

Very basic health, literacy, and other social-services information may also be an important part of effective and useful media in developing democracies. The West Africa Non-Governmental Organization Network (www.wangonet.org) is among the newest of Africa-based web portals dedicated to imparting such information, while seeking to evoke local participation.[17] Success stories of new ICTs in realizing development goals are increasing, and some of the most promising have been documented by groups working in the field.[18] And while most discussions of human rights and media focus on basic civil and political liberties, media may promote or obstruct the realization of economic, social, and cultural rights. Active media strategies are crucial, for example, to disseminate information and to evoke engagement that is central to the success of poverty reduction programs.[19]

Governments can encourage "public service" media content by buying advertising, or, as was for many years the case in the United States, mandating a certain number of public-service announcements for which it can also offer (but should not impose) appropriate content. And democracy-building activities must not be equated with "nation-building" formulas that demand only "positive" news that bolster the image of certain politicians or parties.[20]

Mass media's role in shaping public opinion about conflict can be crucial and is continually vexing.[21] Especially when strife is driven by stereotypical group perceptions that are too easily manipulated on the basis of historical fears or prejudices, alternative media can challenge both fixed beliefs and rumors that may spark or sustain cycles of violence. In wartime, even "mature" media in the most established democracies often exhibit chauvinistic and jingoistic bias. Pro-imperial US media roused public support for the US invasions of Cuba and the Philippines at the close of the nineteenth century. The tendency was again glaringly evident by even a cursory viewing of America's Fox News or MSNBC networks during the American-led invasion of Iraq in March–April 2003.

Media may dampen or fan incendiary situations during domestic strife. Rwanda's Radio Télévision Libre des Mille Collines (RTLM) actively promoted that country's 1994 genocide by broadcasting calls for the extermination of its Tutsi citizens. Prosecutions for inciting crimes against humanity through broadcast media have been pursued by the United Nations International Criminal Tribunal for Rwanda (ICTR) in Arusha, Tanzania.[22] A Belgian citizen, Georges Ruggui, is serving a twelve-year sentence imposed by the ICTR for his work at the pro-genocide broadcaster. And in November 2002 the popular Rwandan singer Simon Bikindi was extradited to Arusha to face charges of complicity to genocide for composing and performing songs demonizing Rwandan Tutsi and urging their murder. More recently, the ICTR convicted Ferdinand Nahimana, founder of the RTLM, Jean-Bosco Barayagwiza, board member of the Comité d'initiative of the RTLM, and Hassan Ngeze, chief editor of Kangura, for crimes against humanity, genocide, and incitement to genocide among others.[23]

When media clearly incite conflict, and local authorities cannot or will not intervene (or in fact might be those propagating the incitement), very difficult decisions on whether and how external actors should seek to block mass media dissemination of messages inciting violence must be considered. Balkans' radio stations and newspapers judged dangerous to civic peace have been closed by UN administrators, as was at least one Iraqi newspaper by American occupation authorities in mid-2003.[24] Electronic jamming of broadcasts is sometimes possible. Attacking media outlets (as US forces did overtly to harsh criticism in Belgrade during the Kosovo conflict, and in more ambiguous circumstances during the invasions of Afghanistan and Iraq) should remain a final, desperate option. Violence against media outlets must be reserved only for the most extreme cases when it is firmly believed that silencing those voices will halt incitement of serious and perhaps widespread crimes.[25]

Yet it must be recognized that information interdiction is an ephemeral and superficial solution. In the long term, providing alternative information is likely to be more productive, especially in reshaping attitudes that underlie conflict and promoting values that respect human rights. The notion that peacebuilding information is effective in reducing conflict is the foundation for many such efforts. Civic education, voter education, conflict resolution, and human rights campaigns utilizing various media have been undertaken in many countries to promote tolerance and respect among communities, sometimes using song, live performance, and radio and television dramas or soap operas to deliver information. These are often identified as among the most popular offerings on externally funded "peace radio."

Various UN agencies, governments, and NGOs have all funded peacebuilding media.[26] One of the most detailed case studies of "peacebuilding" media is of Burundi's Studio Ijambo, a radio production organization. Studio Ijambo ("wise words" in the local Kirundi language) was launched in 1995 expressly to counter virulent reporting that was applauding and encouraging some of the worst violence in Burundi's long-running civil war. The U.S.-based NGO Search for Common Ground, which has broad experience in conflict resolution education and media, received U.S. Government and private funding to help launch the group. The story of its beginnings, growth, and impact is described on the Radio Netherlands' website, which includes an extensive section on "hate radio" and "peace radio."[27]

An evaluation of Studio Ijambo's development and impact was conducted for the US Agency for International Development in 2001.[28] Its introduction relates that in 1995 the extant Burundian media not only reflected the country's deep ethnic divide but actively promoted it, and its members "tried to rival each other over calls to kill, or in advancing their mutually macabre ideologies generating mutual terror and distrust based on historical fears."

The report identifies five "interrelated areas of peace building in Burundi" (intergroup relations, social and political mobilization, political elite negotiations, public institutions and processes, and mass or elite conflict behavior) on which Studio Ijambo produced positive effects. The programming found to be most effective in changing behaviors (as reported by 270 interviewees in Burundi) was a long-running soap opera that incorporated peacebuilding themes and a news magazine–format program that highlighted individual experiences. This certainly corresponds to global experience that human rights, democracy, or development messages embedded in other programming are often better received than those served in overtly instructional formats.

The report also states that it is "more definitive and visible" that Studio Ijambo's media training, which has helped produce high-quality independent programming, has also positively influenced the overall media culture in Burundi. Highlighting the results of journalism training as the project's most verifiable outcome also reflects the extreme difficultly of gauging the "preventive impact" of media or other interventions.

Community radio in many countries is thriving, helping to deliver development information and often becoming a focus for local mobilization and participation in political and resource decision making.[29] New technologies are increasing the capacity and utility of such local broadcasting. Community radio stations often receive content for rebroadcast via the Internet or on compact disk or cassette tapes. Direct satellite radio receivers are becoming small and cheap enough for widespread use. The British Freeplay Foundation distributes windup radios and supports content development for community radio.

The American NGO Internews is one of the best-funded media support groups, working in about thirty countries worldwide on a variety of health, media support, conflict resolution, and democracy promotion activities. One of its projects in Africa, called Local Voices, aims to promote the broad media engagement in disseminating HIV/AIDS information, emphasizing radio as the most effective mode of transmission in the African context. Describing the project, Internews explains, "By interweaving AIDS messages into a variety of popular programs—from music programs with young audiences to political talk shows that reach policy makers—*Local Voices* will have cross-cutting impact that significantly improves public awareness and dialogue."[30]

Getting the message right in local terms is an important challenge even when effective means of delivery are available. The United Nations has launched a new multi-country radio and television drama series for Africa, "Heart and Soul," which focuses on five themes: HIV/AIDS, environmental protection, gender, governance, and human rights. Inclusion of the last two topics is a welcome departure from most development media programming, especially that funded by IGOs, which has typically avoided directly addressing such issues.[31]

In countries that have not yet begun democratic transitions, or those with limited or restricted media, surrogate external media can be important sources of more balanced or accurate reporting. During the Cold War, Radio Free Europe, Radio Liberty, and other outlets, often broadcasting in the vernacular, proved enormously popular among peoples in Eastern Europe and the Soviet Union whose domestic media was tightly controlled. Radio Free Asia, an autonomous US-funded service launched in 1995, draws large audiences in Burma, China, and elsewhere.[32] The BBC, VOA, and other external broadcasters remain widely popular in authoritarian states or where local media is for various reasons simply not trusted. These services also have a long record of providing development and rights information alongside news and other feature programs.

INTERNATIONAL ASSISTANCE

Supporters of media for human rights and democracy must not conclude that the existence of an apparently open media indicates that continued engagement and support to the media sector are not required. Media in developing countries often struggle for their commercial survival. And in societies without established traditions of press freedom, uneven or irresponsible reporting standards cast doubt on media credibility and erode public trust. Opportunities to encourage the dissemination of information on human rights, democracy building, and political participation through local media should be an important part of any program supporting emerging democracies.

Some groups have detailed their strategies and approaches. The Open Society Initiative for Southern Africa's vision of how media can support an open society is laid out in its guidelines for media-related grants. It emphasizes assistance that improves access to and control over means of communication for marginalized groups. Its guiding principles are to support local initiatives that:

- promote the right of all people to communicate
- play a role in holding those in authority and power accountable to those they are supposed to serve
- encourage the free flow of diverse and relevant information through mass media
- support the development of mass media that are accessible to and/ or controlled by the people these media seek to serve
- enhance the long-term sustainability of nongovernmental mass media[33]

The Open Society Initiative for Southern Africa's guidelines reflect the perspective of those who seek to promote a more open, responsive, and participatory media as a tool for social change. They also reflect the guiding assumption of the parent organization, the Open Society Institute, that information access is a key element to democratic empowerment in open societies.

Other bilateral, multilateral, and NGO efforts are under way to help make media more effective in specialized areas. The World Bank has sponsored research and training for media in reporting on corruption and other economic issues; in 2002 the World Bank published a book on media reporting on economics.[34] The International Federation of Journalists (IFJ) sponsors a special project, Promoting Accountability, that offers numerous tools and resources to help media investigate and illuminate the operation of societal institutions, and to perhaps expose malfeasance.[35]

MEDIA SKILLS FOR HUMAN RIGHTS ADVOCATES

"Eternal vigilance is the price of liberty" adorns the masthead of several newspapers around the world. Media theorist Marshall McLuhan neatly turned this conventional wisdom to the age of mass media consumption by warning that "the price of eternal vigilance is indifference."[36] In the four decades since McLuhan's turn of phrase, compassion fatigue, outrage fatigue, and desensitization to suffering have been identified as unfavorable outcomes among consumers of reporting on humanitarian crises and human rights abuses.

But McLuhan's "indifference" must be recognized not as the result of eternal vigilance, but rather of feelings of powerlessness and resignation in the face of enormous and complex problems. All sectors of society need to gain better skills to present their problems, to suggest solutions, and to demand action through the media. Efforts to help NGOs, social justice advocates, parliamentarians, political parties, and progressive governments to become more effective communicators will help broaden the voices heard in mass media. This can also help build constituencies for media freedom by convincing more groups that open media are useful for them. Training on media strategies and advice in using new ICTs are among the areas that can help societal actors understand how media work and how to present information in a manner the media can easily use. Some very good training materials in this area are available on the Internet.[37]

It is crucial for human rights advocates to master the rhetorical and technical skills necessary to move their ideas and information to their intended audiences, including capacities in message formulation, preparing press releases and other publicity materials, and interview and public presentation skills. To pierce an audience's "indifference," an effective message must offer a solution and action that addresses the problem presented. A few basic principles of working with media include credibility, clarity, and proximity:

- The essential qualities of *professionalism, impartiality, reliability,* and *consistency* establish credibility, and demonstrate seriousness, competence, and sincerity.
- It is essential *to communicate a simple, clear, and consistent message that states the problem, suggests solutions, and demands action,* backed by timely and accurate information.

- Advocates must actively establish *proximity* to engage target audiences in human rights issues and to "sell" a human rights story effectively in a competitive media marketplace.

Advocates must make the story of human rights come alive for reporters and editors, and through them, for their audiences in order to help generate awareness and pressure to end human rights abuses. Advocates should help media find people whose experiences offer stories of "human rights with a human face." Wherever possible, it is useful to find linkages—for example, of trade, aid, or tourism—that can help spur outside interest in a particular human rights situation, in other words, establishing "proximity" to a target audience. Media may sometimes be interested in reporting human rights violations on a stand-alone basis. But there is a greater chance of exposure if some proximity can be established between the type or location of abuses and the media outlets' audiences, in other words, answering the classic question, Why should we care?

It is also imperative to make the best use of new communications technologies that allow ever cheaper, faster, easier, and more secure means to collect information, to distribute it widely, and to create or join human rights and other advocacy networks around the globe.

Governments and other institutions produce voluminous information that is disseminated through various outlets. Their official status commands media attention and some credibility, deserved or not. Their resources allow them to use multiple conduits: official news agencies, government press conferences and briefings, diplomatic representatives abroad, special visits for sympathetic media or elites, and sometimes use of well-paid lobbyists around the world. In the information struggle there is unlikely ever to be a level playing field. Human rights activists often have a huge disadvantage when facing blizzards of information—often biased propaganda, and sometimes disinformation and outright lies—coming from those who do not want abuses revealed or publicized.

Activists must counter this handicap first through the quality of their efforts to provide credible and timely information. They must achieve an acknowledged level of accuracy and reliability that makes even the much smaller amount of information they can provide far more powerful. And they must take advantage of newer and cheaper information technologies that can help narrow the gap even further by empowering even individuals to reach large audiences.

Advocates from human rights groups in many countries employ a wide variety of tactics in their efforts, from grassroots activism to media campaigns to lobbying lawmakers and other opinion leaders. These activities help generate the publicity and pressure that might convince a government to halt human rights abuses from a desire to avoid a bad international image or perhaps to maintain smooth relations with countries that say that human rights are an important part of their international policy. Potential damage to reputation and loss of investment, aid, trade, or tourism can be strong incentives to ameliorate abuses.

How victims of human rights abuses or humanitarian crises are represented also deserves careful consideration. Political or partisan perspectives sometimes define "worthy" or "unworthy" victims.[38] Media often seek "pure" victims whose stories are of unambiguous and undeniably uninvited suffering, and most usually choose children to convey this.[39] Human rights advocates should recognize these propensities but also strive to provide ample context and urge media to report more than only the most poignant images of suffering.[40]

ACTIVE OPEN MEDIA: HUMAN RIGHTS COVERAGE AS A CORE RESPONSIBILITY

The news media's role as a witness and unflinching recorder of events remains their central function. But this role should be informed by journalists' keen awareness of human rights and humanitarian issues, and an understanding that respect for human rights is the bedrock for a peaceful and prosperous society.[41] News media that are vigilant watchdogs, and that give voice to the marginalized as well as the powerful, fulfill both their professional responsibilities and an important moral role in which their power is used toward achieving greater social justice.

This ongoing work of the media is of cardinal importance to the evolution and preservation of a political culture that protects and promotes human rights under the rule of law. Unless ruled by the most benevolent of despots, societies lacking active open media are likely to display lower and less informed levels of citizen participation in public decision making. And societies with a restricted or docile media are more susceptible to bad governance and rights abuses, in the first instance because leaders need not account for their actions.

The existence of active open media is nowhere a guarantee that rights will be respected. Yet freedom of expression is a foundational right, without which few other rights will ever be fully enjoyed. Working to ensure that active open media exist everywhere should be a goal shared by all human rights and humanitarian advocates. And advocates should strive also to gain competencies that make best use of media access by shaping and delivering effective human rights messages that will fill the media vessel with content that can help bring positive change for all.

NOTES

[1] The pluralist view of media describes a "fourth estate" watchdog that exercises "eternal vigilance" over societal actors to serve as a counterweight to powerful interests (see more on Marshall MacLuhan's contrarian take on eternal vigilance later in this essay). The muckraking tradition of crusading and investigative journalists taking on corporations, governments, religious groups, and other entrenched interests is indeed alive and thriving in many parts of the world. To fulfill this role meaningfully and on a long-term basis, media must be free, independent, diverse, and professional. A benchmark definition regarding the roles of media in democratic systems is the 1991 Windhoek Declaration on free, independent, and pluralistic media.

[2] These conditions are rarely fully realized in developed countries, and too often remain notable by their absence in developing lands. Complementing the watchdog function is the media's "public interest" role. Public or civic journalism proponents argue that even private media should take up similar roles of identifying societal problems and encouraging debate about their solution. The role of public or civic journalism is still contentious, especially in the United States. The International Media and Democracy Project website, www.imdp.org, offers discussion and "how to" guides regarding the practice of public journalism. Media's watchdog, civic forum, and public-interest roles, pursued vigorously, produce the ideal of what is here described as an "active open media."

[3] For a discussion of news sources and how they affect reporting, see Lawrence Soley, *The News Shapers: The Sources Who Explain the News* (New York: Praeger, 1992). The use of the terms *terrorism* and *terrorist* has long evoked much debate. During the months preceding the US-led invasion of Iraq in March 2003, many media reports helped create an impression of inevitability regarding the war by using such words as "impending" conflict. See Robert K. Elder, "Seeking Neutrality in the Media's War of Words," *Chicago Tribune*, 19 February 2003.

[4] A typical but well-presented example of this argument is offered by Bilahari Kausikan, "Asia's Different Standard," *Foreign Policy* 92 (Fall 1993): 24–42.

[5] For useful information on Florence Nightingale and the media and more on her life story see Country Joe McDonald's "Florence Nightingale Tribute," users.rcn.com website (accessed 31 August 2004).

[6] For the texts of Governor Cosby's "burn order" and his warrant for Zenger's arrest, see Doug Linder, "Famous Trials," law.umkc.edu website (accessed 31 August 2004).

[7] Two accounts of the Zenger trial and its importance in the development of press freedom in America are William Lowell Putnam, *John Peter Zenger and the Fundamental Freedom* (Jefferson, NC: McFarland and Company, 1997); and Paul Finkelman, ed., *John Peter Zenger: A Brief Narrative of the Case and Trial of John Peter Zenger* (Naugatuck, CT: Brandywine Press, 1997).

[8] For basic information on the American Anti-Slavery Society, see Department of State, *USIA: Basic Readings in U.S. Democracy,* usinfo.state.gov/usa/infousa/facts/democrac/18.htm (accessed 31 August 2004). For Anti-Slavery International, the current successor to the Anti-Slavery Society, founded in Britain in 1787, see "The History of Anti-Slavery International, www.antislavery.org/homepage/antislavery/history.htm (accessed 31 August 2004).

[9] Some of Nast's cartoons may be viewed at Jim Zwick, ed., "Political Cartoons of Thomas Nast," in *Political Cartoons and Cartoonists,* boondocksnet.com website (accessed 31 August 2004).

[10] For Tweed's comment, see Spartacus, "New York," www.spartacus.schoolnet.co.uk/USAnewyork.htm (accessed 31 August 2004); see also Seymour Mandelbaum, *Boss Tweed's New York* (Chicago: Ivan Dees, 1990).

[11] "Democratisation and the Mass Media," conference sponsored by the World Association of Christian Communications and the Rockefeller Foundation, Bellagio, Italy, April 2001, offered many interesting perspectives on this issue. For another interesting perspective, see Sean O'Siochru, "Rethinking Media and Democracy: What about 'Democratic Media,'" *The Bulletin of the European Institute for the Media* (March 1997).

[12] Abbott Joseph Liebling, "Do You Belong in Journalism?" *New Yorker*, 4 May 1960. For example, in the early days of World War II, the *Chicago Tribune's* isolationist publisher William McCormack suppressed reporting by the newspaper's correspondent in Berlin, Sigrid Schultz, who warned of the looming genocide against Europe's Jews.

[13] How communications are transmitted can determine how they are perceived. The impact of broadcast media differs from print media. How people engage with interactive media is today a moving target subject to lively debate.

[14] Africa is the least networked continent. Yet thousands of African and Africa-related NGOs and institutions are now web-enabled or exist only as virtual entities. Most African governments are now online, and some are making efforts to develop "e-government" capacities to deliver information and services to citizens. See Economic Commission of Africa, National Information and Communication Infrastructure (NICI), "Africa on the Internet:

An Annotated Guide to African Web Sites," www.uneca.org/aisi/nici/country_profiles/africacontent.htm (accessed 31 August 2004).

[15] For the full report, see www.freedomhouse.org/research/pressurvey.htm.

[16] For a useful guide with substantive information on reporting various rights, framed largely in an Indian context, see British Council, *Press and People: A Manual of Human Rights Reporting in India,* britishcouncil.org.in website (accessed 31 August 2004). For a detailed explanation and examples of reporting on humanitarian issues, particularly in conflict situations, see *The Crimes of War Project*, www.crimesofwar.org (accessed 31 August 2004), founded by Pulitzer Prize–winning journalist Roy Gutman.

[17] A plethora of websites exists in related fields. A reasonable compendium may be viewed at USAID, Promoting Democracy and Good Governance, usaid.gov website (accessed 31 August 2004).

[18] The Institute for International Communication and Development, www.iicd.org/, and the World Bank's Information for Development, or "infoDev" program, www.infodev.org, cooperate to produce a series of ICT/Development success stories.

[19] Ann Hudock, "Hearing the Voices of the Poor: Encouraging Good Governance and Poverty Reduction through Media Sector Support" (Washington, DC: World Learning, May 2003), worldlearning.org website (accessed 31 August 2004).

[20] The bitterly divisive clashes over the New World Information and Communications Order (NWICO) in the 1970s and 1980s still scar discussion over media roles in promoting democracy and human rights. There is no argument here for the official imposition of media "responsibilities" or mandating coverage of certain areas or issues. In the long run, far worse than open but sometimes irresponsible media are media controlled by or compliant to the powers that be.

[21] The broader issues of how media report on civil wars and humanitarian disasters in the developing world are addressed in Colin Scott, Larry Minear, and Thomas G. Weiss, *The News Media, Civil War and Humanitarian Action* (Boulder, CO: Lynne Rienner, 1995).

[22] Radio Netherlands offers a history of RTML and the prosecution of some of its staff. See Radio Netherlands, "Hate Radio: Rwanda," rnw.nl website (accessed 31 August 2004).

[23] ICTR Press Release, 3 December 2003, ictr.org website (accessed 31 August 2004).

[24] Richard A. Oppel, Jr., "Iraqis Get the News but Often Don't Believe It," *The New York Times*, 5 August 2003.

[25] Radio Netherlands offers extensive coverage of hate media/peace media issues, with particular emphasis on radio. See Radio Netherlands, "Contracting Hate Media," rnw.nl website (accessed 31 August 2004). A leading NGO involved in peace broadcasting is Search for Common Ground. See also a very useful short article by experienced BBC broadcaster Gordon Adam,

"Radio's Peacekeeping Potential in Humanitarian Crisis," in *Somalia, Rwanda, and Beyond: The Role of the International Media in Wars and Humanitarian Crisis,* ed. Edward Girardet, Andrea Bartoli, Jeffrey Carmel (Geneva: Crosslines Global Report, 1995).

[26] See Ross Howard, Francis Rolt, Hans van de Veen, and Juliette Verhoeven, *The Power of the Media: A Handbook for Peacebuilders* (Geneva: European Centre for Conflict Prevention, 2003).

[27] Francois Laureys, "A 'Trait d'union' in a Divided Country," Studio Ijambo, Burundi, 12 February 1999, rnw.nl website (accessed 31 August 2004). Studio Ijambo information is also available on the Search for Common Ground website. For information on other peace radio work, see Fondation Hirondelle: Media for Peace and Human Dignity, "Radio Okapi: The Project," hirondelle.org website (accessed 31 August 2004).

[28] USAID and Management System International (MSI), *Media Intervention in Peace Building in Burundi* (Washington, DC: MSI, March 2002), usaid.gov website (accessed 31 August 2004).

[29] The World Association for Community Broadcasting, www.amarc.org/, promotes and supports community radio worldwide. For a description of the impact of one community radio station, see Roger Thurow, "In Impoverished Niger, Radio Provides Missing Links In Chain Of Development," *The Wall Street Journal,* 10 May 2002.

[30] Interviews, internews.org website (accessed 31 August 2004).

[31] UNDP, "Heart and Soul Dramatizes HIV/AIDS and Other Issues for Millions in Africa," *Newsfront,* 3 October 2002, undp.org website (accessed 31 August 2004). Health Unlimited, Project Great Lakes Africa, a British-based NGO, works in several African countries to produce health-related radio and other media programming. The Johns Hopkins Bloomberg School of Public Health Center for Communications Program offers an impressive array of health-related media materials, jhuccp.org website (accessed 31 August 2004).

[32] See Irrawaddy Reporters, "Shortwave Radio a Lifeline for Burmese," *The Irrawaddy,* 1 August 2003, irrawaddy.org website (accessed 31 August 2004).

[33] The Open Society Initiative for Southern Africa, osiafrica.org website. See also The Soros Foundations' Network Media Program, soros.org website.

[34] See, for example, Rick Stapenhurst, *The Media's Role in Curbing Corruption* (Washington, DC: World Bank Institute, 2000). The World Bank Institute also offers training in economics and business journalism and has conducted several seminars in Africa. See also World Bank Institute, *The Right to Tell: The Role of Mass Media in Economic Development* (Washington, DC: World Bank Institute, 2002).

[35] See Promoting Accountability in Africa: IFJ Site for Journalists Covering Corruption, ifj-pa.org website (accessed 31 August 2004).

[36] Marshall McLuhan, *Understanding Media: The Extensions of Man* (New York: McGraw-Hill, 1965).

[37] This section is adapted from training materials developed by the author for media training seminars for the Columbia University Human Rights Advocates Program offering practical media advice to human rights advocates. (The paper, since revised, is available on request from the author [TL69@columbia.edu].) Two excellent sources of media training materials are offered by CIVICUS, www.civicus.org/new/civicus_toolkit_project.asp (accessed 31 August 2004); and the Human Rights Connection, www.hrconnection.org/media/media2.htm (accessed 31 August 2004).

[38] See Noam Chomsky and Edward Herman, *Manufacturing Consent: The Political Economy of the Mass Media* (New York: Pantheon, 1988).

[39] See Susan D. Moeller, "A Hierarchy of Innocence: The Media's Use of Children in the Telling of International News," *The Harvard International Journal of Press and Politics* 7, no. 1 (Fall 2001): 36–57; and Mike Jempson "Children and Media—A Global Concern," *The Communication Initiative,* June 2003, comminit.com website (accessed 31 August 2004).

[40] Rony Brauman, "When Suffering Makes a Good Story," in Girardet, Bartoli, and Carmel, *Somalia, Rwanda, and Beyond.*

[41] See International Council for Human Rights Policy, *Journalism, Media, and the Challenge of Human Rights Reporting* (Versoix, Switzerland: The International Council for Human Rights Policy, 2002).

14

Non-State Actors
and the Challenge of Slavery

Kevin Bales

INTRODUCTION

One significant change in the nature of political action that has taken place over the last fifty years is a shift from established political parties toward non-state issue-based campaigning groups, away from nation-state politics toward global politics. Before the Second World War formal politics tended to take place at the level of the nation state and within a context of competing sovereign nation states. The nation state was, indeed, a defining feature of life in the early twentieth century. In democratic countries political action normally occurred through the vehicle of ideologically driven political parties that competed for power. These parties operated with a bundle of policies and programs that had grown from the social and political theories of Hobbes, Locke, Rousseau, Hegel, Mill, Marx, and Weber, who assumed the primacy of the nation state. Only Kant, with his notion of cosmopolitanism, could be considered an exception.[1]

After 1945 nation states and broadly based political parties continued to predominate, but movements that concentrated on the achieve-

This chapter was first presented to the Columbia University Human Rights Seminar, and a version of this chapter was first published in Kevin Bales, *Understanding Global Slavery* (Berkeley and Los Angeles: Univ. of California Press, 2005).

ment of goals that transcended nation-state borders emerged as well. These movements highlighted such issues as the global environment and respect for universal human rights, issues that had not been adequately taken up by political parties.

The shift away from nation-state based politics toward these issue-based concerns (connected to what Anthony Giddens calls "life politics"[2]) reflects a growing awareness among the citizenry that the things which most directly affect our lives often transcend national boundaries and the reach of national political parties and governments. The result has been a decline in the membership of political parties and a tremendous growth in campaigning organizations such as Greenpeace, Friends of the Earth, the peace movement, and Amnesty International.

State politics and class-based politics are not dead, given the importance of resources generated by tax regimes and the impact on a broad range of issues that occur within national boundaries. Organizations concerned with global social and environmental issues, however, are now key players in both national and international forums. They are unlike political parties in that they are not democratically elected and do not have territorial constituencies. While they have come to resemble governments and business in their bureaucratic organization, they are unlike states and other non-state actors (NSAs) in the nature of their organizational goals. In this chapter I look at the first major human rights organization and campaign and use the history of the anti-slavery movement to chart the evolution of the organization and the influence of NSAs. On the basis of that examination I argue, first, that NSAs have always been important in human rights advocacy; second that bureaucratization has been a key stage in the acquisition of influence by NSAs; third, that NSA activity and interaction, which have increased in the new phase of globalization, redefined slavery; and finally, that defining slavery as a moral issue, as opposed to an economic one, enhanced and enhances the global networking for human rights and the protection of human rights._Given that many human rights have only emerged as expressions of such a redefinition, it is important to trace the transformation of how slavery was popularly conceptualized in the first great human rights campaign.

SLAVERY AND THE FIRST HUMAN RIGHTS CAMPAIGN

If there is a pathfinder for the development of NSAs as a potent force for political change, it is the various incarnations of the anti-slavery movement. The sheer size of the anti-slavery movement of the eighteenth and nineteenth centuries is mostly forgotten today. Likewise, the reality of this campaign as the world's first human rights campaign (and organization) is rarely remembered. A very brief look at the history of this movement can illuminate the origins and the role of NSAs in addressing human rights.

While Greek and Roman philosophers held that slavery was against "natural law," a view echoed by Aquinas,[3] the first organized and long-lasting group operating as an NGO with the aim of altering both state policy and public perceptions of human rights was a committee organized by the British Quakers in 1783.[4] This committee was charged with promoting the total abolition of the slave trade and gradual emancipation. The committee petitioned the parliament and published some anti-slavery tracts, and in 1786, it decided to publish a long essay by Thomas Clarkson, an Anglican and recent Oxford graduate.

The resulting pamphlet was very well received, and Clarkson become a minor celebrity. Then, Clarkson dedicated his life to building up the anti-slavery movement, using the fifty thousand Quakers in Britain as the base on which to build. In 1787 the original Quaker Committee evolved into the nondenominational Committee for Effecting the Abolition of the Slave Trade, with Clarkson as its secretary. The crucial element was that his "vision was of one unified plan of action engaging widespread participation and directed toward destroying the legal basis of a centuries-old commercial enterprise."[5]

The movement built up slowly; Clarkson was equally involved in fund-raising, research, public speaking, and publishing. Fund-raising involved soliciting money from rich individuals; research meant spending months interviewing the sailors and businessmen in the slave ports of Bristol and Liverpool. The necessary public-awareness campaign, in a time without media that reached the majority of the public, was especially arduous. Clarkson would travel up to ten thousand miles by horseback over a period of ten to twelve months in order to speak in hundreds of towns and cities. Possibly the most powerful graphic image showed how slaves were packed on board ship that the committee published as a poster—it is an image that most of us are familiar with today even if we do not know that it originated with Clarkson. In the process of this campaign the committee evolved into the *Society* for Effecting the Abolition of the Slave Trade, and ultimately, in 1824, into the Anti-Slavery Society (which continues today as Anti-Slavery International).

It is important to recognize that key aims of the Anti-Slavery Society were primarily located within the state political system—particularly the enactment of laws, first, to end the slave trade, and second, to emancipate all slaves. However, if those were strategic aims, then tactical work involved other NGOs, especially businesses. This was the case with the widespread sugar boycott of the 1790s. An estimated 300,000 people in Britain refused to use West Indian sugar, though it is difficult to see any effect on government policy or trade, except for a significant increase in the importation of East Indian (or non-slave) sugar. But whether acting within or without state politics and policies, a critical dimension of this original human rights campaign was its intention to bring about a shift in values by raising public awareness. Put another way, the key to the success of this campaign was to bring about a redefinition of slavery in the public mind. Whatever philosophers had written, to the best of our understanding, slavery for the majority of the population in the eighteenth century was an *economic* issue. By the mid-nineteenth century it was generally seen as a *moral* issue, and the core of this redefinition was the privileging of the slave's point of view. For the British anti-slavery movement this is captured in the campaign's other widely known and powerful graphic image, the chained slave on one knee raising his arms and asking, "Am I not a man and a brother?"

A Second Mass Campaign

The history of the anti-slavery movement may be unique, possibly only due to longevity, in its ability to repeat itself. At the end of the nineteenth century the role of the researcher-activist in the mode of Clarkson was taken up by E. D. Morel. Like Clarkson, Morel began his work independently and then came to a close working relationship with the Anti-Slavery Society (at that point known as the British and Foreign Anti-Slavery Society). His aim was the exposure and eradication of the widespread enslavement of the people of the Congo. This campaign was important for demonstrating that a public could be brought to action over events far removed geographically and over events that directly touched supporters as consumers.

King Leopold II of Belgium, acting in a personal capacity, established the Congo Free State in 1884 and subsequently ran it as a private business. This enterprise was based upon slave labor, and with the rubber boom at the turn of the century millions of people were placed under permanent or temporary enslavement. The death toll was horrific; up to ten million people were killed or died of abuse and disease over a forty-year period.[6]

Like Clarkson, Morel began his research on the quayside. By studying shipping manifests he came to understand that the "trade" between Europe and the Congo was all one way—deducing that only slave labor could produce such a volume of imports without having any noticeable requirement for goods in the return trade. What was different in the design of this campaign was the effective use of public media, which did not exist before. With mass circulation newspapers as the primary organs for generating public awareness, the campaign to end slavery in the Congo became what we would now think of as a public relations battle. On one side were the anti-slavery activists and investigative journalists who fed hundreds of articles to the newspapers. On the other was King Leopold's sophisticated and better financed public relations team, generating hundreds of counter-stories and purchasing the cooperation of large numbers of journalists and editors.

In this public relations battle the anti-slavery forces had one significant advantage, a new technology that left the public with little choice in morally defining the colonial exploitation of the Congo as evil—photography. This was especially effective because photographs could now be reproduced in newspapers. John and Alice Harris, who had been missionaries in the Congo, returned with extensive photographic evidence of torture and mutilation of forced laborers. Made into slides, they showed them at over six hundred public appearances over two years. It was the early twentieth-century equivalent of a well-made documentary, shown to a fresh audience. After their work with Morel and the conclusion of the campaign, the Harrises went on to direct the Anti-Slavery Society for many years.

Conviction vs. Responsibility—the Process of Bureaucratization

So far I have presented the early anti-slavery movement as the pathfinder for the development of modern NGOs, particularly those concerned with human rights. But if we are to understand the development of the role of such NGOs, we need to place them within the larger theme of the development of organizations, and especially the bureaucratization process. If we are trying to discover why NGOs have more or less influence, more or less power, or more or less ability to alter the activities of states, then we should consider their level of bureaucratization as an indicator of this ability. Max Weber, in his classic work on bureaucracy, explained that as a form of organization the bureaucracy is:

> superior to any other form in precision, in stability, in the stringency of its discipline, and its reliability. It thus makes possible a particularly high degree of calculability of results for the heads of the organization and for those acting in relation to it. It is finally superior both in intensive efficiency and in the scope of its operations and is formally capable of application to all kinds of administrative tasks.[7]

It is interesting to note that the first bureaucratized organizations were non-state organizations: universities and religious bodies. But it was the bureaucratization of states and businesses that set the tone for modernity, as well as a context in which political action took the form of allegiance to ideologically driven political parties that competed for power on broad platforms, as mentioned earlier. The transformation of NSAs into their current role as near equals in the interplay of states came about, in part, because of their bureaucratization. This required a resolution in one of the basic tensions within the organization of NSAs—the contrast between conviction (the leadership of charismatic individuals) and responsibility (collective leadership following strategic goals).

The early anti-slavery movement was marked by a mixture of the two, but it maintained its continuity and effectiveness through its bureaucratic structure rather than through the personality of Thomas Clarkson. In many ways the test of any organization, whether state or non-state, is its ability to withstand the loss of the leader who personifies the organization's convictions. This was demonstrated when Clarkson suffered a mental and physical breakdown in 1793 and retired from most anti-slavery work for ten years. The committee forming the core of the anti-slavery organization continued to function, albeit at a reduced rate, and was ready to carry through the major campaigns that followed Clarkson's return in 1804. Similarly, in spite of the abolition of legal slavery in most countries by the 1870s, the Anti-Slavery Society continued in a reduced size and was ready to provide an organizational structure to support the campaign against the Congo slavery in the 1880s. Such stability and continuity are crucial to the empowerment of non-state organizations addressing human rights.

Organizations like Amnesty International are known for their highly bureaucratic and hierarchical structures. What differentiates these campaigning bureaucracies is their aim. While the goals of states and businesses concentrate on continuity, expansion, and profit, these human rights bureaucracies add moral aims. They are the reification of conviction within structured responsibility. They also face unique problems because of their moral aims. When these goals are finite, like the eradication of slavery, it is possible to reach an end. This is anti-thetical to bureaucratic structure, since bureaucracies tend to be self-replicating and continuous. While businesses can turn to new areas of profit making, and governments to other forms of regulation and over-sight, the organization with an achievable moral goal can find itself facing self-determined extinction. The Anti-Slavery Society continued after the Congo Reform Association. Upon King Leopold giving up control there, it withered away. A moral aim is also a hostage to for-tune in that it is determined in part by the public perception or defini-tion of its achievement. The Anti-Slavery Society spent the 1950s to 1980s in something like "stand-by mode" as it faced a public that was convinced that slavery no longer existed. Its bureaucratic structure and core of supporters (some of them descendants of the original Quaker organizers), who believed otherwise, kept it afloat. Compare that stability to the collapse of the Campaign for Nuclear Disarma-ment in Britain, an organization with hundreds of thousands of sup-porters, at the end of the Cold War. While its moral aim of ending the threat of nuclear proliferation and war was far from achieved, by the early 1990s the public was convinced it had been. Given a more cha-otic (less bureaucratic and hierarchical) internal structure, Campaign for Nuclear Disarmament could not adapt quickly or mount an educa-tional campaign to counter this perception before it had hemorrhaged supporters and resources.

Yet even the bureaucracy with moral goals can follow the tactical approach of business bureaucracies when its raison d'être is threat-ened. The business with a shrinking market diversifies; a business with an expanding market concentrates and improves product to remain ahead of the competitors that will be drawn to a growing market. In the 1970s and 1980s the Anti-Slavery Society, faced with a shrinking "market," diversified into such issues as child labor, female genital mutilation, and unfree forms of marriage, while maintaining a con-centration on slavery. It is instructive that it diversified with hesita-tion and that it was quickly surpassed in size by organizations whose mission reflected the economies of agglomeration. If the Anti-Slavery Society is the neighborhood custom tailor crafting responses to a key single issue, then Human Rights Watch is the department store of moral goals. As public and state awareness and recognition of slavery and human trafficking began to dramatically increase in the late 1990s, the Anti-Slavery Society also saw the "invasion" of its market. Groups as varied as Amnesty International, the American Central Intelligence Agency, and the Vatican announced their own investigations of, and policies on, slavery. This diversification is to be expected of any successful organization, for it is indicative of the third main force driving the establishment of powerful NSAs in human rights—globalization.

GLOBALIZING NON-STATE ORGANIZATIONS

The redefinition of an issue in moral terms sets out the intellectual justification for the formation of an NGO. The bureaucratization of the activity addressing that issue establishes an NGO with some stability and the potential for continuous operation. But the longevity, size, and power of a NSA are all dependent on the arena in which it operates. Confined within the boundaries of a nation state, with its range of activity restricted to what the state allows, NGOs often define themselves in relation to the state, both in identity and aim, and try to alter state policies.

The ongoing process of globalization has created a very fertile context for NGOs concerned with human rights. They are not restricted to nation-state boundaries (except by choice), and most important, their organizing intellectual paradigms center on moral concepts that are generalizable to all people. The object of their work is normally the alteration of a human activity that transcends cultural boundaries, and their potential "market" is the world population. Their challenge is to bring about a public redefinition of their issue as a moral issue, not locally but globally.

Much of the writing about the globalization process has focused on the ongoing changes in businesses and the world economy, especially those recent advancements in information technology and the rise of neo-liberalism, but globalization has equally affected non-state organizations. There are two key themes within the globalization process: (1) the erosion of control by nation states; and (2) the functional integration of dispersed (economic) activities.[8] These characteristics have suited human rights organizations admirably, creating a context for potential growth. These characteristics have also fostered NSAs that might be thought of as anti-human rights, especially criminal organizations.

Dispersed economic activity and the loss of governmental control are relevant and apply to the newer forms of slavery as well. Slave holders disperse both slaves and slave-based activities. In Brazil slaves are "recruited" in densely populated, economically depressed regions and then shipped over one thousand miles to the fields where they will make charcoal. The charcoal, in turn, will be shipped another one thousand miles to steel mills for use. In Southeast Asia women are enslaved in Burma or Laos for use in Thailand or shipment to brothels in Japan or Europe. Slaves from Mali are found in Paris, slaves from the Philippines are found in London and Saudi Arabia, and Eastern Europeans, especially women, are being dispersed as slaves around the globe. The profits generated by slavery also flow indiscriminately across national borders. Governments (like many individuals) that still conceptualize slavery as a legal status of titled "ownership" linked to the nation state, are at a loss to regulate this trade. It was only in early 1999 that the United Nations met to begin developing new conventions to address this globalized "trafficking of persons."

Organized criminal groups are also globalized NSAs of significant scale and play an important role in slavery and human trafficking. The UN estimates that human trafficking now ranks as the third largest profit center for transnational criminal groups, after the trade in drugs and in weapons. The number of such criminal groups in Russia alone is estimated to be between five thousand and eight thousand, involving up to three million people.[9] Organizationally, however, these groups are simply businesses, some bureaucratic in nature and others centered on a leader. While they operate within a context of higher risks and threats to the stability of the organization than most NSAs, they also work on shorter time scales and are able to achieve goals (profits) quickly. Like other businesses, they do not seek the public redefinition of any issue into moral terms (except occasionally to attempt to reposition an activity, gambling for example, as morally acceptable). They also meet challenges and competition through diversification and concentration, and they consciously make the most of transcending nation-state boundaries.

What is especially interesting is the gray area between NSAs that are criminal businesses, and NSAs, like human rights organizations, that are organized according to moral values. The groups in this gray area can become especially potent when they combine criminal means with the high levels of conviction and strategic moral certainty that characterize NGOs.

The events of 9/11 demonstrated the power of such an NSA in the violent attacks on New York and Washington. While the US government has worked hard to lead public perception to a moral definition of the al Qaeda organization as evil incarnate, it is, after all, an NGO with an agenda focused on (according to its own definitions) moral goals. It has also shown itself capable of transcending state boundaries and carrying on highly dispersed activities. Likewise, it faces the challenge that most human rights organizations confront: the need to convince a sufficient proportion of the global public to redefine certain geo-political or economic problems as moral issues. The survival of the al Qaeda organization depends on many of the factors discussed earlier: how much it relies on the leadership of a single individual, how it has balanced conviction and ideological fervor with organizational structure and stability, the resilience of its bureaucracy, and whether it can alter a sufficient proportion of opinion of its chosen audiences in its favor. In terms of survival al Qaeda has one advantage: unlike most NGOs with a moral agenda, it has devoted a great deal of its human and economic resources to design an organization resistant to attack.

Of course, by using violence as a tactic al Qaeda has removed itself from the general marketplace of non-state, non-governmental actors. This may also be its downfall, since one result of globalization, with its diminution of the importance of nation states, is that NSAs have shifted the focus of much of their activity, and to be successful they must work cooperatively. Violence denies any group access to cooperation with most NGOs. In the past NGOs sought to alter public opinion in order to change the policies of a single government. Today the orientation of action is less toward government and more toward other NGOs or IGOs. At the same time the power of NGOs vis-à-vis that of governments is dramatically increased. Both the UN and many national governments now rely on NGOs to provide the intelligence and structure necessary to develop policy. ILO Convention 182, for example, on the worst forms of child labor was originated and driven to a successful conclusion by a coalition of NGOs. Recent policy announcements by the Economic Community of West Africa States, while apparently authored by national governments, were supported by NGO and IGO staff. In the

United States, two coalitions of NSAs—the chocolate industry on one hand, and human rights organizations on the other—were parties to a major new protocol (note the adoption of diplomatic language).

This agreement, the Protocol for the Growing and Processing of Cocoa Beans and Their Derivative Products in a Manner that Complies with ILO Convention 182 concerning the Prohibition and Immediate Action for the Elimination of the Worst Forms of Child Labor was signed by the major North American and European chocolate companies along with the international trade associations of cocoa producers and users on 19 September 2001 and witnessed by a number of human rights and child labor groups, as well as labor unions.[10] A side agreement offered by the chocolate industry was that the issue of forced labor would also be considered to be part of the agreement. The protocol committed the cocoa and chocolate industry to three key actions: (1) to fund independent research into the extent and types of child and forced labor in cocoa production; (2) to fund and participate in the formation of a new foundation (now called the International Cocoa Initiative) that will include human rights, child labor, and trade unions on its board and that will fund and support projects in cocoa-growing regions that will reduce child and forced labor and help to liberate and rehabilitate those who have been victims; and (3) to bring into being an independent system of inspection and verification that will remove child and forced labor from the product chain at the farm gate. The protocol has been hailed as a breakthrough in that, for the first time, an entire industry has collectively taken responsibility for abuses of human rights anywhere along its product chain. Note that it is an agreement between sets of NSAs.

The government stood as a guarantor and participant to the protocol agreement, but it is worth asking how much longer an official blessing will be needed to "legitimize" such agreements. Indeed, at the meeting establishing the foundation mandated by the protocol, the role of government as participant was excluded without discussion. The near future will see struggles as NGOs seek institutional roles commensurate with their power.

NGOS AND THE ERADICATION OF SLAVERY

This brief review of the evolution of NSAs, particularly NGOs concerned with human rights, points to a few thoughts about where these organizations might be going. In the work of Anti-Slavery International and its American sister organization, Free the Slaves, we have identified several mechanisms by which slavery might be eradicated. One of these is the elaboration of grassroots organizations that directly liberate and rehabilitate slaves. At the present time, in several countries, such organizations are literally freeing slaves and creating situations in which re-enslavement is less likely to occur at a rate far beyond that achieved by state governments. These organizations usually have little or no support from the developed world and rely on scant local resources. While most national governments have both the resources and the laws on the books to eradicate slavery, decades of urging them to do so has had little effect. Anti-slavery organizations will continue to invest in pushing governments to enforce their own laws, but they are also looking for a multiplication of grassroots groups and their effectiveness.

To maximize that effectiveness, it is necessary to take on board the lessons of past campaigns and the histories of NGOs. In the developed world we live among and through bureaucracies in the way fish live in water. Bureaucracies are both ubiquitous and provide most of our sustenance. It is easy to forget that in some parts of the developing world, organizations are much less likely to be bureaucratic in nature. For example, when the International Cocoa Initiative looked at farmer cooperatives in the Ivory Coast as a possible mechanism for reducing enslavement in the production of cocoa and other commodities, it was found that these cooperatives have functioned more like a depot and less like an organization in the way they centralized produce for sale. In sociological terms they met none of Weber's criteria for identifying a bureaucracy.[11] This is not to say that cooperatives will not be effective against agricultural enslavement, but the work with cooperatives will need to begin at an organizational level. This requirement is mirrored in the rapid expansion of capacity building projects being carried out by IGOs, NGOs, and states.

In terms of reducing slavery, capacity building takes several forms. One of the most basic is providing a safe space in which grassroots organizations can operate. When governments fail to enforce their own laws against slavery, they also often fail to enforce laws that will protect human rights workers, or indeed may actively work against NSAs to their detriment. The power of NGOs in the developed world can extend to protect NGOs and activists in the South. This has been shown historically and in the recent past. In early 2000 Anti-Slavery International worked closely with national NGOs and grassroots organizations in Nepal to bring about new legislation banning the traditional forms of debt bondage known as the *kamaiya* system. Mixed delegations of Nepali, Indian, and European representatives visited all major political actors and state organizations. The overt participation of Anti-Slavery International increased the safety of local actors in a country that had imprisoned members of any "troublesome opposition." If there was a significant error in this cooperative approach, it was to underestimate the influence it would bring to bear on the state: the law abolishing *kamaiya* was brought in by decree rather than legislation, and it occurred much more quickly than expected. Grassroots organizations in the countryside were not prepared for the harsh reaction of landowners and the tens of thousands of refugees that would be driven from their homes.

While NGOs tend to view themselves as secondary in importance to states, their influence is often more important in achieving human rights goals. In the United States the passage of the Trafficking Victims Protection Act in late 2000 was also dependent on the information and guidance provided by NGOs, which were later called upon to help train law enforcement in implementing the act and to do the needed research on the best ways to address human trafficking. It should be noted that the majority of experts on this issue are located outside the state law-enforcement agencies. This fact points toward one of the advantages bureaucratic NGOs bring to human rights: they are not encumbered by an excess of democracy internally or by the abrupt changes that can occur in policy and personnel with changes of government. In spite of a lobbying and advocacy role, the operation of most human rights NGOs *outside* the political system of parties and elections is also crucial to their job of protecting human rights.

Politics is about winning the support of constituents and voters, and voters are defined by their physical location within the nation state. Electoral success requires addressing first the concerns of voters, and these rarely rank the human rights of "foreigners" above their own material concerns (in their own countries slaves are politically voiceless). For most politicians in the North there is little incentive to do anything about slavery, as it has neither economic implications nor salience with constituents. Only a handful of politicians recognize a moral imperative.

The job of NGOs is, as it has always been, to bring about a redefinition in public perception. To alter policy, this means translating that public redefinition into voter demand. That requires, in turn, making the issue real to voters and pushing it up on the list of priorities. Since most slavery occurs in the developing world, a close working relationship with grassroots organizations is imperative. For the majority of voters, issues require a human face and clear, single-sentence encapsulation; otherwise, the issue falls into the pool of concerns too big, too complex, or too distant to worry about. Grassroots organizations provide that face and story. If there is one hopeful note concerning the shallowness of voter response, it is that in terms of human rights the political processes of the developed world are less and less important.

The bureaucracies freed of nation-state borders by the process of globalization have wasted little time in building constituencies that transcend the political systems limited by those borders. The bureaucracies whose organizational goals could be maximized by this shift moved most quickly to do so: transnational corporations and transnational criminal organizations. But following them has been a number of coalitions of NGOs whose organizing philosophical positions give them one advantage over businesses or criminal groups. Businesses and criminal groups have the organizational goal of maximizing profit, and this inevitably leads them into competition as they expand into new markets. Human rights organizations also compete for resources (grant money, supporters) but do so while pursuing virtually identical ultimate goals (the protection and elaboration of human rights). This means that conflict within the community of human rights NGOs is more apparent than real. The squabbling may never stop, but it is a form of communication and negotiation while the organizations generally move forward together.

But in spite of their differences in approach, the future of human rights protection may rest primarily with these NGOs. The example of the protocol signed by the chocolate industry and witnessed by human rights organizations is instructive. Two national governments are party to this agreement, but the resources that underpin it and the expertise that drives it come from the businesses and NGOs that transcend state boundaries. In this case the effort at moral redefinition pressed by NGOs went first to the constituents of the businesses (the consumers) and only secondly to the constituents of the politicians. This aim helped to overcome a second problem with electoral democracy: its long time scales. Voters can register a single choice only once every two years or so, and that choice is highly restricted and ill-defined. Consumers can "vote" many times a day in a clearly specified manner. At times their choice is also restricted, but choosing not to vote as a consumer becomes a boycott. The same action by a voter is simply self-disenfranchisement.

This link between business and NGOs is critical when the human rights violation under consideration is slavery. Slavery is an economic and social relationship between two people, one of the oldest forms of human relationships. While popular perceptions of slavery focus on its cruelty, the truth is that people are enslaved for economic exploitation and cruelty is simply a tool used to achieve profits. The total estimated value of slave production globally is about $12 billion. This is a mere drop in the ocean of the world economy, but it is important in that some of this production flows into the homes of consumers in the developed world. Only a small minority of the world's slaves is engaged in production that feeds international markets, but again, they are important in that their condition opens the door to public awareness.

CONCLUSION

The history and present work by NGOs against slavery points both to the importance of bureaucratization of such organizations in the past and to their increasing transcendence of nation states in human rights work. Over time, settings outside of government have taken on a greater importance in the work against slavery, and today the links between NSAs in the NGO and business sectors are often of greater salience than links with governments.

The importance of this is that all actors within the field of human rights must come to understand this shifting importance and influence of NGOs and other NSAs. The temptation to think inside the boundaries of existing and historical relationships is great, but these relationships, among governments, NGOs, businesses, and criminal organizations, are evolving as well. The relative power of the latter three is increasing while the power of governments is declining. Those who wish to elaborate and safeguard human rights need to understand the fluid nature of these relationships and to build both internal structures and external coalitions that take advantage of them.

NOTES

[1] I thank Darren O'Byrne for clarifying this process for me. He deals with it in Darren J. O'Byrne, *Human Rights: An Introduction* (New York: Prentice-Hall, 2003).

[2] In ibid.

[3] See, for example, Milton Meltzer, *Slavery: A World History* (New York: De Capo, 1993), 211.

[4] See Hugh Thomas, *The Slave Trade: The History of the Atlantic Slave Trade 1440–1870* (New York: Simon and Schuster, 1997), 491.

[5] Ellen Gibson Wilson, *Thomas Clarkson: A Biography* (New York: St. Martin's Press, 1990), 17.

[6] The history of the Congo and the anti-slavery movement is detailed in Adam Hochschild, *King Leopold's Ghost* (Boston: Houghton Mifflin, 1999).

[7] Max Weber, *Economy and Society* (1921; Totowa, NJ: Bedminster Press, 1968), 223.

[8] See, for example, Peter Dicken, *Global Shift: The Internationalization of Economic Activity* (London: Paul Chapman, 1992).

[9] James O. Finckenauer, "Russian Transnational Organized Crime and Human Trafficking," in *Global Human Smuggling*, ed. David Kyle and Rey Koslowski (Baltimore: Johns Hopkins, 2001), 171.

[10] For the full Protocol, see www.freetheslaves.net (accessed 31 August 2004).

[11] The following are the major characteristics of the ideal-type bureaucracy: (1) It consists of a continuous organization of official functions (offices) bound by rules. (2) Each office has a specified sphere of competence. The office carries with it a set of obligations to perform various functions, the authority to carry out these functions, and the means of compulsion required to do the job. (3) The offices are organized into a hierarchical system. (4) The offices may carry with them technical qualifications that require that the participants obtain suitable training. (5) The staff that fills these offices does not own the means of production associated with them, staff members are provided with the use of those things that they need to do the job. (6) The incumbent is not allowed to appropriate the position; it always remains part of the organization. (7) Administrative acts, decisions, and rules are formulated and recorded in writing (George Ritzer, *Sociological Theory*, 3rd ed. [New York: McGraw-Hill, 1992], 131).

15

Violating Dignity

Welfare Reform, Black Women,
and Non-State Violators

Dana-Ain Davis

INTRODUCTION

Over the last three decades human rights has expanded to incorporate women's, economic, social, and cultural rights. Whereas fundamental rights were first articulated in the Universal Declaration of Human Rights (UDHR), they have since been elaborated in several legally binding instruments.

Although the UDHR is not a treaty, and the United States has not been a party to many human rights treaties, the Clinton administration emphasized international obligations of the United States. On 10 December 1998, the fiftieth anniversary of the UDHR, President Clinton released Executive Order 13107.[1] This order mandates that the United States fully respect and implement its obligations under the human rights treaties that have been ratified. Treaties relevant to the subject of this chapter, poverty and violence against women, that the United States has ratified are the Convention on the Elimination

This chapter was originally presented as a paper at the Columbia University Human Rights Seminar on 6 May 2002 under the title "'De-Essentializing' Welfare Recipients and Non-State Actors' Violations of Women's Rights." The paper benefited greatly from critical reviews by Susana Fried and Zehra Arat. I gratefully acknowledge Peter Juviler, George Andreopoulos, and Mamadi Matlhako for reading an earlier draft of this chapter.

of Racial Discrimination (CERD) and the International Covenant on Civil and Political Rights (ICCPR). Executive Order 13107 calls on the heads of departments to ensure that they protect and promote human rights within their work. This includes monitoring states' actions to guarantee their compliance.

With respect to gender-based violence and economic fragility, human rights advocates in the United States have organized around the principles contained within these documents, educating communities about rights violations in relation to these issues, among others. The purpose has been to inform those who are most in need of asserting their rights that they have certain rights. This is of utmost importance to women and economically disenfranchised populations, as recent shifts in US social policy and economic restructuring have abridged human rights. Activists have been concerned about poor people's rights, because increased poverty has been driven in part by neo-liberal ideology through the hand of welfare reform.

The consolidation of neo-liberal and conservative interests bred such contempt for social support mechanisms that in 1996 the state protracted its historical obligation to protect citizens from poverty by eliminating entitlements. Eliminating federally guaranteed access to public assistance was articulated in the Personal Responsibility and Work Opportunity Reconciliation Act of 1996 (PRWORA).[2] By way of the PRWORA, poor women's rights are threatened by the state as barriers constrain achievement of adequate standards of living. The inherent dignity[3] to which all are entitled is compromised, as are such basic needs as food security and housing stability. Fundamentally, welfare-reform legislation has pushed many, particularly women of color, deeper into poverty. Consequently, the passage and implementation of the PRWORA translates into failure by the United States to enforce at least three Articles of the UDHR, which will be discussed in the next section.

The UDHR lacks the power of a treaty, but human rights groups in the United States find it useful, along with human rights conventions, to measure US performance and marginalization of citizens' rights. Two groups that employ the human rights framework are the Kensington Welfare Rights Union in Pennsylvania and the Women Rights Network in Massachusetts.[4] Both organizations have engaged in documentation efforts and organized communities against violations perpetrated against poor homeless people and battered women, respectively. Traditionally, human rights are defined as individual rights, and violations are recognized if they are perpetrated by the state. This definition is inadequate because it does not account for violations that do not hold non-state actors (NSAs) accountable for violating human rights.[5]

This chapter examines recent welfare reform through a human rights lens, specifically in relation to black women, and elaborates on the category of non-state violators. It examines the links between human rights and welfare reform by presenting cases that explicate how human rights are violated by public-sector actors and NSAs. I am especially concerned with how welfare reform constructs differential rights violations based on race. Therefore, black women are the focus of this analysis because, as others and I have argued elsewhere, they have been presented to the public as welfare cheats.[6] It is well known in the history of US welfare policy that black women have been demonized and castigated since they began to use welfare in the 1960s. The image of welfare became negatively linked to black women. Portrayed as "parasites" and "welfare queens," black women were the source of conservatives' and neo-liberals' loathing, which led to welfare reform's successful passage.[7] These representations solidified public consensus that welfare policy needed revision, because poor black women are considered to be the reason for "out of control spending" and the demise of morality. Thus, it was on their image that welfare was reformed.[8]

Given the racial content of the welfare reform, I ask, How does the state's refusal to provide basic needs to its citizens reverberate in black women's transactions with parastatal and NSAs? In what ways are state policies corroborated or exacerbated by non-state actors as black women attempt to access goods and services necessary to guarantee an adequate standard of living? I do not posit that state and non-state human rights violations result exclusively from welfare reform, but rather that they are facilitated by changes in the welfare policy. In examining the welfare reform and poverty from a human rights perspective, the state's and private actors' violations against the poor can be uncovered in gender and racial terms. Most of the people who are poor are women.[9] An associative racial and ethnic bias is manifested in the overrepresentation of women of color among those who receive assistance. Women of color make up two-thirds of the caseload, and black women constitute just over one-third of the cases.[10] Black women's human rights are violated by the state because their access to material resources is organized along the axis of gender and race. These circumstances reveal that the deprivation of resources is discriminatory and must be understood as such.[11] Under these conditions there are credible threats warranting action.

In examining expressions of violations, I interrogate the meanings of the violations in order to stake out an interpretation that goes beyond normative definitions of violators. I argue that NSAs are just as capable of denying rights as state actors and intend to show this by focusing on black women's everyday experiences.

According to Susana Fried, it is necessary that "new visions of human rights must be rooted in everyday experiences."[12] In the 1970s feminists established that violence against women was one of many strategies of domination. Scholars and activists stressed that women's lived reality of violence was neither unusual nor exceptional.[13]

As a result of international feminist activism, the United Nations adopted the Convention on the Elimination of All Forms of Discrimination Against Women (CEDAW) in 1979. The convention broadened the human rights framework to include women's rights and was the first human rights treaty devoted to the advancement of women's human rights. Later, the committee that oversees the implementation of the CEDAW issued a general recommendation indicating that violence against women be recognized as a violation of human rights.[14] Increases in gender-based violence precipitated the development of another instrument, the declaration on the Elimination of Violence against Women, adopted by the United Nations in 1993. Although there are limitations to these instruments, a discussion that is beyond scope of this paper, both the CEDAW and the Declaration were crucial turning points in expanding the international community's understanding of what constitutes violations of human rights. One major interpretation of these treaties, however, is their applicability in Western democratic contexts.

WELFARE REFORM AS A HUMAN RIGHTS ISSUE

The welfare state may ostensibly be seen as having redeemed human rights violations by offering assistance to those who were failed by market forces—in other words, poor people.[15] Yet, increasingly there has been reliance on market based models to eliminate poverty, which, according to anthropologist Jeffrey Maskovsky, represents a shift away from policies providing universal access for those in need.[16] But reliance on the market to provide basic needs means that people are often left without housing, food, and health care—due either to the inability to access them or to the denial of those resources. With the steady decline of the US economy, resources have become scarce. The demise of welfare as an entitlement program has aggravated this scarcity.

Women who were part of my study experienced poverty and privation squarely situated within the implementation of welfare reform in New York State in 1997. Their stories underscore the importance of analyzing everyday encounters with the objective of shifting the locus of blame from poor women as "the problem," to violators that impede women's ability to survive.

The Personal Responsibility and Work Opportunity Reconciliation Act

The US welfare system was reformed in 1996, when President Clinton signed the PRWORA, limiting assistance to individuals who up until that time had been assured of federal responsibility to provide assistance for those living at or below poverty levels. With the signing of the act, a new program, Temporary Assistance to Needy Families (TANF) replaced Aid to Families with Dependent Children (AFDC), the federal entitlement program for women and children that had existed since the 1930s.[17] Through TANF, states receive a fixed amount of federal monies to provide assistance to poor families with children. The act also replaced Home Relief, the program for single adults without children, with a program for the same population that must now be funded by state dollars (known in New York as the Safety Net Program).

While ardent critics challenged the merit of several elements of the PRWORA, two stand out as particularly problematic. The first concerns work. Recipients are now required to work in exchange for aid. The work that TANF or Safety Net recipients most often do, however, comes with neither the promise of full-time permanent employment nor worker protections.[18] The second issue is the imposition of time limitations on the receipt of assistance, which is federally capped at five years.[19] These policies, among others, have ultimately reduced the total number of people receiving aid.

In this regard, many posit that welfare reform has been successful. For example, in New York City, according to the New York City Human Resources Administration, the number of those receiving public assistance dropped from 776,264 in April 1998 to 423,969 in April

2003.[20] While some have found employment, the caseload reduction can also be attributed to the punitive measures used against recipients, such as sanctions and case closures. Sanctions are denials of support for specified time periods. Case closures may occur under any number of circumstances, including noncompliance with rules regarding engagement with work or work-related activities and administrative problems. Decreasing caseloads in no way indicates poverty reduction. And, although these measures have been touted as motivating poor people to achieve economic independence, researchers have questioned the impact of these tactics on those in need of assistance.[21]

Human Rights Violations

A human rights framework can be employed to invoke policy critiques. Here, I briefly examine just three rights that the TANF violates. Based on the foundational principles of the UDHR, the point is to illustrate a set of rights that poor people need to have protected, but they are not.

First, TANF violates the right to an adequate standard of living, which is addressed in Article 25 of the UDHR and includes the right to have food, clothing, housing, and medical care.[22] Since most human rights are connected to the maintenance of adequate standards of living, the TANF legislation actually imposes difficulty for those receiving assistance to live according to minimum standards. This is primarily due to the time limits imposed by the legislation. Adequate standards of living imply that people should not live in poverty. However, federal law only permits the receipt of aid for a lifetime maximum of five years, after which support may be terminated. Thus, protections to maintain adequate living standards are jeopardized. The cessation of benefits is linked to time, not poverty reduction. Termination of benefits, as well as sanctions, predestines recipients to experience barriers to the supports (cash and food stamps) necessary to sustain adequate standards of living.[23]

TANF also violates the right to work. Article 23 of the UDHR states that everyone has the right to work and the right to free choice of employment.[24] However, the act mandates that TANF recipients must work or be engaged in work-related activities. The rights to work and the free choice of employment are violated by policies that force people to work but do not factor in the type of job recipients may want. Further, a work-first policy, as it is known, compels recipients to participate in exploitative programs in which the "jobs" they *must* take offer little or no chance of advancement or permanent employment. Workfare program participants do not receive a salary, as they are working off their grant. Alternatively, formal employees get paid to do the same work. Further, since New York does not recognize these workers as employees, the right to unionize is obliterated. Since work placements are mandatory, failure to comply, even under the situation when work may not be available, means that recipients can be lawfully sanctioned and lose their benefits, which then would mean there are violations of the rights to food, shelter, and health care.

The third human rights violation that welfare reform breaches concerns education. Economic restructuring necessitates higher levels of education to secure employment that provides a living wage. Yet higher levels of education are not accessible for some people receiving TANF because related policies restrict the type of education and training that can count as work to one year of job training or vocational training, although it is up to the states to interpret the rules. While federal legislation established that education and job-training activities can meet the TANF work requirements, no more than 20 percent of a state's caseload engaged in education and training activities can count toward the state's work requirement. This means that 80 percent of a state's caseload is denied access to education, suggesting that education is discouraged. Even those few who are encouraged to go to school or receive training tend to gain skills through work or work-related activities and training programs that prepare them mainly for service-sector employment, which traditionally has low wages. Researchers report that welfare leavers are primarily concentrated in service and clerical jobs.[25] Many of those mandated to participate in various educational or training programs do not receive the skills that will move them out of poverty. To the degree that educational attainment is necessary to compete in a highly skilled job market, the denial of such opportunity undermines the recipient's ability to realize economic stability. Thus, Article 26 of the UDHR, which states that education shall be directed to the full development of the human personality, is violated.

The Race and Gender Dimensions of Welfare Reform

Many have made the point that welfare policy accentuates racial and gender discrimination, and their arguments are supported by research. For example, Susan Gooden's study of the interaction between recipients and caseworkers in Virginia found that white women were more likely to receive helpful interactions and encouragement to go to school from their caseworkers than black women.[26] Other research has shown that more white recipients leave the welfare system with employment, while minority recipients leave the system because their cases have been closed.[27] Journalist Jason DeParle found that white women left welfare rolls at much higher rates than black or Latina women, indicating that white women were more successful in their transition into the labor force.[28]

There are other ways in which poverty and welfare reform are marked by race. Black women are slightly more likely to be clustered in low-wage jobs than white women, 41 percent and 38 percent respectively.[29] The labor market has been more accommodating to white women's needs, as they are the primary beneficiaries of higher wages and employment that offers flexible work options, such as child-care benefits. According to some policy analysts, poor women (of color) are increasingly being *forced* into a low-wage labor market, while white women are remaining home, albeit in small increments.[30]

While violations existed prior to the welfare-reform legislation, the very fact that individuals are no longer entitled to government support heightens the potential for abuses. Moreover, previous rights violations against poor women took place within a structure that was designed to help people; now, violations exist within a social and political climate that is avowedly non-protectionist. Correctives to these violations are essential as the actualization of rights relies on standards that are nondiscriminatory.

Parastatal and Non-State Violators

A state may be considered to be violating human rights when it does not offer protection. For the poor, this protection translates into access to the market. The federal welfare-reform law was represented as a measure that would increase welfare recipients' independence by providing them with employment and paths to employment. However, many have reported that access to decent jobs has not been realized.[31] New bureaucratic policies geared to decreasing the number of people on the rolls contribute to the hardships felt by the recipients, and their quality of life is adulterated. The New York City Welfare Reform and Human Rights Documentation Project assessed the impact of welfare reform and concluded that the city created deliberate barriers, making it more difficult for eligible families to access food stamps.[32] Another study addresses the role that the sanctions and participation in welfare-to-work assignments play in causing women to lose, or almost lose, their housing. The findings of a recent report reveal that blacks are more likely to experience housing vulnerability than other racial/ethnic groups, having been evicted at higher rates and having had to take in boarders to help pay the rent.[33] Blacks are twice as likely to be homeless. These and other hardships have been linked to the punitive nature of welfare reform.[34]

While these studies emphasize the role of the state, I will turn to the violations by parastatal and non-state actors, drawing on my own research. The research was conducted in Laneville, a small city in upstate New York, for twenty-three months between 1998 and 2000. It involved participant observation and collecting life histories of twenty-two battered women who received welfare. Of the twenty-two women, thirteen were black, and it is their interactions that are the center of this discussion. The women lived at Angel House, a shelter for battered women, where they were allowed to stay for up to ninety days, as mandated by state law. In New York State, shelters are reimbursed at a daily rate by the Department of Social Services. While some women may have the funds to pay the daily rate themselves, this was not the case among any of the women interviewed. Given the unique payment scheme, most women who go to shelters must apply for social services, if they are not already receiving assistance. For black women who are battered, poor, and turn to the state for assistance, violations occur in public and private spheres.

Anticipating that welfare policies would inflict dilemmas on recipients, organizations around the country began to monitor the state welfare systems to determine the extent of violations against poor people.[35] The Unitarian Universalist Service Committee began monitoring the Massachusetts welfare system for human rights violations in 1995, the year Massachusetts initiated its own welfare reforms.[36] By 1997 the project had expanded to include California, Connecticut, New Jersey, and Washington, and documented the impact of federal welfare reform. The project was organized around several Articles of the UDHR, and the Department of Social Services of each state, as parastatal agencies, were held accountable for violating rights because the state explicitly authorized the reduction of welfare caseloads and the denial of benefits to those in need.

Following the Unitarian Universalist Service Committee project, several welfare reform–monitoring projects were initiated. In New York the Welfare Reform Committee at the Eleanor Roosevelt Center at Val-Kill, located in Dutchess County, New York, developed one such project. The effort involved twenty-five human service organizations and thirty monitors, who documented violations arising from welfare-to-work programs. At the end of 1998 the committee produced its first monitoring report detailing violations of human rights that resulted from changes in welfare laws and regulations and their implementation by the Dutchess County Department of Social Services.[37] Their findings showed that clients' human rights were denied due to:

- arbitrary decision-making that led to sanctions;
- lack of information given to clients;
- lack of timely response to inquiries resulting in late applications and loss of available benefits; and
- failure to reconsider decisions once appropriate client documentation was provided and refusal to review negative decisions when circumstances revealed client's needs.

Under these circumstances the Dutchess County Department of Social Services failed to protect the recipients, and the recipients' right to achieve self-sufficiency was hindered by the welfare-reform policy. Another example of parastatal violations concerns a young woman who was interviewed for my research project.

Case #1—The Department of Social Services as a Parastatal Violator

The 1996 Welfare Reform Act contains provisions requiring minor mothers to live with a parent or legal guardian in order to receive benefits, except under certain circumstances such as violence. This first case shows how in implementing this policy the rights of a young woman were violated by a caseworker at the River Valley County Department of Social Services (RVCDSS).

Leslie is an eighteen-year-old African American woman. She was pregnant in 1999 and applied to the RVCDSS for cash assistance, Medicaid, food stamps, and housing. During her meeting with a caseworker at the RVCDSS, it was revealed that she had experienced violence by both her mother and her boyfriend only after the caseworker informed Leslie she would have to live with her mother. Leslie specifically asked to invoke the family violence option, which would have precluded her from having to live with her mother and would have made her eligible for social services, but she was denied.[38] Ineligibility meant Leslie would have no source of income to support herself and no Medicaid to cover her health needs, although she had a high-risk pregnancy, and no food stamps (even though Medicaid and food stamps can be secured through emergency measures). The caseworker accused Leslie of lying about the abuse in her life to circumvent the welfare-policy mandates, that Leslie only said she experienced violence as a strategy to secure a TANF grant. The caseworker refused to refer Leslie to the Domestic Violence Liaison that could have exempted her from welfare mandates for a specified period of time. Leslie felt dejected and desperate. She was angry and afraid, and she said that the caseworker did not listen to her story carefully.

In Leslie's opinion the worker conferred upon her the identity of being a welfare fraud, presumably because she was young, black, and pregnant—without ever saying so. The ideological habit of characterizing a young black pregnant woman as a fraud is so common that she need not even be specifically referred to as such. Yet the weight and meaning of the unspoken term has several consequences. Not only is access to assistance denied, but being "flagged" as a welfare fraud reproduces the habit of presuming that welfare frauds exist.[39] In the interest of denying benefits, Leslie was in some way constructed as being fraudulent.

The paradox lies in the fact that identity construction is also a strategy used to *provide* social services, not just to deny them. For example, Lipsky argues that to justify the provision of social services, individuals are categorized based on deficits. He makes the point that government-operated social-service institutions constantly engage in identity construction of clients. Caseworkers have a great deal of autonomy in translating policy and determining who will and who will not benefit from the provision of support from the Department of Social Services.[40] Creating negative categories to *justify* the provision of service is contradictory to the current retrenchment of services, and instead, clients are constructed in ways that deem them ineligible for services.

Following the meeting with the caseworker, Leslie filed a human rights abuse claim, and subsequently the decision denying her social services was reversed. This report was part of a welfare-reform documentation project where welfare recipients self-report violations by the Department of Social Services. Filing the human rights abuse form was important in legitimizing Leslie's claim of violation. Cumulatively, forms such as that filled out by Leslie can be used as evidence that such violations are not random events. Clearly based on the response of the RVCDSS, filing the complaint asked the department to respond to individual need, but there must be systemic correctives that operate on behalf of all recipients. However, human rights monitoring and the documentation process on a local level are of value in identifying how the public sector violates rights; they also serve as an instrument to facilitate interventions.

NSAs as Violators

We have seen how a public entity violated a woman's rights by denying access to social services supports. Yet, violations do not only occur in the public sphere. There are NSAs, who also commit significant violations within the context of welfare reform and undermine women's dignity. Despite media spin positing the successes of welfare reform, the cases analyzed in this section illuminate rights abuses by those other than the state or its associative partners.

The foundation of human rights is in fact based on the argument that there are essential rights, universal entitlements for every woman, man, youth, and child to fundamental freedoms and protections. Yet, some women on welfare are characterized as lazy, cheaters of the welfare system, and parasites living off the largesse of the state. The extension of this ideology leaks its way to private actors operating in public spheres.[41] Those on the periphery of state structures are not immune to sociopolitical representations of issues and people.[42] Therefore, non-state private actors are just as prone to obfuscating human rights. They may be found in the private sectors of the market economy and include landlords and employers.

In Leslie's story we find that the River Valley County Department of Social Services was a parastatal violator, one that initially refused to provide Leslie with access to resources she needed. Other women I interviewed had similar interactions with caseworkers. But violations by NSAs were just as frequent. For example, in Laneville a landlord rejected a woman's application to rent an apartment *because* she was battered and on welfare. His justification was that welfare paid too little and her former batterer might "cause trouble."

Infringements of this type, denial of housing by private actors, are far less documented but still reflect violations of poor women's rights. In the interest of further elaborating how NSAs violate women's rights,

I offer two incidents of the infringement of the rights of black battered women on welfare, involving violations related to housing and employment, respectively.

Case #2—The Retailer Violating the Right to Housing

Joanne was a twenty-eight-year-old African American woman with one child, who is five. She lived with her son's father until September 1998. When he had beaten her in the street, she came to Angel House for refuge. With no home and no source of income, Joanne applied for social services and received cash assistance, food stamps, and a housing allowance. Securing housing was essential, given that Joanne could only remain at Angel House for ninety days and whatever housing she found, because it was being paid for by the RVCDSS, required approval by the agency.

Near the end of her ninety-day stay, Joanne found an apartment. However, the apartment lacked a refrigerator, and therefore could not be certified as habitable by the RVCDSS until it was equipped with one. To "purchase" a refrigerator, the RVCDSS provided Joanne with a cost-estimate form to be completed by a retailer. Upon receipt of the completed estimate form, her caseworker would authorize payment for the refrigerator, and the apartment would be considered suitable for living.

Housing is difficult to secure in Laneville for a number of reasons. First, rental properties are scarce and rents are on the rise. The average fair-market value of a one-bedroom apartment in River Valley County is $710 per month,[43] but the monthly allowance for shelter for a family of two is $469. Second, the city is divided by an "invisible redline" that keeps the primarily poor black and Latino residents on the North side and the wealthier, primarily white residents on the South side of the city. As a black woman with little income, Joanne would not easily find housing.

Joanne's search for a retailer that would complete the cost estimate was complicated by the number of establishments indicating that they "did not do estimates because it was too much trouble." Refusal to complete the form prevented Joanne from moving. Finding an apartment with a refrigerator probably would have put Joanne over the housing allotment, or she could move to an apartment in a less desirable part of the city that came fully equipped. With no income, the latter option was the most probable.

We might posit that the barriers making it difficult for Joanne to move violated her right to live in a domicile that met her minimum safety standards. And who was at fault? Fault lay with the RVCDSS *and* the retailers because Joanne experienced a violation of her right to shelter and an adequate standard of living.

Case #3—The Employer Violating the Right to Work

The mandatory-work component of the Welfare Reform Act of 1997 has placed a number of women in the position of being exploited by employers. Since recipients are required to work and often receive their work referral from the Department of Social Services, employers know who among their staff receives support from Social Services. Supervisors have to sign forms verifying that the recipient has come to work and can use this power to intimidate workers and force them to do things that are beyond their job descriptions. Women are at risk for sexual harassment, because employers or supervisors can report them to their caseworker if they fail to do what an employer/supervisor wants.[44] If a woman rejects the supervisor, she may receive a poor report by the employer and end up being sanctioned by the Department of Social Services. If she attempts to stop harassment by indicating that she will file a harassment charge, she risks being fired. This is precisely what happened to Lydia.

Lydia, an African American woman, struggled to meet the mandatory-work requirements. Although she worked part time, the number of hours did not add up to the thirty hours of work per week or work-related activities that are required of recipients. Therefore, Lydia was mandated by her caseworker to attend a training program. In so doing, she was able to compensate for the additional fifteen hours. However, her part-time job was based on a flexible schedule, and her hours changed from week to week. Participating in the training program meant that Lydia needed a fairly regular schedule to accommodate the training program. The supervisor was unhappy with this arrangement and said that if Lydia could not work when they needed her, maybe she should not work at all. But Lydia persevered and continued to arrange her schedule around her employer's needs. Then one day Lydia called in sick. Despite her medical excuse, Lydia's employer used her absence against her. She was asked to come in to the office for a meeting, in spite of her illness. During the meeting she was told she could be fired for missing work and would be reported to her caseworker for noncompliance. Under the threat of being fired and reported and not knowing her rights, Lydia quit the job. She also lost her benefits. In this case the employer violated Lydia's right to work under favorable conditions and to be protected against unemployment.

In the social marketplace Lydia's status as a woman on welfare was a subordinating dimension of her interaction with the supervisor. The tendency to be threatened with job loss and/or to be reported to one's caseworker can be viewed as an indicator of the low value placed on her worth because she was a woman on welfare.

The examples provided here highlight the importance of capturing transgressions of black women's rights in various sites. Within the scope of human rights practice, the infringements they face are situated outside of the state. But the complex relations among state, parastatal, and non-state actors, and poor women are evident, and the state should investigate violations in all spheres, since it is the state that has mandated policies that involve implementation by non-state agents.

In the last two cases the concept of state responsibility has been expanded to "include not only actions directly committed by states, but also states' systematic failure to prosecute acts committed either by low-level or parastatal agents or by private actors."[45] Both represent critical concerns for ordinary women on the local stage where local articulations of abuse occur. Nonetheless, the practices of local NSAs are still the responsibility of the state, as it must not fail to protect people. Failure to protect amounts to collusion. In this context collusion is captured in the concept of due diligence, which maintains that governments are obligated to exhibit the commitment necessary for the investigation, prosecution, and punishment of violations.

By magnifying sites of transgression beyond the state, which bears primary responsibility of abuse, we find that it is not the sole perpetrator of abuse and violations of dignity. The scope of human rights practice must necessarily attend to the situations such as those described in this chapter if the human rights framework is to be rendered responsive to gender-based and race-based violations.

CONCLUSION

At the intersection of violence, poverty, and race are obstacles to achieving self-sufficiency. This consequence takes on added meaning when women's utilization of the reformed welfare system is folded in to a human rights analysis. What black women face, as anthropologist Mary Anglin argues, is structural violence.[46] In her analysis structural violence is the withdrawal of social supports not only by the state but by NSAs as well. By not problematizing these situations there is risk of supporting a contradiction. On the one hand, principles of equality, and requisites for actors to protect all rights, are understood as priorities. On the other hand, if certain categories of violators are viewed as less important than others, then some violations are dismissed, creating a hierarchy of human rights protection.

As I have shown, private NSAs who are embedded in public spheres participate in the cycle of violations. But how often are they held accountable? How often are their violations documented? Although it may be a challenge to analyze the violations of private NSAs within a human rights context, it remains necessary, if links are to be made between state policies and their translation by NSAs. It is further necessary if advocates seek to locate credible threats of violations and hold these agents accountable.

Methodologically, human rights documentation processes are primarily concerned with reporting facts that will bring about change. Individual cases are investigated through witnesses and victim interviews, and abuses are proved not only based on patterns of transgressions but also on demonstrating state failure to protect against the abuses. The requirements of building a case for state responsibility of private actors such as retailers or employers are fraught with barriers and complications, because the institution that has been traditionally seen as the duty bearer to guarantee human rights is the state. However, there can be positive state responsibility with regard to NSAs that can help eliminate, or at the very least diffuse, violations. By placing the abuses such as those described within mainstream human rights practice, it is possible to build public consensus on the idea that the experiences of women like Leslie, Joanne, and Lydia were in fact authentic violations of rights that need to be protected. In other words, definitional exceptionalism—that is, exempting these infractions from interrogation because they do not meet normative definitional standards—poses problems among women for whom inferior material status is prevalent. Hence, human rights practice should aspire to work around the parameters of limited definitions. Toward that end, some interventions are outlined below.

On a practical level, welfare reform–monitoring projects must capture the everyday infractions that many NSAs subject poor black women to. Documentation cannot be limited to the injurious confrontations with the state agencies, such as the Department of Social Services. Such monitoring allows for the assessment of the pervasive nature of such violations and their gender and racial biases. Clearly, advocates can assume constructive roles as mediators between social actors and non-state violators and engage in documentary projects to actualize a human rights agenda.

Given that the impact of poverty is amplified by the apparent excessive advancement of capitalism, the human rights approach can serve as a counterpoint to the diluted ideas of public responsibility for economic inequality. Welfare advocacy ordinarily focuses on entitlements to welfare support based on eligibility of those entitlements, but the aspiration of human rights is to transform the circumstances that allow poverty to fester. To make changes, aspirations alone are insufficient. The nature of the obligation to protect must be strengthened on local and even supra-local levels. Therefore, active local implementation of human rights treaties to mitigate local infractions by private actors is warranted. Parastatal entities such as city councils and boards of supervisors can independently implement treaties, bypassing federal ratification. These entities can, in turn, investigate violations within their districts. One successful example of local implementation can be found in San Francisco, California. The City of San Francisco passed an Ordinance adopting the CEDAW as city law. This placed the city under obligation to conduct a gender analysis of select governmental agencies. As a result, the San Francisco Department of Public Works had to examine the relationship between placement of streetlights and the safety of women and girls. In another instance the Department of Juvenile Probation recognized the need for gender-specific services.[47]

The success of San Francisco's active stance motivated New York City human rights activists to organize around the implementation of two treaties, the CEDAW and the CERD, by the New York City Council. The treaties would oblige the New York City government to identify gender and racial discrimination in policymaking efforts. Ultimately, this strategy could oblige the governmental agencies to pressure entities that provide goods and services to the recipients to protect, rather than violate, rights and to mobilize those who are marginalized to challenge NSAs to act in the interests of poor women.

NOTES

[1] The White House Office of the Press Secretary, Executive Order 13107, Implementation of Human Rights Treaties (Washington, DC: The White House, 10 December 1998), available online.

[2] The Act—P.L. 104–193, 104th Congress, H.R. 3734, 22 August 1996. 110 STAT. 2105—consists of nine titles addressing Aid to Families with Dependent Children (AFDC); benefits for legal immigrants; the Food Stamp Program; SSI for children; child care; the Child Support Enforcement Program; modifications to the child nutrition program; Social Services Block Grant; and miscellaneous issues.

[3] The word *dignity* may be understood as a state of being in which one is esteemed, honored, and valued. The complexity of the word *dignity* lies in the non-materiality of it, that is, a state of dignity is one that is intangible. For a legal discussion of the term as it is understood in Tort Law, see Richard Delgado, "Words That Wound: A Tort Action For Racial Insults, Epithets, and Name-Calling," in *Words that Wound: Critical Race Theory: Assaultive Speech and the First Amendment*, ed. Mari J. Matsuda, Charles Lawrence III, Richard Delgado, Kimberly Williams Crenshaw, 89–110 (Boulder, CO: Westview Press, 1993): 104.

[4] The Kensington Welfare Rights Union uses human rights education, organization, documentation, and litigation to protest economic human rights violations. It collected data that established the basis for a series of reports exposing violations. For the reports, see the group's website, www.kwru.org. The Women's Rights Network used human rights documentation to examine the Massachusetts government's practices on child custody and visitation cases involving domestic violence. See Carrie Cuthbert, et al., *Battered Mothers Speak Out: A Human Rights Report on Domestic Violence and Child Custody in the Massachusetts Family Court* (Wellesley, MA: Battered Mothers Testimony Project, Wellesley Centers for Women, Wellesley College, 2002), www.wcwonline.org website (accessed 18 June 2003).

[5] For example, in 1993, human rights groups claimed that the government of Ecuador violated human rights when oil exploration by the ARCO Corporation threatened indigenous communities with the loss of their land and sources of food. See FIAN International Secretariat, *Economic Human Rights— Their Time Has Come* (Heidelberg, Germany: FIAN International Secretariat, 1995): 20.

[6] Race has been an important explanatory variable in the analysis of the development of US social policy. On race and welfare, see Jill Quadagno, *The Color of Welfare: How Racism Undermined the War on Welfare* (New York: Oxford Univ. Press, 1994); Ronald Walters, "The Democratic Party and Politics of Welfare Reform," in *Social Policy and the Conservative Agenda,* ed. Clarence Y. H. Lo and Michael Schwartz, 37–52 (Malden, MA: Blackwell Publishers

Ltd., 1999); Walter Stafford, Diana Salas, and Melissa Mendez, *Race, Gender, and Welfare Reform: The Need for Targeted Support* (New York: The New York Univ. Robert F. Wagner Graduate School of Public Service, The Roundtable of Institutions of People of Color, Women of Color Policy Network, 2002).

[7] Political-scientist Ange-Marie Hancock discusses how the public identity of marginalized groups is constructed by political elites. Her analysis centers on the construction of black "welfare queens" to make the point that the incipient representations reveal a "politics of disgust." See Ange-Marie Hancock, *The Public Identity of the "Welfare Queen" and The Politics of Disgust* (New York: New York Univ. Press, 2004).

[8] For an analysis of the historical use of welfare racism, see Kenneth J. Neubeck and Noel Cazenave, *Welfare Racism: Playing the Race Card against America's Poor* (New York: Routledge, 2001).

[9] A study by the NOW Legal Defense and Education Fund found that 60 percent of adults who were poor in 2001 were women. See NOW Legal Defense and Education Fund, "New Poverty Statistics Show Poverty Is Still a Women's Issue" (New York: NOW, October 2002), www.nowldef.org website (accessed 10 November 2002).

[10] US Department of Health and Human Services, *Characteristics and Financial Circumstances of TANF Recipients October 1999–September 2000,* Temporary Assistance for Needy Families (TANF) Program, Administration for Children and Families (Washington, DC: Office of Planning, Research, and Evaluation, 2002).

[11] Barbara Gault and Annisah Um'rani, "The Outcomes of Welfare Reform for Women," *Poverty and Race* 9, no. 4 (2000): 1.

[12] Susana T. Fried, ed., *The Indivisibility of Women's Human Rights: A Continuing Dialogue* (New Bruswick, NJ: Center for Women's Global Leadership, 1995), 56.

[13] See Charlotte Bunch, "Violence against Women Is a Violation of Human Rights," *Women in Law and Development in Africa News* (1992): 4; Charlotte Bunch and Roxanna Carillo, *Gender Violence: A Development and Human Rights Issue* (New Brunswick, NJ: Center for Women's Global Leadership, 1991).

[14] Hussaina J. Abdullah, "Religious Revivalism, Human Rights Activism, and the Struggle for Women's Rights in Nigeria," in *Beyond Rights Talk and Culture Talk: Comparative Essays on the Politics of Rights and Culture*, ed. Mahmood Mamdani, 96–120 (Capetown, South Africa: David Phillip Publishers, 2000), 117.

[15] For a historical overview of the welfare state and welfare policy in the United States, see Frances Fox Piven and Richard Cloward, *Regulating the Poor: The Functions of Public Welfare* (New York: Vintage Books, 1993); and Mimi Abramovitz, *Regulating the Lives of Women: Social Welfare Policy from Colonial Times to the Present* (Boston: South End Press, 1997).

[16] Jeffrey Maskovsky, "Sexual Minorities and the New Urban Poverty," in *Cultural Diversity in the United States,* ed. Ida Susser and Thomas C. Patterson, 322–40 (Malden, MA: Blackwell Publishers, 2001), 322.

[17] In the 1930s the program for widows with children was called Aid for Dependent Children (ADC). In the 1960s the program was expanded to provide assistance for family members, notably mothers, and was renamed Aid to Families with Dependent Children (AFDC). See Linda Gordon, *Pitied But Not Entitled: Single Mothers and the History of Welfare* (New York: Free Press, 1994).

[18] For an in-depth discussion of welfare-to-work programs in New York City, see Dana Davis, et al., "Working It Off: Welfare Reform, Workfare and Work Experience Programs in New York City," *Souls: A Critical Journal of Black Politics, Culture, and Society*, 5, no. 2 (2003).

[19] While federal funding cannot be used to support the states' caseload after five years, states may opt to provide assistance for a shorter or longer duration, the latter only being possible if state funds are used.

[20] New York City Human Resources Administration provides data on caseloads. See "HRA Facts: April 2003" (New York: Data Analysis and Research Office of Policy and Program Analysis), www.nyc.gov website (accessed 31 August 2004).

[21] Rebecca Gordon of the Applied Research Center has documented the negative consequences of sanctions and case closures. See Rebecca Gordon, *Cruel and Usual: How Welfare "Reform" Punishes Poor People* (Oakland, CA: Applied Research Center, 2001).

[22] Article 25 addresses social protections related to standards of living and emphasizes the special care and assistance needed by mothers and children in this regard.

[23] While this is in fact the case across the country, New York is unique because the New York State Constitution, Article XVII, obligates New York to provide aid, care, and support of the needy. The Article was adopted in 1939. See New York State Constitution (Albany, NY: Department of State, Division of Administrative Rules), www.state.ny.us (accessed 31 August 2004).

[24] Article 23 of the UDHR addresses rights concerning the free choice of employment and favorable work conditions.

[25] Sarah Brauner and Pamela Loprest, "Where Are They Now? What States' Studies of People Who Left Welfare Tell Us," *New Federalism: Issues and Options for States*, no. A-32 (Washington, DC: Urban Institute, 1999).

[26] Susan Gooden reports that while white women indicated that caseworkers encouraged them to go to school, black women were told that they should go get a job. White women were also more likely to receive transportation assistance, while black women received none. See Susan Gooden, "All Things Not Being Equal: Differences in Caseworker Support toward Black and White Welfare Clients," *Harvard Journal of African American Public Policy* 4 (1998): 23–33.

[27] Ramona Ortega, *Assessing the Intersection of Race and Welfare Reform for New York City Households* (New York: Urban Justice Center, 2001); and Sarah Karp, "Work Preparation Falters: Minorities Off Welfare Get Few Jobs," *The Chicago Reporter* (January 2000), www.chicagoreporter.com website (accessed 31 August 2004).

[28] See Jason DeParle, "Shrinking Welfare Rolls Leave Record High Share of Minorities," *New York Times,* 24 July 1998, A1.

[29] The Women Employed Institute prepares fact sheets using government statistics to examine women's economic status in relation to gender and race for education, employment, occupational status, etc. See Women Employed Institute, "Working Women's Economic Status" (Chicago: Women Employed Institute, June 2002).

[30] Stafford et al., *Race, Gender, and Welfare Reform,* 8.

[31] Equal Rights Advocates is an advocacy group located in California. Its 1999 survey of welfare recipients in three California counties about the welfare reform in the state reports the failings in California's Work First program. See Doris Y. Ng and Ana J. Matosantos, *The Broken Promise: Welfare Reform Two Years Later* (San Francisco: Equal Rights Advocates, 2000), www.equalrights.org website (accessed 9 October 2002).

[32] See Cybelle Fox, *Hunger Is No Accident: New York and Federal Welfare Policies Violate the Human Right to Food* (New York: New York City Welfare Reform and Human Rights Documentation Project, 2000).

[33] See Dana-Ain Davis et al., *The Impact of Welfare Reform on Two Communities in New York City* (New York: CUNY, October 2002), 66.

[34] See, for example, Abby Pritcher, *Human Rights Violations in Welfare Legislation: Pushing Recipients Deeper in Poverty* (New York: Urban Justice Center, 2002).

[35] Welfare reform ushered in criticism from the advocates of battered women and anti-poverty programs, who connected poverty and violence. These advocates pointed out that policies that mandate work, require training, and force women to seek child support, could pose tremendous harm to women. See Ellen L. Bassuk, et al., "The Characteristics and Needs of Sheltered Homeless and Low Income Housed Mothers," *Journal of the American Medical Association* 276, no. 8 (1996): 640–56; and Washington State Institute for Public Policy, *Family Income Study* (Olympia, WA: Washington State Institute for Public Policy, 1993). These reports provided a context for national data that linked women's victimization rates by an intimate partner to household income. See Callie Marie Rennison and Sarah Welchans, *Intimate Partner Violence* (Washington, DC: US Department of Justice, Bureau of Justice Statistics, May 2000).

[36] Unitarian Universalist Service Committee, *America's Forgotten Families: Voices of Welfare Reform,* Welfare Reform and Human Rights Monitoring Report (Cambridge, MA: Unitarian Universalist Service Committee, May 1998), www.uusc.org website (accessed 31 August 2004).

[37] Eleanor Roosevelt Center at Val-Kill Welfare Reform Committee, *Welfare Reform and Human Rights Monitoring Report* (Poughkeepsie, NY: Eleanor Roosevelt Center at Val-Kill, July 1998).

[38] Those who work on behalf of battered women argued that welfare reform would create hardships for battered women if they had to participate in mandated employment or work-related activities. The central issue was that women would experience retaliation as they decreased their economic and

social dependence on their batterers. Moreover, if women were prevented from participating in work or work-related activities due to injury, fear, or barriers imposed by batterers, they could be sanctioned or lose their benefits for non-compliance. Consequently, women's poverty would deepen, especially if the strict time limits applied. Of equal concern was that the loss of benefits might force women to stay with their abusers. One strategy to address these concerns was an amendment to PRWORA in the form of the Family Violence Option (FVO [Sec. 402(a) (7)]). See Demi Kurz, "Women, Welfare and Domestic Violence," in *Whose Welfare?*, ed. Gwendolyn Mink, 132–51 (Ithaca, NY: Cornell Univ. Press, 1999); and Jody Raphael, "The Family Violence Option: An Early Assessment," *Violence against Women* 5, no. 4 (1999).

[39] For a broader discussion on the role of ideology and its reproduction, see Michael Billig, *Banal Nationalism* (London: Sage Publications, 1995).

[40] Michael Lispky, *Street Level Bureaucracy: Dilemmas of the Individual in Public Services* (New York: Russell Sage Foundation, 1980).

[41] Consider, for example, reports by blacks of being followed in stores, not because they have done anything wrong, but because preconceived ideas about race inform interactions in public spheres.

[42] For a discussion on how public opinion on poverty is shaped by the media, see Rosalee A. Clawson and Rakuya Trice, "Poverty As We Know It: Media Portrayals of the Poor," *Public Opinion Quarterly* 64, no. 1 (2000): 53.

[43] In 1999, in order to afford housing at that cost, one would have to have an annual income of $28,700. See National Low Income Housing Coalition, *Out of Reach* (Washington, DC: National Low Income Housing Coalition, 1999), www.nlihc.org (accessed February 2000).

[44] See, for example, Gordon, *Pitied But Not Entitled,* 35.

[45] Michele E. Beasley and Dorothy Q. Thomas, "Domestic Violence as a Human Rights Issue," in *The Public Nature of Private Violence: The Discovery of Abuse*, ed. Martha Albertson Fineman and Roxanne Mykitiuk, 323–46 (New York: Routlege, 1994).

[46] Mary Anglin argues that structural violence marginalizes persons in ways that deny them opportunity. See Mary Anglin, "Feminist Perspectives on Structural Violence," *Identities* 5, no. 2 (1998): 145–51.

[47] For human rights projects located in the United States, see Dorothy Q. Thomas and Krishanti Dharmaraj, *Making the Connections: Human Rights in the United States* (San Francisco: Women's Institute for Leadership Development for Human Rights and the Shaler Adams Foundation, 2000), 15.

16

Non-State Actors
and Religious Freedom in Europe

Willy Fautré

INTRODUCTION

Throughout the second half of the twentieth century Western European countries took part in the elaboration of international instruments that increasingly guaranteed the basic principles of freedom of religion and belief.[1] They also demonstrated a high degree of creativity in conceptualizing and setting up international human rights monitoring and implementation mechanisms. The European scene is worth focusing on because a number of major forces threatening, inhibiting, or safeguarding religious freedom in relatively open societies can be identified and highlighted. It is also a privileged field of investigation because it provides a source of reflection on the significant interactive role played by religious and secular non-state organizations dealing with religious freedom matters, state actors, and supra-state actors.

Christian historical churches and Judaism have naturally and easily benefited from the elaboration of international instruments that increasingly guaranteed the basic principles of freedom of religion and belief in Western Europe, where democracy finally prevailed after the fall of the last dictatorships in Greece, Spain, and Portugal around the middle of the 1970s. The settlement and development of new religious movements in Western Europe (evangelicals, Pentecostals, Jehovah's Witnesses, Mormons, Hare Krishna, and so on) was, however, always accompanied by social and political mistrust. Their integration into the existing religious landscape, which was and still is mainly influenced by a dominant church, either Catholic or Protestant, remains slow and difficult. Secular humanism has also emerged as an additional factor impeding the social accommodation of new religions, especially in French-speaking and German-speaking countries and regions of Western Europe.

In the Soviet Union the Bolshevik revolution brought the Communists to power in 1917. All religions, whether historical or new, were dramatically oppressed for more than seventy years. Thousands of churches were destroyed; clerics were massacred, imprisoned or deported to labor camps; and atheism was imposed in all spheres of society and at all levels of state education. In the aftermath of World War II, religions fell under the yoke of Communism and its atheist propaganda in Central and Eastern European countries that had been "liberated" from the Nazi occupation by the Soviet Union. The spaces of religious freedom were restricted in these new Communist states. This situation prevailed until 1989–90.

Since the fall of Communism in Central and Eastern European countries, the general concept of religious freedom, tolerance, and nondiscrimination has been gaining more and more ground, mainly under the influence of the human rights implementation mechanisms of the OSCE, the Council of Europe, and the EU. At the beginning of the 1990s historical religions in former Communist countries started to regain their freedom, while nontraditional minority religions continued suffering various forms of hostility not only from the state but also from the dominant religions (Orthodox, Catholic, and Lutheran). State and non-state actors (NSAs) started launching anti-cult campaigns against the development and the "invasion" of "foreign cults," usually perceived as a threat to the national identity.

In Western Europe the latent social mistrust toward non-historical minority religions suddenly became a political issue when the Order of the Solar Temple committed a number of mass suicides and homicides in the mid-1990s.[2] The anti-cult offensive was triggered in French-speaking and German-speaking countries, and then spread to other countries. Parliamentary inquiry commissions on cults were set up, as were lists of (possibly) harmful cults. Special laws and decrees were passed. Campaigns warning against cults were sponsored by governmental agencies and specific state-sponsored mechanisms were put in place to fight them.

National parliaments have the responsibility not only to guarantee freedom of religion and belief but also to protect individuals and society against possible misuse of this same freedom. They also have the power to outline the legal framework regulating the relations between state and religions and to entrust its implementation to a particular ministry or state agency.[3]

However, the activities of these state actors are under the scrutiny of a number of supra-state actors involved in the implementation of international standards. The interactive relations between state actors and supra-state actors generate a dynamic process intended to reduce restrictions on religious freedom as well as to regulate state interference into internal matters of religions. The main supra-state actors on the European continent are the United Nations, the OSCE, the Council of Europe, the European Court of Human Rights, and the European Parliament. Of all the European supra-state institutions, the one most influential in practice is the European Court. Of particular importance is the Amsterdam Treaty (1 May 1999). Superseding the Maastricht Treaty of 1992 framing the EU, the treaty stipulates that relations between member states and religions or world views in the EU remain under the authority of the states.

NON-STATE ACTORS INHIBITING FREEDOM OF RELIGION AND BELIEF

NSAs inhibiting freedom of religion and belief can be split into three categories. Cult-awareness groups (CAGs)[4] and counter-cult groups target new religious movements. Some faith communities are also a source of concern as they fuel interreligious and inter-communal conflicts on the European territory. Nationalistic, extreme-right movements and parties are also responsible for religious intolerance, in particular anti-Semitism and Islamophobia. CAGs comprise governmental agencies[5] and non-governmental associations also commonly called anti-cult organizations.[6] These private groups have set as their objective to determine in what way religious movements harm or might harm individuals, families, and society. The founders and members of such groups may have been directly involved in problems related to cults as former cult members or relatives of cult members, or they may be professionals (psychologists, medical doctors, lawyers, journalists) who have been requested to put their skills at the disposal of those who seek their assistance. Occupational or ideological considerations can also motivate secular humanists, freemasons, atheists, communist and socialist politicians, defenders of traditional religions (as in Russia, Poland, Germany, Belgium) to join CAGs. The distinction between these two categories is, however, not always very clear. Some cult-awareness activists may have more than one motivation, including material advantages (lawyers, psychotherapists, or journalists). CAGs are favored by the media because they can provide horrifying stories of victims or defectors. These activists are also consulted as experts in court cases. In concert with supporters in various governments, CAGs contribute to the restriction of religious freedom of new religious movements, to religious discrimination, and to intolerance.

Counter-cult groups (CCGs) in Europe are opposed to religious diversity and to "religious competition" in "the free market of religions." They can originate from majority faiths (Catholic, Orthodox, or Lutheran churches) that want to stop a hemorrhage of faithful to new Christian or non-Christian religious movements. They are also to be found in Protestant minority faiths (such as evangelical churches) that warn against non-Christian religions.

Members of CCGs are likely to include the leadership of a church,[7] clerics,[8] theologians, and former cult members who have joined the new faith. CCGs are meant to defend the doctrine of their denomination against heresies or deviating teachings and to defend themselves against other faiths that attract their faithful. While it is legitimate to defend one's faith, combating other faiths with illegitimate means (false rumors, defamation, hate speech, violence[9]) and with the help of the state[10] is a breach of religious freedom and religious peace. Secular humanism, which is particularly influential as a world view in European French-speaking countries, also has a counter-cult policy as part of its missionary work and its fight against religious obscurantism.

FAITH COMMUNITIES

Europe has been the scene of religious wars in the past. Conflicts between faith communities have not fully disappeared yet, especially in the Orthodox world. While there is interreligious dialogue between the leaders of historical religions in Western Europe, leaders of some Orthodox churches in Central and Eastern Europe rejected contacts with the Roman Catholic Church.[11] Traditionally, historically, and politically, Orthodox churches have always taken a negative stance on religions that "invade" their territories. In countries where they are the dominant religion, the Orthodox churches are an essential component of the national identity. Some churches are also cradles of extremist nationalism, religious and cultural protectionism, intolerance of religious diversity, and resentment of competition for the faithful. Hence, the hostility of those churches to the presence and the pastoral activities of the Roman Catholic Church, Protestant denominations, and new religious movements.[12]

In Bosnia and in Kosovo wars opposing Orthodox populations to Muslim populations claimed innumerable victims in the 1990s. In Romania, Ukraine, and Russia[13] interreligious conflicts oppose groups of Orthodox believers to Eastern-rite Catholics or to Protestant missionaries. Disputes arise among Orthodox churches over competing claims to national supremacy and the role of state religion in the country.[14]Anti-Semitism permeates some Orthodox churches. In Belarus the government has done little to counter the spread of anti-Semitic literature. In March 2000, for example, a Minsk court dismissed a complaint filed by Jewish organizations against the Orthodox Initiative (a state-owned publishing house) for publishing an anti-Semitic book containing the "Protocols of the Elders of Zion" and blaming Jews for societal and economic problems in the country. The book remained on sale at the main Orthodox Church bookstore.

Islam is a minority religion in almost all the European countries except Albania, Kosovo, and Bosnia. The right to change religion is largely impeded at all levels in Muslim communities, from the leadership down to the family level. Mixed marriages tend to be discouraged or prevented, unless the non-Muslim party converts to Islam. Due to the conflict between Palestine and Israel, the main locus of anti-Jewish speech and deeds is moving from the Muslim world to Western Europe through the Muslim diaspora. In Europe, Muslim extremists carry the banner of anti-Semitism[15] and constitute a physical threat to Jews. In France during October 2000, the month following the outburst of the Second Palestinian Intifadah, more than one hundred anti-Semitic attacks, ranging from graffiti to harassment and firebombing, occurred across the country. On 10 October 2000 a synagogue in Trappes was burned. Between October 12 and 14, 2000, local authorities in Strasbourg uncovered several Molotov cocktails that had been planted in a synagogue. Three synagogues in the Paris suburbs of Bagnolet and a Jewish shop in Toulon were firebombed.[16] In Belgium, attacks, both verbal and physical, occurred, mostly in Brussels and in Antwerp, especially in locations with concentrations of Arab/Muslim and Jewish populations.[17] An increase in attacks was stimulated by the events of 9/11 and the reactions that followed. Anti-Semitism, historically a Christian phenomenon in Europe, is now also a Muslim phenomenon, and not just in the Middle East.

The anti-Semitic mindset is reinforced by West European media reporting of the Palestinian-Israeli conflict. An example is the battle of March–April 2002 in the Jenin refugee camp on the West Bank. TV stations and leading newspapers in Western Europe reported a "massacre" of three thousand Palestinians, though, as Harold Evans points out, "the main propagator of this story, Saeb Erekat, has been shown time and time again to be a liar. . . . In fact, there was no massacre, no mass graves. Human Rights Watch has since put the death toll at a total of 54, including, on their count, 22 civilians—the Israeli say three."[18] Apart from some faith-based communities, other NSAs sow hatred against Muslims and Jews. All over Europe nationalistic, extreme-right movements and parties favor a climate of anti-Semitism and Islamophobia.[19] This results in insults, physical aggressions, destruction or damages to property of Jews[20] (Jewish cemeteries, synagogues) and Muslims,[21] not only by extremist activists but also by ordinary citizens, members of "non-extremist" political parties, and intellectuals.

NSAS PROMOTING FREEDOM OF RELIGION AND BELIEF

NSAs promoting freedom of religion and belief include research-oriented groups (ROGs), human rights organizations, and faith-based defense organizations. ROGs contribute to a better understanding of new religious movements, to nondiscrimination, and to religious tolerance. ROGs consist primarily of academics (historians or sociologists of religions) but also accommodate the same actors as the CAGs (lawyers, doctors, psychotherapists), although the latter group's motivation is different. ROGs perceive themselves as seekers of objective information. Their methods include participative observation, interviews, questionnaires, and comparative studies with other religions that share common problematic characteristics (such as pedophilia, questionable recruiting methods, and so on).

The most widely known ROGs in Europe are INFORM[22] or CESNUR.[23] They are open to the outside world and make information available to churches, secular agencies, academics, government departments and agencies (including the police), the media, and other actors of the general public. They organize international conferences, seminars, and roundtables; and give talks in schools, universities, clubs, and church groups. They may also be called as experts in court cases, for or against a movement, or as advisers by governmental agencies.

ROGs are often targeted by CAGs and CCGs because ROGs are critical about their methods of investigation, some of their theories (brainwashing), and their biased and unscientific approach to the cult issue. In countries where CAGs are the privileged interlocutors of governmental agencies and the media, ROGs tend to be excluded from the public debate.

Human rights organizations rarely monitor freedom of religion and belief in Europe. The reason is historical. The development of the human rights movement in Western European societies in the 1960s was concomitant with social events that marked a rupture with the post–World War II society. One of the characteristics of those societal movements was the rejection of any traditional established authority over society, including the Catholic Church. Commitment to human rights, then incarnated by Amnesty International, attracted members who were politically more left than conservative and who were not very interested in defending the rights of believers of established religions.

Amnesty International defended religious prisoners of any denomination in communist countries in the 1960s, 1970s, and 1980s. Jehovah's Witnesses objectors to military service still benefit from Amnesty International support as prisoners of conscience. But Amnesty International does not deal with religious discrimination and intolerance toward new religious movements. Nor does it question the nature of the political systems, especially in Western democracies, that maintain the privileged position of a historical church in the state and the discrimination generated by such a status.

The International Helsinki Federation (Vienna),[24] a transnational actor, has a better record in this regard. Its annual report, to which its member associations contribute, includes a section on religious freedom and intolerance. However, although the commitment of human rights organizations to religious freedom is widespread in former communist countries,[25] it is very limited in Western European democracies.[26] Keston Institute (Oxford)[27] upholds the rights of Christians and other religious believers in the communist and former communist world to practice their chosen faith. A few years ago the Rome-based Italian branch of Aid to the Church in Need,[28] a transnational Catholic organization, started to publish a yearly report on religious freedom around the world. Human Rights without Frontiers Int. (Brussels) has been monitoring freedom of religion and belief around the world for several years on a daily basis. Its information encompasses both historical religions and new religious movements.[29] The interdenominational Forum 18, based in Oslo, Norway, covers the former communist Eastern Europe and USSR.[30]

Faith-based Defense Institutions

Faith-based institutions linked to Catholicism, Orthodoxy, Lutheranism, Judaism, and Islam can to some extent promote freedom of religion and belief, equality of religions, religious diversity, religious tolerance, interreligious dialogue, and religious peace through local common activities, seminars, and international conferences, even if they are motivated by personal interests. In the aftermath of the publication of parliamentary reports on cults and of anti-cult media coverage in many European countries, a number of targeted religious groups felt the need to react to acts of defamation and false accusations associated with the discrimination and the intolerance they claimed to undergo. They have tried to open a dialogue with the public authorities and journalists to correct the misrepresentation of their movement. They have gone to court. They have lobbied human rights organizations, ROGs, national parliaments, and international institutions (OSCE, Council of Europe, European Parliament).[31] There have been attempts to create coalitions of such religious minorities, but they have had a rather short and not very productive life because, at some time, they have found themselves unable to defend movements whose beliefs and practices are in sharp opposition to their own.

BREACHES OF FREEDOM OF RELIGION AND BELIEF, DISCRIMINATION AND INTOLERANCE

This section deals with direct institutionalized discrimination caused by two-tiered systems, with discrimination and intolerance caused by state anti-cult policies with the passive or active complicity of some actors in abuses by state actors and NSAs. Most relationships between states and religions in Europe take the shape of a two-tiered or multi-tiered system in which religious entities ranked in the upper category have either privileges or more rights than those ranked in a lower category. These inequalities enshrined in laws or in constitutions inevitably lead to various forms of institutionalized discrimination. State actors (legislative and executive powers) creating or upholding and operating two-tiered or multi-tiered systems, which are in essence discriminatory, are either supported by or under pressure from religious NSAs (one or more dominant religions) and can count on the passive complicity of a supra-state actor, the EU.[32]

State financing of religions is a major source of institutionalized discrimination. In some countries only a limited number of religions is subsidized by the state with the income tax of *all* citizens.[33] In other countries the state finances a small number of religions with the income tax of their faithful according to their personal choice while other religions cannot enjoy state financial support and the income tax of their members can only be allotted to the state.[34] This means the state contributes to the financial viability and development of some religions but not of others. Religious classes in public schools only concern recognized religions, and not always all of them. When no exemption possibility exists,[35] ethics classes are the only "choice" left to Jehovah's Witnesses, Hindus, Sikhs, Buddhists, and so on.[36]

In countries with a two-tiered or a multi-tiered system, chaplaincies in hospitals, in the army, in prisons, and in other institutions are limited to state-sponsored religions. In countries where there are state anti-cult policies, tax exemption on property[37] and access to public media are denied to minority religions called cults, positions as civil servants are made impossible for members of cults,[38] and courts usually rule against members of cults in child custody issues related to divorce cases. Despite their numerous discriminatory aspects, the two-tiered and multi-tiered systems are tolerated and are not questioned at the political level in the EU.

Discrimination and Intolerance Caused by Anti-Cult State Policies

The setting up of a sect observatory by law and campaigns sponsored by public authorities, with the complicity of NSAs such as CAGs and CCGs, is another form of institutionalized discrimination, because only "bad" religions are targeted, but not harmful or illegal practices of all

religions. Such a measure based on prejudices has entailed a lot of negative consequences for the targeted movements and their members (see
next section).

In Europe the highly publicized criminal activities of some cults in
the middle of the 1990s led to parliamentary debates, the creation of
parliamentary commissions, the publication of parliamentary reports,
lists of cults, the setting up of state-sponsored cult observatories and
agencies fighting against cults, the distribution of literature warning
against cults, and so on. In the aftermath of the installation of these
new state anti-cult policies and activities, many cases of intolerance
and discrimination in the public and private sectors were reported.
They were ignored by almost all secular human rights organizations in
Europe, in particular by those covering cases of discrimination and
intolerance.

France and Belgium were the hardest hit by the wave of non-state
societal intolerance and discrimination against so-called cults, which
also swept other countries. For several years complaints have been pil-
ing up: libel and slander; stigmatizing reports in the media; victimization in the neighborhood, at the work place, and at school; damage to
individuals' and academics' reputation; loss of jobs or promotions;
bankruptcy of businesses offering alternative therapies complementary to orthodox therapies; loss of visitation rights or child custody in
divorce settlements; inability to rent facilities for religious ceremonies
or meetings; unilateral and unfounded closure of bank accounts of cults
or of individuals affiliated with them; police surveillance and interro-
gations, prosecution for alleged illegal practice of medicine; imprisonment; and even bomb attempts.

In France the National Assembly voted in 1998 to create the
Interministerial Mission of Fight against Cults (MILS) and appointed
the head of a CAG (Center against Mental Manipulations) as its chairman. The law also provided for state financing of CAGs despite the separation of state and religions in force in France and gave CAGs the power
to sue cults on behalf of victims. Due to the division of powers and to the
independence of the judiciary, courts have sometimes made a number
of decisions favorable to so-called cults.[39] On 28 November 2002 the
new National Assembly, which was no longer ruled by a Socialist-led
majority, abrogated the law creating the MILS, whose anti-religious policy
was widely criticized around the world and in international forums,
and adopted a new law instituting an Interministerial Mission Fighting

Sectarian Deviances, the mandate and powers of which seem to be much more limited.

In Belgium representatives of CAGs and CCGs, whether religious or secular humanist, were appointed as members of the board of directors of the state-financed cult observatory, officially called Information and Advice Center on Harmful Sectarian Organizations. In March 1999 the French Community of Belgium (one of the federated entities of the Belgian state) launched a campaign against cults. This consisted of fliers; radio and TV spots warning people against cults and gurus; and promotion of the thirty-eight-page richly illustrated brochure "Gourou garde à toi!" (Guru, you'd better watch out!). It also directed people to anti-cult groups. About thirty religious movements from the synoptic table of 189 groups listed in the Belgian Parliamentary Commission's report were targeted as dangerous cults. This campaign was unanimously supported by the francophone media. Several belief groups complain that they and their members were and are still victimized because of that campaign, especially children in schools. On 24 April 1999 the Court of First Instance at Brussels ordered, in an emergency procedure, the French Community of Belgium to stop distributing the brochure. The temporary injunction had been entered on a complaint filed several weeks before by the Anthroposophic Society. On appeal, the French Community was allowed to resume distribution of the brochures, but by then it had run out. This anti-cult campaign by a state actor could count on the support of the media and the passive acquiescence of the dominant religion, the Catholic Church.

In Germany a number of members of the Enquete (Inquiry) Commission on Cults and Psycho-Groups were representatives of the Catholic Church and the Lutheran Church, whose CCGs groups are very active in the media, in schools, and in society in general. A number of federated entities *(Länder)* also produced anti-cult material that is used by Catholic and Lutheran CCGs. In Austria the Ministry of Youth and Environment published a brochure and a CD-ROM warning against cults that is also used by Catholic CCGs.

Legal Battles over Religious Freedom at the European Court of Human Rights

Set up under the European Convention of Human Rights (ECHR) at the Council of Europe, the European Court of Human Rights is a sort of supreme court whose jurisdiction extends over about 750 million people in forty-one countries, from Greenland to Cyprus and from Gibraltar to Vladivostok. Individuals or associations can submit cases to this European institution for any alleged violation of the ECHR, but only after all domestic remedies have been exhausted. The court is the implementation mechanism of the ECHR, which guarantees freedom of thought, conscience, and religion or belief (Art. 9). Other Articles on personal liberty, privacy, freedoms of expression, and assembly and association (Arts. 5, 8, 10, 11) do not directly protect this freedom but can also be invoked in combination with Article 9.

Article 9 consists of two parts. Paragraph 1 states: "Everyone has the right to freedom of thought, conscience and religion; this right includes freedom to change his religion or belief and freedom, either alone or in community with others and in public or private, to manifest his religion or belief, in worship, teaching, and practice and observance." Paragraph 2 states: "Freedom to manifest one's religion or beliefs shall be subject only to such limitations as are prescribed by law and are necessary in a democratic society in the interests of public safety, for the protection of public order, health or morals, or the protection of the rights and freedoms of others." Article 2 of the ECHR's First Protocol establishes that "no person shall be denied the right to education," and that "in the exercise of any functions which it assumes in relation to education and to teaching, the State shall respect the right of parents to ensure such education and teaching in conformity with their own religious and philosophical convictions." Article 14, which prohibits every kind of discrimination based on religion or belief, can be used in combination with Article 9 and the First Protocol.

From 1964 to 2001 the European Court issued twenty-two final judgments in cases against Austria, Bulgaria, Denmark, France, Germany, Greece, Moldova, San Marino, Sweden, Turkey, and the UK. There have been five friendly settlements.[40] Some of these legal battles have been initiated by religious NSAs: a Catholic church in Greece, the Bulgarian branch of Jehovah's Witnesses, an Orthodox denomination in Bessarabia, and a Jewish group in France. Most of the cases were introduced by individuals supported by religious NSAs from the beginning to the end of very long proceedings: twelve cases concerning Jehovah's Witnesses in Greece, Bulgaria, and Germany; two cases involving the national Muslim communities in Greece and Bulgaria; and one case concerning Pentecostals in Greece.

The most important rights involved in these cases were proselytism or the right to propagate one's religious beliefs and to make new members, freedom of religious expression, religious hate speech, various issues related to conscientious objection to military service, denial of registration, freedom of worship, child custody in divorce cases, and state noninterference in internal matters of religions. The European Court is still in its infancy, but it has already been reformed, and more changes are announced due to the increasing number of complaints lodged. However, a number of tendencies can already be highlighted.

A majority of cases concluded by a final judgment or a friendly settlement have been introduced by individuals affiliated with religions that are in the minority in their respective countries—Jehovah's Witnesses (twelve cases out of thirteen), Muslims (two), Jews (one), and Pentecostals (one)—so that the European Court can be seen as their last resort to annul the effects of "bad" or discriminatory laws, to protect themselves against state interference in their internal matters, and to guarantee their rights.

A decision of the European Court concerns only the case it has been requested to judge, and the state is obliged only to implement the court's decision in the said case. In the aftermath of each of the European Court's decisions, no domestic law was abolished or reformed. Experience shows, however, that such decisions can have far-reaching effects that are difficult to outline and evaluate.

The record of the court's decisions shows clearly that the European Court contributes to the implementation of the freedom of religion and belief in the forty-one member-states of the Council of Europe and paves the way to better protection of minority religions. Due to the length and the costs of the proceedings, it is also obvious that the attempts at creating European case law could not be successful without the backing of NSAs (human rights organizations and the concerned religious groups).

CONCLUSION

State actors (legislative and executive powers) create or uphold and operate two-tiered or multi-tiered systems, which are in essence discriminatory, with the support of or under pressure from religious NSAs (one or more dominant religions) and the passive complicity of a supra-state actor, the EU. In some countries they have also singled out a category of minority religions and belief systems (cults) and set up state agencies that they have mandated to fight against them. The limitations of state actors as defenders of rights to religious freedom and nondiscrimination render all the more important not only the monitoring and advocacy of their activities by NSAs, such as human rights organizations, but also the common search for possible solutions. In the case of the institutionalized discrimination caused by two-tiered systems based on two or several categories of religions, two solutions should be worth examining: either a system of total separation between state and religions or a reform of the existing two-tiered systems by introducing a system in which all religious communities and philosophical movements, whatever their historicity or their size, would be registered in the same way by the state provided they respect the basic democratic principles and public order

- by elaborating a financing system that would allow all taxpayers to choose one of the registered religious communities or philosophical movements to which the state would allocate a part of their income tax;
- by granting tax exemption to citizens making donations to registered religious denominations and philosophical movements; and
- by granting equal opportunities to registered religious denominations and philosophical movements in general.

Some religious NSAs practice religious protectionism, combat and violate the individual's right to choose or change religions, indoctrinate youths against other religious communities, stigmatize religious minorities, and issue calls to fight and to violence. Anti-Semitism, Islamophobia, and cult hunting are the three facets of these phenomena but are also the result of the activities of secular NSAs such as extremist political ideologies. In the face of these dangerous deviations, it is the duty of NSAs, whose mandate is to defend freedom of religion and of belief, to identify and analyze them and to make recommendations. It is also up to the state to have the rule of law respected, to prosecute the individual and collective actors committing illegal acts or inciting to religious hatred, and to teach religious tolerance to youths.

NOTES

¹ Among others, the Charter of the United Nations (24 October 1945), the European Convention on Human Rights (3 September 1953), the International Covenant on Civil and Political Rights (3 January 1976), the European Union Treaty of Amsterdam (1 May 1999), the Final Act of the Conference on Security and Cooperation in Europe (1 August 1975), the Declaration on the Elimination of All Forms of Intolerance and of Discrimination Based on Religion or Belief (25 November 1981), and the Concluding Document of the Vienna Meeting of the Organization for Security and Co-operation in Europe (OSCE) (15 January 1989). The dates for the listed treaties are the dates these treaties entered into force.

² In October 1994 a mass suicide-homicide took the lives of fifty-three members of the Order of the Solar Temple in Switzerland and Canada. In December 1995 a similar tragedy involved sixteen members of the Order of the Solar Temple in the Vercors in France. See Massimo Introvigne, "Ordeal by Fire: The Tragedy of the Solar Temple," *Religion* 25, no. 4 (1995): 267–83; Jean-François Mayer, "Apocalyptic Millennialism in the West: The Case of the Solar Temple," lecture at the University of Virginia sponsored by the Critical Incident Analysis Group (13 November 1998).

³ France, Poland, Slovenia, and the former Republic of Yugoslavia (Ministry of Interior), Belgium, Spain, Latvia, Lithuania and Azerbaijan (Ministry of Justice), Belarus, Romania, Slovakia and the Czech Republic (Ministry of Culture), Finland (Ministry of Education), Greece (Ministry of National Education and Religions), Turkey (Directorate of Religious Affairs), Ukraine (State Committee for Religious Affairs), Armenia (State Council on Religious Affairs).

⁴ The terms *cult-awareness groups, counter-cult groups,* and *research-oriented groups* used in this essay have been proposed by Professor Eileen Barker in "Cult-Watching Practices and Consequences in Europe and North America," in *International Perspectives of Freedom and Equality of Religious Belief*, ed. Derek H. Davis and Gerhard Besier, 1–24 (Waco, TX: J. W. Dawson Institute of Church-State Studies, Baylor Univ., 2002).

⁵ Specific state agencies have been created to deal with the "cult issue" in some European countries, including France, Poland, Belgium, Germany, and Austria.

⁶ FECRIS (Fédération Européenne des Centres de Recherche et d'Information sur le Sectarisme/European Federation of Centres Research and Information on Sectarianism) is a transnational network of such anti-cult associations. FECRIS was founded on 30 June 1994 in Paris, following the Congress on Sectarianism in Barcelona in 1993.

⁷ An example is the Anti-Heretic Department of the Greek Orthodox Church.

[8] In Germany, the so-called Sektenberater (cult advisers) hold public conferences and are active in schools and in the media. In France and in Belgium some evangelical pastors see cult hunting against non-Christian denominations as part of their missionary work.

[9] Over several years a splinter group of the Orthodox Church in Georgia carried out more than a hundred violent attacks, mainly on Jehovah's Witnesses but also on Pentecostals and evangelicals with total impunity.

[10] This is particularly the case in Austria, Germany, and in a number of Orthodox countries.

[11] The pope met hostility almost every time he wanted to visit an Orthodox country: Bulgaria, Georgia, Greece, Russia, Ukraine, and others.

[12] This is particularly the case in Greece, where the constitution opens with a tribute to "the holy, consubstantial, and indivisible Trinity." Laws adopted during the inter-war period protect the Orthodox Church against proselytism. Since their promulgation at the end of the 1930s, Orthodox clerics have successfully lodged thousands of complaints against missionary activities carried out by Jehovah's Witnesses and Protestants. In Armenia, Bulgaria, Georgia, and Romania, constitutions stress the historical role played by the Orthodox Church or its privileged position in the state.

[13] In Romania, Ukraine, and Russia there are important Easter-rite Catholic congregations. They have sworn allegiance to the Roman Catholic Church. Under communism they were banned and their places of worship were put at the disposal of the national Orthodox Church. After the fall of communism they started legal battles for the restitution of their property. This is the main source of their interreligious conflict with the Orthodox churches.

[14] Apart from Bulgaria, Romania, Belarus, and other Orthodox countries, Ukraine is the best example of such problems. Most Ukrainian citizens identify themselves as Orthodox Christians belonging to one of three churches: UOC Moscow Patriarchate is the largest, with communities located predominantly in Central, Southern, and Eastern Ukraine; the UOC Kiev Patriarchate, formed after independence in 1991, has the majority of its communities located in the western part of Ukraine; the smallest is the Autocephalous UOC, with its communities located mostly in the West. The Eastern-rite Catholic Church is the second largest faith in the country. The Roman Catholic Church, located predominantly in the west, serves the population of Polish ancestry. The Jewish population is a half million, historically higher in the west, where as much as 10 percent of the population is Jewish. Islam (Crimean Tatars) and Protestant churches are other religious communities of note.

Restitution of property confiscated by the Soviet regime is a source of tension and conflict. Representatives of the UOC Kiev Patriarchate and the Autocephalous UOC allege that governmental preference is given to the UOC Moscow Patriarchate in the east for settling property claims.

Since 1991 increased tensions in interreligious issues in Ukraine have been culminating in acute conflicts, violent actions, and violations of the law.

Inter-Orthodoxy rivalry, raising of crosses near Jewish or Muslim burial grounds, and the visit of the pope caused tensions among some religious groups. Inter-Orthodox rivalry and physical assaults are linked to the relations and a possible unification between the Kiev Patriarchate and the Autocephalous Church.

All four traditional churches in Ukraine have continued to oppose vigorously state acceptance of new religious movements in Ukraine, seeking to block their official registration, foreign missionary programs, and local evangelical activities. See US Department of State, *International Religious Freedom Report 2001* (Washington, DC: Department of State), www.state.gov website (accessed 31 August 2004).

[15] In Sweden, the broadcast of excerpts from Hitler's *Mein Kampf* on Radio Islam led to six months of imprisonment for Ahmed Armai.

[16] See US Department of State, *International Religious Freedom Report 2001.*

[17] In 2002 there were many reports of verbal harassment in Belgium. Jews attending services at the synagogue in Brussels/Forest were assailed by anti-Jewish epithets from hooligans of Arabic descent. On 4 April 2002 three young Jews were attacked as they were leaving the synagogue of the Belz Hasidic community in Antwerp. The attackers were a group of about thirty Muslims who severely beat the young Jews while cursing the Jews, Israel, and Prime Minister Sharon. On 21 April 2002 the chief rabbi of Russia, who headed a delegation of the World Jewish Congress in Brussels, was attacked by a young person of Arabic origin. In mid-November 2002, David Berman, a Jewish teacher in a Brussels public school, was a victim of insults, acts of anti-Semitism, and death threats. The case raised unanimous disapprobation in the media and in political circles.

[18] Harold Evans, "The Voice of Hate" (25 November 2002), www.eurozine .com website.

[19] The term *Islamophobia* refers to unfounded hostility toward Islam. It refers also to the practical consequences of such hostility in unfair discrimination against Muslim individuals and communities, and to the exclusion of Muslims from mainstream political and social affairs.

[20] In Germany, the Federal Ministry of Interior wrote in its 2001 half-year report on politically motivated criminality that two-thirds of such crimes had been committed by right-wing extremists. See IHF Report 2002 on Human Rights in the OSCE Region, www.ihf-hr.org website (accessed 31 August 2004).

[21] The Italian prime minister Silvio Berlusconi proclaimed the superiority of Western civilization over Islamic civilization. His government previously included the Lega Nord (Northern League) leader Umberto Bossi, who had protested the use of public land for mosques for the "Muslim invaders." In Naples two councilors of Forza Italia (Force Italy) and the Alleanza Nazionale (National Alliance) called for the closing of two mosques located in the center of the city. At the European Parliament an MEP from the Lega Nord proposed an amendment to bar Muslims from entering the EU.

In Belgium the Vlaams Blok has become the largest party in several cities by campaigning to reduce the number of mosques and institutionalizing discrimination against Islam. In December 2002 a teacher of Islamic classes was killed by a neighbor in Antwerp, where the extreme-right party got more than 30 percent of the votes at the last municipal and national elections.

In France, Michel Houellebecq, a provocative writer, called Islam "the stupidest religion." He denied inciting racism but argued in court that the Qur'an is inferior to the Bible as a literary work. He was sued by four Muslim groups and a French human rights group after his comments appeared in a magazine interview. He claimed that he had the right to criticize religions and won his case.

In Denmark a poster declaring "By the time you retire, Denmark will be a majority-Muslim nation" helped the Danish People's Party leader, Pia Kjaersgaard, win a place in the ruling rightist coalition in November 2001, shortly after she declared a "holy war" on Islam. In Austria voters swept the party of Jörg Haider, who had campaigned on an anti-Muslim platform, into power in 1999.

[22] INFORM is an incorporated charity that was started in 1988 with funding from the Home Office and further resources from the Church of England and other mainstream churches. It is based at the London School of Economics. Its primary aim is to help the public by providing information about new and/or alternative religious or spiritual movements that is as objective, balanced, and up-to-date as possible. INFORM does not make any judgments about religious beliefs but can say what those beliefs are. INFORM is nonpolitical and nonsectarian. For more information, see the www.inform.ac website.

[23] CESNUR, the Center for Studies on New Religions, is an international network of associations of scholars working in the field of new religious movements. CESNUR is independent from any religious group, church, denomination, or association. While established in 1988 by scholars who were mostly Roman Catholic, CESNUR has had from its very beginning boards of directors including scholars of a variety of religious persuasions. CESNUR International was recognized as a public nonprofit entity in 1996 by the Italian authorities, who are the main current contributors to its projects. It is also financed by royalties on the books it publishes with different publishers and by contributions of its members.

[24] The International Helsinki Federation is an NGO that seeks to promote compliance with the human rights provisions of the Helsinki Final Act and its Follow-up Documents. It supports and provides liaison among forty-one Helsinki committees and cooperating organizations. It criticizes human rights abuses regardless of the political system of the state in which these abuses occur. For more information, see the www.ihf-hr.org website.

[25] International Helsinki Foundation, *Human Rights in the OSCE Region 2002* (events of 2001). Available online.

[26] In the 2002 International Helsinki Foundation Report (events of 2001), religious freedom issues in Austria, Denmark, Finland, Germany, Ireland, Italy,

Sweden, and the UK were not covered, although there would have been a number of things to be said about the cult issue in some of these countries. Belgium, France, and Greece were extensively covered for various particular reasons.

[27] The Keston Institute was founded in 1969 by Rev. Cannon Dr. Michael Bourdeaux. Keston Institute correspondents travel widely through the former Soviet Union and beyond, gathering the latest news on religious freedom from an extensive network of contacts. Keston News Service is an invaluable resource for the media, governments, churches, and many interested individuals. For more information, see the www.keston.org website.

[28] Aid to the Church in Need was founded in 1947 by Werenfried van Straaten, a Dutch Norbertine priest. It was first a relief agency helping German refugees. In 1952 its mandate included pastoral and material help to Catholics persecuted in European communist countries, an activity that contributed greatly to helping Catholics until the collapse of communism in 1989. For more information, see the www.kirche-in-not.org website.

[29] Human Rights without Frontiers Int. distributes information by email on a daily basis and posts it on its website, year after year, country by country alphabetically and chronologically. For more information, see the www.hrwf.net website.

[30] For more information, see the www.forum18.org website.

[31] This is particularly the case for the Church of Scientology (for example, through its Human Rights Office in Brussels) and the Unification Church (through the International Coalition for Religious Freedom).

[32] That complicity is accepted in some provisions of the Treaty of Amsterdam of 1 May 1999, which states that the relations between states and religions or belief systems in the EU remain under the authority of the member states.

[33] In Greece, one religion (Orthodox Church); in Belgium, six religions and secular humanism.

[34] In Spain, the choice is between the Catholic Church and the state; in Italy, between "admitted religions" and the state.

[35] This is the case in the Federal Kingdom of Belgium, in French-speaking public schools (Wallonia and Brussels) but not in Dutch-speaking public schools (Flanders).

[36] Ethics taught in such classes is said to be "non-faith-based," but it usually reflects the secular humanist ideology that several religious movements, such as Jehovah's Witnesses, consider incompatible with their own ethical principles. Ethics teachers are secular humanists, agnostics, and atheists.

[37] In Belgium the tax department denied the group Sukhyo Mahikari an exemption from property taxes on its places of worship on the grounds that it is on the so-called list of cults. This group is officially registered as a religious association in Spain (unpublished material collected during an interview of one of the leaders of Sukyo Mahikari by Human Rights without Frontiers in 2001).

[38] Louis-Léon Christians, lecturer at the Catholic University of Louvain and member of the Belgian Sect Observatory, wrote: "Some Belgian municipalities have made it a requirement for candidates for positions as civil servants to swear a statement that they do not belong to a 'harmful sectarian organization'" ("Liberté d'opinion en droit européen: observations belges (II)— Les limitations [Freedom of thought in European law: Belgian observations II—limitations], *Conscience et Liberté* 58 [1999], 10 n. 1, my translation from French).

[39] In 2002 two administrative courts declared that the Parliamentary Report on Cults lacked any legal value and could not justify the religious discrimination practiced by certain city halls. On 30 May 2002 the Administrative Court of Poitiers canceled the decision on 18 October 2001 by the city of La Rochelle to refuse the location of a communal hall for local meetings of the Jehovah's Witnesses. This decision was based on the cult designation attributed to the Jehovah's Witnesses by the Parliamentary Report on Cults of 1995. On 21 February 2002 the Administrative Court of Rennes constrained the city of Lorient to rent a public hall to the local Jehovah's Witnesses after it had refused to put one at their disposal because they were a cult. The justification of the Administrative Court was similar.

[40] These cases were listed and summed up by Sara Vann and can be found at the www.hrwf.net website (accessed 31 August 2004).

Rethinking the Human Rights Universe

George J. Andreopoulos, Zehra F. Kabasakal Arat, and Peter Juviler

This volume advances the argument that non-state actors (NSAs) have been important players but that their influence and impact on the human rights landscape, as well as their potential, deserve a more comprehensive and systematic treatment. So, how would taking NSAs seriously improve our understanding of the human rights universe and enhance human rights advocacy? In mapping out a strategy for promotion and protection, due consideration should be given to a series of issues that emerge as key components of a new approach. These issues can be clustered as follows: the state/non-state actor distinction, the capacities/accountability nexus, and the balance between active and reactive strategies. While these clusters do not exhaust the existential array of issues on the human rights agenda, they encapsulate recurring themes and challenges. Moreover, they raise critical questions about the current state and future prospects of human rights advocacy.

THE STATE/NON-STATE ACTOR DISTINCTION

Several chapters in the book, addressing issues either at a theoretical level (for example, Arat and Goodhart) or examining specific cases (for example, Gunderson, Martin, Juviler, Davis, and Fautré), point to the interaction between state and non-state actors and alert us to the

problem of setting a false dichotomy between state and non-state actors (or between the public and the private) or seeing the relationship
between these two sets of actors as simply asserting influence on each
other to maximize their self-interest. The lines can be blurred not only
when close collaboration and coalitions are established but also to the
extent of performing each other's functions.

Even the meaning of the term *civil society* has been changing. While
in an earlier period (eighteenth and nineteenth centuries in Europe)
the term *civil society* referred to the domain of private activity that
sustained the rising middle class, nowadays it is viewed as the locus of
"emancipatory counter hegemony."[1] Such a construction has varied
conceptual and policy implications. Civil society can be viewed as the
terrain for resistance and protests, and, more ambitiously, as the arena
in which transnational social movements seek to restrain hegemonic
conduct, as argued by Richard Falk, and in the process reconstruct
political authority in a more equitable and inclusive manner.[2]

The interaction issue is of particular importance here. NSAs de-
marcate their space by reference to state-initiated actions. Moreover,
and in light of some of the above-mentioned developments and trends,
in particular the progressive internationalization of the state[3] and the
transnational networking of NSAs, this space is constantly negotiable,
seeking to adapt to a never-ending stream of opportunities and pressures. This negotiating process is often carried out within a structure
created by international organizations (in which, in some instances,
NSAs have consultative status),[4] where the state/non-state actor distinction is not as clear-cut as it may appear on the surface. One reason
has to do with the fact that many of these NSAs are state-related in a
variety of ways, either because they receive some form of assistance,
or because they operate within a rules-and-regulations framework developed through interstate collaboration. A second reason relates to
the first: while these structures are state centered, the process of interaction (bargaining, signaling, deliberation, and so on) generates its own
dynamics toward the emergence of a suprastatal consciousness whose
exponents cannot be confined to civil society actors alone; it includes
officials of these intergovernmental organizations who, in at least certain issue areas, are transcending the parameters of a state-centric
agenda.

However, not all actors in civil societies are "civil," and ever-
increasing corporate power can undermine the state capacity (or will)
to protect labor rights, deliver social services, and regulate the economy

to meet public needs (for example, access to medicine in the developing world) or set ethical standards for scientific research that has significant human rights implications. Globalization and the internationalization of the state, along with all human activities, can generate pathways to new coalitions formed by transnational social movements and states to deal with a host of critical policy issues, for example, the protection of civilians in armed conflict, the protection of labor rights, and the elimination of anti-personnel land mines. More important, in most, if not all, of these cases, these new coalitions will be challenged by other alliances that contain the status quo–oriented state and NSAs. However, as discussed by Nelson and Lansner, should the news media play its expected checking-and-balancing role by transmitting essential (and alternative) information, the increased public awareness about global injustices and their local implications may even enhance the process that Falk has termed "globalization from below."

More work is clearly needed in this area. At this juncture it suffices to note that the problematization of the state/non-state actor distinction constitutes a useful entry point into analyzing and assessing those trends, trends that cannot be reduced to simple manifestations of material interests or other utility considerations.

THE CAPACITIES/ACCOUNTABILITY NEXUS

What are the implications of the rise in NSA expectations for the capacities/accountability nexus? In the traditional human rights paradigm, NSAs have been perceived as endowed with limited capacities, protective or abusive, while the burden of ensuring accountability fell upon the state. Accountability, of course, refers to the responsibilities incurred by an actor vis-à-vis all entities with whom it interacts in whatever capacity in a particular situation. Under international human rights law, states bear responsibility for abusive conduct perpetrated by non-state entities within their territory (due diligence). Regional human rights courts (European, Inter-American) have issued decisions emphasizing the need for states to exercise due diligence in dealing with human rights violations perpetrated by these entities.

However, the trends of increasing corporate power, concentration of wealth and ownership, global political activism, and international networks display a shift in power and capabilities in favor of NSAs. The increase in NSA capacities is inextricably linked to expectations and calls for the subjection of their activities to greater scrutiny, as convincingly argued by Macklin, among others.

Yet pointing to the positive correlation between NSA capacities and accountability is simply the first step. The broadening of the accountability space will necessitate more work on the sources of accountability (normative framework, legal as well as non-legal), on the mechanisms of accountability (regulatory, voluntary), as well as on the main challenges confronting this expansion. Among the most important challenges would be sorting out the respective responsibilities in state and NSA interactions, enhancing their capacity to abide by human rights laws and/or holding perpetrators accountable. A first step in this direction would be to take a violation-centered approach and provide sound quantitative and sustainable accounting of violations, as Spirer and Spirer argue in their contribution.

PROACTIVE *VS.* RETROSPECTIVE STRATEGIES

In addition to being state-centric, the international human rights regime and the current approach employed in human rights advocacy have been mainly reactive. In monitoring and assessing all types of actors, however, it is vitally important to redress the imbalance between proactive and retrospective strategies and to focus on proactive, protective strategies that will shift the emphasis from ex-post-facto measures to timely monitoring, reporting, and ultimately preventing the abusive conduct. This cannot be an easy task, and what has been proposed so far may not seem revolutionary. Nevertheless, placing the emphasis on the exigencies of prevention would have a profound impact.

To be sure, there are encouraging signs in this direction. For example, two recent initiatives dealing with NSAs, the Global Compact (corporations) and the proposed manual of best practices for engagement (armed groups), irrespective of their ultimate success, are clearly imbued with the spirit of prevention. However, at the same time, the over-reliance on the international criminal justice model (with the ad hoc tribunals and the "hybrid courts") points toward the opposite direction, especially when one compares the tribunals' and courts' annual budgets to the resources available for other human rights activities in the United Nations system. This is not an argument against the use of the international criminal justice model, which, after all, has become increasingly sensitive to the criminalization of human rights violations committed by NSAs. Instead, it is an argument in favor of seizing the moment provided by the open-ended, negotiable character of the relevant normative space to ensure that when it comes to the protection of human rights, it is the prevention of violations that matters and not the identity of their potential sources.

Whether one looks at codes of conduct for corporations (Braun and Gearhart), prior agreements in international clinical trials (Alice Page), or the proposed manual on best practices and seeking ways of engaging armed groups in a human rights dialogue (George Andreopoulos), one thing is becoming increasingly apparent: any effective advocacy in this evolving universe must be premised on the contextualization of the human rights framework, especially in non-adversarial interactions.[5] This does not mean that overarching principles like universality, nondiscrimination, and indivisibility would lose their relevance; rather, it means that any interaction with NSAs should identify appropriate "entry points" for an ongoing dialogue aimed at the protection of human dignity in all its aspects. The dynamic character of this process would reduce the risks of privileging certain standards and normative commitments over others.

HUMAN RIGHTS ADVOCACY:
THE NEED TO TAKE AGENCY SERIOUSLY

In such a context, what does effective human rights advocacy entail? As a starting point, as crucial NSAs, human rights organizations need to revisit the overwhelming emphasis placed on naming and shaming perpetrators of abusive conduct, as well as the disproportionate use of resources for litigation-related approaches. Although their considerable achievements and continuous relevance cannot be denied, those strategies have come to dominate the human rights landscape at the expense of grassroots mobilization initiatives that in the past have contributed to many of the advances that are rightly celebrated today. While several human rights organizations understandably highlight the recent achievements in law enforcement, it should not be forgotten that these constitute only part of the story of the human rights movement. There is another tradition that was set by the anti-slavery movement (Kevin Bales) and followed by the anti-colonial and anti-apartheid movements, as well as the transnational networking of anti-authoritarian activists spawned by the Helsinki Final Act; these examples constitute powerful reminders of the potency and transformational capacity of a politically engaged human rights movement.

In other words, international and national human rights organizations have to put more emphasis on political and grassroots activism and encourage their development. One cannot help questioning what would have happened if the Rwandan genocide was responded to by "a great deal of popular protest" by Americans[6] and other nationalities around the world. By the same token, wouldn't mass protests of the "welfare reform," which mobilized supporters of the welfare state and advocates of social and economic rights, have made a difference?

To be sure, lobbying government officials, or publicizing violations, is important, but it will not go very far if the effort merely reflects the concerns of human rights professionals, or is seen as such. It is one thing to move in the corridors of power and publish detailed and damning reports of governmental abuse, and an altogether different thing to claim mass-based ownership of these concerns, ownership manifested in an increasingly felt pressure from below for change that can also have an impact on the ballot box.

The professionalization of human rights activism has contributed to an artificial separation between "legal" and "political" issues in some of the big debates of recent years, an attitude that has led to a self-inflicted marginalization. As a result, human rights advocates have not only become less effective in constraining the abusive conduct of state actors, but they have not devoted enough attention to strategies for addressing issue areas affected by the conduct of NSAs.

This is particularly troubling when the focus shifts to the debates about economic and social justice issues. Here the lack of substantive interaction between major human rights organizations and social movements associated with the anti-globalization campaigns, or more accurately, with the "globalization from below" campaigns, is instructive. As a report by the International Council on Human Rights Policy noted, "Many of them (i.e. groups participating in these campaigns) would consider that they support human rights or *are* human rights organizations, even though they may not be familiar with human rights law or engage in legal advocacy."[7] There is a tremendous human resource potential associated with the quest for a more equitable distribution of the benefits of globalization upon which the human rights community has barely drawn. As a result, potentially critical networking opportunities with these new constituencies, aimed at building support for a holistic approach to human rights, subjecting the actions of state and NSAs to greater scrutiny, and sustaining resistance to the monopolization of the global agenda by the war on terror, are left unexplored.

The rising profile of NSAs calls for a better understanding of an evolving universe and for different strategies for promotion and protection. These challenges constitute a clarion call to the human rights community to reconnect with its transformative potential. While there are no magic bullets here, taking NSAs seriously necessitates a major rethinking of long-held assumptions and established practices. What is at stake is nothing less than the continuing relevance of the human rights discourse.

NOTES

[1] Richard Higgott, *Coming to Terms with Globalization: Non-State Actors and Agenda for Justice and Governance in the Next Century,* Institute for Globalization and the Human Condition, McMaster Univ. March 1999 (on file with the authors); see also Richard Falk, *Predatory Globalization: A Critique* (Cambridge, UK: Polity Press, 1999).

[2] Falk, *Predatory Globalization.*

[3] This refers to the state's increasing stake in issues that transcend its traditional spatial focus; for a discussion of this issue, see Yoshikazu Sakamoto, ed., *Global Transformation: Challenges to the State System* (New York: United Nations Univ. Press, 1994).

[4] A typical example would be the negotiating process in Rome that resulted in the adoption of the Statute of the International Criminal Court.

[5] We do not include the humanitarian framework, given its different emphasis. Although both frameworks are premised on a fundamental commitment to human dignity, the human rights framework focuses on advocacy, while the humanitarian one focuses on access.

[6] Human rights organizations were actively engaged and tried to persuade the indifferent governments to take actions to stop the genocidal acts in Rwanda. It is reported that Anthony Lake, the national security advisor to the Clinton administration, responded to the lobbying efforts of the Human Rights Watch representative by indicating that no action could be taken "unless a great deal of popular protest began to occur." See David Rieff, "The Precarious Triumph of Human Rights," *The New York Times Magazine,* 8 August 1999.

[7] International Council on Human Rights Policy, *Human Rights after 9/11* (Geneva, 2002), 47.

Contributors

George Andreopoulos is Professor of Political Science at the John Jay College of Criminal Justice and at the Graduate Center, City University of New York. He is also the Director of the Center for International Human Rights at John Jay College. His publications include *Concepts and Strategies in International Human Rights* (Peter Lang, 2003); *The Laws of War: Constraints on Warfare in the Western World* (with Sir Michael Howard and Mark Shulman) (Yale Univ. Press, 1994); and *Human Rights Education for the Twenty-First Century* (with Richard Pierre Claude) (Univ. of Pennsylvania Press, 1997). He is currently completing a book on humanitarian intervention for Yale University Press.

Kevin Bales is President of Free the Slaves, the US sister organization of Anti-Slavery International, and Professor of Sociology at Roehampton University in London. His book *Disposable People: New Slavery in the Global Economy* (Univ. of California Press, 1999) was characterized by Archbishop Desmond Tutu as a "scholarly and deeply disturbing expose of modern slavery." The documentary based on his work won the Peabody Award and two Emmy Awards. Among his other publications are *Understanding Global Slavery* (Univ. of California Press, 2005), and *New Slavery: A Reference Handbook* (ABC-CLIO, 2004). Bales has advised the US, British, Irish, Norwegian, and Nepali governments, and governments of the Economic Community of West African States.

Rainer Braun has worked on the interplay between development policies and human rights in Central America and the United States. He teaches courses on human rights at Columbia University and is pursuing a Ph.D. in political science at the Free University of Berlin.

Dana-Ain Davis teaches in the Department of Anthropology at Purchase College, State University of New York, and is active in issues of welfare reform and battered women. Her research interests include gender, poverty and public policy, black studies, and reproductive rights in both the United States and Namibia. Her publications include *Battered Black Women and Welfare Reform: Between a Rock and a Hard Place* (SUNY Press, 2006).

Richard Falk has been Visiting Professor in Global Studies at the University of California, Santa Barbara, since 2002. Prior to that he was Albert G. Milbank

Professor of International Law at Princeton University. His most recent books are *The Great Terror War* (Olive Branch Press, 2003) and *The Declining World Order: America's Imperial Geopolitics* (Routledge, 2004).

Willy Fautré is Director of Human Rights without Frontiers Int. (Brussels) and Director of the Phare Democracy Programme (European Commission Project). His area of expertise is religious minorities in Europe. He is former chargé d'affaires at the Cabinet of the Ministry of Education for linguistic exchanges between French- and Dutch-speaking communities in Belgium and former chargé d'affaires at the Belgian Parliament on ethnic and linguistic issues in Belgium.

Judy Gearhart is the Program Director at Social Accountability International. Ms. Gearhart has worked on democratization and women's labor issues in Latin America and conducted evaluations for UNICEF and the ILO in Honduras. Ms. Gearhart holds a Master of International Affairs degree from Columbia University, where she teaches a course on human rights and development.

Michael Goodhart is Assistant Professor of Political Science at the University of Pittsburgh. He is author of several articles on human rights and democracy in the global context, and his book *Democracy as Human Rights: Freedom and Equality in the Age of Globalization* has just been published by Routledge. Professor Goodhart was 2004–5 President of the American Political Science Association's Human Rights Section and Book Review Editor of *Polity: The Journal of the Northeastern Political Science Association.*

James L. Gunderson is Chief Legal Officer of Vetco International Limited, a global oilfield equipment and services company. He is President of the New York Chapter of the National Association of Corporate Directors and a frequent speaker on governance and corporate social responsibility. Mr. Gunderson spent most of his career with Schlumberger Limited, where he was Secretary and General Counsel. He has also worked for law firms in New York and Amsterdam.

Peter Juviler is Professor Emeritus of Political Science at Barnard and Adjunct Professor at Columbia University, where he teaches the first human rights course offered at the Harriman Institute. He has published over one hundred articles and several books, including *Freedom's Ordeal: The Struggle for Human Rights and Democracy in Post-Soviet States* (Univ. of Pennsylvania Press, 1998), and, with co-editor Carie Gustafson, *Religion and Human Rights, Competing Claims?* (M. E. Sharpe, 1998), a book also originating in the University Seminar on Human Rights, which Professor Juviler now co-chairs with the other editors of this volume.

Zehra F. Kabasakal Arat is Professor of Political Science at Purchase College, State University of New York, where she also chaired the Women's Studies Program. Her research and publications address a wide range of issues with an emphasis on women's rights and human rights' relation to democracy, development, and Islamic traditions. Her forthcoming books include *Human Rights Worldwide: A Reference Book* (ABC-CLIO) and *Human Rights in Turkey: Policies and Prospects* (Univ. of Pennsylvania Press).

Thomas R. Lansner teaches on international media and policy at Columbia University's School of International and Public Affairs and has served as a consultant to numerous nongovernmental groups. He conducts seminars for media practitioners on human rights, conflict, and election coverage, and trains human rights advocates in media skills. For ten years, until 1990, Lansner was a correspondent, principally in Africa and Asia, for the *London Observer* and other media outlets.

Ruth Macklin is Professor of Bioethics at Albert Einstein College of Medicine in the Bronx, New York. Dr. Macklin is an advisor to the World Health Organization and the Joint United Nations Programme on HIV/AIDS. Her latest book is *Double Standards in Medical Research in Developing Countries* (Cambridge Univ. Press, 2004).

J. Paul Martin is the Executive Director of the Center for the Study of Human Rights at Columbia University. His academic work has focused on the role of external educational and development agents in developing countries, notably Africa. For the last five years this has included teaching and writing on how, using a rights perspective, to maximize the benefits of the presence of multinational corporations for their host communities. His other current writing addresses rights and relations among the major world religious traditions.

Anne Nelson is an Adjunct Professor at the Columbia School for International and Public Affairs. She developed the first journalism school curriculum for reporting on international human rights. She has written and lectured widely on the news media and international affairs and is an award-winning author and playwright.

Alice Page is special counsel to the law firm of LaFollette Godfrey and Kahn, the Madison, Wisconsin, office of Godfrey and Kahn, S.C., where she devotes her practice exclusively to health-care law. Ms. Page, who has a Master of Public Health degree, works extensively in the ethics of human subjects research. From 1999 to 2001 Ms. Page served as a senior policy analyst for the National Bioethics Advisory Commission, an eighteen-member multidisciplinary body, which examined and reported to the president on ethical and policy issues in various matters related to human subjects research. She is the author of "Prior Agreements in International Clinical Trials: Ensuring the Benefits of Research to Developing Countries," *Yale J. Health Policy Law Ethics* 3, no. 1 (Winter 2002), 35–66.

Herbert F. Spirer was most recently Adjunct Professor of International Affairs at Columbia University, where he was assisted by Louise Spirer, an independent scholar. Their most recent publication (with co-editor Patrick Ball) is *Making the Case: Investigating Large Scale Human Rights Violations Using Information Systems and Data Analysis* (AAAS, 2000). Herbert Spirer, with Patrick Ball and Paul Kobrok, also co-authored *State Violence in Guatemala, 1960–1996: A Quantitative Reflection* (AAAS, 2000).

Index

343

Also from Kumarian Press...

Human Rights and Humanitarinism

Aiding Violence: The Development Enterprise in Rwanda
Peter Uvin

Cutting the Wire: The Story of the Landless Movement in Brazil
Sue Branford and Jan Rocha

Dealing with Human Rights: Asian and Western Views on the Value of Human Rights
Edited by Martha Meijer

Famine, Conflict, and Response: A Basic Guide
Frederick C. Cuny with Richard B. Hill

Human Rights and Development
Peter Uvin

The Charity of Nations: Humanitarian Action in a Calculating World
Ian Smillie and Larry Minear

The Humanitarian Enterprise: Dilemmas and Discoveries
Larry Minear

Newer Kumarian Press Titles

Coming of Age in a Globalized World: The Next Generation
J. Michael Adams and Angelo Carfagna

Savings Services for the Poor
Edited by Madeline Hirschland

Transnational Civil Society: An Introduction
Edited by Srilatha Batliwala and L. David Brown

Visit Kumarian Press at **www.kpbooks.com** or call **toll-free 800.289.2664** for a complete catalog.

Kumarian Press, located in Bloomfield, Connecticut, is a forward-looking, scholarly press that promotes active international engagement and an awareness of global connectedness.